PLAYS, PLAYERS, & PLAYWRIGHTS

Marion Geisinger

PLAYS,
PLAYERS,
& PLAYWRIGHTS

AN ILLUSTRATED HISTORY OF THE THEATRE

Hart Publishing Company, Inc. New York City

Contents

ACKNOWLEDGMENTS   9

The Theatre of the Greeks and the Romans   17

The Theatre of the Middle Ages and the Renaissance   67

The Elizabethan Theatre   93

The Commedia dell'Arte   137

The Restoration Theatre   169

The English Theatre of the 18th Century   199

The English Theatre of the 19th Century   243

The Rise of the American Theatre   295

The Russian Theatre   391

The English Theatre of the 20th Century   423

The American Theatre of the 20th Century   517

The American Musical Theatre   653

INDEX   727

Acknowledgments

*Grateful acknowledgment is made to the following sources
which have provided photographs for this work.
The photos appear on the enumerated pages.*

ALINARI—ART REFERENCE BUREAU
Box 137, Ancram, New York
20, 23a, 26a, 32, 45, 46, 48, 54

ALIX JEFFRY
71 West 10th Street, New York, New York
602a, 602b

ART INSTITUTE OF CHICAGO
Michigan Avenue at Adams Street, Chicago, Illinois
166

BRITISH MUSEUM
Great Russell Street, London, W.C. 2, England
23b, 44, 49a, 49b, 49c, 182a, 182b, 183, 188, 217

BRITISH TOURIST AUTHORITY
680 Fifth Avenue, New York, New York
508

GRAPHIC HOUSE, INC.
280 Madison Avenue, New York, New York
598

GUILDHALL ART GALLERY
King Street, London E.C. 2, England
244

HART PUBLISHING COMPANY, INC.
719 Broadway, New York, New York
265, 285, 289a, 289b, 289c, 290a, 290b, 290c, 291

HOUSTON ROGER LTD.
46, Auriol Road, W. 14, London, England
465, 478

JOHN AND MABLE RINGLING MUSEUM OF ART
P.O. Box 1838, Sarasota, Florida
140, 153 and color illustration on cover

JOHN WILLIS COLLECTION
190 Riverside Drive, New York, New York
533, 606, 608, 610, 611, 612, 613, 615, 618, 619, 620, 626, 627, 634, 648, 681, 710, 714, 720, 724a

KENN DUNCAN
853 Seventh Avenue, New York, New York
724b

LIBRARY OF CONGRESS
Washington, D.C.
114

LITTLE, BROWN & CO.
34 Beacon Street, Boston, Massachusetts
553

MAGNUM PHOTOS, INC.
15 West 46th Street, New York, New York
590

MARTHA SWOPE
251 West 72nd Street, New York, New York
630

MINNESOTA THEATRE COMPANY
725 Vineland Place, Minneapolis, Minnesota
623, 624, 625

MUSEUM OF THE CITY OF NEW YORK
Fifth Avenue and 103rd Street, New York, New York
338, 428

NATIONAL PORTRAIT GALLERY
No. 2 St. Martin's Place, London, W.C. 2, England
9, 107a, 107b, 107c, 128, 177, 178a, 179, 193

NATIONAL THEATRE OFFICES
The Archway, 10a Aquinas Street, London, S.E. 1, England
460, 498, 500, 501, 505

NATIONALMUSEUM
Stockholm, Sweden
158, 159

NEW DIRECTIONS
333 Sixth Avenue, New York, New York
582

NEW YORK PUBLIC LIBRARY
42nd Street and Fifth Avenue, New York, New York
5, 7, 9, 11, 17, 37, 41a, 41b, 42, 62a, 67, 71, 75, 78, 83, 86, 93, 95, 99, 116, 133, 134, 137, 139, 148, 150a, 150b, 169, 171, 174, 175, 178b, 180, 186a, 186b, 187, 191, 199, 210, 218, 223, 224a, 230, 243, 257, 275, 295, 303, 304, 335, 337, 356, 361, 365, 368, 370b, 373, 379, 387, 391, 423, 434, 444, 445, 477, 514, 517, 524, 573, 609, 629, 632, 651, 653, 658, 664, 672, 682, 698, 701, 708, 718, 726, 727, 768

OSTERREICHISCHE NATIONALBIBLIOTHEK
1 Josefplatz, Wien, Austria
160

PHOTO SERVICE
1472 Broadway, New York, New York
60, 88, 96, 110, 111, 164, 165, 201, 202, 204, 205, 207, 211, 213, 214, 215, 220, 226, 235, 236, 239, 245, 246, 248, 249, 252, 262b, 262c, 262d, 266, 272, 279, 281, 286, 311, 318, 319, 320, 332, 339, 346, 354, 359, 360, 366, 367, 371, 372, 374, 380, 392, 393a, 393b,

394, 396, 399a, 399b, 400, 402, 403a, 404, 408a, 408c, 409a, 409b,
410, 411, 417, 419, 420, 425, 431, 446, 449, 451, 470, 483, 488,
489, 493, 526, 534, 535, 538, 540, 545, 546, 550, 552, 554, 557,
558a, 558b, 559, 561, 562, 568, 569, 570, 580, 584, 640, 643, 644,
645, 678, 679, 688, 702, 706, 721 and endpaper

STAATLICHE MUSEEN ZU BERLIN
102 Bodestrasse 1/3, Berlin, East Germany
18

"THE MASTER, FELLOWS AND SCHOLARS OF
CORPUS CHRISTI COLLEGE, CAMBRIDGE"
105

UNIVERSITATSBIBLIOTHEK
Universitätsplatz 1, Salzburg, Austria
77

UNIVERSITY OF CALIFORNIA, BERKELEY
Berkeley, California
62b

UNIVERSITY OF MISSISSIPPI
Museum of Classical Archaeology,
By permission of the University of Mississippi
26b

UNIVERSITY MUSEUM
University of Pennsylvania, Spruce and 33rd Streets,
Philadelphia, Pennsylvania
52

VICTORIA & ALBERT MUSEUM
South Kensington, London, S.E. 7, England
130, 241, 262a, 263, 269

WALTER HAMPDEN MEMORIAL LIBRARY
16 Gramercy Park, New York, New York
231, 284, 288, 307, 377, 378, 427, 441, 520, 530, 542, 564, 574,
604, 639, 650, 696, 704, 707, 716

ZODIAC PHOTOGRAPHERS
351 West 54th Street, New York, New York
692, 722

WILLIAM SHAKESPEARE (1564-1616)   The little that is known of Shakespeare's life excites controversy that extends even to his physical appearance. This so-called "Chandos" portrait is believed by some to be the only true picture of the Bard. Most scholars regard this portrait as a romanticized version of the famous, earlier Droeshout portrait in the frontispiece of the First Folio, 1623. The greatest dramatist of all time, Shakespeare remains as relevant today as he was 400 years ago. His extraordinary sense of psychology still makes us gasp in admiration. His plays are regularly performed in all civilized countries of the world.

The Theatre of the Greeks and the Romans

THE BEGINNINGS

Though the origins of all the dramatic arts are shrouded in pre-history, it is universally agreed that the birthplace of the Western theatre was ancient Greece. Aeschylus, Sophocles, Aristophanes, Euripides—the great playwrights of ancient Athens—are still numbered among the greatest playwrights of the Western world.

It is not always realized that all these men were Athenians. Indeed, all the works of the classical Greek theatre which we possess have come to us from Athens; as far as we know, the classical tragedy and the classical comedy were Athenian inventions which grew out of the ancient religious ceremonials celebrated in honor of the god Dionysus. While other Greek city-states no doubt had their own religious festivals, scholars agree that it is to the Athenians that the honor belongs of having transformed these rites into what we today recognize as the basis of the modern Western theatre.

GREEK HORSEPLAY   *A chorus of actors—one-half dressed as horses, the other half as knights—caper to the lively tune of a flute player. This scene, on a sixth-century vase, represents an antic performance called the "Komos" from which Greek comedy sprang. Aristophanes kept a major feature of this ancient revelry, the animal costumes, in several of his plays "Wasps" (422 B.C.),"Birds" (414 B.C.), and "Frogs" (405 B.C.)*

THE FESTIVALS OF DIONYSUS

In the Greek pantheon, Dionysus was a nature god who died and was reborn every year. He was also the god of wine. The rites associated with his worship—which took the form of festivals held several times a year—were characterized by song and dance, the playing of musical instruments, and much flowing of wine. A customary part of the ritual was the chanting of a hymn called a *dithyramb,* in honor of the god.

According to Greek legend, at the moment of his mother's death the yet-unborn Dionysus was snatched from her body by his father, the great god, Zeus. Zeus hid Dionysus in the side of his body until his son was ready to be born. It was this tale that gave rise to the use of the word dithyramb, which literally means twice-born, as a name for hymns performed in honor of Dionysus.

THE DITHYRAMBIC CHORUS

The dithyrambs were traditionally performed by a chorus of fifty men dressed as satyrs. Satyrs were conceived to be half-human and half-animal, and their costume was a shaggy goat's skin embellished by a horse's tail in the appropriate place. The satyr chorus were also

BOAT CAR   The drawing of Dionysus and his satyrs is sometimes called the Thespis Car. Thespis, according to the legend, brought the first tragedy to Attica on wagons in the sixth century B.C.

SATYR CHORUS *This Hellenistic mosaic shows a rehearsal of a satyr chorus conducted by a poet or by a chorus teacher. Some scholars believe that Aeschylus is depicted here; Aeschylus was bald and is known to have taught the chorus. Two young choristers in traditional goatskin loincloths practice the satyr dance under the watchful eye of the old teacher. An elaborately-dressed musician plays the double flute. Behind him an attendant reads from a scroll, while the young actor (right), donning a sleeved goatskin, prepares to play the role of the Papposilinus, the leader of the Satyrs. At the teacher's feet are the heroine's mask and the bearded Papposilinus' mask. On a table at right lies the mask of the hero.*

provided with long animal ears and snub-nosed masks with beards. Protruding from the pelvic region was a prominent representation of a phallus.

THE DITHYRAMBIC FESTIVAL AND THE SATYR-PLAY

The dithyrambic festivals, which were essentially fertility festivals, were originally improvised in a spirit of lively religious fervor. Gradually, these festivals came to be formalized. Sometime during the 7th and 6th centuries B.C., the dithyrambic hymn became a highly developed lyric poem, sung and danced by a skilled chorus at the annual festivals.

Another type of presentation which developed from the dithyrambic chorus was the satyr-play, a form of indecent burlesque in which a mythical hero was presented in some ludicrous situation. It was Aristotle's belief that the tragedy, as a dramatic form, developed out of the satyr-play, although there are modern scholars who disagree. Certainly, the satyr-play came eventually to have a form similar to the tragedy, a drama in which definite episodes were separated by choral odes. The metre used in the satyr-play was the same as that used in tragedy. Until quite late in the history of the Greek theatre, the performance of a satyr-play always concluded a program of tragedies. The satyr-play, incidentally, had absolutely nothing to do with satire, which was a later and quite different development.

THE COMPETITIONS

The transition from the early period of the Dionysian festivals to the time when Greek drama as we know it first appeared is something we know very little about. We do know, however, that it was at the Dionysian festivals that the classic Greek drama first made its appearance, and that long after the religious fervor which originally inspired these festivals had faded, the festivals themselves continued to be the occasions when new dramas were performed.

This seems to have come about in large part because, in the year 534 B.C., the Athenian tyrant, Pisistratus, reorganized the Dionysian festivals and instituted a system of annual competitions in the writing and presentation of dithyrambs and tragedies. Once the competition was established as the method of selecting works for performance at the festivals, the custom of always presenting new works at each succeeding festival was also established.

The rivalry engendered by the competitions was so powerful, and the honor accorded the victors so great, that festival and theatre remained indissolubly linked throughout the history of the Greek classical theatre.

THESPIS (6th century B.C.)

The winner of the first competition that was held—that of 534 B.C.— was the leader of one of the satyr-choruses, a poet and playwright named Thespis.

By the time of Thespis, the leader of the chorus seems to have had a rather special role: he was given lines or passages to perform solo, with the chorus answering him in unified response. Thespis, who originally played such a role in the festival presentations seems to have made a most significant innovation: he it was, according to the Greeks, who first introduced an actor onto the stage.

With this innovation, there was now the possibility of dialogue between the leader of the chorus and the actor. The actor also had the advantage of not being bound to the satyr-role; he might represent a god or hero. Indeed, it was in the role of a god—probably the messenger-god Hermes—that the actor first made his entry into Greek drama.

The name of Thespis, of course, has come down to us in the use of the word *thespian* as a synonym for actor. Actually, the term seems originally to have referred to touring actors, because in ancient Greek vase paintings, Thespis is usually depicted seated on a cart; the tradition was that Thespis would take his actors around in this cart, which they used as a stage or performing platform. Whatever the

AESCHYLUS (525 B.C.—456 B.C.)
Born in Eleusis, near Athens, in 525 B.C.,
the father of Greek tragedy was celebrated in his lifetime as a soldier, citizen,
and poet. His epitaph claims, as his sole
distinction, that he fought in the Battle of
Marathon against the Persians. He died
in the year 456 B.C. at Gela, Sicily. Of all
Greek dramas, the "Oresteia" is the sole
example of the dramatic trilogy which has
survived. This marble bust in the Cap-
itoline Museum in Rome shows the playwright as he was described in literature—
notably in the "Frogs," by Aristophanes—
with a bald head and a wedge-shaped
beard. A legend says that an eagle mistook
Aeschylus's bald head for a rock, and
dropped a tortoise on his pate in order to
break the shell.

SOPHOCLES   The second of the
great triumvirate of Athenian tragic poets,
Sophocles led a long and venerable life as
a statesman and public officeholder, as
well as a poet. Considered "the perfect
man" in his time—he was both handsome
and successful—he was greatly esteemed
by his contemporaries. Celebrated for the
beauty of his voice, he led the boys' chorus
at the victory dance after Salamis. In 471
B.C., he entered his first drama contest
and won his first victory over the great
elder poet Aeschylus in 468 B.C. In writing competition, Sophocles won first prize
18 times and never came in worse than
second.

reason, it seems most fitting to commemorate the first actor in the Western world by dubbing all those who have followed him with his name.

Although Thespis was a playwright, none of his plays have come down to us.

AESCHYLUS (525-456 B.C.)

The first great dramatist whose work is still extant is Aeschylus. He is considered the father of Greek tragic drama.

Aeschylus wrote over seventy plays. Of these, only seven have been vouchsafed to us. All of these are tragedies; the classical comedy was a later development. The burlesque and raucous satyr-plays, of course, were already being presented. Aeschylus was said to have been a master of this form, but only fragments of his work in this genre remain.

Fortunately, the major plays of Aeschylus that have survived were written at various periods of his life, providing us with a picture of his development as playwright and of the development of Greek tragedy to which he made such important contributions.

The Agamemnon, The Choephorae (The Libation Bearers), and *The Eumenides (The Furies)* form a trilogy called the *Oresteia* which tells the story of the house of Agamemnon and the tragedies that befell its members. The other four plays that have come down to us are *The Persians, Seven Against Thebes, The Suppliant Women,* and *Prometheus Bound.*

Aeschylus was nourished on Homer, and his work reflects the grand sweep of Homer's epics. Many critics regard him as the greatest tragic playwright who ever lived, rivalled only by Shakespeare.

Aeschylus began to participate in the competitions in 499 B.C. Five years later, he won first prize; thereafter, he was the most celebrated playwright in Athens. After his death, as a special act of recognition, the Athenians decreed that the rule of presenting only new plays at the festivals might be set aside in his sole case, so that the plays of Aeschylus might continue to be performed.

THE PLAYS OF AESCHYLUS

Prometheus Bound, which is the only remaining segment of a trilogy, deals with the punishment of the titan Prometheus by Zeus, the chief of the Greek gods, for having given the gift of fire to mankind. It is informed by a kind of majestic ambivalence: gratitude to the giver of fire alternates with respect for the majesty of the mighty god who has been defied.

In the *Oresteia,* Aeschylus dwells upon the benevolence of Zeus, as contrasted with the avenging justice of the Furies. In sheer power of great tragic writing, Aeschylus far surpassed his contemporaries. To this very day, *Agamemnon* comes across the footlights with overwhelming power. Cassandra's forebodings of doom, Agamemnon's mighty death-cry, and Clytemnestra's remorseless gloating over the murder of her husband, produce dramatic effects which have made this play a deathless classic. Here were dramatic ideas of such originality that the play has incisive force even 2,400 years later.

AESCHYLUS' INNOVATIONS

Aeschylus inherited a form of drama which was closer to the modern oratorio than to the modern play—a form in which there was but a single actor who intoned long passages of poetry, and a chorus of fifty men whose form of dramatic expression was entirely musical. True, there were dialogue passages between the leader of the chorus and the actor, but these were rather minor portions of the work whose overall tone was still dominated by the chorus.

Early in his career, Aeschylus took the crucial step of adding a second actor to the cast. With this step, he is said to have founded the modern theatre. In the course of his life, Aeschylus gave increasing importance to the actors and to the dialogue passages of his plays, later on, adapting in his own way, Sophocles' addition of a third actor. Aeschylus eventually reduced the number of men in the chorus from fifty to twelve.

 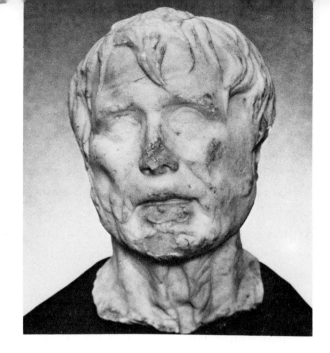

Above LEFT *EURIPIDES   The youngest of the great Greek trio of poets, Euripides, according to legend, was born on the day of the battle of Salamis. Less, however, is known of him than of his two great contemporaries, Aeschylus and Sophocles, though he was probably born in Salamis four years earlier. Unlike his two compeers, he took little part in public life. He first entered dramatic competition in 455 B.C., but did not win first prize until he was past 40. Due to the radical cast of his ideas, his work was unfavorably received in his lifetime. Morose, perhaps a misogynist, he won only five victories (posthumously for the "Bacchae") compared to 18 for Sophocles. Aristotle held him to be "the most tragic of the poets." The bust shown here stands in Mantua.*

Above RIGHT *ARISTOPHANES   (448 B.C.-338 B.C.) The father of Greek comedy, Aristophanes synthesized the elements of the early"Komos" with the burlesque elements of Doric farce, creating the comic masterpieces we associate today with the Golden Age of Greece. His plays satirized every level of society. The statesman, the politician, the philosopher, the popular poet—all were targets for his wit. In "The Clouds," he mocked Socrates; in the "Frogs," he jibed at Aeschylus and Euripides. The public at large suffered in the "Knights." Pericles, Lamachus, Nicias, and Demosthenes were statesmen whom he lampooned. In the "Elezaisousae," he championed the philosophy of communism and women's rights. Although he was never awarded a statue in his honor, this Hellenistic head is believed to be an excellent likeness.*

The contributions of Aeschylus also included the use of painted backdrops and the use of simple properties.

Another innovation was the employment of the chorus to represent a new range of characters. In *The Eumenides,* for example, the chorus represents the Furies who pursue Orestes and threaten Athens with ruin. Robed in black, with snakes wound in their hair, they must have produced a truly compelling effect.

SOPHOCLES (496-406 B.C.)

The first great rival to Aeschylus was Sophocles who first appeared as an important writer in the competition held in 471 B.C. Sophocles did much to humanize both the language and the characters of Greek tragedy. His poetry was flexible and subtle, marvellously adapted to the portrayal of character and emotion in which he excelled.

To Aristotle, Sophocles represented the Greek tragedy in its mature form; and it was on the work of Sophocles that Aristotle's renowned analysis of the nature of tragedy is based.

Sophocles achieved his first major success in 468 B.C., when, at the age of twenty-seven, he won a victory over Aeschylus in the competition. After that, he was to win first prize eighteen times in less than thirty years. He was said to have won second prize very often, and never to have come in third.

Sophocles wrote well over one hundred plays, of which only seven survive: *Oedipus the King, Antigone, Electra, The Trachinian Women, Ajax, Philoctetes,* and the play of his late old age, *Oedipus Coloneus.*

"OEDIPUS THE KING"

Many critics consider *Oedipus the King* the greatest of all Greek tragedies. The action of the play describes how Oedipus gradually comes to realize that he has, in ignorance, killed his father and married his mother. The power of this tragedy is unsurpassed in all literature for the stage. The impact becomes overwhelming when Oedipus, refusing to plead his ignorance, accepts full moral responsibility for his acts, and in a fervor of guilt, blinds himself. Here is flawless structure and high moral purpose.

It was Sigmund Freud who universalized the Oedipus tragedy by ascribing to the drama of Sophocles the psychological interpretation on which most modern psychiatry is based. The *Oedipus Complex* is said to account for a good deal of man's unconscious frustration and neurosis.

"ANTIGONE"

In *Antigone,* Sophocles deals with the conflict between the laws of God and the laws of man. Creon, King of Thebes, has ordained that burial rites not be administered to his nephew, Polyneices, killed during a treasonable assault on Thebes. Antigone, the sister of Polyneices and the daughter of Oedipus, feels that she must follow the laws of God which hold that burial rites must be accorded the dead. Even though it leads to her death, she stands by her belief. The dialogue between Creon and Antigone constitutes a powerful discussion of moral right versus legal right.

EURIPIDES (484-406 & 407 B.C.)

The third great tragic poet of the ancient Greeks, Euripides, did not achieve the early success of his predecessors. He traveled a hard road before his plays were accepted.

Three years after his first victory in the annual competitions, he was once again defeated by Sophocles. Euripides won first prize in the competitions only four or five times, yet the few plays that have come down to us are so good that some of them—*Medea,* for example —are produced again and again in all parts of the world.

Euripides, skeptical of established authority, is considered to have been a more profound thinker than either Aeschylus or Sophocles.

He gave his characters greater psychological insight. He scoffed at the gods, usually portraying them as either immoral or ridiculous, and imputing to them but few of the lofty motives with which they were endowed by Aeschylus and Sophocles.

Euripides, often called a woman-hater, has been attacked for his portrayals of the emotions of women smitten by the grand passion. However, some of the greatest feminine characters in all drama appear in his plays: Medea, Iphigenia, Phaedra, Alcestis, Evadne. Because of his radical ideas, Euripides was satirized by many contemporary voices, among them the playwright Aristophanes.

Of the ninety-two plays composed by Euripides, seventeen tragedies and one after-piece, a satyr-play, survive. *The Trojan Women* depicts the horrors of war and its aftermath. *Hippolytus* introduces the first human, though illicit, love story ever acted in the theatre. *Iphigenia in Tauris* is excellent romantic drama. *Medea* is a powerful study of marital jealousy.*The Bacchae,* perhaps because it was written later in his life when Euripides lived in exile in Macedonia, seems to mark the playwright's return to the religious beliefs which he had rejected in his earlier works.

THE GROWTH OF COMEDY

Tragedy had transported the enrapt audience into the past, creating a mood of sadness, and tragedy had caused the audience to weep. The Greeks were quite ready to see comedy, plays which they could view dry-eyed, with smiles and with uproarious laughter. In 486 B.C., comedy was officially admitted in Athens by the *City Dionysia,* the annual religious festival held in spring.

Early Greek comedy abused and satirized prominent people. This was probably encouraged because it was considered to be healthily democratic.

Classical Greek comedy was divided by the ancient critics into three periods: the Old Comedy, the Middle Comedy, and the New Comedy. Old Comedy, whose great exponent was Aristophanes, has come down to us in plays so topical in their references that they are often somewhat puzzling to the modern reader. The Old Comedies derived, like the tragedy, from the dithyrambs and satyr-plays. They had very little plot and a rather formal structure.

Within this structure, however, they offered a riotous combination of burlesque, obscenity, political commentary, parody, and invective, combined with the most lyrical poetry.

ARISTOPHANES (c. 448-c. 380 B.C.)

Aristophanes was the great writer of comedies. The work which he did which remains to us was produced between 425 and 388 B.C. His earlier work falls into the period of the Old Comedy. His later work marks the beginning of the Middle Comedy. His plays were particularly noted for their outspoken allusions to unpopular people and his allusions to unpopular causes. Several times during the course of his career, he suffered imprisonment; but apparently he was a man of principle and he carried on nevertheless.

The Clouds is an attack on the educational theories of the Sophists, a school of philosophers who were the subject of much popular debate.

The Birds deals with a Utopia which has been set up in the clouds by the Athenians, and is notable for its remarkably lyrical bird chorus.

The Frogs satirizes Euripides and Aeschylus, and features a contest in Hades between the two to determine which of them shall be brought back to earth to save the dying art of tragedy.

THE NEW COMEDY

It was during the end of the 4th century B.C. that the last important development took place in Greek drama. Athens had lost its political importance, but still held the lead in art, science, and philosophy. Comedy shifted from the satirical political themes of Aristophanes to scenes of everyday domestic life. No longer a democracy, Athens was under the domination of Macedonia, and the freedom of speech enjoyed by Aristophanes was no longer possible. The political situation of the day conditioned the creation of the New Comedy.

MENANDER (343-292 B.C.)

The greatest writer of New Comedy was Menander, who wrote over a hundred plays. Of these, more than 1,100 fragments have survived.

Menander presented his first play at Athens around 320 B.C., and he set a standard for comedy which persisted right down to the time of Molière. The comedies of Menander were built around certain typical figures or stock types. Many of the stock characters first created by Menander still appeared on the early Elizabethan stage.

While the costuming of the actors in the New Comedy more closely resembled the clothing of everyday life than it had in the earlier comic theatre, the New Comedy employed the convention of always garbing certain stock characters in certain colors. One such stock character was a roguish slave who always wore a white tunic and a very distinctive mask with red hair. Old men also wore white, but these oldsters were always clean-shaven and had closely cropped hair. Beards were reserved to denote mature manhood or middle age. Young men wore purple; parasites were garbed in black or grey; and old women were presented in yellow or light blue. A courtesan was easily recognized, since that character always had her hair bound up with golden ornaments and brightly colored bands.

By discarding the phallus and wearing costumes similar to the everyday garb of the Greeks, the players of New Comedy developed a more realistic style of acting. Since they appeared in amusing and novel situations, the actors developed individuality in their performances.

It was inevitable that the general themes of these plays should be based on human failings and vanities. The dissolute rake, born of wealthy parents and involved in amorous adventures which were

THEATRE OF DIONYSUS   *Begun in the sixth century B.C., this oldest theatre in Greece underwent successive changes until reaching its present form. The ruins at Athens are Hellenistic; the semicircular playing area was once the round orchestra. The opening of the ancient altar base can still be seen in the center of the mosaic.*

largely engendered by his slave, was a typical figure. So, too, the courtesan, the stern parent, the seduced daughter.

Tragedies of earlier times were still being revived at this period; but the old comedies of the ancient masters were dead and seemingly buried. The New Comedy had taken over.

THE THEATRES

The early theatres of Greece were temporary affairs: merely open areas upon which the chorus danced and sang. The audience sat on rough wooden benches to watch them perform. Behind the perform-ing area, temporary wooden buildings were erected to serve as dressing room, storage room, and backdrop, all in one.

Some scholars believe that Thespis performed in the Agora, or market place, with the audience seated on raised wooden benches to watch. Some time during the 6th century B.C., the sacred precincts of Dionysus were dedicated on the slope of the Acropolis hill in Athens. When the *City Dionysia* began to be held there, the wooden benches were moved to the slope of the hillside. The original performances of all the works of Aeschylus, Sophocles, Euripides, and Aristophanes took place in this sort of makeshift theatre. A stone amphitheatre was not built here until the 4th century B.C.—long after the greatest of the Athenian playwrights were dead.

The typical plan of any Greek theatre came to be an array of seats ranged in curved tiers on the slope of a hill, overlooking a flat performance area, which was called the *orchestra*. The orchestra was usually in the shape of an ellipse—a shape both graceful to the eye and convenient to the spectator. (Note that to the Greeks the word orchestra did not mean a seating place for the audience, but a place where the chorus and actors performed.) Behind the orchestra was a building, with doors through which the actors made their entrances and exits.

Whether the roof of this building was used as a second, raised stage, or whether a raised platform stage was placed behind the orchestra, and the building behind that—or upon it—is a matter over which scholars disagree. Some say that the actors performed on a raised stage of some sort, while the chorus performed on the orchestra, at ground level; others say actors and chorus mixed freely in both areas. In later times (about the 3rd century B.C.), as the chorus was reduced in importance, a separate raised platform stage built of stone became a permanent feature.

In any case, the geographical location of the theatre at Athens gave rise to an interesting theatrical convention which spread throughout Greece and even, later on, to Rome: a character who entered the stage from the left—the side of the theatre which faced inland—was assumed to come from the countryside nearby; a character who en-

tered the stage from the right—the side of the theatre nearest the sea
—was assumed to come from a distant land or from a long journey.

In all the Greek theatres, the audiences were entirely at the mercy
of the weather; no protection was afforded from either rain or sun.
Since performances were held in the early spring and in fall or
winter, the sun was not too grave a problem. It was mainly the rain
that caused trouble.

SCENERY AND PROPERTIES

We are told that Aeschylus used painted scenery in the presentation
of his plays, but there is little knowledge of how he used it.

Certain scenic devices were used in a symbolic sense. A three-
sided screen was erected on each side of the stage. On each of these
surfaces, pictures were painted. The screens could revolve so that any
of the three pictures could face the audience as required.

This simple arrangement of easily changed pictures gave the
audience sufficient understanding of change of scene. When one
screen was turned around, it meant that the scene now represented
was in the immediate neighborhood of the preceding scene. When
two screens were changed, it meant that there was supposed to be a
complete change of locality.

In most of the plays of Sophocles and Euripides, the scenes are
laid before a temple or a palace. The stage buildings, with their
columns standing at the back of the stage, thus formed a very suitable
background. If a backcloth was used, it was in two sections, the
lower part was painted to represent buildings and natural surroundings, and the upper part was painted to represent the sky. This was
done because in many of the plays an actor personified a god, who
often made his appearance on the top of a building. The complicated
tangle of plots and counterplots in the plays of Euripides were usually
resolved toward the end of the play by having a god make his appearance out of the sky.

STAGE DEVICES

The crane was used to hoist mortals up to heaven or gods down to earth. In the case of Trygaeus in Aristophanes's *The Peace,* the crane was used so effectively that Trygaeus appeared to be carried up to Olympus on the back of a giant beetle.

The crane was the "machine" referred to in the expression *deus ex machina.* This machine was used by a playwright to bring a god down to earth to rescue a mortal from an intricate difficulty. The expression *deus ex machina* has come to be applied to any dramatic device introduced by a playwright to bring the action of a play to a timely, if unlikely, conclusion. Thus, by extension, the phrase *deus ex machina* has come to mean the advent of any person or thing that appears suddenly or is introduced unexpectedly to provide a contrived solution to an apparently insoluble dilemma.

THE TROLLEY

Since scenes of violence were taboo in the Greek theatre, all murders were committed off-stage. As all scenes were exteriors, any important action that took place indoors was conveyed to the audience through the expedient of arranging the characters in a set pose on the stage of a trolley, and then pushing the trolley through the stage door and out onto the stage.

TRAP DOORS

Trap doors were used to bring ghosts, Furies, and other subterranean beings onto the stage. Altars, tombs, and statues of gods, being constantly referred to in the Greek plays, were common properties used as part of the settings. In much later times, horses and chariots were brought onto the stage.

The theatre at Epidaurus—the best preserved of the ancient theatres—had a stage which, although only eight feet deep, was seventy-eight feet wide, thus providing ample space for a horse to gallop across stage. In contrast to the rather static performance of the actors, such a rush of movement created a dramatic sensation. Nevertheless, the practice was never widely employed and remained something of a novelty.

COSTUMES

In ancient Greek tragedy, costumes were neither strictly historical nor contemporary. Although the action of the tragedies took place in Homeric times, the producers made no attempt to achieve historical accuracy. Yet the Greeks considered that common, everyday dress was not sufficiently dignified to portray their gods and heroes, so a special costume was evolved. This was a long-sleeved robe decorated with bright colors. Along with this would be worn either the *himation,* a long mantle—usually worn over the right shoulder—that covered most of the body, or the *chlamys,* a short cloak which was flung across the left shoulder. The mask, of course, gave the clue to the character.

The use of buskins, with high soles of six inches to endow the actor with greater height and dignity, is now believed to be a much later practice, not known in classical Greece.

Women characters wore trailing gowns which were longer than those used by men. Moreover, the gowns of women were usually of a particular color. A queen's costume, for instance, was purple. In Greek tragedy, where theatre programs were unheard of, it was imperative that the audience be able to recognize a character without difficulty. Therefore, certain characters were always dressed in a costume of a particular color so that recognition would be immediate.

Color was also used to signify the condition of the character. If the character happened to be in a situation of misfortune or exile, he would be clothed in a mantle of black or gray, which would be draped over his tunic.

A TRAGIC MASK   This great bronze tragic mask of the Hellenistic period was found at Piraeus in 1959 among ruins of a warehouse, believed to have been burned during Sulla's attack in 86 B.C. The contorted brow, the exaggerated eye and mouth openings, and the elaborate headdress are features of the later Hellenistic period.

In ancient Greece, hats were worn only when one went on a journey. Thus, the audience could readily appreciate the change of scene implied when a character wearing a hat appeared on stage.

In tragedies, all male characters wore the same kind of tunic, girdled high under the breast and falling in long, graceful folds. These tunics differed from each other only in their decoration—patterns of varied colors based on floral designs or the shapes of animals or birds.

To differentiate among the gods and the heroes, certain easily recognizable properties were carried. Apollo carried his bow, Hermes his magic wand, Hercules carried his club and lion skin, and Perseus his cap of darkness. Warriors usually appeared in full armor, with a short scarlet cloak draped around the arm. An old man would carry a staff; a messenger of good tidings wore a crown of olives or of laurel. A king would carry a spear and wear a crown; and in addition, a king would also wear a short tunic over the usual long one.

In comedy, the costuming was rather different: the tunics were

GREEK TRAGIC COSTUMES   *Elaborately-patterned stage costumes are illustrated by these figures from Attic vases of the sixth and
fifth centuries B.C. The tiara worn by Andromeda indicates that she
is an oriental princess. The hero from the Pronomos vase holds the
mask of an oriental king.*

much shorter and contained much padding on all sides. The tradition
of the old boisterous Dionysiac festivals was continued by the wearing of the phallus. In the plays of Aristophanes and others the chorus
did not always represent human beings, so special costumes were
required. At various times, the chorus represented birds, fishes, in-
sects, frogs, goats, and even clouds. In *The Birds* by Aristophanes, the
chorus wore a delightfully conventionalized bird costume, complete
with wings and crests.

The buskin was never worn in comedy. A soft-soled shoe, known as the *soccus,* was used, and this kind of shoe has always been associated with comic acting.

MASKS

Tradition has it that Thespis invented the tragic mask, although Aeschylus and others developed its use. In the Greek theatre, a character represented a general type rather than an individual, so a certain number of stylized masks were evolved. A mask indicated by simple outline and shape the general attributes of the particular character who wore it. In the enormous Greek theatre, with its huge distances and its dependence solely on sunlight, facial expression—so important to the actor's craft today—was quite out of the question.

Once the masks had been evolved, they changed only in detail throughout the centuries. The masks varied in size according to the

GREEK CONTEMPORARY DRESS   The long chiton and the short cloak were the basis for stage costume developed in the fifth century B.C.

importance of the character, and the coiffure was built up from the forehead accordingly. Thus, when a mask was intended to represent a king, the hair was built up at the top of the mask, and the actor would gain inches in height and consequently in importance.

Originally, the masks were made of stiffened linen, but it was later found that cork or wood had better acoustical properties. A mask would cover the actor's entire head, and was painted to emphasize the basic expression which the actor intended to delineate. Even the eyes were painted in; only a small hole was left through which the actor could see.

It was once believed that the masks were constructed with small megaphones concealed in the open mouths to amplify the actors' voices, but modern scholars doubt this.

THE ACTORS

The Greek play, as it was finally developed, used only three actors, but there were, of course, many characters, both male and female, and each actor was called upon to play a number of parts. The great advantage of this system was that even the minor parts were excellently played. At any given time, no more than three characters were ever involved in a dialogue. If the three characters were already on the stage and a fourth character appeared, he would have no lines to speak; such a part could be played by a super.

By simply changing the mask, an actor could change his character. This continual change of character put great stress on the powers of the actor's voice, which had to be sufficiently flexible to change with the character, from youth to old age, and from man to woman. Moreover, an actor's voice had to be powerful, since it had to carry outdoors to the furthest reaches of an amphitheatre which held nearly 30,000 spectators.

OLD COMEDY   Several of the distinguishing features of the old comedy characters—the padded jerkin, exaggerated phallus, and grotesque mask—are evident in this terra cotta statuette of a fourth-century cymbalist.

MENANDER   This outstanding writer of the New Comedy was known for centuries only through quotations of his works. Evidently he served as a model for the Roman playwrights, Terence and Plautus. In 1905, a papyrus was discovered in Egypt which contained substantial sections of four of his plays: the "Heros," the "Samia," the "Epitrepontes," and the "Perikeiromene." In 1957, the "Dyskolos" papyrus was found. Translations, with conjectural restorations of the "Epitrepontes" and the Perikeiromene" were undertaken in 1941 and in 1945 by Prof. Gilbert Murray. The text of the "Dyskolos" appears to have first been performed in 317 B.C. when Menander was twenty-five years of age. The head shown here is in the University of Mississippi.

PARASITE MASK   The battered nose, cavernous mouth, and protruding ears of this grotesque mask represent the coarse Sicilian Parasite, a stock role of the New Comedy. This character found particular favor in the plays of the Sicilian playwright Epicharmus (fifth century B.C.) and later in the Roman comedies of Plautus and Terence.

Certain actors specialized in imitating all kinds of weird noises—the rush of the wind, the rush of the sea, and a whole repertoire of animal cries. Some actors would indulge any abilities they had in this direction, as it was always a sure method of attracting applause, though some of the audience considered such displays to be in bad taste and discerning writers deplored this rather cheap method of winning an audience. Aristotle, when writing of the tragic acting of Theodorus, commends the thoroughly natural quality of his voice, remarking that unlike the other actors, Theodorus seemed to speak with his own voice.

Tragic plays were delivered in a loud, sonorous style; all movements were dignified and restrained. A more conversational style was employed in comedy, and in this type of presentation the movements were much more lively.

It was during the 4th century B.C. that the art of acting in Greece reached its highest level. This was due in some measure to the fact that the old plays then being performed were well-known; and since they had already been seen, interpretation by the actors became more important.

The professional status of actors was honorable, almost comparable to that of the priests. To maintain their privileges, about the middle of the 4th century the actors formed a guild, known as the Artists of Dionysus, which included poets, actors, chorus, trainers, and musicians. Among their privileges was their prerogative of travelling through foreign and even hostile states to give performances. Even during the height of the war against Philip of Macedonia, two actors traveled from Athens to Macedonia in order to perform, and were, in fact, instrumental in negotiating the peace.

Another privilege obtained from the city—though not without some trouble—was the actors' exemption from compulsory military service.

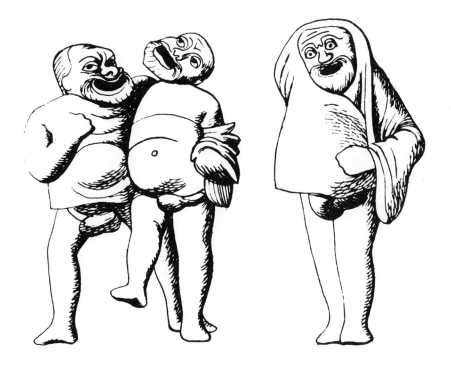

GREEK COMIC CHARACTERS OF THE FOURTH CENTURY B.C.
They wear the costume of Menander's New Comedy: the short jerkin, the large phallus, and the grotesquely-grinning masks.

THE CHORUS

It was under Euripides that the chorus reached its peak of importance. During that period, the chorus for tragedies consisted of fifteen men. The chorus for comedies was larger, twenty-four being the usual number. The chorus was usually characterized as either old men, women, or maidens, and was supposed in a general way to represent the public. They were masked. Their dress was usually contemporary, except when they were called upon to represent such non-human beings as frogs, birds, or Furies.

Normally, the chorus was grouped in a rectangular formation and performed in the circular orchestra. The chorus sang or chanted its

GREEK FARCE   A form of popular comedy known as the "Phlyakes" originated in Italy in the fifth century B.C. The themes remained much the same as in the old Doric farces: there were parodies of myths; the feats of Heracles were the butt of many jokes; and there were burlesques of daily life. The actors in these early farces were called "phlyakes"—gossips—from which the entire body of the popular comedy takes its name. This scene, from a fourth-century vase, shows servants helping the old centaur, Cheiron, up the steps.

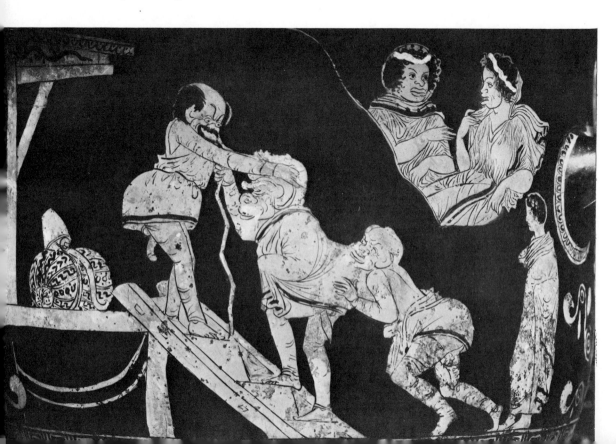

THE TRAGIC ACTOR   This famous wall painting, found in Herculaneum, illustrates the dedication of a mask—most important part of an actor's costume—in a sanctuary of Dionysus. Handsomely costumed, the tragic actor wears raiment characteristic of the late Hellenistic period: white-sleeved robe, broad golden belt, purple mantle—and most representative of the style—the double-soled shoes and the "onkos" (hairdress of the mask). The hairdress is higher than that used in earlier times.

GRECO-ROMAN COMEDY   *This scene, in which a slave appears to be ridiculing a pair of surprised lovers, is on a famed mural in Herculaneum. Depicting a Roman comedy presented before 79 A.D., the slave's mask marks a tradition that goes back to Menander's New Comedy of the fourth century B.C. The role of the slave, first given prominence by that Greek master, was humanized by him. Incorporated into Roman comedy, the character grew louder and more ribald.*

lines, accompanied by the music of a flute. The chorus also danced. In tragic plays, the dance was slow and dignified; in comedies, the movements were more lively, and often were lascivious and coarse.

In those days, singing was done in unison; harmony was unknown. The music was written to suit the words. Both dancing and music were subordinated to the poetry, since the lyrical parts of the play were allocated to the chorus.

The members of the chorus had to be highly skilled. The leader held a position almost as important as that of the actor. The chorus had to be well trained, not only individually but as a group. Since the chorus was such an integral part of the play, expert performance was essential.

THE PUBLIC CHARACTER OF THE GREEK THEATRE

It is important to realize that the ancient Greek theatre was always a public theatre, never a private enterprise. It grew out of public religious ceremonials carried on in the name of and on behalf of the entire community. The Greek theatre never departed from its character of being a public function, involving the community as a whole.

As a consequence, the selection of plays to be performed at the annual festival competitions was up to the state. Months before a festival, the *archon,* the magistrate in charge of the festival, would select the poets who were to present their plays at the forthcoming celebration. Originally, tragedies were presented at the City Dionysia as the spring festival was called; comedies were presented at the Lenaea, the autumn or winter festival. Later on, comedies were added to the City Dionysia, and still later, tragedies were added to the Lenaea.

The number of tragic poets chosen was always three; the number of comic poets grew to be five. The selection was made on the basis of manuscripts submitted by the poets. Certain plays which have come down to us, those of Aristophanes in particular, contain topical references which must of necessity have been written very close to the

THE THEATRE OF ASPENDUS   *The best preserved of all Roman theatres, Aspendus was designed by the architect Zeno, son of Theodarus, a Greek tragic actor of the fourth century. It was built in Pamphylia, Asia Minor, during the reign of Marcus Aurelius in the second century B.C. This drawing shows the highly-ornamented scene wall, the enclosed sides, and the rectangular playing area.*

time of actual performance. It is therefore conjectured that well-established playwrights may have been required only to submit scenarios or outlines of their works rather than detailed scripts, while younger playwrights would have been required to furnish scripts written out in full.

ROMAN COMIC CHARACTERS

Roman comedy owes much of its development to the farces called the Atellana, the Phlyakes, and to the New Comedy of Menander. Naevius, earliest writer of Roman comedies, created from these diverse sources a comedy in which themes drawn from the life of the Roman lower classes predominate. These three terra cotta statuettes from Southern Italy, now standing in the British Museum, represent three types of Roman comic characters: a potter, a politician, and a moneylender. They might easily have come from such plays of Naevius as "Agitatoria" (the politician), "Figulus" (the potter), "Tunicularia" (the man in the small tunic), and "Carbonaria" (the charcoal burner).

THE CHOREGI

Once the selection of poets had been made, arrangements for production began. The state paid for the chorus and three actors (five for a comedy). All other costs were born by a rich and eminent citizen, called the *choregus*. The state had a list of such men; they were called upon to perform expensive and honorable services to the state, such as equipping a warship or sponsoring a play.

Each poet was assigned a choregus by lot. The choregus paid for the costumes, the sets, the training of the chorus, whatever supers, (non-speaking extra actors) were required by the script, and the musicians. Obviously, the assignment of a generous choregus was an advantage to a playwright; that of a niggardly one, a disadvantage. In fact, it was in order to avoid acrimony over the assignments that they were made by lot. Nevertheless, unhappy playwrights often felt that their failure to win the competition at the festival was the result of their being unable to mount their works properly, owing to the assignment of a stingy choregus.

Eventually, it was decided to award a prize to the choregus of the winning play, as well as to its author, and this appears to have solved the problem. The costs of the chorus were one of the greatest expenses a choregus had to bear. He was expected to pay each member of the chorus a wage, provide for his keep, and attend to his training.

In the days of the great poets, they themselves trained the chorus; but after Euripides, the poets no longer took an active part in the production. A special chorus trainer was appointed, who added to the financial burdens of the choregus.

During the Peloponnesian Wars when money was scarce, the authorities permitted two or more choregi to share the expenses of a play. Eventually, at the end of the 4th century B.C., the city assumed complete responsibility and bore the entire cost.

DIRECTION, MUSICAL COMPOSITION, CHOREOGRAPHY

The poet-playwrights were always their own directors. They also

ROMAN SLAVE CHARACTER   This marble statuette in the Vatican Museum shows a slave sitting on an altar to which he has come for refuge. He wears a typical slave costume with certain features, notably the long-sleeved tights and the leggings, taken from the Greek New Comedy. The Roman pallium, his wrap-around garment, is still essentially Greek himation. His mask, too, is essentially Greek. The slipper is the Roman soccus worn by comic actors.

wrote their own music and choreographed their own dances. Aeschylus, a great man of the theatre in every respect, was known to have designed his own scenic effects, as well as to have been the inventor of several theatrical devices which later playwrights continued to use.

When we first hear of the poet-playwright, he was also an actor. Thespis was such. But later, the acting was done only by professional actors. For a long time, particular actors seem to have worked continuously with particular playwrights; later, when this practice became the subject of contention, actors were assigned to playwrights by lot. Finally, at the festivals, prizes were also awarded to the best actors.

THE PERFORMANCES

On the day of performance, the audience arrived at the theatre at

COMIC FATHER MASK   This Roman marble mask, which is now in the University Museum in Philadelphia, points up traditional features of the Greek New Comedy carried over into Roman times: the rolled hair over the forehead, the beard rolled in corkscrew strands, and the highly-arched eyebrows. In the exaggerated style of later Roman masks, the eye and mouth openings are much enlarged.

dawn. Performances started early and continued throughout the day until sundown. There was only one intermission. Five plays were customarily offered in a single day. At the spring festival custom decreed that the day's performance should begin with the presentation of three tragedies, continue with a satyr-play, and end with a comedy.

The performances continued for three consecutive days. The fact that the attention of the audience could be riveted for so long a period of time was a tribute to the art of the performers and the talent of the writers. Perhaps curiosity as to which playwright would win the competition also played a role in securing the audience's attention.

THE FESTIVALS

The dramatic festivals lasted for four or five days; they were splendid and dramatic occasions. The whole first day was devoted to a grand and solemn procession through the city by priests, officials, poets, actors, *choregi,* choruses, and musicians, followed by the populace and the many strangers who had come to attend the celebrations. The participants were attired in brilliantly colored garments, richly ornamented with gold. The procession marched to the temple of Dionysus, from whence they carried out the statue of the deity and set it up in state in the theatre. Announcements were then made of the plays which were to be performed on the following day.

THE PRIZES

The winners of the competition were selected on the final day of the festival by a special jury of ten, who had been seated in places of honor in the front rows of the theatre. When the last performance had ended, each judge wrote down his choice for first place and second place, and placed his ballot in an urn. Only five votes were extracted from the urn, however; a majority vote of these decided who was to receive the award.

The winning poet was then brought to the stage and crowned with a chaplet of ivy; a solemn sacrifice was made, and the proceedings wound up with a grand banquet given by the poet to his actors, his chorus, and his friends.

Originally, the prize for the winning tragic poet was a live goat, that for the winning comic poet, a basket of figs and a jar of wine. Later, money prizes were awarded instead. The victorious poets' names were inscribed in the public archives and carved on a tablet in the theatre.

The lively spirit of the competitions kept the poets striving and stimulated them to their best efforts. Aeschylus, who died at the age of sixty-nine, produced plays right up to a few years before his death; and both Sophocles and Euripides also wrote well into their mellow

LATE ROMAN MASKS   This mosaic by Heraclitus, now in the Lateran Museum, shows masks of the later Roman period, marked by exaggerated eye and mouth openings. In the center is the mask of a woman

years. If a poet was unsuccessful in the competition, he was permitted to revise or rewrite his play and submit the same play at a subsequent festival. Euripides gained several victories with plays which at first had been rejected, and then after revision were successful.

ADMISSION FEES

Originally, performances were given free to the entire population. The consequence was that many people would arrive at the theatre

with elaborately-bejeweled hairdress. On either side of her are masks of an older man and a younger man.

the day before the performance to preempt the best seats. Complaints were heard that many foreigners had also taken prime locations. The city, therefore, decided to charge a small fee and issue tickets for all seats. But it was assumed that all citizens, however poor, were entitled to see the plays. Therefore, in cases of dire need, the city provided the cost of admission.

Since performances were deemed to be part of a sacred festival, even prisoners were released from jail in order to attend the performance. During the several days of the festival, all citizens were expected to be on their best behavior. Any offenses committed during the period were severely punished, and offenders were publicly castigated at the close of the festival.

THE AUDIENCES

In Athens an audience at a single performance could consist of nearly 30,000 people. Such an audience would include strangers and foreigners who had been attracted to the festivals.

Ambassadors and representatives of allied states came to the festival to pay their annual tribute; and sums of money thus collected were dispayed on the stage.

The first rows of the theatre were reserved for these important people, and for various priests, officials, and judges. In the center of the front row, the priest of Dionysus sat on a throne of honor. Lesser thrones were set up for the other officials. Successful generals also sat among the elite.

The remainder of the seats were backless benches built very close together. The rich would come to the spectacle bringing rugs and cushions.

The Athenians were a very lively audience; and to keep order, it was necessary to employ a team of staff-bearers. These men patroled the narrow gangways which divided the audience into twelve blocks. Although it was customary in Greece to relegate females to seclusion, women were nevertheless allowed to view the performances. They all sat together in one place, probably at the back of the theatre. Boys were also admitted; but they, too, had their special place in the auditorium. And even a slave was sometimes taken to the theatre, if he was lucky enough to have a benevolent master.

Aristotle divides the Greek audience into two parts: the refined and cultured citizens, and the rough and ignorant artisans. The poets of that time met, in large measure, the contradictory demands of both of these groups. Superb poetry was linked with simple and sometimes very amusing stage devices; and a study of Greek drama reveals that the sublime in many instances was happily wedded to the ridiculous.

THE ROMAN THEATRE

The Roman republic of the 3rd century B.C. borrowed its drama, like most of its art, from the Greeks. Towards the middle of this century, one Livius Andronicus (c. 284-204 B.C.) presented a comedy and a tragedy in Rome which he had adapted from the Greek and translated into Latin. The success of these performances ensured that future plays presented on the Roman stage would be modeled along the lines of Greek prototypes.

Taken captive as a child, Livius Andronicus had been brought to Rome as a slave. His command of both the Latin and Greek tongues enabled him to become a tutor, which eventually led to his becoming a freedman. He translated tragedies of Sophocles and Euripides, as well as some of the Greek comedies. Naevius, a contemporary of Livius Andronicus, also translated many of the old Greek plays.

In short, the Roman playwrights had the advantage of ready-made material, an advantage which they certainly took.

Plautus (c.254-184 B.C.) and Terence (c.190-159 B.C.) borrowed heavily from the New Comedy of Menander; and in fact much of our knowledge of Menander's works is based on a study of Plautus and Terence.

Seneca (c. 4 B.C.-65 A.D.) wrote tragedy in a style that was to prove a model for all subsequent periods in the theatre. Stage writings of the Elizabethan period in England and of the French theatre in the 17th century are based largely on Seneca's prototype.

PERFORMANCES ON THE ROMAN STAGE

Dramatic performances in Rome did not have the aspect of religious festivals as they had in Greece. Rather, they were considered to be simply a form of entertainment and were usually offered at the public games which the State provided free for the amusement of the populace. Here they were tucked in among such attractions as boxing matches and performances by rope dancers, and it was with diversions of this nature that the Roman actor had to compete.

Theatrical presentations were often made on public holidays, the number of official holidays on which such performances took place increasing steadily through the years until in A.D. 354 there were over one hundred days in the year set aside for that purpose.

Sometimes military victories were celebrated in the theatre, where dramatic presentations might be offered in honor of the achievements of a particular general or of a particular expedition. On certain occasions, the spoils of war were dragged across the stage by hundreds of mules—a spectacle, which though it might have delighted the multitude, was to the intelligent theatre-goer a poor substitute for drama. Cicero, for one, inveighed against this practice.

THE ROMAN PLAYHOUSE

Under the Roman influence, the physical aspects of the theatre changed considerably. The stage, which now was always a raised platform, was provided with a sloping roof which probably acted as a sounding board and improved the acoustics. The stage was also enlarged, and the facades of the stage doors were elaborated with many statues and architectural features.

The use of the chorus declined. In consequence, the orchestra became smaller. Eventually, the Romans abolished the choral part of the performance, and all spectacle took place on the stage.

Moreover, the new theatres built by the Romans were usually erected on level ground instead of on a hillside. It has been suggested that the reason for this was that Romans loved architectural embellishment, and were able to lavish decorative stonework on the facades of their theatres.

The device of raising and lowering a curtain to mark the beginning and end of a play was a Roman introduction. However, instead of being raised to open a play as it is in the modern theatre, the Roman stage curtain was lowered. A slit trench was excavated in the floor of the stage to house the curtain during the performance; and when a play started, the curtain descended into this trench. Details of the mechanical arrangements for operating the curtain are not available; but probably pulleys were attached to the roof of the stage and the ropes went through to the rear of the stage buildings.

Since dramatic performances were conducted in Rome throughout the year, huge and colorful canvas awnings were stretched across the tops of the open theatres to shelter the audience from the elements.

Roman theatres were erected throughout the empire and some—such as the one at Orange in southern France—have survived almost undamaged to the present day.

THE ROMAN ACTORS

The Greeks had laid great stress on unity of production. Actors, chorus, and musicians worked together as a team. The Romans attached more importance to individual performances by the leading actors.

Until the 1st century B.C., Roman actors played without masks, and each player specialized in one particular kind of role. The result was that the original three actors of the Greek tragedies, who played many parts and who switched from one character to another by merely changing masks, gave way to a troupe of specialists. In Roman times, each performer would become expert in some particular type of role, whether it was that of a woman, an old man, a youth, or a parasite; and of course, each developed great skill within the confines of his particular role. Versatility was neither demanded nor developed.

Because they had given up the mask, the Roman actors had to develop facial expression, which led to even further specialization. In Rome, the art of acting reached its height during the 1st century B.C., at just about the time when the writing of plays fell into decline.

The greatest actor the Romans produced was Roscius (d. 62 B.C.), who specialized in comedy. His talent was such that his name has since become associated with perfection in acting, so that the English-speaking theatre has known an American Roscius, an Ohio Roscius, a Dublin or Hibernian Roscius and a Young Roscius. The period of Roscius was unfortunately short-lived, and soon the acting profession

ROMAN AMPHITHEATRE   *This Pompeiian fresco in the Museo Nazionale in Naples is the only pictorial representation extant of a Roman stone amphitheatre. The theatre is believed to have been built in Pompeii around 80 B.C., and was initially used both for circus performances and for formal drama. Later, stone theatres were constructed solely for theatrical presentations. This scene is believed to represent—not an actual performance—but a riot which took place in 59 A.D. (Note the figures outside the arena.) Clearly visible at the top of the picture is the "velarium," an awning which could be drawn over the spectators to protect them from the sun. The small booth in center foreground is believed to be a refreshment stand.*

in Rome lost its status.

After Roscius' time, actors were considered entertainers rather than artists. In large measure, this development was due to the formation of permanent troupes which consisted of foreign slaves. A manager could treat his actors as he wished; flogging was the reward of many who were not well received and who brought discredit to their manager. However, a few of the actors were still freedmen, and these, on occasion, received civic honors.

An important dramatic innovation of the Roman theatre was the appearance of women on the stage, a thing unheard of in the days of Greek preeminence.

CENSORSHIP

In addition to being places of entertainment, theatres were the only public places where slaves and people without civil rights could meet. Such individuals were debarred from both the Forum and the Senate, and the theatre served them as a convenient rallying place.

The theatre was, naturally, also a convenient instrument for affecting popular opinion. Mindful of this, the authorities tightened their control over the theatres and passed many laws imposing restrictions on the actors. During the Empire, actors were treated little better than slaves; and both Julius Caesar (d. 44 B.C.) and Augustus enforced laws which, in effect, deprived actors of their civic rights.

THE DECLINE OF TRAGEDY AND COMEDY

During Empire times, tragedy and comedy declined. The public sought and got farces, burlesques, and pantomimes—short pieces akin to the vaudeville shows and music hall theatre of our own time. In the place of tragedy, solo performances were presented by tragedians or by famous personalities. The Emperor Nero, himself, delighted in giving tragic recitations; he appeared on the stage as Apollo, as Hercules, as Orestes, and as the blinded Oedipus, accompanying him-

THEATRE OF MARCELLUS   *This amphitheatre was begun in 13 B.C. by Julius Caesar and completed by Augustus in 11 B.C.*

HEARST GREEK THEATRE   *William Randolph Hearst gave this 8,000-seat theatre to the University of California in Berkeley in 1903.*

self on the cither—a behavior which shocked conservative upper-
class Rome even more than his worst excesses of cruelty, since by
his day, the majority of actors in Rome were slaves.

THE CLOSET DRAMA

As the public lost interest in the tragedies and comedies of Greek
tradition, upper-class literary playwrights developed the closet drama
—a form of play designed for reading rather than performance. The
tragedies of Seneca (4 B.C.-65 A.D.) were closet dramas, and were
probably never performed on the stage. This type of drama, preserved
in Latin manuscripts, was rediscovered during the Renaissance, and
exercised a profound influence on the playwrights of the 16th century.

THE MIMES

As the plebeian Roman audience cared little for literary drama, pre-
ferring spectacles and vaudeville presentations, the mime farces offered by troupes of traveling players became very popular. The mime
shows mirrored the low life of the times. Certain stock types were
developed: there was the fat, talkative fool, the stupid rustic fool,
and the foolish old man, to name but a few. These easily recognizable
characters were portrayed by mimes both male and female, who
usually improvised dialogue to fill out standard plot situations,
Roman mimes were not required by convention to be mute, as our
modern mimes are. The mimes were so well received that in time
they became the principal features of the day's entertainment. The
chief reason for their success was the intensely human quality contained in their vulgarity.

The mime tradition is one of the oldest and most persistent in the
Western theatre. It originated in ancient Greece, flourished in Rome,
persisted during the Dark Ages with the wandering bands of mounte-
banks and players who constituted the theatre of that period, and
reappeared as a full-fledged and most influential art form in the

Italian *Commedia dell'Arte* troupes of the 16th century. These troupes, as we shall see, passed on the traditional plots and characters of their improvised theatre to the playwrights of the 17th and 18th centuries. Offshoots of the tradition still exist in the British Christmas pantomimes and the Punch and Judy show.

THE DEGENERATION OF THE ROMAN THEATRE

The Romans loved bloodshed and violence. To satisfy the craving of their audiences for mayhem, Roman actors were expected to exchange realistic kicks and blows with their fellow actors and to acquire proficiency in such feats as boxing and knife throwing. In the theatre, mock battles were presented by scores of "warriors" in full armor. In time, in order to satisfy the bloodthirstiness of the Roman populace, this mimicking of violence gave way to the real thing: gladiatorial fights and the baiting of live animals became features of the Roman theatre.

In the days of the Empire life was cheap; and slaves, captives, and robbers were thrown in public spectacles to wild beasts who had been made ferocious through starvation. Sometimes the unfortunate victims were part of a drama which culminated in an execution. During the time of Trajan (c. 53-117 A.D.), a magician dressed as Orpheus was torn to pieces by wild animals. On the day the emperor Caligula (12-41 A.D.) was murdered, a robber was brought onto the stage during the performance of a pantomime and actually nailed to the cross, the audience apparently enjoying his slow and painful death. In later times, robbers and slaves were replaced as victims by the early Christian martyrs. It was through such degenerate spectacles that drama decayed and the Roman theatre collapsed.

The theatres themselves, however, continued to flourish. They had become a very popular feature in the life of the Romans, and their numbers grew from only forty-eight under Augustus (63-B.C.-14 A.D.) to over a hundred under Constantine (c. 288-337 A.D.). These theatres were very large, and each was capable of holding tens of thousands.

EARLY CHRISTIAN OPPOSITION TO THE THEATRE

The early Christian leaders were opposed to theatres and actors in general; and as Christianity spread throughout the Roman world, the early Church began to have some influence on the civil legislation of the Empire. In the 4th century A.D., the so-called *Canons of Hippolytus,* presumed to be the work of the leader of the Christian Church at that time, prohibited the clergy from attending the theatre. Moreover, if an actor wanted to become a Christian—or even to marry a Christian woman—he was obliged to quit his profession.

The Church forbade theatrical performances on Sundays and on religious festival days. St. John Chrysostom (c. 347-407 A.D.) in the East, and St. Jerome (c. 347-419) in the West continued to issue edicts on the evils of the theatre. Yet despite this growing opposition, theatres continued to exist; and during the last years of the Empire there was actually a lessening of official restriction. This may have been due to the fact that the wife of the Emperor Justinian—the Empress Theodora—had herself been an actress before becoming Justinian's mistress and subsequently his wife.

THE END OF THE THEATRE IN ROME

By A.D. 400, the theatres were doomed—and not because of early Christian opposition. Rome was sacked by the invading Goths; and in order to find a scapegoat for their defeat, the authorities blamed the slack Roman defense on the degeneration caused by the loose morals prevailing in the theatre.

However, when Rome was sacked once again in A.D. 467, a theatre was still there. Theodoric, who invaded Italy in 488, found it expedient to continue the theatre; and it was granted further years of grace until 568 when the Lombards—a hard, tough Germanic people from the North—descended on Italy. Although the Lombards did not conquer Rome itself, for many, many years after their arrival in Italy there was no mention anywhere of theatres in Rome.

The Middle Ages
and the Renaissance

TOURING COMPANIES

After the decline of Rome, theatrical performances did not suddenly come to an end. Although the actors were obliged to leave the theatres they had formerly played in, they formed small companies which took to the roads, and wandered through the countryside from hamlet to village to city, performing at weddings, baptisms, and other private festivities.

Members of the clergy who officiated at these events, were, however, ordered to leave the scene before the actors began their performances, the Church being much alive to the purported evils of the stage.

THE WANDERING MINSTRELS

For centuries during the Middle Ages, actors wandered the roads, along with acrobats, rope dancers, and tamers of wild beasts. The best of these itinerant performers became minstrels, the well-paid servants of nobles and kings. The others, little better than vagabonds, performed here and there for a pittance.

The earliest English poem we have recounts the story of a famous minstrel named Widsith, an epic singer who wandered across Europe, through Egypt and Persia, and even as far as India.

By the time Christianity had reached England in the 6th century, the minstrels were well established. Their songs rang with the praises of great heroes and warriors, the continuous warfare of the medieval period assuring them of a constant supply of material.

Wherever they stayed, wandering minstrels were usually made very welcome. To the great houses and castles of the nobility they had virtually a free right of entry, for in addition to providing entertainment, the minstrels brought with them news of foreign parts—news which they no doubt carefully colored to suit each particular audience. Sometimes, indeed, an itinerant minstrel would please some king or noble so well that he would settle down permanently in his service.

The Church, however, looked with disfavor on the activities of the minstrels; the bishops were continually issuing orders prohibiting the clergy from welcoming minstrels or watching their performances. In 1312, a priest of Ripon, England, was charged with breaking the canons in this respect. Nevertheless, despite the edicts of the bishops, the lower clergy generally looked forward to the minstrels' visits. Even bishops, on occasion, received them favorably; and it is recorded that minstrels were usually assured a warm welcome in the monasteries, for being only human, the monks much appreciated the news and entertainment which the minstrels brought them.

By the 11th century, the minstrels were popular among all classes, and gave performances in taverns, castles, guild halls, and marketplaces. At august festivities such as royal weddings, minstrels would appear in great strength; 426 were numbered at the marriage of Margaret of England and John of Brabant in 1290.

Some of the more famous minstrels actually became rich. Rahere (d. 1144), chief minstrel to Henry I of England, is reputed to have made a fortune. When he quit his profession, he had enough money to found the great priory of St. Bartholomew of which he became the first head.

MEDIEVAL MINSTRELS   In this drawing, the minstrels wear the typical parti-colored costumes of the period. The ancient instruments of the Middle Ages which they carry are: (from the left) trumpet, vielle, cymbals, hand organ, harp.

SCHOOLS FOR MINSTRELS

At Beauvais, Lyons, and Cambrai, schools for minstrels flourished. Here minstrels would repair from all over Europe, especially during Lent, when no performances were given. In these schools, the minstrels would learn new songs and pick up fresh news and material.

The first requirement for a successful minstrel was, of course, a pleasing voice. Given this, his chances for success would be greatly enhanced by the possession of a pleasing personality. Needless to say, he would also have to know how to accompany himself on an instrument. Musical instruments in common use were the harp and the vielle, a type of violin. Trumpets were used for the sounding of fanfares, and to punctuate the dramatic moments of a performance. Other instruments of the era were hand organs, cithers, bagpipes, drums, and cymbals.

When several minstrels performed together, they sang alternately, in the form of a dialogue based on question and answer. Many of the old illuminated manuscripts show illustrations of minstrels, musicians, and other entertainers. They are portrayed wearing the usual costumes of the period, but brighter and bolder in color and design

MEDIEVAL FOOL   In typical motley, the jester wears a close-fitting hood. The peaks, representing asses ears, are thought to have derived from the ancient Roman mime, Mimus Calvus.

than the clothing of the general population. One can well imagine these minstrels presenting a pleasing, colorful entertainment to the simple, illiterate people of their day, making use of certain tried and true stage properties, such as that old favorite, the ass's head. In these performances, animal mimicry reached a fine art.

TOWN MINSTRELS

In the beginning of the 15th century, there were small groups of minstrels in the service of the municipal corporations of the larger towns such as London, Bristol, York, Canterbury, Shrewsbury, and Norwich. These performers wore the town livery, and played at local festivities and celebrations. The *waits*, as they were called, also had other duties to perform, including the very odious chore of piping the watch at certain fixed hours of the night.

TERENCE PLAY   This illustrated title page of a manuscript of a play by Terence (c. 1400), preserved in the Bibliotheque Nationale in Paris, is evidence of a continuing secular tradition in a time dominated by religious drama. The reader (shown below) is receiving the play from the poet. In the amphitheatre (above), he reads from the manuscript as three masked jongleurs mime the poet's words before the spectators. Note the masked figures, and those wearing peaked caps who are believed to be inheritors of a comic tradition that goes back to the ancient Roman mimes.

With the invention of printing in the 15th century, the popularity of the minstrels began to wane as the wider distribution of books began to lure away their audiences. Minstrelsy was at its height during the 11th, 12th and 13th centuries, but had quite disappeared by the end of the 16th. This is not to say that the lower class of entertainer did not continue in the marketplace along with jugglers and acrobats. Some of the best of the minstrels were no doubt absorbed into the companies of stage players that were established in the early 16th century.

THE ORIGINS OF THE ENGLISH THEATRE

Though the importance and popularity of the minstrels during the Middle Ages cannot be gainsaid, the development of the theatre in this period owes more to the activities of the people themselves. The Middle Ages was indeed the great period of amateur theatricals. Apart from the folk drama which arose from very ancient celebrations connected with farming and the land—such as the May Day festivals, the performances by mummers, and the celebrated Sword Dance—the chief contribution to the development of the theatre came from the Church.

The religious drama which developed during the Middle Ages began in a very simple way, and soon established its own conventions. It brought to the common people the pageantry and entertainment necessary to relieve the monotony of the daily round and the common task. From 970 onward, there are records which show the introduction of drama into church services. These dramas probably came about through the desire of the clergy to render the incidents in the life of Christ more real to the congregation.

LITURGICAL DRAMA

During the Easter morning service, a short, simple scene was played before the altar. A seat representing the Holy Sepulcher was placed

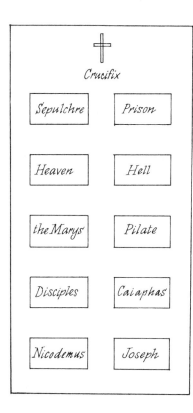

Crucifix

Sepulchre | Prison

Heaven | Hell

the Marys | Pilate

Disciples | Caiaphas

Nicodemus | Joseph

MIRACLE PLAY PLAN   *This diagram shows the mansions of the "Resurrection," a 12th-century miracle play. The placement of the settings was determined by the interior structure of the church, and became fixed by tradition.*

where all could see. Two priests dressed as angels stood on either side. Three women would enter the church and wander up to the angels. One of the angels would then ask "Whom do you seek in the Sepulcher, O Christian women?" The women would reply "Jesus of Nazareth, who was crucified, O heavenly ones." The angel would then point to the Sepulcher and say "He is not here. He has risen even as he foretold. Go announce that He has risen from the Sepulcher." Then choir and congregation would burst out singing *"Te Deum Laudamus"* together, while the church bells chimed out in climax.

This little scene must have had a tremendous effect on the congregation. Though the dialogue was chanted in Latin, and the angels' wings were not very convincing, the impact of the scene, heightened by the earnestness of the players, must have been tremendous on an unlettered and simple peasant congregation.

The success of these small beginnings was followed by other short scenes presented in church. In one, the meeting of Mary Magdalene and Christ in the garden was presented. Still another mini-drama showed Peter and John running to the Sepulcher; another portrayed the incredulity of Thomas.

Later, at Christmas, other scenes were introduced, depicting the shepherds and the three kings at the Manger. The dialogue, at first chanted in Latin, in time came to be spoken in English. Gradually, the religious play evolved quite separately from the service. The actors were people of the Church: priests, nuns, choirboys. The costumes consisted of the usual ecclesiastical dress: surplices, cloaks, and chasubles.

CHURCHES AS THEATRES

The whole interior of the church was used as the theatre, and short scenes were played in various parts of the building. The setting in each case symbolized the particular scene. For certain scenes which were played again and again, and which were deemed to be an integral part of the service, a permanent structure was built in the church. Thus, instead of being represented by a seat, the Sepulcher became a wooden or iron construction, complete with hinged lid. The beautiful interiors of the early churches provided plenty of opportunity for dramatic effect; and the lighted candles, carried by the actors, heightened the dramatic emphasis of individual scenes.

In the 12th century Resurrection play, each scene was called a "mansion." The scenes were arranged to be played in different parts of the church, and the places where each scene was played became fixed by tradition. The situs of the crucifix was generally fixed at the altar.

The play would begin with the actors performing one scene, perhaps near the entrance of the church. Then, having played that scene, they moved on to the next location where they would play another scene. They would proceed in this manner around the church.

The contents of these religious plays varied considerably, and would at times include incidents from the Old Testament. When in time the number of scenes increased, and the congregation which the plays attracted became very large, it became necessary for the plays to be produced outdoors on the church steps.

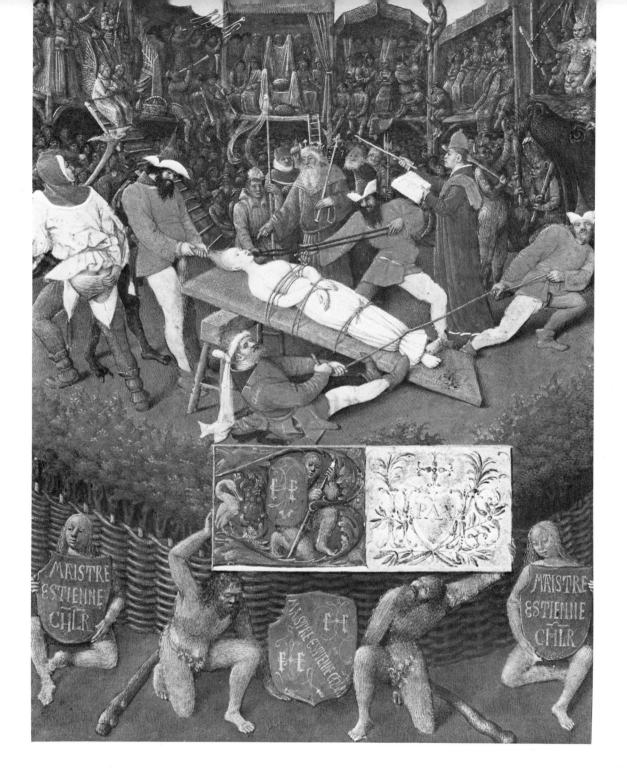

THE MARTYRDOM OF ST. APOLLONIA   *The medieval religious drama, an outgrowth of the simple liturgical plays originally performed within the church, is illustrated in this famous 15th-century miniature by Jean Fouquet entitled "The Martyrdom of St. Apollonia." On a raised platform stage in a large open area (the "platea" or simply the "place"), the martyred saint is being tortured. The multiple stage settings (the mansions), are arranged in a semi-circle, from Heaven (to the left) to Hell (on the right). The dominant figure, holding a book and a pointer and standing (in the right foreground), is believed to be the prompter.*

GUILD PRODUCTIONS

The main development of the theatre during the 13th and 14th centuries was the taking over of the drama from the Church by the citizenry. This situation developed because the church authorities resented the enormous popularity and appeal that the ecclesiastical performances had for the common people, in contrast to the regular church services. The Church understood well enough the latent power of the drama; but the Church felt that the people who watched the plays were not spiritually uplifted, but had rather come to the church to be entertained. Whether or not this judgment was true, the Church stopped producing plays and prohibited the clergy from taking part in them.

The plays, however, were a part of the Easter celebration, and the people demanded their entertainment. The vacuum was filled by the craft guilds who took over the responsibility of production. So it happened that the craft guilds who had the responsibility for the repair of bridges and roads and the building of chapels and charitable institutions took turns building scenes and effects, providing the actors and costumes, and producing the plays. The net result was that the spectacle moved from the steps of the church into the marketplace and into the guild hall.

The guilds took their responsibility for production very seriously. They spent considerable sums on scenery, on costumes and on effects; they even paid the actors for taking part in the performance. A man at Coventry, for example, was paid three shillings and four pence for playing God. Another was paid four pence for cock-crowing. At Hull, a certain Jenkins Smith received one shilling and one pence for taking the part of Noah.

MIRACLE PLAYS

As more scenes from the Old Testament were added, the plays grew in length. They grew and grew, until performances actually lasted several days. The dialogue had more affinity with the daily life of the

BELIAL AND THE DRAGON'S MOUTH   *Traditionally, Hell was represented by the medieval scenic artists as a gargantuan monster's head, known as the
Hell Mouth. (Some scholars suggest that it derived from the Biblical monster Le-
viathan.) In this illustration from a medieval manuscript in the Studien-Bibliothek
in Salzburg, three heavenly hosts try to keep the devil where he belongs.*

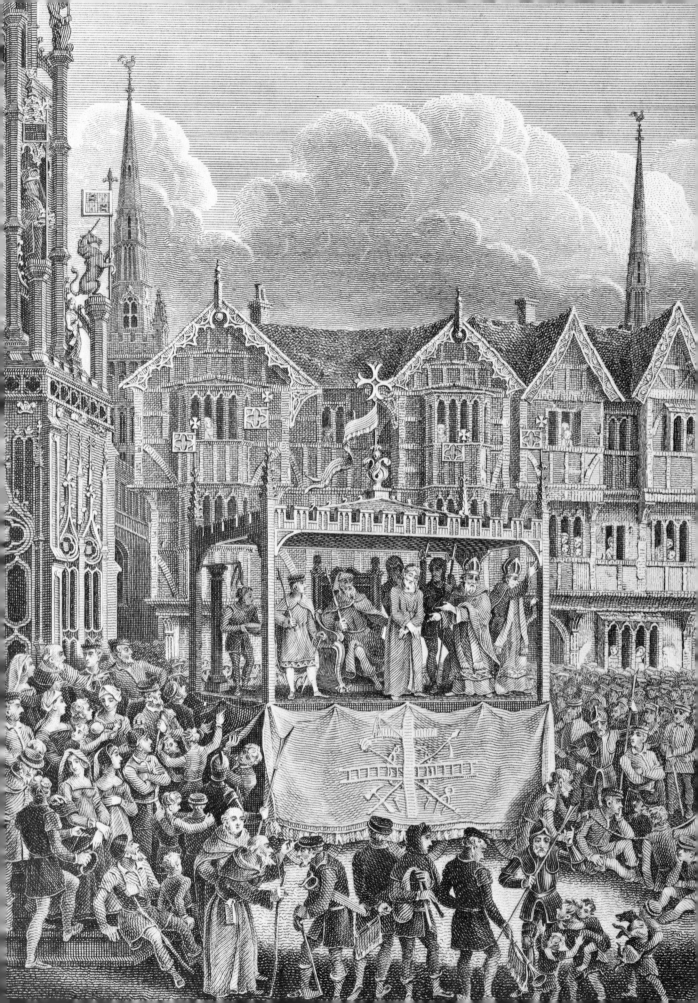

MEDIEVAL MYSTERY PLAY   This engraving by David Jee to illustrate Sharp's "Dissertation on the Pageants or Dramatic Mysteries Anciently Performed at Coventry," is a conjectural representation of a medieval mystery play. It shows Jesus before Pilate in a scene from the Coventry cycle of Biblical history plays. The individual set pieces, or "mansions," were built on wagons, or "pageants," a form of setting especially popular in England and Holland. The audience was stationed in groups throughout the town square. Wagon followed wagon around the square, each halting in turn before the next group of spectators to perform its own segment of the play cycle, so that the audience, remaining stationary, saw the whole play unroll before it in sequence.

people, and therefore was more easily managed by the unsophisticated amateur players.

The plays, following the tradition of earlier church performances, had separate settings erected for each scene—scenes which were built of wood and canvas, and were placed on elevated stages for all to see. If one imagines a modern fairground arranged in a rectangle with all sideshows distributed along the sides and with perhaps one or two of the shows in the open space, one might get a better idea of how miracle plays were staged during the Middle Ages.

THE PROMPTER

A painting by Jehan Fouquet shows an incident from one of the French miracle plays. Behind the central group of actors, the several stages for the various scenes in the play can be seen. One of the most prominent figures in the painting is the prompter; he is seen standing among the actors with a book of the play in one hand, and a stick in the other. The prompter was very important because there was extant only one complete Ms. of the play. Each of the actors was given his own lines to commit to memory. He had no idea of the rest of the play, neither did he know who would speak before him or after him. It was thus necessary for the prompter to indicate the sequence, by pointing his stick at the actor whose turn it was to speak next.

STAGING DEVELOPMENTS

In the middle of the marketplace there was an open space which was used for various scenes, especially those scenes for which there was no particular setting. The open space would also serve to house a stage set, if necessary. In the Fouquet miniature, the king has left his throne which had been set on one of the stages. He then descended the steps to the ground, and he joined the group of actors in the center area. Since much more movement was possible by using this central area, a further development had been made in the history of the theatre.

There was very little scenery used in these presentations. The audience simply had to use its imagination to visualize the place where the action of the play was supposed to occur. Since many stage conventions of the Elizabethan Theatre derived from those developed during the Middle Ages, it is obvious that the paucity of scenery in Shakespeare's theatre was simply an inheritance from an earlier period—a convention to which the British audience was accustomed.

THE MOVABLE WAGON-STAGE

In England, instead of using set stages around a marketplace as they did on the Continent, the scenes for a mystery play were built on wagons. A contemporary description reads:

> . . . *a highe place made like a howse with ij rowmes, being open on ye tope: the lower rowme they apparrelled and dressed them selves; and in the higher rowme they played: and they stood vpon 6 wheeles.*
>
> *They first beganne at ye Abbaye gates: & when the firste pagiente was played at ye Abbaye gates, then it wàs wheeled from thence to the pentice at ye highe crosse before ye mayor; and before that was donne, the seconde came, and ye firste wente in-to the watergate streete, and from thence vnto ye Bridge-streete, and soe all, one after an other, tell all ye pagiantes weare played.*

Something of this old arrangement still survives in the Lord Mayor's show held in London, where the pageants are only tableaux and there is no acting or dialogue.

THE HELL MOUTH

One of the most popular scenes in the miracle play was the Hell Mouth. This portrayed an assortment of demons rushing about making horrible noises. The effects were created through the use of fire-works and flaming spars on which powdered resinous pitch had been thrown. When this was set afire, clouds of smoke and flame belched forth from the Hell Mouth.

These demons appeared in most of the scenes. As they had no lines to speak, there must have been great competition for these parts. One suspects that the apprentices, being younger and more agile, were given most of these devil parts; and when they came into contact with the older citizens—perhaps their masters—the deviltry was no doubt more realistic.

HUMOR IN THE MIRACLE PLAYS

Although the plays were based on incidents from the Bible, a good deal of comic byplay crept into the script. Often a short interlude of invented stage business, probably involving some form of slapstick, was inserted into a script at a convenient spot. Such scenes would evoke an immediate response from the audience. The characters that played such scenes were usually either devils or shepherds.

MEDIEVAL DEVIL MASKS   *As seen in these drawings, these false faces were grotesque and fearsome. They were often animal-like, with snouts of beasts and with a variety of large horns.*

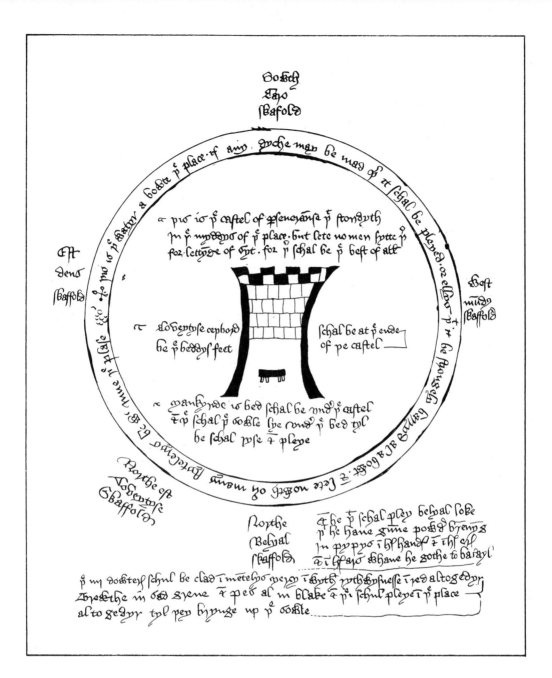

MEDIEVAL STAGE PLAN   *This plan shows the arrangement of the mansions in "The Castle of Perseverence," an early 15th-century morality play. The circle in this plan represents a ditch which was to be filled with water or "stronglye barryd" (fenced off). It contained within its perimeter the playing area; the castle is in the centre with "mankynde is bed" (a bed for mankind) below it. The outer circle shows also the various mansions placed at symbolic compass points: God is in the East, the World is to the West, Belial (Hell) is North, Caro is South, and Covetous to the Northeast.*

RENAISSANCE STAGE   The Trechsel edition of the plays of
Terence, published in Lyon in 1493, was illuminated by a series of
woodcuts illustrating the stage settings for the plays. Among these
woodcuts is this illustration of an Italian "theatrum." The simple medieval trestle stage has been transformed into a sculptured and mag-
nificently-detailed edifice. A stairway on the left leads to the galleries.
Three tiers of spectators watch a performance of a comedy by Terence.
The musician sits before the proscenium in which three curtained
alcoves, each representing a house, are the outgrowth of the medieval
mansions.

On the other hand, the playing of saints and other sacred figures was very stiff and reverential and resolved itself into a series of formal, stilted movements.

THE ACTORS IN MIRACLE PLAYS

In England men and boys were used to play female characters, a convention that lasted right up to Restoration days. On the Continent, however, women occasionally took part in miracle plays; for example, at Metz in 1468 a young amateur actress appeared as St. Catherine, and performed in a major role in which she recited a great number of lines.

Players in miracle plays had to be ready for their daily stint at 4:30 a.m. Since the entire cycle of plays lasted two or three days, these actors must have found it very fatiguing, especially as they had to repeat their performance at every stop on the route of the wagon stage sets. On the other hand, on the Continent where the miracle plays took place in fixed booths on the market square, the actors were more fortunate. After their own performance was over, they could join the rest of the audience to watch the remaining scenes.

THE MORALITY PLAY

The morality play, which developed in the later years of the Middle Ages, had one central figure representing Man. All the abstract qualities of vice and virtue were then characterized by other actors. Since the morality play was more ethical in theme than religious, the development of this genre tended to remove the influence of the Church on the drama. The staging of the morality play was similar to that of the miracle play, but fewer scenes were used.

Perhaps the best-known example of the morality play is *Everyman*. In Cornwall, certain amphitheatres were set up in the country where morality plays were performed. There are records of a play called *The Castle of Perseverance* which was performed during the reign of Henry VI. These records inform us that Mercy was dressed in white, Ruthlessness in red, Truth in a sad green, and Peace all in black.

RETURN OF THE PROFESSIONAL ACTOR

During the 15th century, the professional actor once again began to make an appearance. It is quite possible that the professional wandering entertainer occasionally assumed a role in the miracle plays. The cycles of the miracle play were so long that interludes of pure entertainment would have been welcome to both players and audience. It is very likely that professional advice in acting was frequently sought by and given to the producers of the miracle plays.

THE RENAISSANCE

The 15th century saw a great change in the social life of Europe, reflected in substantial measure in the treatment of the miracle plays. Pageantry became more important; the spoken drama declined.

Performances took place more often in the banqueting hall than in the marketplace. With the invention of printing and the consequent renaissance of learning, and the establishment of many colleges and educational centers, the ruling class became more dominant. The miracle plays gradually declined in popularity, and drama rediscovered its old form. Scholars began writing plays, using for subject matter much of what they had read in classic Roman literature.

Probably the first Italian writer of tragedy in Italian was Gian Giorgio Trissino (1478-1550). His best-known play was *Sofonisba* published in 1515, but first performed in 1524. Other dramatists of the time were Rucellai, Il Cinthio, and Dolce. Torquato Tasso (1544-1595), a great writer of pastoral plays, was widely translated. His *L'Aminta* had tremendous influence outside Italy for many years.

Ludovico Ariosto (1474-1533), whose great epic poem *Orlando Furioso* is more famous than any of his dramas, was probably the most important of the Renaissance playwrights. Some of his dramas survive, and are highly regarded in Italy even today.

Niccolo Machiavelli (1469-1527) and Pietro Aretino (1492-1556) were among the best of the comedy writers, the former being especially known for his *Mandragola*.

RENAISSANCE STAGE DESIGN

Italy was the center of the Renaissance. New theatres were built in the cities of Vicenza, Mantua, Milan, Naples, Florence, and Venice, all of which contained famous academies. Private performances of plays written by local scholars were performed in these theatres. Great artists such as Raphael, designed theatres and scenery, setting standards which have not been surpassed even today.

THE TRAGIC SCENE BY SERLIO   *Serlio's tragic scene differed from the comic in the use of palaces on the painted flats and backdrop, instead of simple houses. The basic principle of lath-and-canvas constructions intermixed with painted cloths, and the use of a perspective backdrop, remained the same for both scenes.*

THE TEATRO OLIMPICO AT VICENZA   *This Renaissance masterpiece, begun by Andrea Palladio in 1580, was completed after his death
by Vincenzo Scamozzi in 1584. Built along Roman lines, it was the first permanent theatre to be constructed since classical times. The auditorium*

(cavea), where the spectators were seated, is a semi-ellipse, which afforded
better sight lines than the Roman half-circle. The orchestra (left foreground)
and the playing area (in front of the scene wall) are classical in style. The
wall (scaena frons) with its central portal (Regia) and its four smaller entry-
ways is modelled after the Roman amphitheatre at Orange, France.

The architects of the Renaissance modeled their work on the ancient classic principles expounded by a manuscript by Vitruvius, a Roman architect of the 1st century B.C. This manuscript gave detailed information about the architecture of the Greek theatre; and the architects of the Renaissance modeled their work on the ancient classic principles expounded therein.

One of the fascinating discoveries of the Renaissance was the use of perspective. Artists and architects—in those days there was little difference between the two—vied with each other in producing stage settings in which painted perspective was employed to the full.

In the early 16th century, Sebastiano Serlio (1475-1554) produced a work on theatre architecture based very closely on the manuscript of Vitruvius. From Serlio, we have illustrations which show the principles of stage setting to be used in tragedy, in comedy, and in pastoral drama. All plays of that time could be placed within these categories.

The scene for a tragedy, according to Serlio, should be a street of grand palaces with a dignified archway in the background and many statues and architectural adornments associated with grandeur.

In contrast, comedy should be played, said Serlio, on an everyday street scene which would contain an inn, some shops, and many balconied windows at greatly varying levels. This was essentially a lively and human setting, much closer to reality than that of the tragic scene.

Differing from both of the above, the pastoral scene should emphasize, according to Serlio, the lyrical qualities. It was to be a landscape with trees in the foreground, and a rocky path wandering between the cottages of laborers—a scene which prevalent everywhere in Italy.

Serlio's published works and others in similar vein eventually found their way to England and formed the basis of stage design in the 17th century, a period during which Inigo Jones was designing the scenery for the Court masques.

THE INTERLUDES

By the 16th century, the miracle plays had all but fallen into disuse, except in a few isolated instances. Filling the gap were companies of professional players which had been formed to give performances of the "Interludes," as they were called, in halls and in inns. The interludes were short comic pieces based on everyday life. These interludes more closely resembled variety sketches or vaudeville sketches than plays, and the entertainment was greatly relished by the people of the times.

THE SCHOLAR-PLAYWRIGHTS

After printing became more universal, scholars in England were busy studying the ancient works of Greek and Roman drama, and then writing plays based on classical principles. The first plays of the scholar-playwrights were performed at the universities. Written without any practical knowledge of the theatre, these works seem to us to be stilted and pedantic. It was left to Shakespeare to infuse into drama that profound knowledge of life which, together with his practical knowledge of stagecraft, yielded dramas which have remained, and are likely to remain, models for all time.

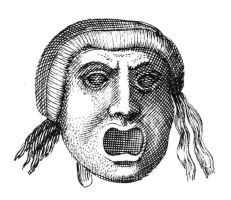

The Elizabethan
Theatre

INN-YARD PLAYS

From about the middle of the 16th century on, traveling companies of players began to give performances on stages set up in the court-yards of certain inns in London. These inns were large and important establishments, and they were also used as stations by the great network of public carriers plying their trade over the entire country. When one started a journey by public carrier, or when goods were dispatched from one town to another, the inn was the inevitable starting place. Here horses were hired, goods were transferred from carrier to carrier, and there was much bustle and excitement. In the beginning, actors took turns with the carriers in leasing the use of the courtyard; but later on, when performances attracted large audiences, the proprietors of certain inns gave up the business of acting as terminals and concentrated on the presentation of drama.

The inns in those days were generally of a standard design. The edifice was built in four sections around a rectangular courtyard. There were entrances at both the back and the front for wagons and horses. The courtyard itself was open to the sky; and around it on the walls of the inn, two or three galleries were constructed at different levels. These galleries were roofed over, but were open at the sides.

A stage would be set up at one end of the courtyard, somewhat near the stairs which gave access to the galleries. At the back of the stage there probably would be a curtain. Behind this curtain there would be some space which the actors could use as a dressing room. Sometimes the gallery immediately above the stage would be used in the action of the play. This gallery was generally reserved for the actors. A courtyard could comfortably hold some three or four hundred people, who would pay a penny or two pence to stand and watch the performance. The nobility and the wealthy who were attracted to these inn-yards plays would buy seats in the galleries which surrounded the stage. Often, a simple platform or ramp would be constructed in parts of the courtyard so as to afford a better view of the stage; and now and then a seat would be provided on the ramp on payment of a further sum.

The innkeepers reaped quite a harvest in providing refreshment to the audience. The innkeepers also retained the admission fees to the galleries, so that the income of the actors depended on the admission fees they could glean from admission to the courtyard.

In some towns the innkeeper was quite an important person. Sir William Davenant's father, owner of the Crown Inn, Cornmarket, was an alderman at Oxford, and eventually became Mayor of the city. But in London the innkeepers were not quite so highly respected. Had they wielded more influence, they might have helped to mitigate the growing hostility of the City Fathers toward the players.

PURITAN AND CIVIC HOSTILITY TOWARD THE THEATRE

All through the early history of the theatre, actors had to contend with prejudice and hostility from civic and religious authorities. During Elizabethan days, the inveighing of the Puritans against stage presentations and the calumny heaped upon the players were of the same stripe as the charges made by the early Christian pre-

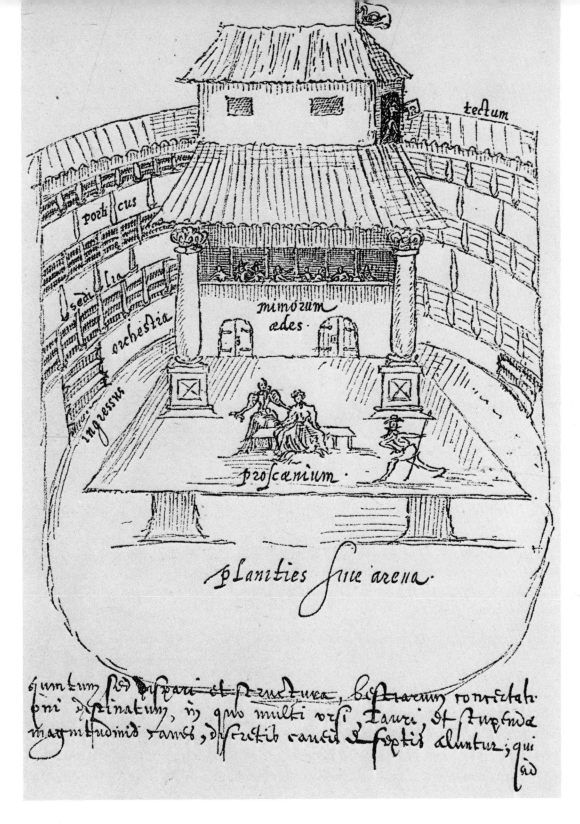

THE SWAN THEATRE   *Although it is called "The de Witt Sketch," this famous drawing is really a copy of Johann de Witt's original, made by a friend, Arend van Buchell, to whom he had sent the sketch in a letter describing his visit to London in 1596. It is the only contemporary representation of the interior of an Elizabethan playhouse and corroborates references from written material. Here are the open stage, the pillar-supported canopy, the three galleries for spectators, and the topmost hut from which heavenly noises and other sound effects emanated.*

THE GLOBE THEATRE   *Visscher's panorama of London, in which this detail of the theatre appears, was published in Amsterdam in 1616; but the precise date of the scene which is represented is uncertain. It is believed that the engraver worked from secondary sources. Whatever material was at his disposal, however, he was satisfied that the Globe was a polygonal building. The original Globe's end came on June 29, 1613, during a performance of Shakespeare's "Henry VIII." Burning cotton wadding, used to fire a gun that signalled the King's entrance, set fire to some straw; and shortly thereafter, the theatre was consumed in flames.*

lates. The theatre was accused of fostering ungodliness, idolatry, lewdness, profanity, and evil in general. The mere fact that players were pretending to be what they really weren't was in itself damnable. Moreover, there was a general complaint that Sunday performances were violating the sanctity of the Sabbath.

The City Corporation complained that the public performance of a play gave idlers the opportunity to congregate and create disorders. Furthermore, they objected to what they termed an "unthrifty waste of money of the poor." The City Corporation also made much of the accidents that occasionally happened on the stage or amongst the audience: "sundry slaughters and maimings of the Queen's subjects have happened by ruins of scaffolds, frames, and stages, and by engines, weapons, and powder used in plays."

About 1570, the Lord Mayor as well as the Corporation were all Puritans; and in consequence, the players suffered a double attack. Had not the players foreseen this danger years before, the Lord Mayor would have taken means to stop all performances. When forming their companies, the players had placed themselves under noble patronage and had named their companies after their patrons; and so a certain company was known as "The Earl of Leicester's Men," another as "The Queen's Men," still another as "The Admiral's Men," and so on. Thus, attempts by the City to regulate the players were parried by higher authority, usually through the Privy Council.

TOURING COMPANIES

However, in times of plague the City Fathers had their way and stopped all performances. During a hot summer in London and other cities, open sewers and conduits that ran in the streets would do their deadly work. A plague would strike, and then all public gatherings would be prohibited on the ground of curtailing infection. At such times, groups of players would take to the road and tour the country.

From 1573 to 1587, there were twenty-three touring companies that had given performances in Stratford. The young Shakespeare must have seen plenty of acting in his boyhood. These companies also gave private performances at court, and in noble households, and at universities. These groups of itinerant actors held great appeal for all classes of the community. It is interesting to note how Shakespeare included in his plays characters and episodes that would appeal to all the members of his audience, the scholar, the courtier, the poet, as well as the common people.

In 1572, a statute provided that all strolling players who had not been licensed by a lord should be treated as vagabonds. Many of the touring companies traveled and performed under license and permission from their patrons, but there may have been unlicensed companies who were liable at any moment to be hauled before the magistrates and charged with vagrancy.

THE FIRST PUBLIC THEATRES

All through the 16th century, the players had been having a bad time, what with the plague and the assaults of the City Fathers. In 1556, as a countermeasure, the leading player of the Earl of Leicester's Men, James Burbage, launched a new project. Burbage had formerly been a carpenter and decided to use his combined skills to build a public theatre for plays just outside the City limits, at Shoreditch.

In those days Shoreditch was a rural region. There was a pleasure ground nearby at Moorfields which had been set aside for sport and for picnicking. The area was close enough to the City to attract an audience, but above all, it had the great advantage of being outside the jurisdiction of the City Corporation. There is little information about this playhouse except that it was called by the simple name of "Theatre." Probably it did not differ greatly from theatres of a later day, concerning which we are better informed. It was a wooden structure, probably circular in plan.

The Earl of Leicester's Men did very well here, and crowds flocked to their performances. The very same year, another theatre was built quite near the first one. It was called the Curtain, and was also managed by the astute Burbage.

In his early twenties, when Shakespeare first came to London, he went to live at Shoreditch and was soon at work at one or the other of the two theatres.

In 1596, another theatre called the Blackfriars was opened in the City. Although this playhouse stood within the City limits, it was

AN ELIZABETHAN STAGE   In this woodcut from the frontispiece of the 1632 edition of "Roxana," a play by William Alabaster, we have one of the few bits of pictorial evidence of what an Elizabethan stage looked like. It is believed to represent a Cambridge student's performance of the play on a temporary stage. Unlike the "de Witt" sketch, the stage is tapered in shape, and is enclosed by a railing. Whether a curtained inner stage and the gallery above for actors or spectators actually existed has been a matter of controversy amongst scholars.

nevertheless outside the jurisdiction of the City Corporation since it was situated on Crown property. Its name derived from the fact that the plot on which the theatre was erected was part of the old abbey of the Black Friars, which had become Crown property after the Reformation. Other theatres built outside the city limits on the south bank of the Thames were the Rose, built in 1587, and the Swan, built in 1596.

THE SWAN

This theatre was situated near some landing stairs for boats. It probably took its name from the great number of swans that frequented the north bank of the river Thames nearby. A rough sketch of the Swan theatre, made by a visiting Dutchman, one Johan de Witt, is still extant. This drawing shows that the designer of the early theatres wanted something that had the elements of the rectangular inn-yard with its galleries, and something of the circular arena in use for the then popular sport of bull-baiting.

The stage was square and projected well into the arena or pit. Around this roofless arena, there were covered galleries, very much as in the old inn-yards. The rear part of the stage was roofed over, either with tiles or with thatch. At least one gallery was provided at the rear of the stage for use in staging the plays. There was a central opening in the rear wall, with a curtained alcove or inner stage.

Above the roof of the stage there was a small hut or turret which may have housed some primitive stage machinery. From the turret, a trumpeter blew warning blasts announcing the commencement of the performance; and from this turret, too, a flag flew which could be seen from across the river, indicating that a performance would be given that afternoon.

THE GLOBE THEATRE

Upon the death of James Burbage, his two sons, Richard and Cuthbert, carried on at the Theatre; but owing to some difficulty about the renewal of the lease by the landlord who owned the ground, the Burbage brothers decided to move elsewhere In 1598, they formed a syndicate with some of the Lord Chamberlain's Men who were playing at the Curtain. The actors were William Shakespeare, John Heming, Augustine Phillips, Thomas Pope, and William Kemp.

By the end of the year they employed carpenters and laborers to pull down the Theatre and salvage its timber and fittings. These were to be used in building the new theatre which was to be called

ELIZABETHAN PLAYHOUSE   *Traditional features were the open stage (partially roofed over), the curtained "tiring house" (behind), and the balconies, used by both spectators and actors.*

the Globe. The new edifice was to be built at bankside on the south bank of the Thames, and constructed in accordance with the latest stage developments.

By this time, Shakespeare had written about twelve of his plays, including *Romeo and Juliet, A Midsummer Night's Dream, The Merchant of Venice,* and *Henry IV,* and he was already accounted as the greatest dramatist of his time. But the Globe was yet to witness the full flower of his genius, for Shakespeare's tragedies were to be produced later.

The Globe company contained the leading actors of the day. The theatre outshone all other playhouses in the standard of its plays and in the quality of its productions. The company was organized on a profit-sharing basis. The original syndicate of the two Burbages and the five leading actors was known as the "House-keepers," and these seven received a certain proportion of the income. The rest of the company received shares of the box office receipts, according to their status in the company. When an actor became more important by virtue of his increasing skill, he was promoted to become one of the House-keepers and he received a larger share of the receipts.

When James I came to the throne, he demonstrated his pleasure with the Globe company by allowing the group to call themselves the King's Men. The success of the Globe group was further assured when it acquired the Blackfriars theatre in the city for use as winter quarters, for this theatre was entirely roofed in. With a few braziers of burning coal distributed about the house, the theatre was reasonably comfortable during cold afternoons. Indeed, the company played as often at the Blackfriars as it did at the Globe, for the Blackfriars was a semi-private theatre and attracted a better class of audience. Since admission fees were larger at the Blackfriars, this theatre became more profitable for the actors and the management.

THE FORTUNE THEATRE

The nearby Rose theatre suffered greatly from the competition of the Globe, so much so that the managers, Henslowe and Alleyn, decided to build a new theatre in the city between Golden Lane and Whitecross Street. They called their new enterprise the Fortune. Unlike the circular Globe, the Fortune was a square building. The stage of the Fortune was identical with its famous sister, its dimensions being recorded as forty-three feet wide by twenty-eight feet deep. To get some idea of the great extent of this stage, one might compare it with the proscenium opening of the average theatre in London today, which is just about thirty feet wide.

WILLIAM SHAKESPEARE (1564-1616)

Without question, the greatest playwright who ever lived and the most pervading influence in the history of the theatre was William Shakespeare. Almost 400 years after his death his plays are just as vital as when he lived; and hardly a season passes, either in London or New York, or in smaller playhouses throughout England and the United States, where Shakespeare is not performed. Moreover, translations of Shakespeare's plays have been made into just about every recorded language, and performances of his plays are presented yearly in the far corners of the earth. The vast number of commentaries written about the plays of Shakespeare would alone fill an entire library. Even though the language employed by the Bard of Avon, as he has come to be known, may be archaic in certain instances, the basic quality of his poetic and philosophic insights assure this playwright an enduring place in the history of drama for as long as one can peer into the future.

About the life of this world's most famous playwright much is speculated but little is known for a certainty. The records are scant, and tradition fills in what is lacking in fact. William Shakespeare was born to John Shakespeare and Mary Arden in Stratford-on-Avon, probably on April 23, 1564. The father was a glover who rose to high municipal positions in his native town. As a young boy, Shakespeare apparently enjoyed relative prosperity. He attended a grammar school

Enter Tamora pleadinge for her sonnes
goinge to execution

Tam: Stay Romane bretheren gratious Conquerours
Victorious Titus rue the teares I shed
A mothers teares in passion of her sonnes
And if thy sonnes were ever deare to thee
Oh thinke my sonnes to bee as deare to mee
Suffizeth not that wee are brought to Roome
To beautify thy triumphes and returne
Captiue to thee and to thy Romane yoake
But must my sonnes be slaughtered in the streetes
For valiant doynges in there Cuntryes cause
Oh if to fight for kinge and Common weale
Were piety in thine it is in these
Andronicus staine not thy tombe with blood
Wilt thou drawe neere the nature of the Gods
Drawe neere them then in being mercifull
Sweete mercy is nobilityes true badge
Thrice noble Titus spare my first borne sonne

Titus: Patient your self madame for dy hee must
Saxon do you likewise prepare your selfe
And now at last repent your wicked life

Aron: Ah now I curse the day and yet I thinke
Few comes within the compasse of my curse
Wherein I did not some notorious ill
As kill a man or els devise his death
Ravish a mayd or plott the way to do it
Accuse some innocent and forsweare my selfe
Set deadly enmity betweene too freindes
Make poore mens cattell breake there neckes
Set fire on barnes and haystackes in the night
And bid the owners quench them with there teares
Oft have I digd up dead men from their graues
And set them vpright at their deare freinds dore
Euen almost when theire sorrowes was forgott
And on their breastes as on the barke of trees
Haue with my knife carued in Romane letters
Let not your sorrowe dy though I am dead
Tut I haue done a thousand dreadfull thinges
As willingly as one would kill a fly
And nothing greeues mee hartily indeede
For that I cannot do ten thousand more &c

Henricus Peacham
Anno m° q° q° q°

So far too
Shakspear
Titus
Andronicus
Sc. 2

CHRISTOPHER MARLOWE   A Cambridge scholar, poet, and the greatest of "University wits," Marlowe profoundly influenced the Elizabethan theatre, although he wrote only four plays in his brief lifetime. "Tamberlaine the Great, Part I," written when he was 23, inaugurated the use of highly-charged blank verse as a medium to express the tragic fate of the hero—anticipating Shakespeare's great tragedies. The miniature shown here is generally considered to be a portrait of the poet.

in Stratford, and is reputed to have indulged in occasional mischief as a young man. Actually, the first record of his activities is a marriage document which almost certainly identifies his wife as Anne Hathaway. Speculation about the nature of this marriage is based on the evidence that in May, 1583, less than six months after the November 1582 wedding, a daughter, Susanna, was born. Twins, Hamnet and Judith, born in 1585, made Shakespeare the father of three at the age of 21.

There is no record of Shakespeare's activities until 1592, when he is lambasted as an "upstart crow" in a pamphlet by the apparently envious playwright, Robert Greene. Legend has it that Shakespeare had left Stratford after a deer-poaching escapade to join a group of players in London. In any event, it is clear that by 1592 he was a well-established actor and playwright of enviable reputation and popularity. He seems to have moved in a relatively short time from a country schoolhouse to exalted social and literary circles in the City.

"TITUS ANDRONICUS"   This illustration of a page from a manuscript in "Titus Andronicus" was done by Henry Peachum in 1595. The drawing is believed to be the only known representation of Elizabethan actors in costume, rendered by a contemporary.

His son's success led John Shakespeare to apply successfully for a coat of arms in 1596.

The meager documents that exist establish Shakespeare as a member of the Lord Chamberlain's company and associate him with the Swan Theatre and with Blackfriars. The records do not reveal much of the life experiences of Shakespeare, the man. The best documentation is contained in the plays he left for posterity.

Shakespeare signed his will on March 25, 1616 and died one month later, on April 23, presumably of a fever contracted in a drinking bout with Drayton and Ben Jonson. He started his writing career about 1590, with *Henry VI,* and contributed thirty-six plays in all to the theatre of the world. Though it be difficult if not impossible to track down where his knowledge and skill were acquired, it is virtually indisputable that the poetic range of his expression represents the acme of man's literary achievement.

SHAKESPEARE AND THE SCHOLAR-PLAYWRIGHTS

Shakespeare brought real life to the Elizabethan audiences in his presentation on the stage of such characters as Sir John Falstaff and Mistress Quickly, and in recreating on stage the atmosphere of the tavern and the city street. It is only necessary to read the works of dramatists immediately prior to this great writer to realize the contrast he afforded. His predecessors were primarily scholars and literary men, and their verse seems pedantic and lifeless. By contrast, Shakespeare's verse was vibrant and quite understandable to the folk of his day. He did not write above the heads of his public.

The scholar-playwrights resented the fact that Shakespeare, a com-

BEN JONSON   Bricklayer, soldier, poet, and playwright, Jonson was unrivaled in his time as a writer of satiric comedies. His early plays reflect the limiting conventions of the comedy of "humours," but the characters of his best work have a breadth beyond that narrow scope. Between 1605 and 1612, while writing some of his major comedies, "Volpone" (1606), "Epicene or The Silent Woman" (1609), and "The Alchemist" (1610), Jonson, working with the scene designer and architect Inigo Jones, created a series of eight brilliant court masques. Though Jonson was a difficult man, the regard in which his contemporaries held his wit and the bite of his satire is reflected in the famous epitaph: "O Rare Ben Jonson."

BEAUMONT AND FLETCHER
(1584-1616) & (1579-1625)   *The fore-*
most collaborators of the Elizabethan age
are credited with 53 plays, although it is a
generally held opinion today that only six
or seven of these were of joint authorship.
Their collaboration is remembered chiefly
in the introduction of the "tragi-comedy,"
a dramatic genre that was to dominate the
theatre for the latter half of the 17th
century.

mon actor, could write plays so successfully. Evidence of Shakespeare's popularity is contained in a publication by Robert Greene in which he advises his university friends to give up writing for the stage because the actors had "one, an upstart crow, of their own to supply their needs."

Ten years before Shakespeare was born, John Lyly wrote several plays inspired by the classics, developing a prose style made up of puns and the then fashionable jugglery of words. George Peele, Thomas Lodge, Thomas Nashe, and Thomas Kyd all wrote plays modeled on the works of the Roman dramatist, Seneca. Kyd's *Spanish Tragedy* was one of the most popular plays of the time. Although he wrote some fine poetry, even Marlowe wrote plays that were difficult to act and to bring to life.

On the other hand, with his feet firmly planted on the stage and with his acute powers of observing human nature, Shakespeare recreated, in dramatic form, life in England as he saw it. It was politic, of course, for him to place the action of the plays in foreign countries and to endow the important personages—the nobles and the princes—with foreign names so that there could be no chance of recrimination by some lord who might deem himself caricatured on the stage. But Shakespeare could not resist placing the Elephant, the famous tavern of South London, in the mythical country of Illyria, as he did in *Twelfth Night*.

In one of the scenes in *A Midsummer Night's Dream* which takes place near Athens, Shakespeare introduced a group of rustics who were given uncommon but typically English names, and who behaved exactly as Shakespeare may have seen them deport themselves in the fields and hamlets of Warwickshire.

CHRISTOPHER MARLOWE (1564-1593)

There was one true poetic genius among Shakespeare's immediate predecessors. Christopher Marlowe wrote only four plays, *Tamburlaine, The Tragical History of Doctor Faustus, The Jew of Malta,* and *Edward II,* but he penned these pieces in a glorious blank verse of such lyrical power that no one after him but Shakespeare reached his eminence. Next to the Bard, he is regarded as the greatest Elizabethan dramatist. Unfortunately, he was killed in a tavern fight when he was but thirty-four years old.

BEN JONSON (1572-1637)

Among the dramatists contemporary with Shakespeare, his immediate friends were Ben Jonson, Francis Beaumont, and John Fletcher. Jonson was continually in trouble because he was hot-headed and quarrelsome, and he was sent to prison three times for various reasons. However, he was a fine scholar and wrote some good comedies. In 1598, Shakespeare's company staged Jonson's first success, *Every Man in His Humour.* In 1603, Jonson followed with *Sejanus;* in 1604, with *Eastward Ho* which represented a collaboration with his old friends and rivals, Marston and Chapman. His later plays include *Volpone* in 1606, *Epicene* in 1609, *The Alchemist* in 1610, and *Bartholomew Fair* in 1614.

Jonson was quite overbearing, and at times, he no doubt patronized the Bard for his lack of classical learning. Always envious of Shakespeare's success, Jonson was honest enough to admit Shakespeare's greatness; and when the immortal playwright passed away in 1616, Jonson wrote a sincere memorial in verse.

FRANCIS BEAUMONT (1584-1616) AND JOHN FLETCHER (1579-1625)

Two prolific writers, Francis Beaumont and John Fletcher, worked and lived together. Between them, separately and together, they produced over fifty plays which included romantic comedies, pastorals, and tragedies. They also wrote a new kind of play called the tragic-comedy, which although it contained tragic incidents, had a happy ending. It is not clearly determined exactly when the collaboration began. It is thought that *The Knight of the Burning Pestle* (1609)

The Spanish Tragedie:

OR,

Hieronimo is mad againe.

Containing the lamentable end of *Don Horatio*, and
Belimperia; with the pittifull death of *Hieronimo*.

Newly corrected, amended, and enlarged with new
Additions of the *Painters* part, and others, as
it hath of late been diuers times acted.

LONDON,

Printed by W. White, for I. White and T. Langley,
and are to be sold at their Shop ouer against the
Sarazens head without New-gate. 1615.

"THE SPANISH TRAGEDY"   *Thomas Kyd's play, written about 1585, is one of the bloodiest dramas of the time, and a forerunner of the revenge play, popular in late Elizabethan and Jacobean theatre. This illustration is from the title page of the 1615 edition.*

The Tragicall Historie of the Life and Death of Doctor Faustus.

With new Additions.

Written by CH. MAR.

Printed at London for *Iohn Wright*, and are to be sold at his shop without Newgate. 1631.

"DOCTOR FAUSTUS"   Christopher Marlowe's drama, "The Tragical History of Doctor Faustus," illustrated here by a woodcut from the title page of the 1636 edition, was based on a German medieval legend. It was first performed by the Admiral's Men, c. 1588, with Alleyn playing the title role. In this scene, Mephistopheles, wearing a costume reminiscent of the devil costume in medieval liturgical plays, appears from a trapdoor (at right) in answer to the invocation of Faustus who is safely enclosed in his magic circle.

EDWARD ALLEYN   One of the two best actors of
the Elizabethan age, Edward Alleyn is shown here in a
portrait by an unknown artist. In an age of rivalry
among contending troupes, he joined the Admiral's
Men, and as their leading player, created many of Marlowe's tragic heroes. He amassed a fortune in his lifetime. After retiring in 1604, he founded Dulwich College where this portrait hangs.

may have been their first collaborative work, although more of Beaumont's touch is evident in this play. With *Philaster* (1610), their talent for tragi-comedy was established. Others among their notable works were *The Maid's Tragedy* (1611), *A King and No King* (1611), and *The Scornful Lady* (1613).

OTHER CONTEMPORARIES OF SHAKESPEARE

Thomas Dekker (1572-1632), John Webster (1580-1634), John Ford (1586-1639), Philip Massinger (1583-1640), John Marston (1575-1634) and George Chapman (c.1560-1634) flourished during this period. Dekker wrote some good comedies, among which may be mentioned *Shoemaker's Holiday* (1599) and *The Honest Whore* (1604). Understanding the new realism that Shakespeare was achieving, Dekker introduced many scenes from the low life of his times into his plays.

Webster and Ford wrote tragedies. Webster's most popular plays

RICHARD BURBAGE   The first great actor of the English stage was the son of James Burbage, a carpenter, part-time actor, and builder of the first permanent theatre in London. He probably began acting with the Admiral's Men in 1584. Later, as a member of the Lord Chamberlain's Men, the company to which Shakespeare belonged, Burbage became the first performer to play the great Shakespearean roles of Hamlet, Lear, Othello and Richard III. This painting is believed to be a self-portrait.

SHAKESPEARE AND HIS FRIENDS   This painting in the Corcoran Gallery of
Art, Washington, D. C., depicts a convocation of great Elizabethan figures as imagined
by the Scottish artist John Fade (1820-1902). Depicted are, standing left: Sylvester,

Camden, Earl of Dorset. Seated from left to right: Stow, Beaumont, Fletcher, Ben Jonson (in top hat), Bacon, Donne, Raleigh, Shakespeare. Standing center: Earl of Southampton, Robert Bruce. Seated right: Cotton, Dekker.

THE RED BULL PLAYHOUSE *Illustrated on the frontispiece of "The Wits; or, Sport Upon Sport," written by Francis Kirkman in 1763, is an Elizabethan stage. Some of the features appear similar to the stage depicted in the "de Witt" sketch, notably the gallery at the rear for spectators, which has been a source of scholarly controversy. Of particular interest is the representation of contemporary stage lighting: the chandeliers and the footlights, shown for the first time on an English stage.*

were *The Duchess of Malfi* (1614) and *The White Devil* (1612). Ford is chiefly remembered for *'Tis Pity She's a Whore* (1633).

RICHARD BURBAGE (1567-1619)

Richard Burbage was the son of James Burbage who built the first theatre structure in England.

Richard Burbage played all of Shakespeare's great tragic parts. Shakespeare wrote his plays to suit the actors of his company; he must have had Burbage in mind when writing *Hamlet, Othello, King Lear,* and *Macbeth.*

Little has been recorded about Burbage except that his movements were graceful and that he was perfectly natural on the stage. His musical voice lent beauty to quite commonplace verse.

Besides acting in the plays of Shakespeare, Burbage also appeared in many of the works of Ben Jonson, in Kyd's *Spanish Tragedy,* and in Webster's popular tragedy *The Duchess of Malfi.* Also talented as a painter, Burbage has left several portraits of his fellow actors which now hang in the Dulwich Gallery.

EDWARD ALLEYN (1566-1626)

The other great tragic actor of the time was Edward Alleyn, especially noted for his performance in Marlowe's *Tamburlaine.* Alleyn also played in many of Shakespeare's early works.

When Shakespeare was at the Globe, Alleyn was in partnership with his father-in-law Philip Henslowe. Later, the actor acquired several theatres including the Rose and the Fortune.

A shrewd businessman, Alleyn made a fortune, bought Dulwich Manor for £10,000 and founded Dulwich College. A typical example of the sophisticated Elizabethan, Alleyn was a scholar, a poet, a courtier, and an adventurer. A man of wide interests, he was always ready to break new ground. Very tall and of splendid physique, Alleyn proved imposing in majestic parts.

RICHARD TARLETON (?-1588)

About 1580, the chief comic actor of the day was Richard Tarleton, whose popularity was probably mainly due to his improvisations. The audience would suggest a theme or a verse, and Tarleton would extemporize some doggerel, or cap the given line with another.

Tarleton was also noted for his jigs—humorous dances accompanied by comic patter. The jig usually took place at the end of the play, and was not really connected with it. Tarleton has been associated by many scholars with *Hamlet's* Yorick.

WILL KEMP (1579-1600)

Kemp took Tarleton's place as the leading comic actor, and modeled his style largely on that of Tarleton. He played with Shakespeare's company, appearing in many of Shakespeare's early plays, taking the role of Peter in *Romeo and Juliet* and of Dogberry in *Much Ado About Nothing*.

Possibly because of differences of opinion with Shakespeare, Will Kemp did not remain long with the Globe and left to join the Earl of Worcester's Men. He also traveled extensively on the Continent where he was very popular.

Kemp is chiefly known for his famous wager. He bet that he would dance all the way from London to Norwich, and he did.

ACTING

Hamlet's directions to the players in Act III, scene ii, illuminate the stage transgressions of the day. This speech summarizes Shakespeare's own ideas about acting which, as he put it, should be "natural but not too natural."

> *Speak the speech, I pray you, as I pronounced it to you, trippingly on the tongue: but if you mouth it, as many of your players do, I had as lief the town-crier spoke my lines. Nor do not saw the air too much with your hand, thus, but*

use all gently; for in the very torrent, tempest, and, as I may say, the whirlwind of passion, you must acquire and beget a temperance that may give it smoothness. O, it offends me to the soul to hear a robustious periwig-pated fellow tear a passion to tatters, to very rags, to split the ears of the groundlings, who for the most part are capable of nothing but inexplicable dumbshows and noise. . . . Be not too tame neither, but let your own discretion be your tutor: suit the action to the word, the word to the action; with this special observance, that you o'erstep not the modesty of nature: for any thing so overdone is from the purpose of playing, whose end, both at the first and now, was and is, to hold, as 'twere, the mirror up to nature; to show virtue her own feature, scorn her own image, and the very age and body of the time his form and pressure. Now this overdone, or come tardy off, though it make the unskilful laugh, cannot but make the judicious grieve; the censure of the which one must in your allowance o'erweight a whole theatre of others. O, there be players that I have seen play, and heard others praise, and that highly, not to speak it profanely, that, neither having the accent of Christians nor the gait of Christian, pagan, nor man, have so strutted and bellowed that I have thought some of nature's journeymen had made men and not made them well, they imitated humanity so abominably.

. . . And let those that play your clowns speak no more than is set down for them [probably a dig at Will Kemp, whose habit of introducing his own gags on the stage must have caused Shakespeare a deal of annoyance] *for there be of them that will themselves laugh, to set on some quantity of barren spectators to laugh too; though, in the mean time, some necessary question of the play be then to be considered: that's villanous, and shows a most pitiful ambition in the fool that uses it. . . .*

WILLIAM KEMP *Reproduced from the title page of his "Nine Days' Wonder" written in 1600, this drawing shows the actor dancing a morris. The book gave an account of Kemp's memorable dance in 1599, from London all the way to Norwich, which he performed on a wager and won.*

Shakespeare himself played various parts in his own plays. He took the role of the Ghost in *Hamlet,* and of Theseus in *A Midsummer Night's Dream.* These parts portrayed little by way of personal character, but required a dignified and poetic interpretation.

Apart from the writing of his plays, Shakespeare's chief activity was his direction of them. Some of the chief actors who acted under his tutelage were Richard Burbage, Edward Alleyn, John Heming, and Will Kemp. John Heming was later to publish the plays of Shakespeare. William Kemp became the leading comic actor of his day, outshining Robert Wilson, John Singer, and Thomas Pope, who also were regarded as very talented clowns.

THE BOY ACTORS

When Shakespeare was writing his plays, all female parts in plays were acted by boys and men. Women had never achieved any importance in the theatre of the past, which had always essentially been a masculine domain. Though women had appeared in the Roman theatre, they never took major roles but were simply singers or dancers.

This in part was a reflection of the mores and manners of the day. During Elizabethan times, women were very much in the background in everyday life. It was not until Restoration days that they came to act on the stage. In Shakespeare's time female roles were taken by boys who could easily don a woman's costume, put on the necessary makeup, and pass as a woman. Since these young boys could hardly have sufficient experience of life to do justice to the interpretation of female roles, Shakespeare arranged for the most difficult parts to be assigned to male characters.

Typically reflecting this procedure is the opening scene of *Twelfth Night,* in which the Duke Orsino discusses his mistress at length. When she finally appears, her character has already been so well established in the minds of the audience that there is little she need say to portray the role. Shakespeare employed another useful device: he contrived to make his heroines assume male attire. For example, Portia appears in *The Merchant of Venice* as a lawyer. When one considers the dress of the time, it will be seen that a youth with a slight figure could easily portray a woman in man's costume. In the man's costume, the padded doublet or full breeches or trunk hose would quite conceal a feminine figure. Conversely, the woman's costume, with its enormus skirts and padded sleeves, could easily conceal a boy's figure.

The boy players were thoroughly expert at female impersonations. Some of them even continued with their feminine roles even after their voices had become masculine. The part of Lady Macbeth was probably played by one of these senior boys, who would naturally be much more experienced and much more capable of playing a more difficult part.

Unfortunately, there is little record of the boy actors, although some undoubtedly continued to play female parts until they were middle-aged. Probably the best known of these boy actors was Nat Field (1587-1620), who did not play women's parts in Shakespeare's company. When, in 1608, the Globe company took over the Blackfriars Theatre, the Globe retained the leading boy actors, William Ostler and John Underwood, but little more than their names is known about them.

No doubt these boys were a constant problem to the companies, for they were getting older all the time and their voices would crack, and they would have to be replaced. Suitable boys must have been scarce; that is probably why there are rarely more than two or three female characters in any one of Shakespeare's plays.

COMPANIES OF BOY ACTORS

Apart from the boys who served an apprenticeship with the regular companies, there were two troupes composed entirely of boy actors. The Choir Boys of St. Paul's played near the St. Paul's Cathedral; the Choir Boys of the Chapel Royal played at the Blackfriars Theatre before the Globe company acquired it. These boy companies were evidently extremely popular in London and probably created serious rivalry with Shakespeare's company at one time, as is illustrated in Hamlet's discussion with Rosencrantz which concludes:

> *Hamlet: Do the boys carry it away?*
> *Rosencrantz: Ay, that thy do, my lord; Hercules and his*
> *load, too.*

"Hercules and his load" is a reference to the Globe, where a sign outside the entrance of the theatre showed Hercules holding up the world.

Ben Jonson wrote plays for the Chapel Royal boys, while Marston and Dekker wrote for the boys of St. Paul's. There was great rivalry between Jonson on the one hand, and Marston and Dekker on the other, and they attacked each other in successive plays. The popularity of these boy companies did not last, however, and the public soon deserted them for the regular companies.

ELIZABETHAN STAGING

The stages in those days were well supplied with trapdoors, used not only in the action of certain plays, such as the gravediggers' scene in Hamlet, but also for passing small pieces of scenery or furniture onto the stage. This would be done in full view of the audience, but at the same time some action would take place on another part of the stage in order to distract the attention of the audience.

Shakespeare's plays were not split up into separate scenes as they are usually played today, but were played with a continuous flow of characters coming on and going off the stage. It would often happen that certain characters in a scene would still be carrying on a dialogue when players in the following scene had already come into view. The changing atmosphere of successive scenes—from comedy to tragedy, from the bustle of the public square to the more intimate interior—was created almost entirely through dialogue. When, as it sometimes happened, a definite break was required, a sense of interval was effected through the introduction of a dance or procession, or by the use of rhyming couplets, the latter convention remaining until well into the 18th century.

A study of *Hamlet* yields much information about the acting and staging of plays in Elizabethan times. It is quite possible by reading a play carefully to reconstruct the way in which it was staged.

For example, in Act I, scene iv, Hamlet confronts the ghost of his father. As Hamlet says earlier, this scene takes place on "the platform," which means the gallery above the stage. The Ghost appears and does not speak, but beckoning Hamlet to follow, makes an exit. Hamlet does so in spite of protestations from his friends, Horatio and Marcellus. After Hamlet goes, Horatio and Marcellus deliver six lines of dialogue, which gives the Ghost and Hamlet just sufficient time to descend the stairs onto the main stage where they make their entrance. Now the Ghost begins to speak. After the Ghost has made his long speech, he makes an exit, presumably through a trapdoor. This fits in perfectly with the old notion that ghosts were subterranean beings.

At this point Horatio and Marcellus make their entrance. After some conversation with Hamlet, they are sworn to secrecy about the night's happenings. The Ghost echoes the order to take an oath, the stage directions reading, "Ghost cries under the stage."

When *Hamlet* is read bearing in mind the facilities of the Elizabethan stage, one gains some idea of the continual flow of movement in this play. As performed on a modern stage, *Hamlet* does not seem quite as convincing. Some change of setting, accomplished with a drop curtain, is usually necessary to separate two scenes in modern-day performances of *Hamlet*.

ELIZABETHAN COSTUMES

Since they formed almost the only feature of decoration on the stage, the costumes worn by the players were most important. Actors who played nobles and princely characters wore the very richly decorated dress of the period. The fools and clowns wore the garb generally in use by the common people.

Eastern characters, such as Othello, usually wore a turban and some kind of long, baggy trousers gathered in at the ankle. The short coat worn by the Near Eastern characters would be ornamented according to the Elizabethan concept of Saracenic style.

For friars and similar characters, robes and gowns of a special kind were used. In Henslowe's diary we find that a costume for Cardinal Wolsey cost the company £38 12s 2d. for "coats, velvets, satis, and lace," a princely sum in those days. The costumes for the female characters were also expensive. In one instance, £9 was spent on a taffeta gown. In another, a skirt of silver camlet cost £2 15s.

The women's dress of the period, as worn by the boy players, was very rich in decoration. The curious stilted shape of the figure was obtained through use of a leather corset which had two semi-circular side pieces projecting out at right angles to the bodice. The petticoats and the skirt were drawn in over the side pieces, making the skirt bunch out at the waist and then fall in long straight folds to the ground. The boys could easily manage these rather stiff and all-concealing costumes.

Red was the fashionable color for hair, no doubt because Queen Elizabeth wore a wig of red hair. Since most of the ladies of the court

ELIZABETH I   *This drawing is based on a portrait of the Queen in elaborate court dress. The "cannon" sleeve, long stomacher, and the farthingale (hooped petticoat) were characteristic of the mode of the day.*

JAMES I AS A BOY   *This drawing is based on a portrait painted in 1574, which shows James I wearing engorged pantaloons, called "venetians," a style imported from Venice.*

ELIZABETHAN COSTUME   *This drawing shows the typical trunk hose, doublet, and ruff. The nonchalant drape of the cloak was characteristic of the studied pose of the gallants of the age.*

COUNTRYWOMAN'S COSTUME   *The drawing shows the ruff and the farthingale, typical of Elizabethan dress.*

aped the Queen, and donned a red wig, the boys' use of wigs of this hue carried conviction.

To give the finishing touches to the richness of the costumes, a good deal of stage jewelry was used. Shakespeare inserted a considerable amount of pageantry in his plays, and the richness of the costumes enhanced the many processions and formal dances which punctuated the performances at the Globe and at the other theatres. The costumes of the numerous heralds, with their surcoats and heraldic devices, helped achieve a dramatic and pleasing spectacle.

For Elizabethan actors, costumes were the great expense, and they generally spent a considerable portion of their earnings in providing additions to their wardrobes.

MUSIC IN THE ELIZABETHAN THEATRE

An important aspect of Elizabethan productions was the music, and Shakespeare, for one, employed innumerable songs in his plays. The stage directions in *The Tempest* call for a small orchestra, and at the end of *Much Ado About Nothing* Benedick asks the pipers to strike up for a dance.

In de Witt's sketch of the Swan, the word *Orchestra* is written under the first gallery at the left side of the stage, which would seem to be a very suitable place for the musicians. The stage directions of Shakespeare's plays called for music and a flourish of trumpets for the many processions. If a character was killed on the stage, a procession was formed to bear off the body; and no doubt there was considerable stage business not explicitly mentioned in the stage directions. At the end of the various acts it was customary to present a formal dance in which all the players took part.

ARTIFICIAL STAGE LIGHTING

In England during Shakespeare's time, artificial lighting was used for the first time. Although the Globe was open to the sky and performances were given only on summer afternoons, the stage balcony fell in the shadows, and therefore in some scenes candlelight could be used for effect.

In *Romeo and Juliet* the balcony became Juliet's bedchamber.

Probably some lighted candles were put on stage to denote that the action was taking place at night.

In the first scene in *Hamlet,* which we presume took place on the balcony, Horatio makes reference to "the morn, in russet mantle clad, walks o'er the dew of yon high eastern hill." This might indicate the use of a concealed lighting effect, which in fact the Italian stage was using previous to the era of the Elizabethan theatre.

In the case of the Blackfriars Theatre, artificial lighting was necessary because the playhouse was roofed in. Probably the chief source of illumination were chandeliers holding numerous candles, much like the lighting that must have been used for performances held at Court.

COURT PATRONAGE OF THE THEATRE

The development of Shakespeare's art, and the development of the Elizabethan theatre were bound up with the growth of Court influence on the drama. Henry VIII happened to be fond of pageants, masques, and dramatic diversions; and when Elizabeth came to the throne, she developed a taste for plays. Shakespeare's company continually played in Court where they elicited patronage from various nobles who saved the theatre many times from extinction at the hands of the city fathers.

Some of Shakespeare's plays are said to have been written by order of the Queen. There is an old tradition that *The Merry Wives of Windsor* was the outcome of her wish to see Falstaff in love. There is no doubt that *The Merry Wives* is not of the same quality as the other plays in which the immortal Sir John appears, but we can only guess what Shakespeare thought of *The Merry Wives of Windsor.*

ELIZABETHAN MASQUE   The painting, "Sir Henry Unton's Wedding" (c. 1597), hanging in the National Portrait Gallery, illustrates an early Elizabethan masque. Sir Henry is seated at the table (center); his wife (at the right end) is being addressed by a masked huntsman. In the ritualized dance in the foreground, the children represent the Cupids of Night and Day. Other principal masquers are Mercury, and Diana and her huntresses, who carry either a garland or a bow and arrows.

KNIGHT MASQUE   *Costumes in all their glory, in such late Court masques as "Brittania Triumphans," were eagerly awaited by the audience. This sketch of a Knight Masquer's costume by Inigo Jones illustrates the finery in which masque characters were often clothed. The headdress was composed of feathers and jewels.*

COURT MASQUES

As performances at Court increased, it became apparent that the needs of the Court audience were quite different from those of the public audiences. The public craved plenty of dramatic action, passionate acting, and low comic relief. The Court audiences desired a more poetic spectacle in which the ladies and the gentlemen of the Court could take part.

There is a hint of this Court influence in one of Shakespeare's last plays. In *The Tempest*, Prospero conjures up a masque to celebrate the betrothal of Miranda to Ferdinand. It has been suggested that in the writing of this play Shakespeare was influenced by the masques that were especially written and produced for the Court. It has been presumed that *The Tempest* was written in 1611. Some years earlier, Ceres and Juno were characters in a masque written by Samuel Daniel. Nymphs called *naiads,* and reapers performing a country dance appeared in other masques which Shakespeare,

MASQUE SETTING   The sketch for "The Forum of Peace" by Inigo Jones illustrates a setting for the masque, "The Triumph of Peace" (1634), which was produced in collaboration with the dramatist James Shirley. According to a contemporary viewer, the perspective setting displayed "sumptuous Pallaces, Lodges, Porticos, and other noble peeces of architecture."

through his connections at Court, may have witnessed. Some writers even suggest that Shakespeare's explanation of the abrupt ending of the masque in *The Tempest*—the dissolving of "the cloud-capp'd towers, the gorgeous palaces"—is a direct reference to the scenic devices of Inigo Jones. While the speech has a deeper philosophical meaning, it is certainly possible that Shakespeare was influenced by the scenic splendor of the Court masques of his day.

Around this time Ben Jonson began writing exclusively for Court performers, and he produced a large number of masques which were a combination of spectacle, dance, and formal recitation. In these performances no great acting ability was required. In effect, these masques were a dramatization of the courtly qualities of beatuiful and dignified appearance, of refined speech, and of graceful mien.

INIGO JONES (1573-1652)

Artist and architect, Inigo Jones produced the masques and designed the scenic backgrounds and the costumes famous in his day. Jones had studied art in Italy, and he returned with a store of information about the Italian theatres, which by then had developed the art of staging to a great extent. The Italians had evolved stage devices for moving elaborate scenery. They had developed colored lighting and many other elements in the theatre which we associate with much later times.

A large number of sketches, diagrams and plans limned by Inigo Jones have survived and give us information about the staging of the masques. Considerable sums were spent. A single masque produced for the Queen cost as much as £3000.

Ingenuity as well as lavishness was displayed in some of the devices for moving scenery. This was usually done in full view of the

PLATFORM STAGE   The illustration from the title page of William Haithorne's English translation of "Roman Comique," by Paul Scarron, published in 1676, shows strolling players on a platform stage set up in a marketplace. The stage is similar to the illustration in "The Wits" frontispiece, though the details of the picture may be French. Open-air performances by itinerant troupes continued through the latter part of the 17th century.

SCARRONS
COMICAL ROMANCE
OF
A Company of Stage Players.

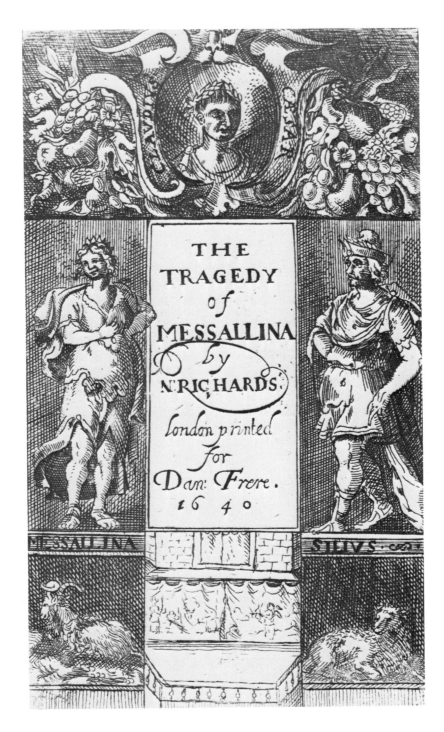

THE "MESSALLINA" FRONTISPIECE   The title page of N. Richards' tragedy, written in 1640, is interesting for the tiny etched panel (below center) which gives some idea of the Elizabethan theatre of the day. The stage is tapered in shape, and has a low railing around it. It is evident there was also an inner stage which could presumably be opened and closed by the curtains.

audience. In fact, the movement of scenery was an integral part of the masque. Gods and goddesses appeared and then vanished at will through the medium of clouds which moved across the scene.

This emphasis on setting irritated Jonson, and finally resulted in his quarreling with Jones. However, Jones was in the stronger position, and he continued to direct the masques while writers other than Jonson provided the scripts.

THE LEGACY OF THE ELIZABETHANS

Within the space of fifty years, drama had developed from the pedantic, lifeless verse of the scholar-playwrights to the greatness of Shakespearean tragedy, full of deep penetration of character and set forth in a language that reached heights of perfection that have never since been approached. Acting, too, reached heights of greatness. Burbage was the Thespian paragon of his day; what other actor had had a *Hamlet,* an *Othello,* and a *Lear* written especially for him?

The masques, with their sumptuous settings and costumes, and under the brilliant direction of Inigo Jones, achieved new levels of esthetic endeavor. The tradition of spectacle bequeathed by the Elizabethans played a large part in the theatre of later centuries.

The Commedia Dell'Arte

ORIGINS OF THE COMMEDIA

The Commedia dell'Arte, which arose in 16th century Italy and died out in the early 18th century, was a theatre of improvisation, performed by traveling troupes of actors who worked with a basic repertory of stock characters, plots, jokes, bits of business, and dialogue which they drew upon as needed. This was the theatre which gave us Harlequin, Columbine, and Pierrot. It represented a new incarnation of the ancient mime theatre which began in early Greece and which flourished in imperial Rome.

With the final dissolution of the Roman theatre in the 6th century, actors took to the road, traveling from place to place in small companies, performing at fairs and festivals, in villages and castles, for whatever they could earn—much like the traveling jugglers and minstrels of the same period. Certain features of the Commedia dell'Arte appear to have an ancient ancestry: the wearing of the phallus by the character Pantalone seems to be a direct survival from the ancient world; the character of the Captain is almost an exact counterpart of a character in one of Plautus's comedies; even the

137

fact that the Commedia dell'Arte players were masked suggests some ancient survival.

THE PLOTS OF THE COMMEDIA

Since the theatre of the Commedia dell'Arte was improvised, we have no actual scripts of their performances. We have, however, quite a number of *scenerii,* or plot outlines which were collected during their period of activity, as well as a compilation of jokes, set speeches, prologues, bits of action, and dialogue put together to serve an actor's purpose in a variety of spots.

This material makes it evident that many of the plots and situations used by the Commedia dell'Arte were based on old Roman and Greek comedies: the plays of Terence and Plautus, in particular. Typically the stories were farces; romantic intrigue, cuckoldry, and knavery were favorite themes. Other subjects were mistaken identity, avarice, the conflict between old husbands and young wives, or between bombastic old pedants and shrewd peasants or wily valets. Everything from buffoonery, rascalry, and braggadocio to tender sentiment and romance was within the range of this theatre. But the preeminent theme was marital infidelity. Young wives of old men and virtuous daughters of rich merchants engaged in involved and complicated love intrigues. The valets and the servant-maids engineered the innumerable ridiculous situations; and while doing so, engendered secondary love affairs, so that there was a continual interplay of plot and counterplot. In short, the subject matter for the Commedia was human weakness exposed by a sharp but playful invention.

THE ACTORS OF THE COMMEDIA

The actors of this improvised theatre needed immense skill; they developed immense style. Brilliant teamwork was essential, as each player had to be prepared to pick up the lines tossed to him by his fellow players and respond to them instantly, wittily, and appropri-

GIUSEPPE DOMENICO BIANCO-
LELLI   *This portrait of the foremost
Harlequin of the 17th century hangs in
the Museo Teatrale in La Scala, Milan.
Biancolelli is shown here in the costume
of "The Doctor." Born in Bologna in
1640 of a family of improvisators, he first
appeared on the stage in 1661. His talents
as dancer, acrobat, and mime, attributes
necessary for the playing of Harlequin,
and his keen wit soon brought him into
the public eye. From 1654 until his death
in 1688, he played in Paris (in French) as
a member of the Théâtre Italien.*

ately—and still continue to advance the action of the play. Only the
use of stock characters and stock plots made such an enterprise possible. Nevertheless, it would be truer to call the players of the Commedia dell'Arte actor-playwrights rather than just actors.

The characters were fixed by tradition: there were lovers and
sweethearts, bombastic or foolish old men, knavish servants, a boast-
ful captain, and a variety of dupes, braggarts, and intriguers. In
general, each actor would choose one stock character from the repertory and portray him throughout his career, improving and refining
his characterization by adding bits of business and dialogue throughout the years. The actors had an extensive repertoire of speeches,
wisecracks, and gags which could be used in any given situation.

HARLEQUIN AS BEGGAR   Now in the Ringling Museum, Florida, this 18th-century painting by Giovanni Ferretti shows Harlequin in a characteristic pose. He wears a stylized costume of a uniform, geometric pattern. The dexterity and suppleness required of the performer is hinted at in this posture. Of the entire Commedia troupe, Harlequin in particular had to display great physical agility because of the acrobatic feats expected of him.

The speeches were so fashioned that they could be lengthened or compressed, according to need.

STYLE OF PERFORMANCES

The actors could easily mime their story, thus making it clear to the audience without giving away any information to the other characters. They also had an extensive repertoire of amusing tricks and acrobatic stunts. They would turn themselves into fountains, or imitate statues, remaining motionless and unseen by other characters until the denouement of the plot required them to resume their own characters. Syringes for the squirting of water, and other properties today associated with the circus or variety stage, were greatly in use.

Although players were never at a loss for words, it might sometimes be effective to use some byplay as a relief to the spoken show. The comedians also had stock cues which simplified the entrances and exits of the various characters, ensured smoothness of playing and gave the performance a dramatic form.

In order to cue in the actors, it was only necessary to post a copy of the scenario in the wings before the performance. This bare outline of the plot served as a guide to the actors in their comings and goings on the stage. The actors cooperated so closely and understood their roles so well that they were able to perform whole plays this way without a script.

THE COMPANIES

The necessity that all members of a troupe be thoroughly familiar with each other's style and routines tended to hold a company together. The players often intermarried; and the traditions of the craft were handed down from father to son, and from mother to daughter. Thus a Commedia company was often a family in the literal sense of the word.

The most famous actors of the Commedia dell'Arte were Flaminio

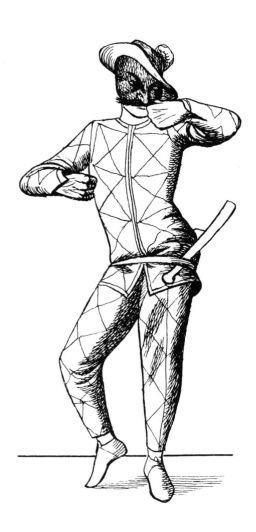

HARLEQUIN   *This drawing shows the stylized motley of the harlequin with his wooden batte.*

Scala, Andreini, Biancolelli, and Riccoboni, all cultured men, distinguished as poets and writers. Probably the original writers of much of the dialogue, these actors composed scripts which were handed down through generations of players. The most famous company was probably the Gelosi, of which Scala and Andreini and Andreini's wife, the lovely Isabella, were members. She was a cultured, witty, and beautiful woman; and the heroines of these plays were generally named Isabella after her. The art of these great comedians was refined to such a high standard that their work had a direct influence on the theatre of Europe for nearly 200 years.

The entertainment provided was enjoyed by all classes of the community. The actors of the Commedia travelled all across Europe and met with universal success, even though they often spoke no tongue but their native language. Music and pantomime made their meanings clear, even to those who could not understand the dialogue, and the subject of their comedy—the frailties and vanities of mankind —was universal.

The companies were continually meeting opposition from either the Church or the civic authorities, so they had to be continually on the move. They traveled through most of the countries of Europe —Austria, Germany, France, Spain, England—and wherever they performed they left behind ideas which were adopted into the theatres of those countries. Perhaps the most profound influence was felt in France.

CREATION OF CHARACTERS

The characters of the Commedia dell'Arte were of two main types: the comic characters who performed the most important parts in the plays; and the "straight" characters who provided the love interest, lending a romantic interpretation to their roles. Since they were constantly being recreated by individual actors, the interpretation of the traditional characters varied somewhat with different companies.

THE COMIC CHARACTERS

Arlecchino originally somewhat of a numskull, a servant, a simple native of Bergamo. He was the most famous character of the Commedia dell'Arte. Although guileless, he was full of pranks and always extremely agile. Harlequin was usually played by an actor who was also a clever dancer and acrobat. In many old prints, he is seen on stilts, walking on his hands, and generally spending a considerable time in the air.

In the 17th century, a famous Harlequin named Dominique or Biancolelli gave a new interpretation to the character. This Harlequin, no longer a rather stupid creature, was clever and shrewd. While his character was interpreted almost entirely in mime, he exhibited occasional flashes of verbal wit.

BRIGHELLA   Stock character of the
Commedia dell'Arte with money pouch,
dagger, and guitar.

His distinctive costume was originally a simple tunic and breeches
with numerous patches which were supposed to indicate his servile
status. In the 17th century, the motley patches became symmetrical
diamond shapes of red, blue, and green, separated by yellow or gold
braid.

Harlequin wore a black mask which had a bristly moustache and
sometimes wore a beard. At this belt hung his magic sword-bat. He
usually wore a skullcap or a large-brimmed hat decorated with a
hare's foot to symbolize his fleetness.

In spite of the changes the character underwent, there has always
been something gay about Harlequin that has captured the imagination of writers, musicians, and artists throughout the centuries. Even
today, whenever an actor in the traditional Harelquin costume appears on the stage, we anticipate something wonderfully amusing
will follow.

Brighella was also a native of Bergamo, and also a servant; but unlike Harlequin, he was always wily and clever, and continually busy at some sly mischief. Brighella was a singer, a musician, and a dancer, always ready to tackle any undertaking whether it was serenading his master's mistress or baiting some old man. As soon as his craft and rascality had earned him some money, he was content to laze and loaf until necessity forced him to engage in some further trickery. Brighella looked ferocious and indulged in frequent knife-play—provided he was dealing with someone older or weaker than himself.

His mask was olive-colored; it bore a hooked nose, moustache, and a beard. His costume was a short tunic, trousers which had green braid trimmings along the seams, a short cloak, and a soft hat with a green border. At his belt, Brighella always carried the symbols of his character—a money pouch and a dagger.

SCAPINO   *Stock character of the Commedia dell'Arte in loose-fitting costume with wooden sword.*

MEZZETINO *Stock character of the Commedia dell'Arte often depicted as a musician. Striped tunic and trousers were common.*

Scapino, a servant and a companion of Brighella, was also always ready to put out his hand for money; but where Brighella would draw his dagger, Scapino would flee danger in a rapid exit. In common with the other comic characters, Scapino was continually involved in amorous intrigues, both on his own account and on his master's. The character was not of the first importance, being actually a variation on Brighella. Though Scapino's costume seems to have varied considerably, it followed the general tradition of the costume of a valet: a small cape with a short tunic and loose trousers. Scapino's garb was usually decorated with green and white stripes to indicate it was some kind of livery.

Mezzetino was another familiar of Brighella's, with similar but milder characteristics. At the end of the 17th century, his costume was redesigned in France by the actor Constantin who played the character without a mask. Mezzetino's costume was similar to Scapino's, but with stripes of red and white instead of green and white. In the early 18th century in France, Mezzetino was a great favorite and appears in many of Watteau's paintings.

Pantalone, the dupe, a respectable citizen of Venice, was usually a retired old businessman. Money was his ruling passion, and his avarice constantly brought him trouble. Pantaloon sometimes had a young wife or a daughter who was engaged in a love affair behind his back—sometimes even before his very eyes. Occasionally, Pantaloon would fall in love himself, but always with some young maiden who was an incorrigible flirt who used him for game. It was transparent that her favors were promised only to extract money from the old fool.

Pantaloon's traditional costume was a short red jacket and the tight-fitting trousers to which he had given his name. He also wore a long trailing cloak or gown of black, similar to that worn at one time by the Venetians as a sign of mourning when the Turkish pirates succeeded in despoiling them. A small brimless cap, slippers, and the all-important money pouch at his belt, completed Pantaloon's

PANTALONE   *A comic character of the Commedia dell'Arte in traditional costume of red tights and long black coat.*

THE CAPTAIN   *Il Capitano was a stock character of the Commedia. Prevailing opinion is that the character developed during the Italian Renaissance, born of the hatred the conquered Italians had for their Spanish overlords. At first, the captain cut a dashing figure; he was on occasion a lover, and not given solely to the bombastic posture for which he is most frequently known. However, he was gradually vulgarized; and representations of the mid-17th century show him in more grotesque costume. In that later period, his hat plumes grew bizarre; his sword was exaggeratedly present, as was sometimes a gun. Most importantly, his round-eyed and bulbous-nosed mask made him a creature intended for ridicule. In this woodcut from the "Compositions de Rhetorique" of Tristano Martinelli, he is caparisoned in typical elegant Spanish military dress.*

costume. Shakespeare mentions "the lean and slippered Pantaloon with spectacles on nose."

In some early engravings, the phallus is discernible, a relic of the days of the ancient theatre; and Pantaloon's mask is brown, with a long hooked nose, gray moustaches, and a short white beard with two absurdly long points.

The Captain was the classic braggart; as he strutted about armed with a long rapier and twirling his moustaches, he looked so forbidding and so ferocious. He had been away to the wars where he had performed deeds of prodigious valor, but strangely enough, all his victims were alive and well. His long-winded, bombastic talk was punctuated with strange oaths acquired in foreign lands. Of course,

The Captain was really an abject coward, and Harlequin and his fellows had only to make the clinking noise of men-at-arms offstage for the Captain to collapse with fright and pretend to be dead.

A very famous Captain was Francesco Andreini who played with the Gelosi troupe in Paris in the 1570's. He had been a soldier, and for a time had been a prisoner of the Turks. No doubt, in his interpretation of the character he drew on his own experiences.

Originally, The Captain, like his fellows, was a native of Italy; but in the 17th century when the Spanish Army dominated the rest of Europe, The Captain became a Spaniard. His costume followed the military dress of the times, and changed with each successive period. In the early 17th century, The Captain wore tight-fitting clothes decorated with stripes, a plumed felt hat, and high boots. His mask was flesh-colored, with a large hooked nose, and great bristling moustaches. One of The Captain's most important properties was his great sword—which was never unsheathed—but which was worn with the point thrust aggressively upward.

SCARAMOUCHE   A comic character of the Commedia dell'Arte, this intriguer generally appeared in short black cloak and cap.

PANTALONE   "The grand seigneur of the Masks," as this comic character of the Commedia was known, Pantalone is seen here in the costume which remained constant throughout theatrical history. He wears tightfitting trousers and vest, a black flowing cloak (zimmara), soft slippers, a soft black hat, and a pointed grey beard. The protuberant phallus is believed by some scholars to be a carry-over from the ancient Roman mimes.

COVIELLO SINGING   In this 17th-century Italian print, Coviello, a native of Calabria, plays the guitar and sings with a Sicilian friend. Although he is usually associated with Pantalone as one of the stock old men, he occasionally appears as a "zanni" with Pulcinella.

THE DOCTOR *This comic character of the Commedia dell'Arte is drawn here in his traditional black costume, the badge of his profession.*

The Doctor was another dupe. A product of the University of Bologna, he was the embodiment of all the foolish, pedantic professors in the world. His knowledge of letters, medicine, philosophy, astronomy, and the law was profound; but his knowledge of life, gained solely from books—which he generally misquoted—was shallow indeed. He had learned everything about life, but understood nothing. He was continually meddling in other people's affairs and pontificating. Naturally, he provided Harlequin and his fellows with great sport. Like his old friend, Pantalone, he was occasionally assailed by the gentler passion, with the result that he was caught in countless ridiculous situations.

His costume was the black dress of the man of letters or the man of science of his day. Though he originally wore a long black cloak and a small hat, in the 17th century the cloak tended to become shorter and was worn over a black tunic, while the hat became enormously large with a great, wide brim. Around his neck he wore a large ruff, and under his arm or in his hand he always toted a huge book, or a treatise. His mask, curiously enough, covered only his nose and forehead, and was either black or flesh-colored. To round out the character, *The Doctor* always wore a mustache and a short pointed beard.

Scaramouche, originally a variation on The Captain, was of much lighter caliber. Scaramouche was more adroit, less bombastic, and something of a musician and dancer. He appeared in a completely black costume, and as played by Fiorillo in the 17th century, wore no mask. In with the valets, he was continually involved in picking pockets and dodging blows. Like the Captain, in order to impress the ladies and to scare peaceful citizens, Scaramouche bragged of his imaginary feats of prowess.

Pulcinella, from whom the English Punch has evolved, is considered by many scholars to be the direct descendant of a Roman comic character known as *Maccus;* some ancient statuettes have similar characteristics, including the same great hooked nose and round belly. Puncinello's hunched back is a more recent development.

PULCINELLA   *A Neapolitan creation of the 16th century. The exaggerated humpback, sagging belly and hooked nose, as well as the ruff and high hat, were developments of the 17th century.*

PULCINELLA WITH A COOKING POT   In this 18th-century painting
attributed to Giovanni Domenico Ferretti, the character of Pulcinella wears the
classic costume of the zany: a loose-fitting, white garment and a conical-shaped hat.
The hooked nose, humped back, sagging belly and highly-exaggerated tall hat were
later developments of the character.

PEDROLINO   *In his loose-fitting white costume derived from the dress of the 16-century zany, this character wears the large buttons added in the 18th century.*

Punchinello was usually represented as an old bachelor, sensual and cruel, but with a sense of humor and flashes of wit. His costume, based on the traditional dress of the peasants of Italy, was white. Like those of the other characters, this costume was changed in France during the 17th century to red breeches and a green-trimmed jacket. Punchinello wore a ruff and a tall conical hat, sometimes a skullcap. His mask was chiefly all nose, although it was sometimes adorned with a moustache and beard.

Pedrolino (Pierrot) was another valet, but a trustworthy one. Pierrot was a rather simple character; when encouraged by Harlequin to engage in trickery, he was invariably the only one to be caught and punished. Originally, Pierrot was closely related to Pulcinella and

Brighella; but in France, Pierrot developed into a more attractive and elegant personality. His costume was a simple white tunic, loose trousers with a large ruff, and a soft felt cap. In the 18th century, Pierrot sprouted large buttons on his tunic, and long sleeves that concealed his hands. He also acquired a strange quality of sadness. Played without a mask, Pierrot's face usually was powdered white.

THE LOVER   His talent lay in his handsome face. His costume reflects the fashionable dress of the day.

INNAMORATA   This 17th-century character traditionally wore the dress of the day.

THE STRAIGHT CHARACTERS

The Lovers were known by various names such as Fabio, Ottavio, Silvio, Leandro, Lelio, and Flavio. The only characteristic of these

THE FANTESCA   The costume of the 16th-century maidservant originally indicated her status, but the costume gradually began to resemble the dress of the mistress.

BALLERINA   Her talents were confined to musical interludes and epilogues. After an etching from Jacques Callot's "I Balli di Sfessania", 1602.

men was their being in love and serving as foils for the comic characters. The Lovers were always good-looking and elegant, and were dressed like the young gallants of their time. The actor had to interpret the part in a poetic and cultured manner, appearing just a trifle ridiculous. The Lovers (or *Innamoratos*) were often played by men of birth and position. Sometimes the noble before whom the actors performed would play the part; or the part might be played by the director of the company himself. The Lovers acted without masks.

The Innamoratas were also known by various names such as Flaminia, Lavinia, Aurelia, and Isabella. Women first appeared on the stage as actresses during the 16th century, and were welcomed with joy in France; but women were not allowed to play in the Papal States until the 18th century. The numerous names of the female Lovers derived from individual actresses who had their own particular characteristics. Isabella, the celebrated wife of Andreini and the leading actress in their company—the *prima donna*—was renowned for her beauty, her cultured wit, and her poetic writings. She made of her character the idealized type of a woman in love. Her costume was the elegant dress of the period.

None of the Innamoratas wore masks.

The Soubrette, confidante to the Innamorata, had many names such as Liletta, Smeraldina, Olivetta, Francheschina, or more popularly, Columbine. The Soubrette, a buxom wench, was a servant girl usually in love with one of the valets. She was on close terms with Harlequin, and would willingly enter into the intrigues hatched by him and his companions. The Soubrette had a ready wit, and her lines were sometimes outrageous. She was often required to disguise herself in the costume of a cavalier, of a doctor, or even of Harlequin. Originally, her costume was that of the common people of the 16th century, distinguished by a large white apron. Later, in France, her dress became indistinguishable from that of her mistress.

HARLEQUIN SETS OFF TO BATTLE   *A typical comic scene from the "Recueil Fossard," a collection of early prints of the Commedia dell'Arte. Here Harlequin, in an obvious parody of Don Quixote, is ready for action: his armour is on backwards; a cooking pot (called a "marmite") serves as a helmet; and as he sets off to battle on his donkey, his blunted lance is held aloft. According to the subscripture, he is willing, like Hercules, to take on Hell for the sake of his "dear Mistress, the beautiful Francisquine."*

The *ballerinas* and *canterinas*—the dancers and the singers—could sing and play several instruments. They sometimes performed acrobatic feats or danced on a tightrope, and would perform during the intervals of a play. Sometimes, they would tell the story of a play in an epilogue which was sung.

SCENERY OF THE COMMEDIA

As they could not expect to find a theatre in every town they visited, the comedians usually carried around with them a portable stage with curtains, along with their considerable stage properties. In many old

COMIC SERENADE   *A characteristic mise-en-scene, from one of the earliest documents extant on the Commedia dell'Arte (the "Recueil Fossard" in the National Museum in Stockholm). This invaluable group of engravings, unearthed in Sweden in 1928 by Agne J. Bejier, presents figures of the Commedia as seen around 1577 and offers indisputable evidence of their costumes. The costume of Harlequin, consisting of triangular or diamond-shaped patches in a formal design, clearly derives from the irregular patchwork seen here. Pantalone's long cloak (zimmara), his soft cap (which alternates with a fez-like cap), and the typically loose-fitting garb of the early Zanni are clearly visible. In this print, Harlequin, Pantalone, and a Zanni (generic type of servant-comedians) are simultaneously serenading an unseen lady.*

prints, these portable stages can be seen set up in the marketplace. They were usually just simple square platforms with a decorated curtain as background. The characters entered upon the stage by mounting short ladders at the side.

Throughout the 16th and 17th centuries, since the Italians were ahead of the rest of Europe in stage technique; we can be sure that the comedians, all practiced professionals, had the ability to make full use of scenery and stage machinery whenever these were avail-

Troisième Journée.
Le Malade imaginaire, Comedie representée
dans le Jardin de Versailles devant la Grotte

MOLIÈRE PERFORMANCE   This engraving by Le Pautre represents an open air performance of "Le Malade Imaginaire," given at Versailles in 1674 for King Louis XIV

Dies tertius.
Dokesinoson, seu Æger imaginarius, Comædia acta
in Hortis Versaliarum ad foras Cryptæ.

and his court. The comedy was first performed at the Palais-Royal in February, 1673
with Molière playing the hypochondriac, Argan.

able. The actors of the Italian Commedia were experienced in the use of colored lighting, fireworks, and fountains which provided spectacular effects during their performaces. The settings, usually of an architectural nature, would represent a street or marketplace in perspective.

In France, in the 17th century, the comedians used a great variety of settings, interiors, and outside sets, either architectural or in the form of a pastoral landscape. At the Hôtel de Bourgogne theatre, the Commedia actors maintained a permanent architectural setting, in the center of which stood a large arch. Behind this arch, interchangeable backcloths representing various scenes were placed.

When they performed at Palladio's famous classical theatre at Vicenza in Italy, they had an elaborate permanent setting with three archways allowing perspective views of streets of solidly constructed wooden houses. The characters could be seen in any street; yet being invisible to each other, several could appear simultaneously and continue quite naturally with their involved plotting. There were two further doorways at the side of the arches, so there were many ways of ingress and exit.

INFLUENCE IN FRANCE

Although the Commedia dell'Arte was popular everywhere in Europe, it was in France that this style made its greatest impact and even affected the legitimate stage. In the 1570's, several great troupes visited Paris, among which were the Ganassa and the Gelosi. The Gelosi troupe, which numbered among its players the renowned husband and wife team of Francisco and Isabella Andreini, was the outstanding troupe of its time. The popularity of these companies in Paris was so great, it paved the way for visits by other Italian troupes.

By the 17th century, the Italian Commedia was well established in Paris, popular alike with the court and the public. In 1658, when the great French comic playwright, Molière (1622-1673), first obtained permission to settle in Paris, he was assigned to share a theatre with the Commedia dell'Arte troupe led by Tiborio Fiorilli (1608-1694), which was already resident in that theatre. For several years, Molière's troupe and Fiorilli's used the theatre together, giving their performances on alternate nights.

Many of Molière's early plays show the influence of the Commedia dell'Arte. It is hard to say whether this derived from Molière's contact with Fiorilli's troupe in Paris, or whether he had already been much influenced by contact with other such troupes during his many years of touring the provinces.

In 1680, when the national theatre company of France—the Comédie-Française—was founded, the Commedia dell'Arte troupe then resident in Paris had attained such high status it was given a theatre of its own at the same time. The Hôtel de Bourgogne, where they had already been playing for some time, was now renamed the Comédie-Italienne in order to distinguish it from the Comédie-Francaise, the French theatre.

Seventeen years later, in 1697, the Commedia was expelled from France because the players were sufficiently imprudent to offend the king's mistress, Madame de Maintenon, by presenting a play called *La Fausse Prude,* which the audience delighted in believing referred to that lady.

In 1716, when the Italian comedians were allowed to return to the French capital, tastes had changed and the days of the harlequinade were by and large over. In spite of this, the Comédie-Italienne maintained their company by turning to the production of comedies written in French by young French playwrights. The most outstanding of these dramatists was Pierre de Marivaux (1688-1763) who gave his name to a whole style of French comedy known as *marivaudage.* Marivaux had been much influenced by the Italian Commedia in his work.

Even before their expulsion from France, the Italian comedians had begun to introduce French songs and bits of French dialogue into their performances. Now they performed entirely in French. Increasingly, French actors joined the troupe, until it became entirely

French and the company was finally simply absorbed into the French theatre.

The last of the great Italian Harlequins, Carlin Bertinazzi, was seen by the great English actor-manager, David Garrick, on his visit to the Continent in the 1760's. Garrick is said to have considered Bartinazzi one of the best actors in Paris.

INFLUENCE IN ENGLAND

From France, the influence of the Commedia dell'Arte passed to England. Charles II, having spent part of his exile in France, must often have seen such comedy performed in Paris. After his return to the English throne, the King gave an Italian company permission to play a season in London, during which they proved very popular. Samuel Pepys, in his *Diary,* mentions having seen "Polichinelly"

MOLIÈRE (JEAN-BAPTISTE POQUELIN) (1622-1673)   The greatest writer of French comedy and a supreme "man of the theatre," Molière was actor-manager of his own troupe for 15 years. He laid the groundwork for the formal establishment by Louis XIV of the Comédie Française, also called the "House of Molière." Through his master-works—SCHOOL FOR WIVES (1662), TARTUFFE (1664), THE DOCTOR IN SPITE OF HIMSELF (1666), THE MISANTHROPE (1666), THE BOURGEOIS GENTLEMAN (1670), THE IMAGINARY INVALID (1673)—he singlehandedly raised comedy to the level of the classic tragedies of Corneille and Racine. Molière is shown here in a famous portrait with one of his Commedia dell'Arte figures, Sganarelle. The painting is based on an engraving by Simonin.

COMMEDIA PERFORMANCE   *This oil painting by Marco Marcola in the Art Institute of Chicago depicts an open-air performance of a Commedia dell' Arte troup in Verona in 1772. Arlecchino is shown bowing before his innamorata.*

several times, in 1666. No doubt Charles enjoyed these performances, which used women players as well as men, and he was partly responsible for the acceptance of actresses on the English stage which for so long had allocated female roles to young boys.

If the Commedia made its impression on actors and playgoers under Charles II in the 17th century and on David Garrick in the 18th, it appears to have made an impression on English playwrights considerably earlier. A Commedia dell'Arte company had been in England as far back as 1527. Shakespeare and his audience must have known of them, as Shakespeare refers to Pantaloon in *As You Like It* in terms which he clearly expects his audience to understand. The comic letter scene in *Twelfth Night* might easily have been a scene played by the Italian comedians. Indeed, it is not hard to see something of the Commedia's Captain, Harlequin, Brighella, Columbine, and the Doctor in Shakespeare's Sir Toby, Sir Andrew, Fabian, Maria, and Malvolio.

THE LEGACY OF THE COMMEDIA DELL'ARTE

The stock characters of the Commedia dell'Arte have passed into our literary tradition. Punch, in our Punch and Judy shows, is just a version of the Commedia dell'Arte's Punchinello. Indeed, many of the characters and situations used in European puppet theatres today are survivals from the old Commedia.

The traditional British Christmas pantomime still uses characters and material based on this tradition, and many of the Commedia's jokes and routines still survive among the low comics and entertainers of the burlesque theatre, the music hall, and among the clowns of our circuses.

A different sort of comic tradition also developed from the Commedia dell'Arte: the comedy of manners. In England, the plots of William Congreve and Richard Brinsley Sheridan—in France, the style of Marivaux and of the great Molière—owe much to the complicated intrigues of the Commedia dell'Arte.

The Restoration Theatre

LINKS WITH THE PAST

From 1642 to 1660, during the regime of the Commonwealth Protectorate under Oliver Cromwell, all the theatres in England were closed and all stage performances were prohibited by Parliament. During this long lapse of regular performances in London, most of the professional players took to the road and performed at the big fairs held all over the country. Occasionally, private performances were given. Cromwell's new regime was not very welcome in certain parts of the country, and so it is probable that performances went on unchecked in these places.

Thus, it would be wrong to assume that when the theatres were finally reopened after a hiatus of eighteen years there was a complete break with the traditions of the past. In 1660, when the monarchy was restored with the accession of Charles II and the playhouses were reopened, there were still a number of players alive and active who had begun their careers during the reign of Charles I. Among these, it was Sir William Davenant who was primarily responsible for providing the link with the past.

169

SIR WILLIAM DAVENANT (1606-1668)

Born in Oxford in 1606, the son of an innkeeper, Davenant was considered by many to be a natural son of Shakespeare who had often stayed at the inn. Davenant's mother was known as a great beauty and a very witty woman. At all events, Davenant had Shakespeare for a godfather. Inheriting his mother's wit, he achieved fame as a poet and dramatist, became Poet Laureate in 1638, and was knighted by Charles I in 1643. In his early years, Davenant lived in noble households and at Court where he became acquainted with the best manners of his time.

After quarrelling with Ben Jonson, Inigo Jones, producer of Court masques turned to Davenant for material. Davenant supplied what was wanted, and rose rapidly in favor with the Court. *The Temple of Love,* a masque performed in 1634 at Whitehall for Queen Henrietta Maria and her ladies, put his star in the ascendancy. Three years later Jonson died. Davenant succeeded him as poet in the service of the Court, being awarded a patent by Charles I. Although the position was not clearly defined, it can be assumed that Davenant was recognized as holding the office of Poet Laureate, whereupon his influence with the Queen became greater. He was later granted a patent to build a theatre in which to present "plays, musical entertainments, scenes, and other like presentments."

Davenant proposed to introduce the spectacle and scenery of the Court masques into the public theatre. However, because of political difficulties and perhaps also owing to some disagreement about the site of the new theatre, Davenant's playhouse was not erected until more than twenty years had passed.

At the beginning of 1640, Davenant wrote his last masque. In this work, all the art of Inigo Jones and his assistant, John Webb, brought to a climax the pride and beauty of court pageantry.

Later that year, Davenant became manager of a company of players at the Phoenix Theatre in Drury Lane, a playhouse also known as the Cockpit. He replaced the previous manager, William Beeston, who had presented an unlicensed play containing some topical allusions

SIR WILLIAM DAVENANT (1606-1668)   The major theatrical figure of the 17th century, William Davenant succeeded almost single-handedly in keeping the theatre alive during the Commonwealth. A patent from Charles I, granted to him in 1639, permitted him to present theatrical entertainment privately. His dramatic operas: "The Siege of Rhodes" (1656), "The Cruelty of the Spaniards at Peru" (1658), and "The History of Sir Francis Drake" (1658), successfully evaded the Puritan ban and at the same time established Davenant as "the father of English opera." With the Restoration in 1660, Davenant was issued a monopoly warrant by Charles II and founded the famous Duke's Theatre.

that gave offense to the Queen, in consequence of which Beeston had been arrested and the theatre closed. The Queen, knowing of Davenant's wish to have his own theatre, appointed him to "govern, order, and dispose" the players and their plays and productions. The Phoenix, however, was a small theatre, and there was obviously not sufficient room here for Davenant to carry out his schemes of painted scenery and elaborate stage machinery.

Davenant remained in charge of the Phoenix for just about a year; then he was forced to flee to the countryside to avoid being arrested by the Parliamentary soldiers. Davenant held a position in the royal army at this time. He was apprehended at Faversham and brought to London, where he was detained for two months. After his release, he eventually reached France. In 1642, the year in which all the theatres were closed, he returned to England, joined the King's forces, and remained with his sovereign until the defeat of the royalists at Marston Moor in 1644. Once again, Davenant escaped to France. However, ill luck dogged him; while he was sailing to America in 1651, the ship he was on was captured by a Parlimentary frigate and Davenant was brought back to London and confined in the Tower. Tradition has it that it was Milton who finally secured his pardon and his ultimate release from prison.

In 1652, Davenant found himself a free man, but without any position and practically penniless. No doubt he used his knowledge of the stage in some of the private performances that were being surreptitiously given during the period of Puritan rule; he must certainly have kept in touch with his old friends of the theatre.

At this time, there was a quiet but constant protest against the closing of the theatres, particularly among scholars and writers. In 1656, Davenant, using all his tact and political genius, actually approached the Commonwealth Secretary of State, suggesting that stage presentations would be beneficial to the administration of the day because of their moral value. Although this argument failed to convince, Davenant in the same year gave a private performance in a hall at the back of his own house. The play itself constituted a plea for the opening of the theatres. In the course of the argument, Aristophanes and Diogenes made their appearances, and we can be sure that Aristophanes won the day.

The success of this venture encouraged Davenant to more ambitious efforts. He followed in 1656 with *The Siege of Rhodes,* an opera with scenery designed by John Webb. The stage on which the performance took place was only eighteen feet wide and nine feet high, and the several scenes were changed by easily movable flats or sliding panels. Through sheer simplification, Webb successfully applied the ideas and innovations of the masque stage to a more intimate setting. The scenes were built with only three sets of wings and a backboard, and these sparse properties could easily be changed without machinery.

In 1658, Davenant finally got permission from the authorities to reopen the Phoenix, his old theatre. His opening production, which he again called an opera, was entitled *The Cruelty of the Spaniards at Peru* (1658). As this was quite in line with Cromwell's hatred of Catholic Spain, it no doubt pleased the authorities. This so-called opera was merely a series of declamatory speeches with songs and musical interludes delivered against a background of painted scenery. Although only a slight piece, it was the thin edge of the wedge.

Davenant was getting closer to his goal and he became a bit bolder, following up in 1659 with a production of the second part of his earlier work *The Siege of Rhodes*.

This play created open opposition, especially since it came on top of a surreptitious attempt to bring Charles II back from exile, and once again Davenant found himself in prison. However, he still retained some influence in high places, and in August of 1659 he was released. Thereafter performances were resumed at the Phoenix early in 1660 without much hindrance.

Sensing the changing political atmosphere, Davenant left for France soon thereafter to join the royal entourage. When King Charles II returned to England in May, 1660, Davenant returned with him in triumph. As a figure of importance, he was now in a position to carry out his long-cherished ambition of presenting his plays publicly in a manner for which he had worked and struggled for many years.

THOMAS KILLIGREW (1612-1683)

One other man was to have a similar opportunity. Thomas Killigrew had been a dramatist before the exile, the author of two tragedies: *The Prisoners* and *Claracilla*. In 1647, Killigrew followed the King into exile on the Continent. While there, he wrote poetical works of a fanciful nature which proved very pleasing to the Court audiences. Exile also provided Killigrew with the opportunity to travel and see first hand the technical achievements of the theatres of France and Italy.

After the King and Court returned to England at the time of the Restoration, Killigrew was rewarded for his loyalty to the Crown by being appointed groom of the royal bedchamber to the King and chamberlain to the Queen. His talents received recognition when he was given, along with Davenant, the opportunity of reopening and managing a theatre in London.

*THOMAS KILLIGREW (1612-1683)
Courtier, playwright, manager, man of
the theatre, and faithful attendant to his
king, Thomas Killigrew followed Charles
II into exile. With the King's triumphant
return in 1660, Killigrew got permission
for himself and Davenant to be the "dic-
tators of the theatres of London." On May
7, 1663, he opened the Theatre Royal in
Drury Lane with a revival of "The Humourous Lieutenant." Killigrew's taste in
plays primarily ran to romantic tragedies
of love and honor, with such long-forgot-
ten titles as: "The Parson's Wedding,"
"The Prisoners," "The Princess," and
"Cecilia & Clorinda." He managed Drury
Lane until 1674 when, exhausted by internal strife, partisan audiences, defecting
actors, and serious financial problems, he
turned over the theatre to his son Charles.*

THE PATENT THEATRES

The right to own and manage a theatre—and along with that the
exclusive right to present dramatic entertainment to the public of
London—was secured by the issuance of Royal Patents to Davenant
and Killigrew. These Royal Patents established a legal monopoly on
dramatic production in London. Thus, when the theatre of London
was reopened in 1660 after a hiatus of eighteen years, there were—
and could be by law— only two theatres in the city.

The patent rights to these two theatres continue to this day, and
are held at present by the Drury Lane Theatre and the Covent Garden Theatre, although they no longer give the patent holders an
exclusive monopoly. The original monopoly right held, more or less,
for nearly 200 years, until it was finally broken in 1843. Both the
enforcement of the monopoly and the inevitable efforts to circumvent
it affected the history of the English theatre throughout two centuries.

THE DUKE'S THEATRE   *This edifice in Dorset Garden was a baroque masterpiece designed by Christopher Wren, England's greatest architect. The theatre opened in 1671 under the management of Thomas Betterton and Charles Davenant.*

INTERIOR OF THE DUKE'S THEATRE   *The apron stage, the double proscenium doors, and the stage boxes were characteristic of Restoration theatres. Note the musicians' box above the proscenium arch.*

THE KING'S PLAYERS AND THE DUKE OF YORK'S PLAYERS

Upon receipt of their patents, Killigrew and Davenant each formed his own company. Killigrew's group was known as the King's Players, and performed at the new Theatre Royal in Drury Lane which Killigrew had built in 1662. Davenant's group was known as the Duke of York's Players, and first performed at a theatre in Salisbury Court. Later, Davenant converted a tennis court at Lincoln's Inn Fields into a theatre and set up his productions there.

For the next few years, however, things did not go too smoothly. There were long periods when the theatres were closed again, once during the years of the Great Plague (1665) and once after the Great Fire of London (1666).

There was some outward rivalry between the two companies, although their relationship was actually a friendly one. Killigrew's company kept to the traditional simple stage of Shakespeare's time; Davenant's company made use of painted scenery and mechanical devices, borrowed from the court masques which Davenant had produced before the Commonwealth.

WILLIAM CONGREVE (1670-1729) Foremost among writers of Restoration comedy, Congreve won initial acclaim when "The Old Bachelor" was successfully staged in 1693 with an illustrious cast that included Thomas Betterton, Mrs. Barry, Mrs. Bracegirdle, Mrs. Mountfort, Doggett, and Wilks. The following year, his next two plays, "The Double-Dealer" and "Love for Love," firmly established his reputation as the leading dramatist of the Restoration. Discouraged over the poor reception given his last and best play, "The Way of the World," Congreve retired from the theatre. His plays are prized for their stylistic elegance and for his understanding of feminine psychology. Millimant, in "The Way of the World," is considered one of the most ingratiating heroines of the English stage.

ABOVE LEFT: WILLIAM WYCHERLEY (1640-1716)   *Coarser than the plays of his later contemporaries, Wycherley comedies set the style of wit and sparkling dialogue that characterized Restoration Comedy. He had a modest success with his first play, "Love in a Wood," written in 1671. Better known, however, are his two major comedies: "The Country Wife" (1674), a study of sexual foibles, and "The Plain Dealer" (1676), a satirical comedy reminiscent of Moliere's "Le Misanthrope."*

ABOVE RIGHT: GEORGE FARQUHAR (1678-1707)   *Unsuccessful in his lifetime, George Farquhar lived a tragic and unhappy life, dying prematurely at the age of 29. His early works "The Constant Couple," "Love and a Bottle," "The Inconstant," and "Twin Rivals" (1702) are hardly remembered. More familiar are "The Recruiting Officer" (1706), and "The Beaux' Stratagem" (1707), characterized by the lively wit and vivid characterizations of the comedy of manners. Farquhar's later plays also reflect the increasing taste for sentimental comedy that was to predominate in 18th-century drama.*

SIR JOHN VANBRUGH (1664-1726)
Vanbrugh's plays, though they fall historically among the last works of the Restoration drama, are a descent into farce from the brilliant word play of Congreve. "The Relapse" (1696), Vanbrugh's first play in its patent immorality, is close to the conventions of early Restoration comedy. His later plays show signs of the sentimentalism that characterizes the moral tone of plays in the 18th century. "The Provok'd Wife" (1679), his great work, revealed a fortuitous combination of wit and plot that made it immensely successful, and kept the play popular well into the 18th century. The character of Sir John Brute in this play was a favorite of David Garrick's, and is considered today a classic role in the repertory of Restoration comedy.

Finally, Davenant decided that his theatre at Lincoln's Inn Fields was not large enough to house the scenery he wanted, so he determined to build a new theatre at Dorset Garden. This playhouse, designed by Christopher Wren, was very elaborate and ornate. It opened in 1671. Unfortunately, Davenant, who died in 1668, did not live to see it.

After Davenant's death, the management of his theatre was carried on by his wife who was a shrewd business woman, and later by his son, Charles Davenant, in partnership with some of the leading actors of the company. Killigrew's company also carried on when he passed away; his son, Charles, took over as manager.

THE AUDIENCES DURING THE RESTORATION

It was mostly gallants of the town and the Court who attended the theatre in Restoration days. The common people still regarded the

THE LAUGHING AUDIENCE   *Hogarth, the master satirist, affords a glimpse of the theatre patrons of Nell Gwynne's day. Miss Gwynne must have often seen such faces when she acted in the Theatre Royale.*

theatre as an appurtenance of the Court. The old Puritan influence still remained very strong; few of the stolid middle class ever attended the theatre.

The young gallants went regularly to the theatres, not only to see but to be seen. The auditorium was illuminated as brightly as the stage itself. Witty conversation and intriguing gossip flowed continually through the audience throughout the performance of a play. People would come and go at all times, regardless of what was going on, on the stage; sometimes in the middle of a scene an argument in the pit would lead to a duel. It is recorded that during a performance of *Macbeth,* a young gallant met his end at the point of a sword. Such were the conditions under which the players performed. Yet they went from strength to strength.

RESTORATION PLAYS

The first productions of the two companies were chiefly the old mainstays: Shakespeare, Beaumont and Fletcher, Ben Jonson, and their contemporaries. Davenant was too busy at management to do much writing himself, so new productions were chiefly adaptations and translations. For the young gallants of the Court who constituted the theatre-going public at this time, these works seemed largely dated and out of style. Occasionally a tragedy or a poetical work set in a distant land met with their approval. But the great vogue of the period was for comedy; and the great contribution of the Restoration playwrights to the English theatre was the Comedy of Manners.

The Restoration Comedy or Comedy of Manners depicted the world of its audience, a moneyed and elegant world, a world of wits and rakes, of fops and dandies. Plots revolved around the eternal subjects of attempted seduction and adultery, and the seeking of fortunes through the manipulation of marriage alliances—all counterposed to the successful working out of a romance. The interplay of greed and wit, vanity and flirtation, scandal, backbiting, frivolity and badinage was set in a silken world of courtly gallants and beautiful, witty young ladies of the upper class. The plots had all the stylized and complicated intrigue—none of it to be taken really seriously—of the old Commedia dell'Arte farce, but the subject of the comedy was really the hypocrisy, vanity and double-dealing of the elegant world which was itself the comedy's chief audience: human frailty behind a charming mask of wit, intelligence, and elegance.

The chief of the Restoration playwrights were: William Congreve (1670-1729), William Wycherley (1640-1716), Sir George Etherege (1635-1691), Sir John Vanbrugh (1664-1726), John Dryden (1631-

RESTORATION SCENERY   The spectacular sets used in the Duke's Theatre is illustrated by these two scenes from the 1673 edition of Settle's "The Empress of Morocco." Elaborate scene changes were made possible by a series of painted flats and back shutters, the flats running through grooves in the stage floor to meet in the center or to remain apart as wings, lending perspective in depth. The curtain was used principally at the beginning and the end of a performance to mark the start and close of the action. Rarely was it used during the performance itself. The scene was changed in open sight of the audience. The use of flats behind the proscenium arch facilitated quick scene changes without the actors' having to move. Actors frequently required to "go within," did so, going to the stage rear as flats closed in behind them.

INTERIOR OF A RESTORATION THEATRE   No actual plan of
the interior of the Duke Theatre remains, but the engravings from the 1673
edition of Settle's "Empress of Morocco" offer invaluable evidence of what the
interior must have looked like. The proscenium arch displays a formal pattern
in place of the usual supporting pillars at the sides. Above, there is a kind of
truncated half-roof, above which stand two statues which might represent
the muses Thalia and Melpomene. The curtained center window and those
at either side, with a violin, fife, and drum depicted on the ledge below,
indicate that this may have been the music room. The deep and wide apron
stage, cut off in the drawing, is just visible in front of the proscenium frame.
The proscenium doors, one of the most important features of the theatre, can
just be seen, with the stage boxes above them.

1700), and Thomas Otway (1652-1685).

The earliest of these was Sir George Etherege, whose *The Comical Revenge; or Love in a Tub* was produced in 1664. This was followed by two other plays: *She Would if She Could*, in 1668, and his best play, *The Man of Mode: or, Sir Fopling Flutter,* in 1676.

Of John Dryden's dramatic works, the two best known today are the comedy *Marriage à la Mode* (1673) and the tragedy *All for Love* (1678).

William Wycherly's *The Country Wife* (1675) is still performed, as are Congreve's *Love for Love* (1695) and *The Way of the World* (1700). These two are considered the masterpieces of the Restoration Theatre.

George Farquhar's best-known work is *The Beaux Stratagem* (1707). *The Recruiting Officer* (1706) was for a long time an active part of the English repertory. Farquhar's *The Constant Couple* (1701) was famous in its day for offering the actress Peg Woffington the opportunity to appear in a "breeches" part, that is, a young man's role.

Sir John Vanbrugh, whose most successful play was *The Provoked Wife* (1697), was also an architect. He was the designer of Blenheim Park, the estate of the Duke of Marlborough, which eventually became the home of the Duke's most eminent descendant, Sir Winston Churchill.

Thomas Otway's *Venice Preserved* (1682) is generally considered the best work of tragedy which the Restoration period **produced**

THOMAS BETTERTON (1635-1710)

The most famous actor of Restoration times was Thomas Betterton, who dominated the scene until the beginning of the 18th century. According to most writers of his day, Betterton excelled in both tragedy and comedy.

We have little information about his early life, except that he was born in 1635, the son of an under cook to Charles I. He was somewhat precocious, took early to reading and study, and as a young man was apprenticed to a bookseller, John Rhodes, who had a great love for the stage. One of Betterton's fellow apprentices happened to be Edward Kynaston, who also became a well-known actor. Probably these two young men started acting during the period of surreptitious private performances under the Commonwealth. Rhodes, for his part, reopened the Cockpit Theatre as soon as the Restoration took place, and Betterton became a member of his company. When the issuance of the theatre patents forced Rhodes to close down, Betterton went to Davenant.

In 1660, Betterton signed a contract with Davenant of which we still have record. The terms of this contract provided that the total receipts of the house were to be divided into fifteen shares, of which three were to go to the management for rent and the building of scenery and costuming and properties, while seven went to Davenant for the maintenance of the costumes of the women players and to pay his own personal expenses; the other five shares were to be divided among the actors.

It is interesting to note that in this particular contract there is a clause which provides for the perpetual maintenance of a private box in the theatre for Thomas Killigrew, indicating that although the two companies showed outward rivalry, the two managers themselves—Davenant and Killigrew—were on very good personal terms.

Betterton soon played leading parts in Davenant's company. In Pepys's *Diary,* we read that in 1661 Betterton played Hamlet. The entry runs "To the Opera, and there saw 'Hamlet, Prince of Denmarke,' done with scenes very well, but above all, Betterton did the Prince's part beyond imagination."

This was the most successful tragedy that the company put on for many years. The take at the box office was considerable, and the company gained a high reputation.

About the same year, one of Davenant's plays, called *Love and Honour,* was presented. For this production the records refer to "the King giving Mr. Betterton his Coronation Suit in which he acted the part of Prince Alvaro." The Duke of York and Lord Oxford also

ANNE OLDFIELD (1683-1730)   Discovered by George Farquhar in an English tavern reciting lines from Beaumont and Fletcher while she did household chores, Mrs. Oldfield was hired to appear at the Drury Lane in 1699. She achieved her first success as Lady Betty Modish in Colley Cibber's "The Careless Husband," and created Mrs. Sullen in Farquhar's "Beaux Stratagem" (1707), and Lady Townley in Cibber's "The Provok'd Husband" (1727). Until her death in 1730, she reigned as leading comedienne at the Drury Lane, limning with unparalleled ability the contemporary ladies of fashion.

MRS. ANNE BRACEGIRDLE (c. 1663-1748)   Trained by Thomas Betterton, Mrs. Bracegirdle became the successor to Mrs. Barry as England's leading actress. She is said to have first appeared on stage at the age of six as a page in Otway's "The Orphan." Her greatest successes were in the plays of Wm. Congreve, serving as a model and an inspiration for many of his characterizations. She created Angelica in "Love for Love," and Milliaman in "The Way of the World." Here she is seen in this mezzotint as "The Indian Queen." In what is historically described as a "wicked age," she was admired for the propriety of her private life as much as for the excellence of her acting.

MRS. ELIZABETH BARRY (1653-1713)   The first great tragedienne of the English stage, Mrs. Barry began her apprenticeship under the unsuccessful tutelage of Sir William Davenant. This was followed by a more auspicious alliance with the Earl of Rochester (a notorious rake, but a man with an instinctive genius for the theatre). In 1678, under the sponsorship of the Earl, she was presented at the Theatre Royal as Isabella, the Queen of Hungary, in "Mustapha," an occasion that brought her some recognition. It was in 1680, however, when she appeared as Monimia with Thomas Betterton in Otway's "The Orphan," that she established a lasting reputation as England's leading actress. She created Isabella in Southerne's "Fatal Marriage," and Belvidera in Otway's "Venice Preserv'd." She is seen here as Lady Randolph in "Douglas."

BETTERTON AS HAMLET   This engraved frontispiece of "Hamlet" in
Nicholas Rowe's "Shakespeare" (1709) is thought to represent Betterton in the part.
It gives some indication of design, costume, and stage business of the time. The
overturned chair (on the appearance of the Ghost) was a traditional piece of
business until 1783.

loaned the clothes they wore at the King's coronation to the actors. Unquestionably, a close relationship had developed between the players and their audience; and just as surely, the King maintained a special interest in the theatre.

In 1664, Betterton played in *Henry VIII*. A writer of the time says "The part of the King was so right and justly done by Mr. Betterton, he being instructed in it by Sir William, who had it from old Mr. Lowen, that had his instructions from Mr. Shakespeare himself." Mrs. Betterton also appeared in this production.

Because there was such a constant presentation of new plays and old revivals, there could have been few rehearsals and the actors must have been under great strain. In those days a play seldom ran more than a week. It was quite common, in fact, for a play to have only one performance, due no doubt to the limited audience. Pepys, in 1664, writes of *The Bondman*: ". . . it is true for want of practice many of them forgot their parts a little, but Betterton and my poor Ianthe (Mrs. Betterton) outdo all the world."

Betterton wrote three plays himself, and played in them with his wife. These productions were successful and had many revivals.

After Davenant's death, Betterton took over the management of his company. In 1671, they moved to the new theatre in Dorset Garden which Davenant had commissioned Christopher Wren to design. With another leading actor, Henry Harris (c. 1634-1704), they formed a management which also included Lady Davenant and her son Charles, who was by then acting with the company. This theatre project was successful. In 1682, when the two patent companies united, they were also able to draw on the new plays of Killigrew's company.

The chief qualities of Betterton as an actor were dignity and sincerity: he had the ability to interpret a part judiciously and he got himself across to his audience, quite able to give the impression of being natural. His stage presence contrasted favorably with that of other actors of his day, who had a common tendency to "tear a passion to tatters," to quote Shakespeare's much-borrowed phrase.

Pepys and other writers of the time continually make mention of successors taking Betterton's parts and proving a disappointment to the audience.

A description of Betterton:

> *. . . a great head, a short thick neck, stoop'd in the shoulders, and . . . fat short arms, . . . his left hand frequently lodg'd in his breast, . . . his actions very few, but just. . . . His aspect was serious, venerable, and majestic. . . . His voice was low and grumbling, yet he could tune it by an artful climax which enforc'd universal attention even from the fops and orange girls.*

Betterton appears to have been a man as highly respected for his moral character as for his dramatic powers. Until his death in 1710, he continued to act intermittently. Among the distinguished people of his day, he was able to count many friends; and when he passed away, he was buried in honor in Westminster Abbey.

BENEFIT PERFORMANCES

Among the institutions of the Restoration theatre that survived until the 19th century were the benefit performances. A leading player would have one performance during the season from which he would receive the entire proceeds, after basic expenses had been deducted.

In 1709, a famous benefit performance was given for Betterton. The play was Congreve's *Love for Love*, and Betterton played Valentine. The evening was attended by a great gathering of distinguished people, which overflowed the pit from gallery to gallery, and spilled onto the stage itself.

The benefit system began during the period when the income of the company was shared out between the actors and the manager. At first, benefits were offered in order to do honor to an outstanding actor or actress. During the 18th century, however, an actor's benefit night became his chief source of income for the year. The system of

MARGARET HUGHES (1643-1719)   *The distinction of having been the first actress on the English stage falls to Mrs. Margaret Hughes. On December 8, 1660, at a converted tennis court called the Vere Street Theatre, she is said to have appeared as Desdemona in "The Moor of Venice," Thomas Killigrew's version of Shakespeare's "Othello."*

sharing out the company's profits suffered abuse at the hands of dishonest managers; and finally, the entire method of payment was discarded in favor of the payment of regular salaries.

LEADING ACTORS OF THE RESTORATION

Some of the other important actors of the time were Michael Mohun (1620-1684) who began his career in the time of Charles I, Edward Kynaston (1640-1706), Henry Harris, Betterton's co-manager, and Charles Hart (d. 1683). William Mountfort (1664-1692) was accounted the leading comic actor. Others known for their comic roles were Joseph Haines (d. 1701), James Nokes (d. 1696), Thomas Doggett (1670-1721), and John Lacy (d. 1681).

THE FIRST ENGLISH ACTRESSES

One of the most notable innovations which the Restoration brought to the English theatre was the actress. The English tradition, at least since Elizabethan days, had been to have women's parts played by boys and young men. During its period of exile on the Continent, Charles's court had become habituated to the Continental custom of permitting actresses to portray women's roles.

The first presentation of an English actress on an English stage took place the very first year the theatres of London were reopened—1660—when the King's Players presented *Othello* with an actress in the cast. In order to forestall undue surprise, the audience was apprised during the prologue that a female would appear in the play. During the epilogue the inquiry was made: "And how do you like her?" The applause that followed ensured the establishment of the actress on the English stage.

One of the first women to appear on the English stage was a Mrs. Coleman, who played in Davenant's production of his opera *The Siege of Rhodes*. Even after women had become accepted on the stage, they were customarily referred to by their last names only—as Mrs. Barry or Mrs. Bracegirdle, for example—an effort no doubt to maintain a proper sense of propriety.

Whatever the formalities, the ladies' presence on the stage led to a renewed interest in the theatre—especially for the young gallants of the Court and the town, who became interested in the charms of the leading performers.

NELL GWYNNE (1650-1687)

The most famous of the actresses who graced the Restoration stage was Nell Gwynne. Although she played for only a short period and chiefly in comedy parts, she rose to great eminence and became the mistress of King Charles II. Pepys found her to be a lively and witty creature; it is probable that she had greater powers as a personality than as an actress.

NELL GWYNNE (1650-1687)   Nell Gwynne started life hawking herring in the streets, and running errands in a brothel. A brief turn as an "orange girl" ended when Charles Hart, of the Drury Lane, became Nell's sponsor and presented her, at 15, as Cydara in Dryden's "The Indian Queen." She later appeared in "The English Monsieur," "The Humorous Lieutenant" and most notably, as Florimell in Dryden's "The Mayden Queene" in 1666. Her acting days were eclipsed, however, when in 1669, at the age of 19, she became the mistress of Charles II and abandoned the theatre for a life at court.

COSTUMES FOR JAMES I AND QUEEN ANNE   Designs by Inigo Jones show sovereigns in elaborate costumes designed for court masques.

OTHER RESTORATION ACTRESSES

Betterton's wife, whose full name was Mary Sanderson Betterton (d. 1712), seems to have been a very clever actress. She played many roles opposite her husband. In the field of comedy, Mrs. (Susanna) Mountfort (1667-1703) gave ideal interpretations in the new comedy of manners, and exhibited a commendable robustness and vivacity. A great tragic actress of the time was Mrs. (Elizabeth) Barry (1658-1713).

The end of the 17th century saw the rise of the celebrated Mrs. (Anne) Bracegirdle (1673-1748), an extremely capable actress. She would deliver prologues and epilogues, which in those days were written for special performances, and she achieved fame also for her singing and dancing. Mrs. Bracegirdle also appeared in tragic parts and won a great success in a play written by Mrs. Aphra Behn (1640-1689), who was probably the first Englishwoman to write for the stage.

FOREIGN COMPANIES

From the time of the Restoration on, certain foreign companies of players also performed in London. While in exile in France, the royal court of Charles II had developed a taste for French drama; and so companies from France frequently visited England to give performances, and they proved to be very popular. Even more popular was the Commedia dell'Arte which visited London at various times. In 1683, *The* Commedia dell'Arte played at Windsor before the King.

THE RESTORATION THEATRES

The development of the theatre at this time paved the way to the modern stage.

Theatre buildings by and large conformed to certain general principles. The stage projected into the center of the auditorium as it did in Shakespeare's day, but the stage also extended backward to an equal depth past the proscenium arch. Two stage doors were built into either side of the heavy and ornate proscenium. These portals were used by the actors. Above these doors there were boxes usually occupied by the audience, but sometimes used in the play itself when a balcony scene required their use. The stage boxes on one side of the theatre were reserved for the orchestra.

In the Duke's Theatre, a special box was provided for the orchestra at the top of the proscenium arch. From time to time efforts were made to place the orchestra in the pit below the stage, but this arrangement always met with the disapproval of the audience who liked to have nothing between themselves and the players.

RESTORATION SCENERY

The scenery was composed of a painted backcloth hung across the back of the stage, and painted canvas flats or wings, standing at either side.

Sometimes the scenery across the backstage was formed of sliding panels which travelled in grooves on the floor. By this device, a setting could be changed simply by sliding a new set of panels into view, or sliding one set away to reveal another one behind it.

There was a curtain behind the proscenium which when lowered concealed the scenery. After the customary prologue was delivered by an actor or actress standing on the forestage, or apron as it was called, the curtain rose and revealed the setting. The curtain did not descend until the end of the play. During the play, all scene changes were made in full view of the audience. During such scene changes, songs and musical interludes would be presented.

RESTORATION COSTUMES

While vaguely historical costumes were sometimes worn by male players, actresses invariably appeared in the dress of the latest vogue. Perhaps, when necessary for the plot, there was a bare suggestion of the garb of another period, such as a plumed headdress or some small concession in the details of a frock. Historical accuracy in stage costume was not established until well into the 19th century. Until then, even Shakespeare was usually played in the contemporary dress of the day.

LIGHTING DURING RESTORATION DAYS

Lamps and candles served the Restoration theatre for illumination. As far back as 1598, the Italians had used glass oil lamps which could be filled with colored liquid, and so be made to reflect colored light, to create stage effects. At the court masques of Charles I, colored lighting, too, had been used extensively, but the colored lighting was of a somewhat different type from that employed by the Italians. Strips of colored silk were placed in front of groups of candles and lamps situated behind the scenes; and from these, there emanated something of a colored hue which suffused the stage.

General lighting was provided by great circular fittings holding many candles, which were hung above the apron. These chandeliers also illuminated the auditorium. Probably there were additional candles around the boxes and galleries.

Some form of footlights came into existence about the time of the building of the new theatre at Dorset Garden in 1671. These footlights consisted of six oil lamps at the edge of the stage. The lamps were placed in the center of the stage, and they could be controlled to suit the action of the play. A night scene, for example, required some diminution of the lighting. The great chandeliers, of course, would shine on brightly; but the lowering of the footlights rendered sufficient concession to reality to convince the audience that the action was taking place at night time. To reinforce the illusion, in a night-time scene one of the actors would carry a candle.

THE CANDLE SNUFFERS

Restoration days saw the establishment of an amusing stage convention—the invisible candle snuffer. In those days, the tallow candles that were used needed constant attention in order to make them burn brightly. Two attendants usually looked after the candles; one was on the stage and the other was in the auditorium. No matter what action was taking place on the stage, should a candle begin to splutter, one of the attendants would walk onto the stage, quite unmindful of the actors, and attend to it. Having concluded his task, he would make a dignified and noiseless exit. His appearance on the stage on such occasions was accepted in the same matter-of-fact way that scene shifters were accepted—as a necessary part of the impedimenta of the theatre. Far from decrying the appearance of the candle snuffer on the stage—perhaps at the most dramatic moment of the play—the audience, on seeing a light fail, would actually raise a shout for him; and woe betide him if he were not soon forthcoming.

The English Theatre
of the 18th Century

CHANGES FROM RESTORATION DAYS

With the opening of the 18th century, English theatres began to attract much larger audiences. Not only had the population of Britain increased from six million in 1650 to ten million in 1800, but the theatre now began to be patronized by the members of the rising middle class. The loose morals and permissive behavior of court circles, which had chiefly patronized the theatre in Restoration days, gave way to tighter standards under Queen Anne. As the theatre became less voluptuous and more respectable, the interest of court circles waned considerably as a consequence. In time, the growing middle class, which formerly had had little interest in the stage, began to dominate the theatre public. This change in audience brought with it a change in the nature of theatrical entertainments.

However one may regard the court circles of the days of Charles II, it cannot be gainsaid that the nobility appreciated wit and poetry, and had reasonably sophisticated tastes in art. The same judgment does not apply to the stolid, unimaginative middle class of Queen Anne's day. It was, therefore, more or less to be expected that the bright comedy of manners would give way to productions which were less sophisticated, more spectacular, and unquestionably more sentimental.

The increase in public interest brought in its train, of course, the building of new theatres and the enlargement of those already in existence. This was the period when many new playhouses were built, both in London and in all the larger towns of England. The fashionable resorts of Bath, Tunbridge Wells, and Brighton enjoyed a great expansion in stage facilities, and even the provinces witnessed a thriving theatrical activity.

During Restoration days, the small, select group which had formed the audience had demanded a constant change of bill and a continual flow of new plays. In Betterton's day, plays were usually put on for one or two nights. A production very rarely ran for a week. During the 18th century, however, the larger public made it possible for a play to run for a considerably longer time: forty or fifty performances were not uncommon.

Although there was a change in the kind of play needed to meet the demands of the new audience, the theatre as an art did not evidence any marked development. The actual mounting and presentation of plays showed little radical alteration, and the design and structure of the playhouses were not altered significantly. The early 18th century was essentially a period of expansion rather than one of change.

COLLEY CIBBER (1671-1757)

Much of our knowledge of the theatre of the first half of the 18th century is derived from Cibber's famous *Apology for the Life of Mr. Colley Cibber, Comedian*. Cibber began acting in 1690 with Thomas Betterton's company, and became the most popular personality in the theatre during the first three decades of the 18th century. Although he did not have the qualities of a great dramatic actor, Cibber was a fine comedian. Moreover, he knew how to write successful comedies. Added to these theatrical gifts was the executive capacity of an excel-

COLLEY CIBBER (1671-1757) *This noted actor-manager-playwright is remembered principally for his famous memoirs "Apology for the Life of Mr. Colley Cibber, Comedian," an enlightening account of Restoration acting, which was published in 1740. In 1700, Cibber also penned a notable adaptation of "Richard III." His play "Love's Last Shift; or, the Fool in Fashion" is said to have started the 18th-century vogue for sentimental comedy.*

lent manager, which he demonstrated as one of the co-managers of the Drury Lane Theatre.

THE PATENT THEATRES

The Drury Lane—or more properly, The Theatre Royal at Drury Lane—was one of the only two theatres in London at the opening of the 18th century. The other was the rebuilt theatre at Lincoln's Inn Fields. Both theatres continued to operate under the exclusive royal patents granted by Charles II upon his return from exile in 1660.

Ownership of these patents was bought and sold; often, shares in the theatre patents were sold like shares in a corporation. One of the principal shareholders in the company at Lincoln's Inn Fields was Christopher Rich, a lawyer of unpleasant temperament who found that operating a theatre was more lucrative than practicing law. Christopher Rich started to rebuild the Lincoln's Inn Theatre, but the revised structure was not completed until shortly after his death in 1714. Control of the Lincoln's Inn Theatre then passed to Rich's son, John Rich, who was to become one of the leading personalities of the early 18th century theatre.

JOHN RICH (1692-1761)
Remembered principally as a great Harlequin, the actor-manager of the original Covent Garden presented the first mute Pantomime or Harlequinade on the English stage. His success in such entertainments as "Harlequin Doctor Faustus" and "Harlequin Sorcerer" compelled his rival Garrick at Drury Lane to add similar amusements to the end of the bill.

JOHN RICH (1692-1761)

John Rich made his first stage appearance in the prologue of Farquhar's *The Recruiting Officer*, the first play to be presented at the newly rebuilt Lincoln's Inn Theatre when it was opened in 1714. The following year, he made an attempt at acting tragedy, which was a failure. Thereafter, he appeared only in his own pantomimes; and it is upon his performance as a mime and his development of mime as a medium that Rich's fame as an actor rests.

Under Rich's management, the new theatre began a successful policy of presenting a form of performance quite new at the time. The presentation was composed of music, spectacle, dancing, and mime. Rich took some of the characters from the *Commedia dell'Arte* and adapted them to conform with English conventions. He used these characters in comic scenes based on allegorical plays, and the lives and loves of various gods and goddesses.

At first only dialogue was used; but gradually music was introduced and the form relied heavily on recitative and arias.

However, the comic part of the opera was presented entirely in mime. The miming presented the adventures of Harlequin and Columbine, Clown and Pantaloon. John Rich himself played Harlequin, using the stage name "Lun," the name of a noted French comedian, and he became famous for his dancing and miming in that particular role. It was said that Rich developed his powers of miming because he unfortunately had a poor voice, and because his tones were rough and uncultured. But whatever the reason he took to playing pantomime, all writers of the period are agreed that his actions and gestures were so expressive that he had little need to speak.

Rich also made great strides in staging. He transformed scenes with surprising effect. At the touch of Harlequin's magic bat, huts and cottages would be transformed into palaces and temples. As he made another gesture, some of the characters would turn into animals or be transformed into pieces of furniture. Gods and goddesses were continually descending to earth or being whisked up to the heavens. All this folderol greatly intrigued the audience, and was accomplished through the ingenious use of machinery and trapdoors. Sound effects, too, played a great part. There was much thunder, many rain storms, loud roaring of seas, prodigious fire and lightning, and great flurries of paper snow. Of course, all this was highly acceptable to a naive audience, and Rich enjoyed many years of success. His rise was a constant source of irritation to Drury Lane, and Cibber felt obliged to follow suit in some form.

As far back as 1702, Drury Lane had presented an entertainment which consisted of dancing and action accompanied by music. This production was called *The Cheats of Scapin or the Tavern Bilkers* and was created by John Weaver, a Shrewsbury dancing master. Although at the time Weaver's creation was considered something of a novelty, the success of Rich's policy at Lincoln's Inn demanded that Weaver produce something more spectacular. In 1717, Weaver presented ballets, as we would call them today, one based on the theme

LINCOLN'S INN FIELDS THEATRE   *The old theatre on Portugal Street, which had fallen largely into disuse after John Rich left it for Covent Garden in 1732, subsequently became a barracks, an auction room, and at the time of this illustration, a china warehouse. It was pulled down in 1848.*

of Mars and Venus, and another on that of Orpheus and Eurydice. Still later, Weaver drew on Cupid and Bacchus.

These productions were offered in addition to the serious plays presented on the same program. Cibber and his co-managers felt the need to apologize for these light aberrations, which as Cibber said, "we generally use as crutches to our weakest plays."

JOHN GAY (1685-1732) The success achieved by the poet and satirist with his ballad-opera "The Beggar's Opera," first produced by John Rich at Lincoln's Inn Fields, London in 1728, was so overwhelming, it led to the now famous pun that it made "Gay rich and Rich gay."

THE BEGGAR'S OPERA

Today, John Rich is probably chiefly remembered as the man responsible for the first production of John Gay's *The Beggar's Opera,* which opened at the Lincoln's Inn Theatre in the winter of 1727-28, and ran for 63 nights. Colley Cibber was mortified, for he had been offered the "Newgate pastoral," as it was called by Swift, and had declined to produce it. The receipts from the run of *The Beggar's Opera* were £11,000. Upon the heels of this great success, theatre managers presented the play throughout the provinces, achieving runs of 40 and 50 nights.

Rich now began to look about for another playhouse. His plans were to build a new theatre which would house a much larger audience, and the site he chose was in the Covent Garden.

COVENT GARDEN

It was through public subscription that Rich raised the money to build his new theatre. The 50 subscribers made three payments of £100, so that Rich came into a sum of £150,000. In return, each subscriber was to receive a royalty of two shillings for every performance and, as a special bonus, free seats anywhere in the house—except behind the scenes. When it is realized that in Restoration days the public was permitted, on payment of a fee, to venture behind the scenes to see the actors, it can be understood how important a step had been taken. Now even the privileged shareholders were confined to the front of the house.

The new theatre opened in 1732, the first vehicle being a revival of Congreve's *The Way of the World*. The new theatre had a large auditorium, but the stage itself was somewhat small, since seats were placed on the apron.

Seats on the apron stage brought in half a guinea each—twice as much as any box seat. Seats in the orchestra, then called "The Pit," remained at half a crown. Seats in the lower gallery were priced at two shillings, and seats in the higher gallery at one shilling.

In those days, seats were neither numbered nor reserved. A notice on the apron stage announced: "Servants will be allowed to keep places on the stage, and the ladies are desired to send them by 3 o'clock." In other words, any person who could afford a servant might send someone as early as 3 o'clock in the afternoon to sit in a chair on the stage, and thus save a place for his master.

Performances began at 6 p.m.; and when, at the appropriate hour, the doors of the theatre were thrown open to the waiting crowd, a veritable stampede would follow. As all the seats were backless benches, and since there was no central aisle, a wild hurdle would ensue as everyone would clamber excitedly over the benches to get the best places. And, of course, in such a melée the ladies, with their large skirts, would be at a distinct disadvantage. Often they would lose their hats, and sometimes even their shoes in the struggle. Once seated, they would spend quite a time collecting themselves and rearranging their clothes.

The competitive spirit thus engendered by this wild scramble for

COVENT GARDEN THEATRE   Built by John Rich, this famous playhouse opened December 7, 1732, with Congreve's "Way of the World." The company was headed by James Quin. The interior of Covent Garden is seen here presumably as it appeared toward the end of the century after extensive remodeling in 1784 and 1792. The proscenium doors are still greatly in evidence, as are the stage boxes.

seats would put the audience in fine fettle. The play would either have to start with a bang or the actors would meet with a noisy reception. The audience had been keyed up, and what they craved was action and spectacle rather than wit and poetry.

Although the new theatre at Covent Garden proved a success from the very beginning, Rich kept the Lincoln's Inn Theatre going, but transferred the patent to Covent Garden. Drury Lane and Covent Garden now became "the legitimate theatres," which had the monopoly of the spoken word. Legally, other theatres in town were allowed to present only pantomime, spectacle, and musical shows but there was no hard and fast application of this rule. Even the Drury Lane Theatre was forced at times to present pantomime instead of Shakespeare, in order to hold its audience and remain economically viable.

HENRY FIELDING AND THE HAYMARKET

The Haymarket Theatre, where Fielding's company played, had acquired a reputation for burlesque, opera, and the musical show. Fielding had written some brilliant satirical pieces for the stage, among which his best known effort was *Tom Thumb the Great*. This play ridiculed the type of tragedy that was being continually paraded on the boards at that time, a species of drama in which all the characters seemed to be killed off in the last scene. As long as Fielding confined his satire to the contemporary stage, he was safe; but when he ventured into politics, he started to tread on very dangerous ground. It is said that because of the content of one of Fielding's plays, Robert Walpole, the chief government minister of his day, brought about the passage of the Licensing Act of 1737, which gave the Lord Chamberlain the power of censorship over all plays performed within the city of Westminster. Thus fettered, Fielding soon gave up writing for the stage and devoted his whole time to the penning of novels.

PEG WOFFINGTON (1714-1760)

The year 1740 saw the debut at Covent Garden of the celebrated

Peg Woffington. She had appeared in London earlier at the Haymarket, when at the age of fifteen she performed as a member of the juvenile troupe of the famous Madame Violante. After three years of touring the country, Miss Woffington eventually settled down in Dublin where she achieved great fame, especially in playing the part of Sir Harry Wildair in Farquhar's *Constant Couple*.

On coming to London, Peg Woffington called at the home of John Rich nineteen times without giving her name. Each time, she was refused an interview. When Rich finally came to know who his persistent caller really was, he invited her in and acquired her services for Covent Garden at the modest salary of £9 per week. In private life, John Rich was something of an eccentric. Peg, recording her visit, describes him lounging on a sofa with a cup of tea in one hand, from which he took occassional sips, and a book in the other, surrounded by no fewer than twenty-seven cats, which walked all over the sofa, climbed onto the lap and shoulders of the famous man—and even sipped his tea.

Peg made her debut in the role of Sylvia in *The Recruiting Officer,* a part in which she appeared in male costume in several scenes. This suited her sparkling and vivacious personality, and she began to play men's roles in other plays. From then onward, the "breeches" part was an accepted convention, and most leading actresses were prepared to occasionally assume a male role.

MRS. CIBBER (1714-1766)

Some years previous to the appearance of Peg Woffington in London, another famous actress had begun her career at Drury Lane. Susannah Cibber was a sister of the composer, Thomas Arne, and the wife of Colley Cibber's son, Theophilus. Trained by her father-in-law, she played in both comedy and tragedy. Her voice was of such fine quality that it is said that Handel arranged contralto parts for her in his *Messiah*.

At this time, there was a good deal of cooperation between the two patent theatres, and actors would play at both theatres by cordial ar-

MARGARET WOFFINGTON IN BREECHES   A gifted come-
dienne, Peg Woffington, as she was called, became the rage of London in
1740 when she appeared as Sir Harry Wildair, the first of her famous
"breeches" parts, in George Farquhar's "Constant Couple." The comely
actress is pictured here speaking an Epilogue, dressed "in the habit of a
Volunteer reading the Gazette containing an Account of the Last Action
at Falkirk," allegedly delivered after a performance of Beaumont and
Fletcher's "The Scornful Lady," at Drury Lane in 1746. However, some
opinion holds that this illustration represents the actress in the part of Sir
Harry Wildair, a role which she continued playing (as the 1755 Playbill
indicates) until the end of her career.

THEATRE ROYAL in *Covent-Garden*,

This prefent *Thurfday*, being the 20th of *November*,
Will be prefented a COMEDY, call'd

The Conftant Couple;

Or, A TRIP to the JUBILEE.

Sir *HARRY WILDAIR*

By Mrs. WOFFINGTON,

Colonel *Standard* by Mr. SPARKS,
Vizard by Mr. RIDOUT,
Alderman *Smuggler* by Mr. ARTHUR,
Beau *Clincher* by Mr. SHUTER,
Young *Clincher* by Mr. COLLINS,
Dicky by Mr. COSTOLLO,
Conftable by Mr. MARTEN, *Tom Errand* by Mr. BENNET,
Angelica by Mrs. DYER,
Lady *Darling* by Mrs. COPIN,
Parly by Mrs. PITT,
Lady *LUREWELL*

By Mrs. HAMILTON.

With DANCING
By Mr. GRANIER, Mifs HILLIARD,
and OTHERS.

To which will be added a FARCE, call'd

The VIRGIN UNMASK'D.

Coupee by Mr. SHUTER.
Quaver by Mr. LOWE,
Blifter by Mr. MARTEN,
Goodwill by Mr. REDMAN, *Wormwood* by Mr. STOPPELAER,
Mifs *Lucy* by Mrs. BAKER.

Boxes 5 s. Pit 3 s. Firft Gallery 2 s. Upper Gallery 1 s.

To-morrow, will be prefented a Tragedy (*Not Acted thefe Two Years*) call'd rangement. In 1742, John Rich acquired the services of Mrs. Cibber. She played in tragedies opposite James Quin, then Rich's leading tragic actor.

DAVID GARRICK (1717-1779)

In October, 1741, a new star arose at the Goodman's Fields Theatre, an advent which caused such a sensation that the receipts of both Drury Lane and Covent Garden immediately showed a precipitate decline. David Garrick had arrived. At age twenty-four, he was playing Richard III, and was billed as "a gentleman who never appeared on any stage." This was not strictly true, as for several years he had gained experience in amateur theatricals and had even played in provincial theatres under an assumed name. By descent half French and half Irish, Garrick was the son of an army captain. He had received a good education, he and his brother having been the first pupils at a private school set up by Dr. Johnson.

David Garrick was rather short, but he was extremely handsome. He had the good sense to acquire the foundations of his art in the provinces, under an assumed name, so that when he made his debut in London he had sloughed off all his amateurishness and had acquired the requisite Thespian polish to take London by storm.

The plain fact is that Garrick had developed an entirely fresh approach to acting. The play-going public, now a bit tired of the rather heavy, declamatory style of such leading actors as Wilks, Booth, and Quin, were enchanted by Garrick's fresh and natural approach. In consequence, the Goodman's Fields Theatre played to such crowded houses that the two patent theatres were obliged to do something quickly or else suffer disaster.

After going through the necessary legal formalities, the two legitimate theatres successfully invoked their monopoly rights, with the result that Giffard, the manager of Goodman's Fields, had to cut the season short and close the theatre. Whereupon Fleetwood, the wealthy irresponsible youth who then managed Drury Lane, persuaded Garrick to join his company, luring the actor with what, in those

*DAVID GARRICK (1717-1779)   From his sensational debut in
"Richard III" in 1741 until his retirement from the management of the
Drury Lane in 1776 (three years before his death), Garrick established
a very great career as actor-manager.*

days, was the colossal salary of 600 guineas a season.

Garrick seized his opportunity and set forth on a series of roles in
Shakespearean and contemporary plays which he interpreted in his
novel and exuberant manner. Not surprisingly, he met with some
opposition from Macklin, who until then had been the leading actor
in the Drury Lane company. Macklin's performances at that time
belonged strictly to the old traditional style. However, Macklin himself was later to come under Garrick's influence, and was to revolutionize the portrayal of Shylock by investing him for the first time
with genuinely tragic qualities.

After having quarreled with Rich, Peg Woffington had left Covent
Garden and had also joined the Drury Lane company. She formed an

PLAY BILL *that announced* GARRICK's *first appearance in London.*

———————

[*October* 19, 1741.]

At the Theatre in GOODMAN'S FIELDS, this Day will be performed,

A Concert of Vocal & Instrumental Music,

DIVIDED INTO TWO PARTS;

TICKETS AT THREE, TWO, AND ONE SHILLING.

Places for the Boxes to be taken at the Fleece Tavern, near the Theatre.

N.B. Between the Two Parts of the Concert, will be presented an Historical Play, called the

LIFE AND DEATH OF

KING RICHARD THE THIRD;

CONTAINING THE DISTRESSES OF K. HENRY VI.,

The artful acquisition of the Crown by King Richard,

The Murder of Young King Edward V., and his Brother in the Tower,

THE LANDING OF THE EARL OF RICHMOND,

And the Death of King Richard in the memorable Battle of Bosworth Field, being the last that was fought between the Houses of York and Lancaster; with many other true Historical Passages.

The Part of King Richard by A GENTLEMAN,

(*Who never appeared on any Stage,*)

King Henry, by Mr. GIFFARD,   Richmond, Mr. MARSHALL,

Prince Edward, by Miss HIPPISLEY,   Duke of York, Miss NAYLOR,

Duke of Buckingham, Mr. PATERSON,   Duke of Norfolk, Mr. BLAKES,

Lord Stanley, Mr. PAGETT,   Oxford, Mr. VAUGHAN,   Tressel, Mr. W. GIFFARD,

Catesby, Mr. MARR,   Ratcliff, Mr. CROFTS,

Blunt, Mr. NAYLOR,   Tyrrel, Mr. PUTTENHAM,   Lord Mayor, Mr. DUNSTALL.

The Queen, Mrs. STEEL,   Duchess of York, Mrs. YATES,

And the Part of Lady Anne, by Mrs. GIFFARD.

WITH

Entertainments of Dancing,

By Mons. FROMET, Madame DUVALT, and the Two Masters and Miss GRANIER.

To which will be added, a Ballad Opera, of One Act, called

THE VIRGIN UNMASK'D.

The Part of Lucy, by Miss HIPPISLEY.

Both of which will be performed Gratis, by Persons for their Diversion.

———————

The Concert will begin exactly at Six o'Clock.

CHARLES MACKLIN (c. 1700-1797)
Forerunner of a more natural style of acting subsequently made memorable by David Garrick, Macklin, after years of playing, became famous overnight with his startling portrayal of Shylock. So impressed was Alexander Pope by the actor's unconventional portrayal that he composed his famous couplet: "This is the Jew/ That Shakespeare drew." Two plays by the actor-author, "Love à la Mode" (1759) and the famous comedy "The Man of the World" (1781), continued to be performed well into the 19th century.

attachment with Garrick which eventually blossomed into a love affair. Although their alliance did not culminate in marriage, the affair may have been the cause of Garrick's move to Dublin some two years later. Fleetwood, ever a bad manager, had gotten into arrears with his players' salaries. Garrick led the company in a strike. Matters became progressively worse, and were never quite satisfactorily settled.

In 1745, Garrick left the Drury Lane Theatre and accepted an offer for a season in Dublin. Here he was enthusiastically received by Irish audiences and added further to his laurels.

In June of the following year, he returned to London for a short season with John Rich at Covent Garden, where he earned £300 for playing in only six performances. Five of these were Shakespearean roles, and Garrick appeared as King Lear, Hamlet, Richard III, Othello, and Macbeth. After a period during which management had stressed pantomime and spectacle, drama had come back with a vengeance.

GARRICK VERSUS QUIN

The following season Garrick was re-engaged. Mrs. Cibber was also part of the company, and Garrick began a long and happy partnership with her.

During this season, Garrick and Quin played alternately with each other. For example, on October 20, Quin played Richard III; on

October 31, Garrick played the same part. The public was thus given the opportunity of comparing the differing styles of the two famous actors. One cannot help but admire Rich's showmanship in thus presenting the new style of acting and the old style of acting, side by side, in his theatre.

Here is a contemporary description of Quin:

> *Quin presented himself upon the rising of the curtain in a green velvet coat, embroidered down the seams, an enormous full-bottom periwig, rolled stockings, and high-heeled, square-toed shoes; with very little variation of cadence, and in deep, full tones, accompanied by a sawing kind of motion which had more of the senate than the stage in it, he rolled out his heroics with an air of dignified indifference that seemed to disdain the plaudits bestowed upon him.*

And here is Garrick:

> *When, after long and eager expectation, I first beheld little Garrick, then young and light, and alive in every muscle and in every feature, come bounding on the stage . . . Heavens, what a transition! It seemed as if a whole century had been stepped over in the changing of a single scene—old things were done away, and a new order at once brought forward, light and luminous, and clearly destined to dispel the barbarisms and bigotry of a tasteless age, too long . . . superstitiously devoted to the illusions of imposing declamations.*

Garrick had broken all the rules. He had upset stage convention, and yet by his naturalistic acting, he had completely won the public. Quin, although he was a competent actor in his own way, suffered the humiliation of seeing the box office receipts increase night after night as Garrick performed, while on the nights that he himself took the leading role, the receipts fell proportionately. It says a lot for Quin's good nature that he and Garrick got on quite well together,

QUIN AS CORIOLANUS   The actor is portrayed as he appeared in James Thompson's tragedy which was presented at Covent Garden in 1749. His costume is a variation of the semi-classical dress adopted for Roman characters. The plumed helmet, full periwig, and wide skirt are far from being historically accurate.

and that throughout the entire season there was no sign of open enmity between them.

   At the end of that portentous season, Garrick bought a share of the Drury Lane Theatre. In 1747, he assumed management.

GARRICK'S MANAGEMENT OF THE DRURY LANE

Garrick had persuaded Mrs. Cibber to join the Drury Lane com-

STROLLING PLAYERS
Hogarth's well-known engraving of "strolling players dressing in a barn" tells much about backstage life in the 18th century. Scattered throughout the scene are props and theatrical machinery. Of particular interest are two wave-makers (left) and a flying machine drawn by a dragon (above). Some of the actresses are costumed, apparently getting ready for a performance.

GARRICK AS MACBETH   In the
18th century there was no tradition of
historical accuracy in costuming Shakespeare's tragic heroes. Contemporary dress,
for example, was used for costumes in
both "Romeo and Juliet" and Macbeth."
Here, David Garrick, dressed as a fashionable man of his day, appears in 1768 at
Drury Lane in the character of Macbeth.

pany, which at this time also included Peg Woffington, the lively
Kitty Clive, Mrs. Pritchard, Delane, Yates, and Macklin. At thirty,
Garrick was the leading actor and manager of the most brilliant company of players in the English theatre. Though he ruled the company
with an iron hand, by careful training of the players in his own ways
of acting and by the force of his overriding personality, he achieved a
unity in production which has rarely been exceeded in the history of
the theatre anywhere.

Garrick continued his repertoire of Shakespearean roles with great
success. He also found time to write over forty plays, most of which
attained at least a moderate success.

In 1763, after many years of public acclaim, Garrick suddenly tired of London and set off with his company on a grand tour of France and Italy, where for two years, they played with great success.

In 1765, he returned from his triumphs abroad to Drury Lane, bringing with him many new ideas for revolutionizing the stage. England had always been behind the European theatre in stage technique. Just as Inigo Jones and William Davenant had brought new ideas from the theatres of France and Italy home to England, Garrick returned ready to equip the stage of the Drury Lane with the latest continental innovations.

INTERIOR OF THE DRURY LANE   This is how the theatre looked in 1775 after extensive remodelling by the Adams Brothers. The proscenium door and the stage boxes are just within view at the right.

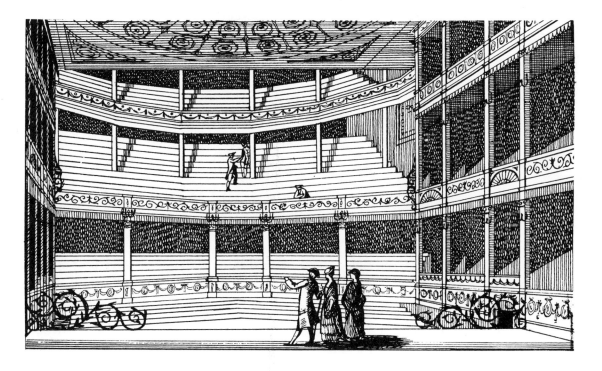

GARRICK'S STAGING INNOVATIONS

The need to accommodate a larger and larger public had brought about certain changes in theatre architecture since the time of the Restoration. The apron stage, or forestage, which projected out into the audience, and upon which most of the action of the play had been performed, was now diminished to half its former depth, so that more people could be seated in the auditorium. For the same reason, the proscenium arch, which had formerly been deep enough to house two or three doors on each side, through which actors made their exits and entrances upon the stage, was now narrowed in depth, so that the new stages had only one door on each side of the proscenium. With the foreshortening of the apron stage and the proscenium arch, the tendency of actors now was to play more and more on the back stage behind the proscenium, rather than in front of it, on the apron. The actors were thus closer to the scenery, but further from the audience.

Garrick realized that because of this tendency some of the finer points of the acting might be lost; but he compensated for this by considerably improving the stage lighting.

LIGHTING

Up to this time, indoor theatres were lit by large, hoop-shaped chandeliers holding vast rings of candles, which hung above the audience in the auditorium and above the actors on the apron stage. One reason that actors had tended to avoid the back stage was that it was very poorly lit.

The trouble with the great hoop-like chandeliers was that they obstructed the vision of the audience in the gallery seats. Garrick's innovation was to remove the chandeliers from the front of the proscenium and place them behind it, over the back stage and out of sight of the audience. Thus, at one stroke he accomplished three things: he gave a clear view of the stage to the whole audience; he illuminated the back stage, which the actors now needed to use because the apron was so much smaller; and, by making the auditorium

GARRICK AS SIR JOHN BRUTE   One of Garrick's favorite comedy parts was that of Sir John Brute in Vanbrugh's "The Provok'd Wife," performed in 1763 in Drury Lane. The part of Brute was known to actors as a "Drag Part," as was any female impersonation when long woman's clothes dragged upon the stage. This theatrical expression survived well into the 20th century and was still used by older actors when referring to "Charley's Aunt."

darker and the stage brighter, he greatly heightened the dramatic effect of his productions.

In addition to moving the chandeliers, Garrick also placed lights behind the wings on a level with the actors. He introduced the use of lanterns and wall brackets as an integral part of the stage setting. These, of course, also provided more light on the stage. Other innovations were the greater use of oil lamps, and the use of colored transparent silks for producing lighting effects in color.

MACKLIN AS SHYLOCK In the Trial Scene from "The Merchant of Venice," at Drury Lane, 1741, Macklin, who had restored dignity to a role that had been treated as crude farce since the Restoration, wears Shylock's traditional long, black garberdine and white necktie. The costume is a convention established in Elizabethan times.

"THE COUNTRY WIFE" This 18th-century costume for the play shows the elaborately powdered wig and the hooped skirt then in fashion.

Garrick also made greater use of footlights. Although footlights had been introduced in England many years before, their use on the stage was not universal; even in the new Covent Garden Theatre of 1732, footlights had not been installed. The total effect of Garrick's innovations was to illuminate the actors much better, and to have less lighting fall on the audience.

SCENERY: THE BEGINNINGS OF REALISM

Up until the middle of the 18th century, stage scenery traditionally consisted of a stylized architectural setting. No matter where the action of a play was supposed to occur, whether in a foreign country, a marketplace, a palace, or a humble cottage, the scenic artist would paint a conventional architectural setting, with virtually no regard for style or period.

Garrick had different ideas. In 1771 he brought over from Europe the scenic artist, Philip James De Loutherbourg (1740-1812), a specialist in scenic effects. De Loutherbourg introduced a bit of realism into his stage sets, actually taking a trip to Derbyshire to make sketches for his rather romantic landscape scenery. He devised methods for producing the effects of fire, moonlight, clouds, rain, volcanoes, the lapping of waves and so on, using concealed lighting behind silk screens as well as sound effects to achieve this. His unusually naturalistic effects were much admired, although his scenery would not be considered naturalistic by modern standards.

Later in the century, another designer, William Capon (1757-1827), produced settings which had some regard for historical accuracy. He produced designs and stage settings in which houses were painted as they might have appeared in the day when the play was set. Capon also paid particular attention to the Gothic style of architecture. Here, one finds the tentative beginnings of the great quest for realism on the stage which was ultimately reached at the end of the 19th century.

COSTUMES

Strangely enough, despite the variety of innovations in theatre design

OLIVER GOLDSMITH (1730-1774)   Goldsmith's first work "The Good-Natured Man" (1768) failed in its debut at Covent Garden. However, his masterpiece "She Stoops to Conquer" (1773) opened there to great acclaim. Frequently revived, the play has become an English classic.

and staging which the 18th century introduced, it produced little change in stage costume which still consisted chiefly of contemporary dress; costumes of an earlier period were never worn, even when called for by the action of a play. Garrick, for example, played all his great Shakespearean roles in the elaborate costume of his own day.

This practice seems to have been demanded by the audience, for when, in 1773, the noted actor Macklin appeared at Covent Garden as Macbeth, clad in an authentic Scottish kilt, he was greeted with boos, hisses, and a storm of disapproval. It is not surprising, therefore, that for a long time no actress would dare to wear anything but the very latest fashion—whatever the period of the play in which she appeared.

In 1734, it is true, a ballet dancer named Mlle. Salle, appeared at Covent Garden without the enormous hoop skirt and the piled-up coiffure which were the fashion of the time. She wore her own hair, unpowdered, simply arranged, and without ornament. She was dressed in a bodice and petticoat, over which a simple roll of muslin had been carefully draped along the lines of a Greek statue. This freedom, dictated by the needs of dancing, seems to have met with the approval of the audience.

Although the performance of such lighter forms of entertainment as pantomime and ballet permitted actors to don special costumes, in the presentation of tragedy the actors invariably wore costumes which were counterparts of the vogue of the day. It was left to the famous Mrs. Siddons, towards the end of the century, to introduce freedom and variety into women's dress on the stage.

GARRICK'S LAST YEARS

Soon after his return from the Continent, Garrick retired from acting, remaining, however, a very active manager at Drury Lane. But the public would not tolerate his retirement and clamored for his return to the stage. Six months later King George III issued a royal command to Garrick to resume acting, and this Garrick could not ignore. He continued performing until his final retirement in 1776, three years before his death.

During his career, Garrick amassed a considerable fortune. He built a large house at Hampton, which still stands, together with the delightful little temple he erected by the edge of a river on his grounds as a tribute to Shakespeare, to whom he owed so much of his success.

Garrick did much to raise the social status of players, who now began to regard themselves no longer as servants of the aristocracy, but as equals.

THE GREEN ROOM

The institution of the green room, the salon in which interested members of the upper classes could meet the players during the intervals between their appearances on the stage, had its origin in Restoration days. This reception room was described by Pepys. It is not known why green was chosen as the particular color for this room, but it is undeniable that the color green was definitely associated with the theatre during the 18th century. Tragedies were always played on a green carpet; the stage curtain itself was green; and the stage attendants, who moved the furniture and changed the scenery, wore green livery.

THE GUARDSMEN

It is chiefly due to Garrick that the theatre banished the snobs of high society from their privileged seats on the stage, which since Shakespeare's day had caused embarrassment to the actors and ill feeling to the patrons of the orchestra. After this reform, the only persons who could be seen on stage were the green-liveried stage attendants and the guards who stood at both sides of the stage as a first line of defense against the onslaught of overexuberant members of the pit.

A story is told that one of these guardsmen was so overcome by the power of Garrick's acting in a certain tragedy that he fell in a faint. Afterward, Garrick sent for the man and, sympathizing with his embarrassment, gave him a guinea. That kind of news got around. The following night, another guardsman collapsed. Unfortunately for him, he had not realized that Garrick had been playing in a comedy, and so the anticipated guinea was not forthcoming.

Guardsmen were also used to keep order outside the doors of the theatre; for in those days there were no policemen to carry out these duties.

Even in early Victorian times, on the occasion of a royal visit to the theatre, a yeoman of the guard would stand at either side of the stage during the performance.

PLAYS OF THE 18th CENTURY

The first 70 years of the 18th century produced few plays of lasting value. Writers had discovered the novel and the essay as new forms for their endeavors. While both Pope and Johnson wrote plays, their dramas were too literary and lacking in vital force to engage the theatre-going public. The neo-classic playwrights of this period created grand and heroic figures which actors such as Booth, Wilks, and Quin interpreted in a heavy, ponderous, declamatory style. Unfortunately, the fresh, romantic approach of Garrick had little counterpart in the writings of the dramatists of the day.

In general, comedy faired better than tragedy during the 18th century, although we are left today with only three comedies from the time which have acquired universal acclaim: Oliver Goldsmith's *She Stoops to Conquer,* and Richard Brinsley Sheridan's *The Rivals,* and *The School for Scandal.*

SHE STOOPS TO CONQUER

She Stoops to Conquer, Oliver Goldsmith's (1730-1774) second play, was first produced at Covent Garden in 1773. Goldsmith's first effort, *The Good Natur'd Man,* had met with only moderate success. Colman, the manager, had accepted his second play, therefore, with misgivings, and delayed presenting it for over a year. At last, owing to the persistent prodding of the eminent Dr. Samuel Johnson, Colman finally put *She Stoops to Conquer* into rehearsal and presented it on March 15, 1773.

It was an immediate success. The press and the public were full of acclaim. The play had humor; and the rather sentimental quality of the happy ending was much appreciated by the audience. But Goldsmith was unable to enjoy his first financial success for long, as he died the following year at the age of 46.

RICHARD BRINSLEY SHERIDAN (1751-1816)

The son of Thomas Sheridan, an actor of the old school who had

"SHE STOOPS TO CONQUER"   In this engraving after Parkinson, Edward Shuter and Jane Green (as Mr. and Mrs. Hardcastle) and John Quick (as Tony Lumpkin) are shown in this scene from Goldsmith's comedy. Although George Colman, manager of Covent Garden, reluctantly produced the play in 1773, it became an immediate success, and has since become a classic of the English stage. The costumes are interesting, since they show the fashion of Goldsmith's time.

played at both Covent Garden and Drury Lane, Richard Brinsley Sheridan was born in 1751. When he was 22, Sheridan married a singer, Elizabeth Linley, who was the daughter of a composer.

In 1775, when Sheridan was only 24, his first play, *The Rivals*, was produced at Covent Garden. The opening night was not a success, but after alterations in both the cast and the dialogue, the play immediately rose in public favor.

The following year, when Garrick retired from Drury Lane, Sheridan managed to raise enough money to buy his share of the patent. He moved into the theatre with his whole family: his wife kept the accounts, his father-in-law became the musical director, Mrs. Linley, his mother-in-law, became wardrobe mistress, and his old actor-father, Thomas Sheridan, was installed as stage manager.

The first full season of Sheridan's management of Drury Lane, 1777, saw the production of his masterpiece, *The School for Scandal*. This brought Sheridan a large amount of money and an international reputation as a playwright.

The same year, Sheridan wrote *The Duenna*, an opera for which Dr. Linley wrote the music. This was produced at Covent Garden. *The Critic,* a comedy based largely on the Duke of Buckingham's farce, *The Rehearsal,* soon followed. The play burlesqued the stage of the earlier days, and in particular the rhyming tragedies of Dryden. Sheridan also wrote *Pizarro,* a tragedy which is but rarely revived and has few lasting qualities, although it did achieve popularity at the time it was written.

When he was only twenty-eight, Sheridan gave up writing for the stage and confined his activities to management. His sparkling wit and social qualities were not to be lost, however, for in 1780 he entered Parliament and distinguished himself as an orator and a master of debate. But as his interest in politics increased, his passion for the

RICHARD BRINSLEY SHERIDAN (1751-1816) In the short span of four years, from 1775 to 1779, Sheridan wrote two masterpieces "The Rivals" (1775) and "The School for Scandal" (1779) that have remained in the repertory of the English theatre. The playwright was the auhtor of seven plays.

"THE SCHOOL FOR SCANDAL"   *This illustration shows the famous Screen Scene, the high point of Sheridan's comedy, as it was performed at the Drury Lane in 1777. Note the proscenium doors and the stage boxes.*

theatre declined, and Sheridan's managership deteriorated. He dressed and lived in a style totally beyond his means, and only when the receipts from his theatre began to fall away and his style of living was endangered did he begin to take renewed interest in the theatre. In 1791, he rebuilt the edifice, making room for 3,600 people, an increase of 1,600 seats. The stage now had a proscenium opening of forty-three feet.

Despite an iron curtain and numerous other precautions, including water taps well distributed throughout the theatre, the building caught fire in 1809 and burned to the ground. Sheridan first heard the news of the fire while in the House of Commons, in the midst of a Parliamentary debate about the war in Spain. It is typical of the man that he stayed on until the House adjourned. When he finally returned to the theatre, he found it only a smoldering shell.

Sheridan was completely ruined by the fire. He remained bankrupt until his death in 1816—a rather depressing end to a brilliant career.

In 1812, Samuel Whitbread, the brewer, built a new theatre on the same site. Although it has been considerably altered, Whitbread's Drury Lane is still a functioning theatre in London today.

SARAH SIDDONS (1755-1831)

During Garrick's last years at Drury Lane, he was continually on the lookout for fresh talent. Owing to his ill health and his declining years, the leading actresses of the company were getting a little out of hand; so Garrick decided to introduce into his theatre a young and beautiful actress who had been achieving some notice in the provinces. Garrick had first heard of Mrs. Siddons when she was playing at a small theatre at Cheltenham. He followed her engagements about the country, and he sent out agents to report about her progress for a whole year before he decided to offer her a contract.

At this time, Mrs. Siddons was 20 and already a mother. She made her debut at Drury Lane in December, 1775, playing Portia in *The Merchant of Venice*. Although young, she was not without experience. Born of a theatrical family—the Roger Kembles, who had quite a provincial reputation—she had first appeared on the stage as a child. Throughout her childhood, she alternated periods of acting on the stage and of going away to school. Her training endowed her with an easy facility for remembering lines, a clear and pleasing voice, and a passion for Milton and the classic poets. Her parents encouraged her talents, and were not a little disappointed when at the age of 18 she married a rather second-rate actor by the name of William Siddons. The young couple left the Kembles and joined another company who were touring the west of England. It was with this company that Mrs. Siddons was discovered at Cheltenham in the summer of 1774.

When at last she arrived at the Drury Lane, Garrick was pleased with her appearance, paid her compliments, and recognized both her promise and her inexperience. Although he gave her every encouragement, her debut was a failure. Poor Sarah was in panic. She walked onto the stage, a tall, slender, rather gawky firgure, and immediately her voice began to quaver. Her lines died off in a whisper, and she became so nervous she completely forgot her stage directions. The play dragged on to a depressing end. Except for one sympathetic newspaper, the press confirmed the public reaction to a disappointing first appearance. The solitary exception was a friend of Garrick's who had seen Mrs. Siddons act in the provinces and who did not wish to mar what he believed was a promising career. In spite of the bad beginning, Garrick decided to continue her engagement on through the season, and she played opposite him in one of his own farewell appearances. Garrick lavished time in giving her instructions. On evenings when she was not on stage, she would watch his acting from the special box he had provided her. Her ineptness, however, continued throughout the season and she achieved no better reception from either press or public. It was no surprise then that when Sheridan took over management at the end of the season, the services of Mrs. Siddons were not retained.

With a heavy heart she set off again with her husband for the provinces, determined at least to make a success in the flourishing theatres of Birmingham, York, Liverpool, and those in the other large towns. After periods of local success, and intermittent illness and confinement, she finally settled down at Bath, which by then had become a center of fashion, elegance, and scandal. Her success among this critical public was immediate. She worked hard and she gave creditable performances in Shakespearean parts and in contemporary plays.

For four seasons she played at Bath; and during this time, her art slowly matured. Her intellectual powers likewise grew, and with increasing experience and the time in which to develop her own approach to acting, she acquired new confidence and the knowledge of her own powers of restraint. In 1780, Thomas Sheridan came to Bath for his health. On seeing Mrs. Siddons act, he was so struck with her development that he hastened back to persuade his son to engage her for Drury Lane.

SARAH SIDDONS (1755-1831)   Leading tragedienne of the 18th century, Sarah Siddons dominated the English stage from her second appearance in 1782 at the Drury Lane in "The Fatal Marriage" to her final performance as Lady Macbeth in 1812, the year of her retirement. This painting was rendered by Gainsborough.

SARAH SIDDONS AS LADY MACBETH   England's foremost tragedi-
enne first played Shakespeare's tragic heroine in 1785 at Drury Lane, a part in
which almost 30 years later she made her farewell appearance.

Sarah Siddons had been a success at Bath. She had many friends in the town, and so she was not easily persuaded to give up the certainty of a small but regular income for the uncertainty of London. She was undoubtedly afflicted by thoughts of her previous failure. It was only after two years that she agreed to accept an engagement from Sheridan and bid farewell to her loyal audiences in Bath, who were greatly disappointed at her leaving. At her final performance, Mrs. Siddons produced on stage her three "reasons" for accepting an engagement in London—her three small children.

At Drury Lane, her first appearance was made in the leading part of Isabella in a play by that name. It was a version by Garrick of Southerne's *The Fatal Marriage,* in which grief and tears were predominant. On the evening of the opening night, her father, Roger Kemble, turned up to allay her fears. Although she was inwardly quaking, she walked onto the stage and immersed herself completely in the part. The role gave her magnificent opportunities for displaying her qualities of pathos and tragedy, and with her now well-matured style, she gave a great performance. The audience was deeply moved. Before the curtain descended, spontaneous applause broke out all over the theatre. Sarah Siddons had returned to triumph.

The press was full of enthusiastic notices. Some critics even adjudged Sarah to be superior to the great Mrs. Cibber. Her success at Drury Lane was now complete, and her future assured. She remained there, playing leading parts, for the next 27 years.

At twenty-seven Mrs. Siddons was tall and slender, with graceful movements, while her head was small, with classic features and dark, compelling eyes.

At the close of her first successful season in London, she went to Dublin, accepting a summer engagement at the Smock Alley Theatre, where she was to join her eldest brother, John Philip Kemble (1757-1823). Kemble, having completed his education in France, had set out to conquer the stage. His first important engagement was in Dublin, and on the strength of his successful seasons there Sheridan booked him for Drury Lane. In the autumn he returned with his sister to London and began a long period of successes.

Like his sister, Kemble was tall, handsome, and dignified in appearance. His style of acting was more like the classic style of the earlier actors than Garrick's easy, naturalistic flexibility. Both Sarah and John found their greatest successes in tragic roles, particularly in Shakespearean plays, and until the early 19th century they remained the undisputed leaders of the stage in England.

Mrs. Siddons made several innovations in women's costume in the theatre. She was the first woman to discard the powdered hair and large hooped skirts of the time. She developed costumes of a simple shape, based on classic models, and designed simply draped headdresses to replace the elaborate, beplumed helmets which until then were the traditional wear of tragic actresses. Her costumes were in no sense historically accurate, but they were no longer of the latest fashion, and were especially designed for acting and the stage.

THE RIOTOUS AUDIENCES

During this period, audiences were lively and vociferous. If they took a dislike to anything or anybody, rather than boycotting the theatre, they would pay for admission night after night in order to vent their displeasure by creating a disturbance. At times, theatregoers would attempt to invade the stage and stop the performance, with the result that riots were common in the theatres of England throughout this century.

In 1738, the ringleaders of a riot at the Haymarket were brought to trial. But the judge declared "that the public had a legal right to manifest their dislike to any play or actor, and that the judicature of the pit had been acquiesced in from time immemorial."

Since this was the attitude of the court, it is hardly necessary to say that the public were indeed quite conscious of their rights, and that criticism was highly vocal and unrestrained. Actors and managers were compelled to bow to the demands of their arbiters. The occasional invasions of the stage by unruly members of the pit made it necessary to provide spiked railings at the limits of the orchestra.

"THE OVERFLOWING OF THE PIT"   A humorous comment on the popularity of seats in the pit is illustrated in this 18-century engraving, after a drawing by S. H. Grimm. Especially interesting is the spiked partition (above right). Spiked railings were commonly used in 18th-century theatres in order to control the unruly audiences.

Decorative ironwork at the front of the Drury Lane stage was really placed there to hinder the destructive efforts of the audience, rather than for esthetic reasons.

One of the most serious disturbances occurred in 1755, when a company of French dancers was being presented by Garrick at the Drury Lane Theatre. During those days, England was drifting into war with France. The audiences in the pit and the galleries showed their disapproval of Garrick's entrepreneurial choice by six nights of prolonged rioting. Garrick appealed to the better instincts of the gathering, and was supported by the fashionable folk who occupied the boxes, but this polarized the audience and the incensed pit and galleries began to fight with the gentry. Upper class gallants jumped into the pit with swords drawn, and blood was shed.

Suddenly, all participants in the melée became united in a common purpose—to wreak as much damage upon the theatre as possible Benches were torn up, scenery was demolished, and havoc ensued. When the dust had settled, the destruction amounted to a loss of several thousand pounds.

Even when things seemed quite normal, the audience of the 18th century English theatre could hardly be said to be well behaved. It was common practice for members of the galleries to pelt unpopular personalities in the pit with orange peels or rotten fruit. Quarrels among people in different parts of the theatre were frequent. Name calling and imprecations were shouted across the seats, and sticks and canes were rapped impatiently on the floor until the curtain rose.

Under such trying conditions, the actors just had to be engaging. Unless they secured the interest of their clients, pandemonium would ensue. Thus it came about that the greatest contribution of the 18th century to the theatre was the development of better actors and actresses.

CHANGES IN THE THEATRE IN THE 18th CENTURY

During this century the use of the large apron stage declined. Scenery became more realistic, and was accorded more space on the stage. The acting lost a certain freedom of movement which was possible on the larger Restoration stage. Moreover, the concentration of light on the actors tended to confine the acting space. During this era many more theatres were built for a theatre-going public which was derived mostly from the growing middle class. However, tastes were quite plebeian, and great drama did not flourish in an atmosphere where mediocrity was appreciated. Few plays of lasting value were written.

The audiences demanded what they deemed to be their money's worth, and therefore a long bill became necessary. This often included a full five-act tragedy, plus a comic piece, plus a ballet or pantomime, along with interludes of dancing or music, and various prologues and epilogues.

MRS ABINGTON   A drawing of the actress as she appeared in the role of Estieania in "Rule a Wife and Have a Wife."

The English Theatre
of the 19th Century

KEMBLE'S MANAGEMENT OF COVENT GARDEN

During the summer of 1802, Kemble and Mrs. Siddons left the Drury Lane Theatre for good. It had become insupportable for them to suffer the continual wrangles with Sheridan over payment of their salaries.

Kemble managed to raise sufficient money to purchase a one-sixth share in the Covent Garden patent. With the interest he acquired, he had the oportunity not only of acting, but, as stage manager, of deciding who should play with him. While negotiations were in process, Kemble made a holiday tour of the Continent and Sarah Siddons went to Ireland. In 1803, they both returned to London to start the new season. Kemble first appeared in *Hamlet*, and was accounted a great success. Mrs. Siddons took the role of Isabella in *The Fatal Marriage*, and she, too, won audience acclaim.

As a manager, Kemble was tactful and considerate. Unfortunately, he had to cope with the excesses of George Frederick Cooke (1756-1812), an actor with a reputation which was second only to Kemble's. Cooke drank heavily and had an uncontrollable temper. Nevertheless,

JOHN PHILIP KEMBLE (1757-1823) *Eldest son of the Kemble family and brother of Mrs. Siddons, Kemble was an actor in the grand manner—at his best in tragic and heavy dramatic parts. His great roles included Cardinal Wolsey, Brutus, Rolla (in Sheridan's "Pizarro"), Hamlet and Coriolanus, a part in which he made his farewell appearance on June 23, 1817. In this portrait by Sir Thomas Lawrence, he is seen as Coriolanus in a costume noted for its historical accuracy.*

when he was sober, and when the part he played was suitable for him, he rendered an extremely fine performance. His passionate and erratic acting stood in marked contrast to the studied calm and dignity of Kemble's style.

The first season went well. Among the plays produced, eleven were by Shakespeare, an indication that public taste was veering more towards drama than spectacle. Though the pendulum was soon to swing back, for the moment acting was the all-important element in the theatre.

MASTER BETTY (1791-1874)

The following season, that of 1804, both Mrs. Siddons and Kemble were eclipsed by a young prodigy known as Master Betty. "The Young Roscius" had sprung into public notice in the provinces, where he had appeared with great success. Although only about 13 years of age, he was playing leading parts with adult actors. His fame swept the country. He had come from Belfast, where a year or two earlier he had seen Mrs. Siddons play. The boy had been so impressed with her acting that he decided to take up a career on the stage. His talent was prodigious, and Kemble engaged him for Covent Garden, where his success with the public was so great that Kemble cast him in the major tragic roles of the theatre.

Apparently Betty's father was a keen businessman. When Betty appeared at Covent Garden, he received 50 guineas a night. On alternate nights he played at Drury Lane, where he commanded an even higher salary. London went completely mad over the boy, to such an extent that Pitt, then Prime Minister, adjourned the House of Commons so that that august assembly could come down in a body to see Betty play Hamlet.

The lad, it is reported, was able to portray emotions well in terms of his body stance and his action; but his face showed little or no expression, and though it may be hard to believe, his lines were delivered in a singsong fashion, a style which had been popular early

WILLIAM HENRY WEST BETTY (1791-1874)   Known as Master Betty or "The Young Roscius," the child prodigy is seen here as Hamlet, the part in which he made his London debut in 1804 at the age of 13. After a brief but spectacular career of several years, he spent the rest of his long life in obscurity.

NEW COVENT GARDEN THEATRE
After the Covent Garden fire of 1808, John Philip Kemble had the theatre rebuilt and enlarged in 1809. The new galleries were semi-circular in shape; the apron was greatly foreshortened; and the proscenium doors and stage boxes were retained within the proscenium arch.

in the 18th century. How, then, despite this grievous fault, did he become so popular? It was probably young Betty's precocity which most enthralled his audience—and the novelty of seeing a tiny, slender figure standing on stage in a place usually occupied by a stalwart tragedian.

However, the public soon grew used to the phenomenon and, pre-

dictably, grew tired of the little hero. When opinion turned, it turned with a vengeance, and poor little Master Betty was actually hissed off the stage during a performance of Richard III.

Betty played a year or two longer in the provinces and then vanished from the stage. His father soon spent all his money, and Master Betty died at the age of 83, in complete obscurity.

THEATRE ROYAL.

The Public are respectfully informed, that

Master BETTY,

Is engaged FOR A FEW NIGHTS ONLY,

And will make his first Appearance

This present MONDAY, September 15, 1806,

IN THE TRAGEDY OF

Tancred & Sigismunda.

Tancred,	- -	Master BETTY.	Officers,	Messrs. HOWELL and
Matteo Siffredi,		Mr. ARCHER		SEYMOUR.
Earl Osmond,	-	Mr. WILKINSON,	Sigismunda,	- Miss NORTON.
Rodolpho,	-	Mr. MORETON.	Laura,	- Mrs. SKINNER.

After which, the Musical Entertainment of,

No Song, No Supper.

Frederick,	- -	Mr. SMITH.	Servant,	- Mr. MORETON.
Crop,	- -	Mr. D'ARCY.		
Robin,	- -	Mr BROWN.	Dorothy,	- Mrs. W. PENSON.
Endless,	-	Mr. TERRY.	Louisa,	- Mrs. MORETON.
William,	-	Mr MIDDLETON.	Margaretta,	- - Mrs. SMITH.
Sailors, Messrs. Howell, Seymour, & Brennen			Nelly,	- Mrs. ARCHER.

PLACES, with Tickets, for the first Night, to be taken at the Box-Office only, from Ten till Three o'Clock, on SATURDAY; and for the succeeding Nights, from Ten till Three, the Day previous to the performance, and not before.

BOXES, 4s. 6d. UPPER BOXES 4s. PIT, 3s. GALLERY, 1s. 6d.

Doors to be opened at Six, and the Performance to begin precisely at Seven.

Days of Performance are MONDAY, WEDNESDAY, THURSDAY, and FRIDAY.

To-morrow, (TUESDAY) the Tragedy of,

HAMLET,

Hamlet, by MASTER BETTY.

JOSEPH GRIMALDI (1778-1837)
The greatest pantomimist of his century, Grimaldi is pictured as the Clown in the English pantomime "Mother Goose." His stylized make-up established the tradition for all such future clowns, who were called "Joeys" after Joseph Grimaldi, creator of the prototype.

JOE GRIMALDI AND MOTHER GOOSE (1778-1837)

In the autumn of 1806, Covent Garden witnessed the advent of the most successful mime of his time: Joe Grimaldi appeared in *Mother Goose* and won renown as the greatest low comedian of the day. Grimaldi's father had been employed by Garrick at the Drury Lane, and so young Joe had been brought up in the theatre. By the time he was in his mid-twenties, he was a highly accomplished and experienced actor. He had played both Drury Lane and Sadler's Wells, chiefly in pantomime. In *Mother Goose*, the principal character was not Harlequin but Clown, and Grimaldi portrayed this character with great skill in dumb show and subtle gesticulation. He was

MASTER BETTY PLAYBILL   An 1806 playbill announces the appearance of "The Infant Roscius" as Tancred in "Tancred and Sigismunda", the then popular James Thomson drama. The program was to be followed the next evening Tuesday, September 16, by "Hamlet".

responsible for the curious costume and makeup which has been adopted and imitated by all subsequent clowns, even those seen today at the circus.

Grimaldi's subtlety of movement was such that even Kemble deigned to take private lessons from him. The same was true of certain gentlemen of the court.

Mother Goose, in the manner of the times, was only part of the evening's program. It was usually preceded by a full-length tragedy, and a comic ballet. The popularity of this pantomime was such that it ran for ninety-two performances, during which period the accompanying plays were changed many times. Thus, the run of *Mother Goose* started a tendency to spend much more money on scenery, costumes, and properties for pantomime than for tragedy. In heavy drama, the personality and skill of the actor were held to be sufficient attraction.

The long bill of those days led to the practice of admitting the public at half price sometime midway through the evening's entertainment. Thus, theatre-goers who only wished to see a pantomime could do so at a lower charge. Because it was possible to gain admission to see Grimaldi at a bargain rate, many enthusiasts were encouraged to witness his performances not merely once, but several times.

THE FIRE AT COVENT GARDEN

In 1808, Kemble's misfortunes began when the firing of a gun on the stage of Covent Garden set some scenery to smoldering. Flames burst out early the next morning, and with great rapidity fire consumed the entire building. Everything in the theatre was destroyed. The valuable scenery, the costumes, the stage properties—as well as Kemble's extensive library of books and manuscripts—all went up in smoke. The tragedy also enveloped Mrs. Siddons, who lost her entire collection of stage jewelry and costumes in the fire, a property of considerable value.

THE NEW THEATRE

Public concern for John Philip Kemble and Sarah Siddons was soon forthcoming, and public subscriptions to rebuild the theatre poured in. While money was being raised for the new building, which was to be raised on the site of the old, the company moved to temporary quarters at the Queen's Theatre in the Haymarket. The payment of insurance claims brought in about half the necessary capital, and within a year the new theatre was fully completed.

The new building, designed in the prevailing classic style, was fronted by a huge Doric portico. Extra space was now available to enlarge the interior, since several neighboring houses had also been destroyed in the fire; and so grand anterooms and salons were added to the new building for "the comfort and convenience" of the public. Two central aisles made the pit more accessible. There were three tiers of boxes and two galleries. The third tier was made up of 23 private boxes. Each of these had its own anteroom, and was furnished with chairs. This was a great innovation at that time, as hitherto the seating accommodations had consisted of rows of backless benches.

The new house was illuminated by 40 glass chandeliers, each holding many candles. Not only had the auditorium been made much grander, but the stage had been considerably enlarged. The proscenium opening was now about 40 feet wide, and the depth of the stage from the footlights to the back wall, nearly 70 feet.

When filled to capacity, the new Covent Garden held an audience of nearly 3,000 people. The entire cost of building and furnishing amounted to over £300,000, a prodigious sum at the time. Less than half of this money had been raised when the theatre started operation, and thus Kemble began at the new Covent Garden under a heavy burden of debt. This led to an increase in admission price and provoked a storm of public disapproval, with the result that Kemble lost favor with the public and soon went into eclipse.

THE O.P. RIOTS

On September 18, 1809, Covent Garden opened with *Macbeth,*

followed by a musical farce called *The Quaker*. No sooner had Kemble appeared on the stage to make the customary opening address than pandemonium broke out. Many in the audience produced hand bells, watchmen's rattles, and all kinds of noisy instruments. Unques-

THE KEMBLE FAMILY IN "HENRY VIII"   *"The Trial Scene," also known as "The Kemble Family," a mezzotint by George Clint after a painting by Henry Harlow, shows the members of this famous acting family on stage. Sarah Siddons as Queen Katharine is seen with her brothers. John Philip Kemble, Stephen Kemble, and Charles Kemble, playing Cardinal Wolsey, Henry VIII, and Cromwell, are seated at the table. Although presented here as a group, it is uncertain that the Kembles ever appeared together in the play.*

tionably the action was premeditated, and certainly organized at least in an underground manner. Placards were produced, demanding the "Old Prices." Other posters proclaimed "Kemble Tremble." The audience kept up a continual chant of "O.P." and a regular

beat of stamping feet and raps on the floor insisted that Kemble restore the old scale of prices.

With admirable self-control, the company occupied the stage and performed the play, although because of the hubbub, the lines they recited were quite inaudible. Night after night, the disturbances continued. Determined not to be beaten by the mob, Kemble had Bow Street runners in the house to arrest the ringleaders. Some of the noisemakers were evicted, some incarcerated, and some brought to trial.

The riots continued, and Kemble was finally forced to put on a program which was composed entirely of dumb show. But the public wouldn't be placated or put off, and the demonstrations went on throughout the season. Kemble, in desperation, even hired prize-fighters to control the audience, but even the presence of those gorillas didn't avail to still the mob who seethed with indignation. Only the darling of the public, Grimaldi, effected a temporary lull in the boisterous proceedings.

The press was divided on the issue. Cartoons were published satirizing the whole affair, and editorials glutted the public prints. Kemble submitted his book of accounts to an impartial committee of influential people, which included the Solicitor-General and the Governor of the Bank of England. He was intent on showing how speculative theatre management really was, and had made up his mind to convince his detractors that he was fully justified in raising admission prices. The committee published its report which confirmed Kemble's contention, but it was all to no purpose, for nightly the cry of "O.P." continued.

Kemble realized he was beaten. He had to bow to public demand. He arranged to meet with 300 of the rioters at a dinner held at the Crown and Anchor Tavern, and he signed a paper agreeing to their demands. A public apology was delivered from the stage, and this was greeted with a placard hoisted from the pits on which was written the words "We are satisfied."

However, when it was all over, it became clear that the disturbances were not entirely due to the increase in prices; for to start with, the admission to the two galleries had remained at the old prices. From the ranks of the pit, the leaders of the riot gave vent to their disapproval, not only to the increased prices of orchestra seats, but also to the innovation of "private boxes" and the employment of a foreign singer. Later, of course, they were vociferous in their damnation of the strong-arm methods used against them by Kemble's mercenaries, the pugilists.

The galleries, of course, followed the lead of the pit; but they, too, had an additional complaint. They claimed that their poor view of the stage in the new theatre was due to the increased height of the galleries, and that this increased height had been necessitated solely by the addition of the extra tier of "private" boxes.

SPECTACLES AT COVENT GARDEN

The private boxes were rented for the season and brought in about £10,000 a year; but when Kemble was forced, in view of the public clamor, to abolish them, the loss of this considerable income had to be made up from somewhere else. Inevitably, Kemble turned to what today is termed "box office draw." Pantomime, burlesque, and the lighter forms of entertainment had become increasingly popular. The minor theatres were booming. It was noted that Astley's Amphitheatre employed horses and other animals to provide entertainment. All of this convinced Kemble to put on, in 1811, a production of *Bluebeard* which featured sixteen horses. The following year, an elephant was introduced on the stage. All this panoply and highjinks greatly appealed to the public.

MRS. SIDDONS' RETIREMENT

In that same year of 1811, Mrs. Siddons retired from the stage at the age of fifty-six. She had been a player for over forty years, and had attained a unique position in the history of the theatre. She was regarded as a lady in the grand manner, and in that role she remained unsurpassed. Sarah Siddons was the first capable actress to lead a blameless and normal life.

Her final performance was as Lady Macbeth. In accordance with the custom of that time, the play was stopped immediately after her final exit in the sleep-walking scene. As a compliment to the *grande dame* of the stage, the audience insisted that the performance come to an end right then and there. Mrs. Siddons was no longer in the script, and there was no point in seeing any more of the show.

After changing her costume, Sarah Siddons reappeared to make a final speech in a verse specially composed for her by her nephew, Harold Twiss. She retired with a comfortable income. She could enjoy her last years in peace and quiet. Even in retirement the stage still attracted her, and occasionally she made brief appearances at benefit performances for other actors. As late as 1819, eight years after her official retirement, she appeared in the popular tragedy, *Douglas*. She died in 1831.

KEMBLE'S CONTRIBUTIONS AS ACTOR AND MANAGER

After the O.P. riots, Kemble never managed to recapture his popularity. Although he continued acting, he was an aging and disappointed man. In 1817, he retired to an ovation which was as great as that accorded his famous sister. He died in 1823. As an actor, John Philip Kemble was of a stately and picturesque appearance. He possessed a rather husky voice, which one overlooked because of his great stage presence. On the stage, his deportment and pose were modeled on Roman sculpture rather than on the realities of Roman life.

As a manager, his reputation rests on his presentation of Shakespeare's plays. He attempted to dress his players in the costumes of the period which they played, and he spent considerable care and time in making the settings similarly appropriate. Kemble was devoted to the classics and kept the great tragedies alive.

DRURY LANE (1808)   Rebuilt by Sheridan in 1784, the new theatre was "planned upon a . . . larger scale than any other theatre in Europe." The number of galleries was increased from three to five, and the auditorium was enlarged to seat 3,600 people. Such large houses forced actors to extremes in order to project voice and gesture. The cavernous hall was referred to by Mrs. Siddons as "a wilderness of a place."

NEW AUDIENCES FOR THE THEATRE

In 1800, there were only ten theatres in London; by 1840, there were twenty-two. This was partly due, of course, to the natural growth of population; but a good deal of the increase in theatre seats can be attributed to the fact that the theatre was now attracting a much broader-based audience. During the first half of the 18th century, as the theatre began to cater to less elevated tastes, the upper classes began to lose interest in it. Polite society, not wishing to rub elbows with the ever-increasing working class patronage, stayed away from what was now considered to be an uncongenial atmosphere.

"GIVING OUT"

Since Restoration days, it was traditional at the close of a play, for the manager of a theatre or his representative, who would often be the stage manager, to announce the repetition of the performance on subsequent nights. This was known as "giving out." How well this announcement would be received usually decided the fate of the production.

The audience was now sitting in judgment, and emphatically expressed its likes and dislikes. The verdict they rendered had great effect on the drama of the day. Several great writers of the time, including Dickens and Browning, were to sit in the pit and hear the hissing and booing that marked the reception of their plays. Quite naturally, men of sensibility might decide to confine their activities to the much safer practice of written publication.

PIRATING

There were plenty of hack writers in the theatre who successfully wrote melodramas, burlesques, and other forms of light entertainment —men of no great talent. Not being able to create an original plot, they would adapt their work from French comedies and farces or from any other source, with the result that much of the drama in England was pirated.

Likewise, the writings of English authors were not sufficiently protected by law. When an author presented a new play to a manager, he received as compensation only a sum agreed upon. The author could not protect himself against the plagiarizing of his material by some other manager, who might send a servant to the theatre to make a copy of the play as it was presented, and who then would show the same work in his own theatre, albeit in a somewhat mangled form. In consequence, there was no serious writing for the English stage for about the first forty years of the century. Finally, the baleful results of this condition became so evident that Parliament, in 1832, passed the Authors Act, which afforded protection to writers.

MONOPOLY OF THE PATENT THEATRES

Those ghosts of the Restoration theatre, the Killigrew and Davenant patents, still persisted; the managers of Drury Lane and Covent Garden held the exclusive right to present spoken drama. Apart from the Haymarket, which was open only in the summer when the two patent theatres were closed, all the other so-called minor theatres in London were obliged to present only "illegitimate" drama—entertainment in which any dialogue that was spoken had to be accompanied by music. The minor theatres obviously felt aggrieved; they were continually at odds with the two patent theatres, which, in turn, did all they could to enforce their monopoly.

During the 18th century two Acts of Parliament were passed which, although they did not define the position very clearly, in practice enabled the monopoly conditions to continue. The Licensing Act of 1737 gave the Crown, through the office of the Lord Chamberlain, unlimited powers to license and censor plays within the confines of the city of Westminster. But each succeeding Lord Chamberlain interpreted the Act differently and wielded his powers accordingly. Some of these ministers read the Act literally and licensed "illegitimate" houses; others sustained the patent theatres to the exclusion of all rivals.

In 1752, a second Act was passed which extended the scope of the earlier Act to all places of amusement in Westminster and elsewhere, and bestowed upon local magistrates the authority to grant licenses at their quarter sessions. There was only vague understanding between the magistrates and the Lord Chamberlain as to the restriction of these newly licensed theatres to "illegitimate" drama. No real definition existed as to how far these theatres were to be confined to pantomime, music, and dancing.

A further Act of 1832 merely confirmed previous enactments, and extended the powers of local magistrates to license "legitimate" theatres outside the twenty-mile limit of London. This third Act greatly increased the number of theatres in the provinces; for although in the larger cities theatres already existed under royal patent, magistrates were now able to license performances of serious drama in any town or city. Thus, companies of actors, unable to work in London because of the monopoly conditions, found new scope for their activities in the provinces.

In 1787, one of the minor theatres had defied these monopoly conditions by putting on *As You Like It*. The immediate result of this was that the patent theatres had the unfortunate manager charged with vagrancy under the original Licensing Act, the theory being actors performing without a license were "vagrants and sturdy beggars."

THE BURLETTA

What was known as the *burletta* was a burlesque-type of musical piece without a word of dialogue. When the plot required some explanation which was too difficult to portray through miming, large pieces of cloth were lowered from the flies on which the story was told in letters big enough for all to read.

The development of the burletta must be regarded as the story of the rise of the minor theatres to the eventual defeat of the monopoly of the patent theatres. When, early in the century, melodrama was introduced from France, it was given a form similar to that of the burletta. In the eyes of the law, such productions were subject to the strictures of the law.

The first manager of the minor theatres to develop the possibilities arising from the vagueness of the law in defining "illegitimate" drama was Robert William Elliston (1774-1831). He rented the Royal Circus, later known as the Surrey Theatre, an edifice in which equestrian displays had been held. Under the title of "burletta" he presented *Macbeth* and other well-known classics. In order to conform with the law and to escape the wrath of the managers of the patent theatres, Elliston largely rewrote the plays he produced into doggerel verse; and to afford his productions more protection, he arranged a continuous piano accompaniment.

What was formerly the dumb show was now being developed into a new form of entertainment. The important question now arose of how much music must accompany the speaking of verse. The encroachments continued. As time went on, the piano accompaniment dwindled until it existed only as a few almost inaudible chords.

Thomas Dibdin (1771-1841), a songwriter, succeeded Elliston at the Surrey. Dibdin presented *The Vicar of Wakefield,* a production that was highly praised, although one writer regretted that "the good old Vicar is forced to sing in order to evade the watchfulness of the proprietors of the two patent theatres."

By 1819, the definition of *burletta* came to include prose comedy, provided the production contained five songs in each act. The minor theatres usually bestowed more care and attention on the scenery and costumes than did the "legitimate" patent theatres. However, in order to attract a full house, the "legitimate" theatre was now forced to concentrate more on spectacle than on the drama in which it held a monopoly. Indeed, in 1831 Drury Lane was showing *Timor the Tartar,* a play which brought horses on the stage. At approximately the same time, Covent Garden put on a spectacle called *The Life and Death of Buonaparte,* a performance which depended almost entirely on the appearance and acting of horses.

On the other hand, during the same period the "illegitimate" theatres were presenting *Romeo and Juliet* and *Katherine and Petruchio* at Sadler's Wells, *Richard III* at the Surrey, and *The Merchant of Venice* at the City Theatre—a topsy-turvy situation if there ever was one. These productions of Shakespeare were arranged to conform with the burletta formula. Nevertheless, perverted as they had to be, their success emphasized the futility of the prevailing law.

EDMUND KEAN (c1787-1833)   "To see Kean act," said Cole-
ridge, "was like reading Shakespeare by . . . lightening!" The actor is
shown here in two guises: as Sir Giles Overreach from Massinger's A
NEW WAY TO PAY OLD DEBTS, the scene rendered by George Clint; and
as Othello, a part in which, a critic of the day noted, "he is too often
in the highest key of passion." The memorabilia include a pass signed
by Kean for a Drury Lane box, and two miniatures of the actor.

THE END OF THEATRE MONOPOLY

In 1832 a group of writers for the stage met under the chairmanship of Lord Bulwer-Lytton (1803-1873). This group drew up a petition to Parliament. The same year, a Bill was presented to Parliament which was intended to free the minor theatres from the monopoly and thus render conditions possible for creative writing for the theatre. The Bill passed the Commons, but it was rejected by the Lords chiefly because of a fanatical speech by the Bishop of London, who attacked the theatres in general as hotbeds of vice and immorality.

Lord Conyngham, the Lord Chamberlain at the time, sympathized with the plight of the minor theatres and interpreted the Licensing Act as a means for extending the interests of the theatre. He granted licenses to many new theatres, and extended the seasons of the Adelphi and the Olympic. He also insisted that the patent theatres limit their performances to spoken dialogue; and as a crowning blow, he made the two patent theatres close during the Lenten period, although the minors were allowed to remain open.

Because of the restrictions on their monopoly, the patent theatres were now running at a loss. Serious drama soon dwindled in their programs, and eventually disappeared completely.

Finally, in 1843, the Theatre Regulations Act was passed. The minors at last had acquired their freedom, and theatre monopoly in England had passed into history.

EDMUND KEAN (1789 or 1790-1833)

In the early 1800's, there began a considerable development in the presentation of plays. Many of the theatre managers were also actors. They now dominated the theatrical scene, and the art of acting itself saw a new development.

COVENT GARDEN PLAYBILL   In 1828, the playbill for a benefit performance for John Fawcett, an eminent actor of the time, announced the appearances of Edmund Kean as Richard II; Charles Kemble, the youngest son of the Kemble family, in ROMEO AND JULIET; *and Mme. Vestris in a popular "breeches part," as MacHeath in John Gay's* THE BEGGAR'S OPERA.

For the BENEFIT of

Mr. FAWCETT.

THEATRE ROYAL, COVENT-GARDEN.

Saturday next, March 29, 1828,

On which occasion an

Act of three of the most Popular Tragedies of Shakspeare

Will be performed.

THE THIRD ACT OF

RICHARD II.

King Richard,   Mr. KEAN,

(His first appearance at Covent Garden in that character.)

Bolingbroke,   Mr. WARDE,

Duke of York, Mr. FITZHARRIS,   Duke of Aumerle,   Mr. RAYMOND,

Earl of Northumberland, Mr. DIDDEAR,   Harry Percy, Mr. HOLL,

Bishop of Carlisle, Mr. EVANS,   Sir Stephen Scroop, Mr. BAKER,

Gardeners,   Mess. Horrebow and Atkins,

Queen, Mrs. FAUCIT,   Blanche, Miss HENRY.

THE THIRD ACT OF

HAMLET.

Hamlet,   Mr. YOUNG,

Claudius, King of Denmark, Mr. EGERTON,   Polonius, Mr. BLANCHARD

Horatio, Mr. SERLE,   Rosencrantz, Mr. BAKER,

Guildenstern, Mr. CLAREMONT,   Actors, Mess. EVANS and ATKINS,

Ghost of Hamlet's Father,   Mr. WARDE,

The Queen, Mrs. FAUCIT.

Ophelia, Miss HENRY,   Actress, Mrs. DALY.

THE LAST ACT OF

ROMEO & JULIET

Romeo,   Mr. C. KEMBLE,

Prince Escalus, Mr. HORREBOW,   Paris, Mr. RAYMOND,

Friar Lawrence. Mr. EVANS,   Friar John, Mr. MEARS,

Apothecary. Mr. MEADOWS,   Page Master WATSON,   Balthazar Mr Irwin

by   Miss JARMAN.

which, (in two acts) The

...'s OPERA

VESTRIS,

(...sitively for This Night only.)

BARTLEY,
...OWS

WILLIAM MACREADY (1793-1873) AS HAMLET   *This part was performed with notable success during his 13-year stay at the Drury Lane, which began in 1823. He was considered by William Hazlitt, the noted 19th-century critic, the "best tragic actor of my remembrance, except Kean."*

One of the brightest stars that ever streaked across the British firmament was Edmund Kean, who in 1814 made his debut at Drury Lane as Shylock. He thrilled his audiences with a new style of highly passionate interpretation. Kean gave full vent to his inspiration, in contrast to the calm, studied, classical declamatory manner of Kemble.

Edmund Kean had grown up in the theatre. At an early age he was a strolling player in the provinces; and so when he came to London, he had had a very considerable amount of experience. At Drury Lane, his success was immediate and overwhelming. He came to play all the great tragic roles—Hamlet, Othello, Lear, and Richard III—and his hold on the public was such that he was able to command a munificent salary. In consequence, he acquired a fortune during his first years in London; but since he deported himself in his personal life rather recklessly and became involved in a scandal, he felt obliged to leave England and went on tour in America.

In the rapidly growing eastern cities of the United States, theatres were springing up at this time. English actors proved very popular and were finding an attractive new field in America. Although Kean met with great success on the American boards, he eventually returned to London and once again made appearances at Drury Lane. The public appeared to distinguish the actor from the man; and his reception in Britain was as warm as in his most popular days before he was involved in scandal. Kean's way of life still estranged him from polite society, and his ostracism exacted its toll. When he died in 1833 at forty-six, he was exhausted and prematurely aged.

WILLIAM CHARLES MACREADY (1793-1873)

Two years after Edmund Kean made his Drury Lane debut, William Charles Macready made his first appearance at Covent Garden. It was the last year of Kemble's management. Macready's style was largely in the Kemble tradition, but was somewhat blended with Kean's passion, plus a touch of the easy, polished acting of the French players he had seen on his trips to Paris.

Macready was a man of considerable intelligence, and he attracted the company of the great writers of the time. Though he played roles in the contemporary drama, he achieved his greatest success in Shakespearean parts.

A man of good taste, Macready raised the standard of production of serious plays. For the first time since the days of Garrick, productions went into adequate rehearsal. For many years previously, actors had been given scripts and memorized their lines more or less in private. An actor was allowed to interpret the part he was given *as he wished* during the actual performance, provided the interpretation was within the bounds of the accepted traditions. Under such conditions, when, for example, Edmund Kean played Shakespeare, the production centered on the solo performance of the star who was merely surrounded by a host of supernumeraries.

When Macready assumed management, he insisted that rehearsals be thorough, that all parts be equally well played, and that the whole production aim at a unified effect. To attain this end, he cast aside the rather mangled forms of Shakespeare's plays that were universally used at the time, and reverted to the original text.

To ensure that his scenery and costumes were harmonious and correct, he employed J. R. Planché, who, apart from being an accomplished writer of the lighter forms of entertainment, was an expert on historical costumes. In 1823, Planché had collaborated with Charles Kemble, who had succeeded his brother, John Kemble, as manager at Covent Garden. The production was *King John*. Here in this production, for the first time in the history of the theatre, costumes of the past were reproduced with reasonable accuracy.

During the monopoly period, Macready had been active manager at both of the patent theatres at different times; but his tenure in both situations did not prove to be financially successful. However, he also played at many of the minor theatres, and he also successfully toured American cities. He retired from the stage in 1851, and died in 1873.

CHARLES KEAN (1811-1868)   *A setting for Charles Kean's production of* HENRY V *illustrates the vogue for historical accuracy in costume and stage setting which was introduced by the designer James Robinson Planché. Kean's productions, as actor-manager of the Princess's Theatre from 1850-1859, were characterized by such lavish settings. He evinced an extreme regard for realistic detail. Kean's method of staging—which combined realism with visual effects— and his handling of crowd scenes profoundly influenced the European theatre.*

CHARLES KEAN (1811-1868)

Much against his father's wish, Charles Kean, the son of Edmund, began acting in 1827. He began his professional career touring the provinces; and for some years he appeared on the American stage. He then returned to London just when Macready was about to retire; and filling the gap, he soon became the leading tragedian of his day.

Unlike other monarchs of the preceding hundred years, Queen Victoria took an interest in the theatre and saw Kean perform in 1849. The Queen was so delighted with his performance that she inaugurated a series of theatricals at Windsor Castle, and appointed

Charles Kean as "Master of the Revels." The direct effect of the Queen's interest in the theatre, together with the more scholarly and tasteful productions of Macready and Kean, brought the upper classes back to the theatre. Theatre-going had now achieved high social stature.

Charles Kean hadn't the brilliant though erratic genius of his father, and was generally considered to be a lesser actor. But as a manager he saw to it that he was surrounded by a first-rate cast. All his productions were mounted with taste, and even with splendor. He continued in the path set by Macready, insisting on historically accurate costumes, and worked out his productions in detail so that the leading actor no longer monopolized the stage. Under Kean's direction, the true intent of a play wasn't distorted in order to aggrandize the talents of a particular star.

Kean took over the management of the Princess's Theatre in 1850, and enjoyed continuous success for nine years there. He then played the provinces, and undertook extensive tours of the United States and Australia. The small theatre he managed made the long run possible. Previously, only spectacular afterpieces and pantomimes ever enjoyed runs of several weeks. During the first half of the 18th century, the usual length of run for serious drama hovered around two weeks, although a production could, of course, be judiciously revived from time to time. In contrast, Kean's productions at the Princess's usually ran for a hundred nights.

MADAME VESTRIS (1797-1856)

What Charles Kean and William Macready did for the production of serious drama, Lucia Vestris and C. J. Mathews did for the development of comedy and burlesque. Lucia Elizabeth Bartolozzi, a charming and delightful creature, possessed of a rich contralto voice, married a famous ballet master, one Armand Vestris, only to be separated a few years later. Although she was a dancer, she made her

MADAME VESTRIS (1797-1856) IN "PAUL PRY"   *The play was presented in the Haymarket theatre in 1825. As manager of the Olympic in 1831, Miss Vestris became the first actress-manageress of the English theatre.*

CHARLES JAMES MATHEWS   (1803-1878) *The 19th-century actor-manager is portrayed as George Rattleton in his own play* THE HUMPBACKED LOVER *presented at the Olympic Theatre in London in 1835.*

Published by E. Glover, No 1 Water Lane, Fleet Street.

M.ʳ AND M.ʳˢ CHARLES MATHEWS.
(LATE MADAME VESTRIS.)

MR. AND MRS. MATHEWS AT HOME   Mme. Vestris with her second husband, Charles Mathews, the younger, is shown in an entertainment. The two presented a series of vignettes in which the versatile couple assumed a variety of characters. This form of entertainment was styled after solo performances given by Charles Mathews, the elder, known as his "At Homes."

first appearance in London, in 1815, as an opera singer. Subsequently, she appeared at the patent theatres as singer and dancer and actress, acquiring great popularity through the magnetism of her personality.

But it is her achievements as a manager which render her position important in the early Victorian theatre. In 1831 she acquired the management of the small Olympic Theatre. She intended to present legitimate drama in accordance with the monopoly conditions which then prevailed. She had the little theatre redecorated in excellent taste, and she contrived to make it a little showcase, more comfortable than the much larger patent theatres. In many ways, Madame Vestris's Olympic was the forerunner of the small, intimate theatres which are to be found in London today.

The Olympic presented comedies and burlesques by J. R. Planché and others, and achieved a quiet revolution in the manner of presentation. For some years previously, characters in comedies had always worn eccentric costumes, and comic acting itself was broad and extravagant. Madame Vestris introduced the use of contemporary costume. When it is considered that the twenty years from 1830 to 1850 was probably the most charming period in the century from the point of view of costume, it can well be imagined that Madame Vestris's productions reached new heights of taste and elegance.

Her small company was chosen with great care. Since none of the productions required a large cast, a high standard of acting was achieved in all the parts.

By this time, stalls were being introduced in the pit. As stated above, the fashionable element of society gradually began to frequent the theatres once again. The Olympic, because of its intimate atmosphere, had great appeal for this segment of society, particularly since it could be assured of a refined and tasteful production.

Madam Vestris introduced the innovation of concluding an evening's program by about eleven o'clock. Before this, theatre programs rarely finished before midnight; and when a bill was particularly long, the show might run until the small hours of the morning.

THE MATHEWS-VESTRIS MANAGEMENT

Charles James Mathews (1803-1878) joined the company of Madame Vestris in 1835, and rapidly became the leading light comedian of his day. His father, generally referred to as the elder Charles Mathews, had been a famous comic actor, known chiefly for his monologues and character studies. Charles Mathews the younger was sympathetic to the policy of his manager, Madame Vestris, and developed a style of acting based on the observation of contemporary manners. He soon succumbed to the considerable charms of his superior, and three years later they were united in matrimony.

Not long after their marriage, they gave up the Olympic Theatre and spent a year touring America. On their return to London, they took over the management of Covent Gardens; but because of the conditions prevailing under the monopoly laws, they were not very successful.

In 1841, the Mathews-Vestris team produced a play by Dion Boucicault (1822-1890) called *London Assurance*. Boucicault, an actor and writer with a thorough knowledge of both French and English stage traditions, was feeling his way in quest of a more realistic contemporary drama which he later developed into a more melodramatic style.

In spite of some excellent productions of Shakespeare's comedies, the Mathews-Vestris management of Covent Garden came to an end in 1842. Some time later, they acquired control of the Lyceum, where they reverted to burlesque and light comedy.

In 1854, Madam Vestris retired. Two years later she died. Mathews continued acting for another twenty years.

SAMUEL PHELPS'S MANAGEMENT AT SADLER'S WELLS

During the period when Charles Kean managed the Princess's Theatre, Samuel Phelps (1804-1878) was in charge at the Sadler's Wells. He had taken over directorship in 1844, after having received his training under Macready.

SAMUEL PHELPS (1804-1878) AS FALSTAFF   *As actor-manager of the Sadler's Wells Theatre, a playhouse formerly used for aquatic melodrama, Samuel Phelps devoted himself principally to the production of Shakespeare, restoring many of the texts to their original versions. From 1843 to 1863, he presented 34 of Shakespeare's plays, a record unbroken until 1923 when the Old Vic completed a cycle of the Bard's plays.*

Before the advent of Phelps, Sadler's Wells had confined its activities to melodrama. Making use of its watery surroundings, Sadler's Wells had a large tank on its stage for aquatic displays. In general, Sadler's Wells had a low reputation as a rendezvous for the rougher element of London. Yet Phelps played Shakespeare successfully for eighteen years in Sadler's Wells; during this period most of the Bard's repertoire was produced, as well as other classic dramas of the past. Phelps performed in the Macready style, and he shone particularly as Falstaff and Malvolio. In contrast to Charles Kean, Phelps stressed good acting. Settings and costumes were accounted to be of less importance in his productions. His success at Sadler's Wells was probably due to the fact that this was the first time that serious drama had been presented at this theatre, which had become known for its surfeit of spectacle.

SCENERY OF THE 19th CENTURY

By the middle of the century considerable development had been achieved in stage settings. During the monopoly period, the scenic artist had had great opportunities, for settings of romantic grandeur played an important part in burletta and melodrama. Since these presentations depended so much on visual appeal, artists designed not only interiors, but whole landscapes.

The scenery used had become more solid; the details more profound than before. Moreover, the constant change of scenery that was required to satisfy audiences demanded development in stage machinery. As settings became more elaborate, the stage roof was heightened to permit the scenery to be hoisted out of sight of the audience.

Devices such as the diorama were evolved—a landscape painted on a continuous backcloth which, mounted on rollers and turned mechanically, gave the audience the illusion of movement in place. The dioramas were especially effective where the action called for an exciting journey or a race.

Although Charles Kean had developed historical accuracy in costume and setting, the scenery was still artificial in the sense that it was painted and not three-dimensional. Interiors were represented by a painted backcloth and several sets of wings, while the ceiling was represented by a hanging painting.

LIGHTING IN THE 19th CENTURY

Early in the century gas light had been introduced. Originally this was used to light up the auditorium, but its employment on the stage shortly followed. The great advantage of this form of illumination was that it could be easily controlled. The candle snuffer now belonged to history. Now, with the movement of a lever, a stage mechanic could subdue or increase the lighting at will.

In 1860, the first use was made of limelight. This produced a strong incandescent light and became the chief means of emphasizing a character or portion of a scene. In turn, limelight led to the use of incandescent lighting, which greatly increased the effectiveness of stage illumination.

CHANGES IN THEATRES

By the middle of the century, great changes had come about in the amenities offered. Upholstered seats were now provided in the boxes and in the stalls. The pit, which had only benches, was gradually moved to the rear of the auditorium.

The crudely printed playbills of former days, which in some cases were a foot or more long and which were printed in ink that smeared at a touch, had now given way to smaller, better-printed programs, which were much more like those in use today.

These refinements, added to the development of scenery and lighting, and combined with the interest of Queen Victoria, brought about a renascence in all aspects of the drama.

CHARLES FECHTER (1824-1879)

A step forward in this new direction was achieved under the management of Charles Fechter, a well-known French actor who first appeared in London at the St. James's Theatre, taking roles in French plays. French companies had always made periodic visits to London, usually playing at the Queen's, the Lyceum, or the St. James's. Mlle. Rachel had acted at the St. James's where she had attracted the fashionable world, in much the way that Sarah Bernhardt was to enthrall audiences at a later time.

In 1860 Fechter appeared at the Princess's in *Ruy Blas*. Later, Fechter played *Hamlet* in English, creating not only a sensation by his acting, but also by his production. In contrast with the traditional style of tragic acting, the Frenchman played the role in a comparatively realistic manner, interpreting Shakespeare's play as a refined, poetic melodrama.

Fechter is also notable as the innovator of the box set, an interior setting with the appearance of solid walls and with a realistic ceiling. He also devised a sinking stage, so that all the solidly-built scenery could be removed to the basement and be replaced there by a new set.

TOM ROBERTSON (1829-1871)

In 1865, a new management made its contribution to the rapidly changing methods of stage representation. Marie Wilton (1839-1921), who had succeeded Lucia Vestris as queen of the light theatre, went into partnership with one H. J. Byron (1834-1884), a writer of light pieces. They took over the Prince of Wales's Theatre, on whose site the Scala now stands. The Prince of Wales's Theatre became the home of a new kind of play, by a rising new dramatist by the name of Tom Robertson.

Robertson had already won recognition for his play *David Garrick*, produced at the Haymarket, in which E. A. Sothern (1826-1881), a well-known actor, had appeared with great success.

CHARLES FECHTER (1824-1879)   The actor is shown as he appeared in his highly acclaimed portrayal of Hamlet at the Princess Theatre in London in 1861. Though costumed in traditional black, his realistic interpretation led him to wear a blond wig.

Robertson's subsequent plays—*Society, Ours, Caste, M. P., Play,* and *School*—were all comedy-dramas based on contemporary life. These plays were peopled with flesh-and-blood characters, drawn with a keen observation of the life of the times.

Because Robertson had been an actor and knew intimately the problems of the stage, his plays dealt very successfully with staging and his characterizations were sound. The realism that he achieved was, of course, only comparative; today, his plays seem stagey and melodramatic. But at the time they were written Robertson's plays gave the public a new representation of mid-Victorian life, with all its social and economic significance. His work was seminal and made possible the later portrayal of social problems on the stage by Sir Arthur Wing Pinero, Henry Arthur Jones, and John Galsworthy. In fact, it is believed that the character of Tom Wrench in Pinero's *Trelawney of the Wells* is supposed to represent Robertson in his early days. This play is also interesting for its portrayal of stage life and the changing conditions of the times in that period.

MARIE BANCROFT (1839-1921) AND SQUIRE BANCROFT (1841-1926)

Three well-known actors of the day, Marie Wilton, Squire Bancroft, and John Hare (1844-1921), performed in Robertson's plays. Marie Wilton married Squire Bancroft, and the two, acting in tandem further developed the realistic method of production which had begun with Fechter. Scenery became thoroughly realistic. Much of the painted architectural detail of interior sets gave way to solid cornices and pillars. Furniture acquired a new dramatic significance. In short, the Bancrofts spent much time and concern in creating a realistic atmosphere, as exemplified by the exact reproduction on the stage in the play *Money*, by Lord Bulwer-Lytton, of a card room in a famous West End club.

The Bancrofts had twenty years of unbroken success. They finally moved to the Haymarket in 1879, where they were responsible for many innovations in management: notably, the restrictions of the program to one play, the raising of the status of the bit player, and the introduction of matinee performances.

MUSIC HALLS

In the 1870's and 1880's, the music halls reached new heights of importance. Originally these halls, attached to taverns, were special saloons in which musical entertainment as well as refreshment were provided. With the passage of the Theatre Regulations Act of 1843 and the abolition of monopoly of the patent theatre, plays could be given at any licensed theatre, although no smoking nor drinking was allowed in the auditorium. But in the music halls—and by 1870 there were over twenty of them in London—smoking and drinking were permitted. Some of these establishments were quite large, such as the Alhambra. Many palatial new theatres were built during the eighties, such as the Empire and the New Tivoli.

The audience of the music halls consisted chiefly of the working class and the male contingent of the middle class, and of course the fare was fashioned to suit their demands. The performers had only

SHAKESPEARE'S "MACBETH"   Henry Irving (1838-1905) is
shown here in a scene from "Macbeth." Macduff is played by Mr.
Alexander.

to amuse, and made no pretensions to artistic performance. These
actors knew what their audience wanted; and if they could provide
entertainment, they were assured of success. The best known of
these actors assumed set characters in which they invariably appeared,
usually garbed in rather eccentric costume and makeup. In their
brief turns on the stage they offered song and dance and comic patter.

Acrobats, jugglers, and contortionists also found their place on the
program. Stars were able to appear at several theatres during the same

evening, repeating their short turns at each and driving off to the next theatre. The music hall songs of those days are still alive today. However, it is the tunes which have chiefly survived, for the words of that time usually seem rather vulgar or trite today. The songs, generally written to appeal to the working class audience, often reflected the social and economic discontent of these people. Stars such as Jenny Hill, Dan Leno, Alfred Glanville Vance, George Leybourne, Herbert Campbell, Albert Chevalier, Gus Elen, Vesta Tilley, and Marie Lloyd were immensely popular and attracted crowded houses to the variety theatres, as they came to be called. This English music hall theatre was the forerunner of vaudeville in the United States.

The rougher elements of the town largely deserted the theatres in favor of the variety houses, so that the theatre became almost the sole domain of the middle class. However, theatres such as Drury Lane, which contained thousands of seats to be filled, could not afford to ignore the drawing power of the variety stars, and therefore engaged them to fill the chief parts in their pantomimes. Whatever the pantomime was supposed to be, the star had little to do except fill the role with his normal music hall turn.

Today, that traditional British entertainment, the Christmas pantomime, still makes use of variety stars to fill the chief parts; although in the last few years, players from the legitimate stage have also been included.

TECHNICAL ADVANCES

From the time when the Bancrofts produced Robertson's plays, stage presentation increasingly became more realistic. In 1880, electric lighting was introduced at the Savoy and brought about hitherto undreamed of developments in the theatre. The great flexibility of electricity made all kinds of realistic effects possible. The new mechanics of illumination were now able to produce sunlight and moonlight.

Germany was in the forefront of producing technical improvements for the stage, and from that country British directors imported the idea of the sliding stage and the sinking stage. These contrivances enabled whole settings to be moved out of sight all at once.

The cyclorama, the revolving stage, and many electrical devices for controlling unusual lighting effects now came into play, with the result that the theatre underwent a dramatic development. The cyclorama, also of German origin, was a plaster half-dome which covered the back of the stage. Light could be thrown on this surface to represent the sky. Since this light cast no shadows, the cyclorama provided a great illusion of depth, particularly if a blue light were used.

The large stages of Covent Garden and Drury Lane were now reconstructed in sections. Each of these sections could be raised or lowered at will, thus enabling huge scenic effects to be rapidly removed and supplanted.

HENRY IRVING (1838-1905)

The greatest figure in the last thirty years of the century was Henry Irving. Like many other actors before him, he served his apprenticeship in the provincial theatres of Dublin, Liverpool, Manchester, and other great cities. By the time he made his London debut in 1866, he was an accomplished actor. Irving's performance as Hamlet in 1874 established his reputation as the leading actor on the English stage. By comparison with the tragedians of the past, his was a fresh and naturalistic interpretation. His acceptance and use of the new improvements in the theatre as they became available, ensured his continuing success. One of Irving's innovations was the blackout, during which scenery could be changed unseen by the audience.

Irving had a wonderful sense of pictorial effect. He managed to interest some of the leading painters of his time in designing for the stage, among them Burne-Jones, Alma-Tadema, Ford Madox Brown, and Gustave Doré.

Some of Irving's productions veered to over-elaboration; he was in the habit of introducing considerable stage business not in the script.

ENGLAND'S GREATEST ACTOR

The House in which the late Sir Henry Irving was born at Keinton Mandeville, Somerset. Sir Henry was born in the room marked with a cross

Born 1838
Died 1905

SIR HENRY IRVING.

Into thy hands, O Lord.
(Becket)

IRVING'S RESTING PLACE.

WESTMINSTER ABBEY

HENRY IRVING (1838-1905)   *Eminent actor-manager of the late 19th century, Henry Irving became established as an actor of the first rank by his portrayal of Mathias in* THE BELLS. *This was a melo-drama by Leopold Lewis based on Erckmann-Chatrian's* LE JUIF POLONAIS *and was produced at the Lyceum Theatre in 1872. As the manager of that theatre from 1878 to 1899, Irving's productions were marked by opulent settings. He had great regard for historical accuracy. At left, Irving is caricatured as Jingle in "Pickwick," the role in which he made his first appearance at the Lyceum. The esteem in which Irving was held is demonstrated by the commemorative postcard above, which celebrates his birthplace and his place of burial.*

As vehicles for his art, Irving preferred to use rather inferior plays and adaptations, although he did perform to great advantage in Shakespeare. He economized on authors, and was thus able to spend more in production. But in spite of his tendency to economy, after a long period of management at the Lyceum, Irving failed financially, and the management was taken over in 1899 by a syndicate.

MRS. PATRICK CAMPBELL (1865-1940)   One of the leading actresses of her day, Mrs. Campbell is seen here as Paula in A. W. Pinero's THE SECOND MRS. TANQUERAY, a role which brought her into prominence in 1893. She was one of the most beautiful women of her time. George Bernard Shaw called her "perilously bewitching." Her correspondence with the famous playwright formed the basis of a play DEAR LIAR by Jerome Kilty, produced in London and New York in 1959.

It is chiefly as an actor and a personality that Irving was respected. He did much to raise the status of the acting profession in England, and was the first actor to receive the honor of being knighted. Irving played in melodrama, and is particularly remembered for his performance in the horror play, *The Bells*. His style was not a passionate one; but by superb timing, his long speeches moved the audience much as it had been moved by Garrick. Irving possessed enormous personal magnetism and held his audiences spellbound. His popularity in England was almost matched by his popularity in America, where he made many tours. His last English tour, in 1905, was cut short by his death a few days later in Bradford. Mourned by a large and devoted public, he was buried in Westminster Abbey.

LILY LANGTRY (1853-1929)

Famed more for her beauty and personality than for her acting, this famous star was painted by Millais and Burne-Jones. She appeared chiefly in modern plays, and achieved tremendous popularity. Oscar Wilde wrote *Lady Windermere's Fan* as a vehicle for her talents.

MRS. PATRICK CAMPBELL (1865-1940)

The dynamic personality of Mrs. Patrick Campbell accounted for her being much sought after as a leading lady. She achieved notable success in Pinero's *The Second Mrs. Tanqueray,* produced in 1893. She is also particularly remembered as the original Eliza Doolittle in Shaw's *Pygmalion*.

ELLEN TERRY (1847-1928)

The leading actress of the last quarter of the 19th century is considered to be Ellen Terry. Born of parents who were well-known provincial actors and close friends of Charles Kean, Ellen first appeared on the stage in 1856 as the boy, Mamillius, in *The Winter's*

ELLEN TERRY (1848-1928)
Her 24-year association with Henry Irving at the Lyceum was considered "one of the glories of the English theatre." The characters shown here include Mme. Sans Gêne, Margaret, Olivia, and Nance Oldfield. A woman of great personal magnetism, Ellen Terry conducted a "letter-box-romance" with George Bernard Shaw, a term used by the noted playwright for their correspondence.

HERBERT BEERBOHM TREE (1853-1917)   During his lifetime, Tree produced 18 of Shakepeare's plays. A gallery of Shakespearean portraits performed by the actor-manager is presented here. A critic accounted him as a "romantic actor of erratic brilliance."

JOHNSTON FORBES-ROBERTSON
*(1853-1937) Noted actor-manager of
the Lyceum Theatre from 1895 until his
retirement in 1913, Forbes-Robertson continued the Henry Irving tradition of
grandiose productions of Shakespeare and
contemporary plays. His* HAMLET, *given
at the Lyceum in 1897, was considered
one of the finest portrayals of his time.*

Tale, presented at the Princess's Theatre. In 1867 she played Katherine to Irving's Petruchio in *The Taming of the Shrew.*

For some years after this, Ellen Terry retired from the stage. Returning in 1875, she played Portia under the management of the
Bancrofts, at the old Prince of Wales's Theatre. After this she rejoined Irving, and a long and happy partnership ensued in which
she played all of Shakespeare's great heroines. Later, she also appeared
in some of the early Shaw plays. This developed into a famous romance with the renowned author, which was conducted almost entirely by correspondence.

Most of the critics of Ellen Terry's day write of the vitality of her
acting. Even in her old age she was able to convincingly portray the
freshness of youth.

THE ACTOR-MANAGER

The last years of the century were dominated by the actor-manager,
who led his company on the numerous tours needed to ensure a

viable income. Each company had its repertoire of plays which was sufficiently large that, when playing a week in a new town, the troupe could present a fresh play each evening. Since there were a variety of parts to be played, and there were a limited number of players in the company, the younger actors would often double in roles during a single evening. It was this experience that provided good groundwork for developing powers of portrayal. The actor-manager usually played the leading roles himself; but as the manager kept a constant eye on the performances of the youngsters, each budding artist was likely to get a chance to play a larger role when he was ready for it.

GEORGE ALEXANDER (1858-1918)

George Alexander had been an actor at one time and understood the stage well. When he assumed managership of the St. James's Theatre in London, he presented a series of modern plays by such authors as H. A. Jones, Sir Arthur Wing Pinero, and Oscar Wilde. His distinguished company included Mrs. Patrick Campbell, Irene Vanbrugh, Marie Tempest, and Henry Ainley.

HENRY BEERBOHM TREE (1853-1917)

Henry Beerbohm Tree was known chiefly for his melodramatic and character parts. Though Falstaff and Hamlet were his most successful roles, he also produced and acted in dramas by Ibsen, Wilde, and Maeterlinck.

He founded a school for acting and was prominent in furthering the interests of the theatre. In fact, he built Her Majesty's Theatre in 1897. Henry Beerbohm Tree was knighted in 1909 by King Edward VII for significant accomplishments in the theatre.

FRANK BENSON (1858-1939)

Heading a company which included most of Shakespeare's plays in its repertoire, Frank Benson traveled all over Britain, and through

Canada and South Africa. For many years Benson organized the annual festivals at Stratford-on-Avon. His organization was superb.

Strangely enough, his company was almost as well known for their prowess at cricket as they were for their acting, and it was waggishly said that he recruited the men of his company with more thought for their skill at the wicket than for their ability on the boards. However, there is no doubt that Frank Benson wielded considerable influence on his contemporaries.

JOHNSTON FORBES-ROBERTSON (1853-1937)

Having served his apprenticeship with Samuel Phelps, and having played under the management of the Bancrofts and at various times with Irving, Johnston Forbes-Robertson assumed management of the Lyceum in 1895. His distinguished appearance and his romantic temperament suited his best roles which were Romeo, Hamlet, and Macbeth.

BRIDGE FROM THE PAST

In summary, it can be said that the Victorians bequeathed to the theatre considerable technical development in advanced lighting, in better settings, in greater realism in scenery, and most certainly in acting, which was freed from the former conventional features and achieved far greater realism. Drama, for the first time, began to deal with day-to-day life.

The era saw the end of the patent theatre monopoly, and thus led to the building of many new theatres in London and in other large cities. Extensive tours were taken by companies throughout England and to other countries throughout the world, particularly to the United States. The advent of actor-managers yielded productions of greater distinction, with more care given to rehearsals and the details of production. In essence, the theatre of Victorian days began to resemble the stage we have today. In many respects then, the Victorians must be accounted as the link from the past with the modern theatre.

The Rise of the American Theatre

EARLY PURITAN OPPOSITION

Of early theatrical performances in America, but few records have survived. It is quite clear in retrospect that the professional stage in colonial days was very slow in establishing itself.

The main obstacle was the strong Puritan prejudice against all forms of display, showmanship, and anything deemed to be "vain." The Pilgrim Fathers who landed at Plymouth Rock in 1620 were, after all, the ideological brethren of the Puritans who shut down the English theatres in 1642. They brought with them to their new country a hatred of all those aspects of English life which they associated with the sophisticated and somewhat loose-living aristocracy. Costumes, make-believe, and the portrayal of tawdry character were frowned upon. The prejudice against the theatre was deeply rooted; and during the whole of the 17th century, only a few spasmodic performances of plays are recorded.

During the early 1700's, strolling players began to arrive from England. The population of the growing towns of America was now about equally divided between the descendants of the early Puritan settlers with their abhorrence of all frivolity, and the later colonists who had a more liberal attitude toward the living arts.

THE EARLIEST PERFORMANCES IN AMERICA

In the South, most of the original settlers were adherents of the established Church of England, so there was greater tolerance in these colonies than there was in the Puritan North. In Charleston in 1703, an English actor, poet, and gentleman, one Anthony Aston, put on a play he had written, and earned the distinction of being the first professional actor to perform in the New World. Later, Aston moved on to give some performances in New York, but ultimately returned to England where he resumed his acting career with his own company at Oxford. Perhaps he sensed that the time was not ripe for the development of the theatre in New York where, in 1709, the Governor's Council forbade "play-acting and prize fighting."

At that time, Williamsburg was the capital of Virginia. Here, in 1716, a contract was signed between William Levingston, a merchant who built a theatre, and Charles and Mary Stagg; but nothing more is known about this venture. Presumably, Mr. and Mrs. Stagg were strolling players who had visited the Colonies with a small company from England, and who then moved on, after giving several performances.

As the population of the New World increased, amateur performances were more frequently given. These usually took place in a courthouse or in some other building which could be used to house a makeshift stage, and which had sufficient seating space to allow a tolerable audience. In 1736, the students of William and Mary College, whose first productions dated back to the beginning of the century, performed the tragedy of *Cato*. This play was followed on successive days by other amateur productions such as *The Busybody,* and Farquhar's *The Recruiting Officer* and *The Beaux' Stratagem*. These productions were some of the favorites of the London stage of that day.

During the 18th century, *Cato* became one of the most popular tragic plays in America. Written by Joseph Addison (1672-1719) in the early years of the century when England was threatened by political tyranny, this play about the noble Roman philosopher whose patriotism and love of liberty transcended life itself, became for the American colonies a symbolic representation of their own struggle for political freedom.

THE ENGLISH TOURING COMPANIES

Though most people in England regarded the Colonies as a Western wilderness, companies of English players were nevertheless willing to tour the country. These troupes took things as they found them, playing in converted storehouses, or even building a theatre wherever they might anticipate a good reception, while avoiding those towns where the Puritan attitude prevailed.

The plays they brought with them were those then in favor on the London stage. The great skill of these players, acquired under the arduous conditions of constant, even nightly, change of bill, greatly impressed their American audiences, and their successes encouraged many of these English actors to settle permanently in America. By the middle of the 18th century, the growth of population resulted in the building of theatres in Charleston, Philadelphia, New York, and Baltimore.

EARLY THEATRE IN CHARLESTON

In 1735 at Charleston, Thomas Otway's (1652-1685) finest tragedy *The Orphan* was staged in the courthouse. As an afterpiece, the pantomime *The Adventures of Harlequin and Scaramouche,* an English version of Italian comedy, was presented.

It was customary at this time to conclude the evening's performance with a short farce or pantomime, which gave the audience time to regain its spirits if a somewhat heavy tragedy had been witnessed. Also, the afterpiece gave the lesser players a chance to shine.

That same season, a ballad opera was given entitled *Flora, or Hob in the Well* which may have been the very first musical production on the American stage. The final production of the 1735 season was a benefit performance of Dryden's *The Spanish Fryar,* in honor of its leading lady, who was known as Monimia after a character which she played with great success in *The Orphan.*

So successful was this short season by these unknown players that a subscription campaign was started for the construction of a playhouse. The founders of Charleston were noblemen who had been granted a charter by Charles II in 1670. They were by no means prejudiced against the theatre, and they led a lively social life with occasional concerts, balls, and other entertainments. The construction of the playhouse, therefore, went ahead without opposition. Early in the following year, the New Theatre in Dock Street opened with Farquhar's *The Recruiting Officer.* A revival of Otway's *The Orphan* with the popular Monimia, Lillo's *The London Merchant,* and a ballad opera *The Devil to Pay,* were the other productions given that season.

During the following winter, revivals of the earlier productions were presented, but after this nothing further is recorded of the company. The theatre may have been used for concerts and balls until it burned down in 1740.

THE MURRAY-KEAN COMPANY

After the fire, Charleston was without a theatre until 1751, when a new theatre was built by subscription for "the company of comedians from New York," a company headed by Walter Murray and Thomas Kean who had performed Addison's *Cato* and other plays in Philadelphia in 1749. In New York, they had converted a storehouse in Nassau Street into a theatre where they played *Richard III, Love for Love, The Orphan,* and *George Barnwell.*

Murray and Kean opened in Charleston in late October, 1751, in *Richard III.* The composition of the company and the standard of their performances remain unknown, but there is little doubt that the performances created an interest in Charleston in the theatre. The ground was thus prepared for the very able and talented players of William and Lewis Hallam.

THE HALLAM COMPANY

When David Garrick and his manager, Giffard, went to the Theatre Royal in Drury Lane, William Hallam became the manager of the Goodman's Fields Theatre in London. Although enjoying some reflected glory from its departed star, Goodman Fields Theatre became a difficult house to operate financially. In a few years, Hallam went bankrupt. But he settled his affairs in such a reasonable manner that his creditors allowed him to retain his scenery, costumes, and sufficient capital to start again. With this rudimentary capital, he formed a small company to send to the American colonies.

William's brother, Lewis (1714-1756), had been the chief low comedian in the company at Goodman's Fields. Lewis's wife played the leading female roles in both tragedy and comedy. Three of the four children of Lewis Hallam were to accompany their parents to America and would later perform with the company: Lewis, junior, then a boy of twelve; a younger son, Adam; and an older daughter, eventually introduced on the stage as Miss Hallam. The rest of the company was composed of efficient players, all willing to leave England for an indefinite period.

Early in May, 1752, Lewis Hallam sailed for America with a complete company, properties, costumes, scenery, and a repertoire of no less than twenty-four plays and their accompanying afterpieces. This repertoire was prepared and cast at the home of William Hallam, who was to remain in England as directing manager.

The roster of plays, all tried and successful pieces on the London stage, consisted of four by Shakespeare, five by George Farquhar, two by Colley Cibber, two by Nicolas Rowe, and others by Bishop Hoadley, George Lillo, Nathaniel Lee, Christopher Bullock, Sir Richard Steele, and Sir Robert Howard, as well as three farces by David Garrick. There was one pantomime.

These plays were thoroughly rehearsed and prepared for production during the company's six week voyage on the *Charming Sally*. Disembarking at Yorktown, the company set off for Williamsburg where application had been made to the Governor for an official license to perform. On being favorably received, Lewis Hallam set about converting an unused storehouse on the outskirts of the town, fitting it with a stage, pit, gallery, and boxes—complete as a "regular Theatre, fit for the Reception of Ladies and Gentlemen."

The theatre was launched on September 5, 1752, with *The Merchant of Venice*. The opening performance was preceded by a prologue written by one of the players, Mr. Singleton, which reminded the audience that the players had come from England as their humble servants, and assured them of the high moral tone of what they were about to witness. Young Lieutenant George Washington may have been a member of that audience for he had developed a taste for theatricals in the West Indies. Certainly he was to see the younger Lewis Hallam in many of his performances in later years.

It was the custom of the company to play on Monday, Wednesday, and Friday of each week. To the townspeople, it must have been a delight to walk to the playhouse on the edge of the woods on a fine evening to see great stories played out and emotions portrayed with skill and sophistication. The accent was on taste and refinement; the makeshift building was made to look as nearly as it might like a small London theatre. The ability of the company and the good behavior of the actors was confirmed by a testimonial given to Hallam by the Governor at the close of the season. This written approbation was to be used as a passport to elders of other towns in which Hallam's company might seek to give performances.

From Williamsburg, the company journed to Annapolis where another theatre had been erected early in 1752. After a short season there, the company continued northward, playing in Maryland and eventually arriving in New York where they settled in a theatre in Nassau Street, a theatre which had been converted by the Murray and Kean company from Philadelphia some time back.

So a year after their first performance in Williamsburg, the Hallam Company opened at Nassau Street with *The Conscious Lovers,* followed by *Damon and Phillida.* Their performances on Mondays, Wednesdays, and Fridays met with great success, and the company ended its season with Congreve's *Love for Love,* playing to a packed house for the benefit of the poor of the city.

Despite the large Quaker element in the city who would certainly attempt to prevent him from giving performances, Hallam decided to take his company to Philadelphia. But before making the move, Hallam sent one of his company, a man by the name of Malone, a man of engaging manners and great powers of persuasion, to Philadelphia to make application to the Governor for permission to play. For this diplomatic mission, Malone was to be rewarded with the parts of Falstaff and Don Lewis, roles that generally were played by Hallam himself. During this era, the custom prevailed that when success in a role was confirmed by both management and audience, the role became the actor's own property so to speak; and while he was a member of the company, no other player was permitted to perform it.

As was more or less expected, the Quakers organized a petition to the Governor for the prohibition of "lewd and profane stage-plays," and their opponents busily collected signatures for a counterpetition. Eventually, Governor Hamilton decided for the players and gave them permission for twenty-four performances on condition that they offered nothing indecent and immoral, and that they would perform one night for the benefit of the poor of the city.

Resistance to Hallam's company by a large portion of the population continued in many towns during the second half of the 18th century. In many cases, the opposition succeeded in getting the Governor's Council to pass an edict prohibiting performances. This did not always stops the players, for their supporters would address themselves to the government in London, which always repealed the edict. In some ways, this action was unfortunate since the theatre began to become associated in the minds of many Americans as an instrument of British control. Thus, it came about that the first Continental Congress in 1774 passed a law prohibiting stage performances.

In Philadelphia, Hallam found a convenient storehouse on Pine Street. After its conversion, he opened with *The Fair Penitent* by

Rowe, and used Garrick's *Miss in Her Teens* as an afterpiece. Needless to say, what with all the excitement generated by the two petitions, the house was packed. Even certain members of the opposing faction attended! The company performed with their accustomed skill. So successful was the entertainment that the Governor granted Hallam an extra six nights.

After the season in Philadelphia, Hallam and his company sailed for the West Indies, but not before they received a visit from William Hallam. It is probable that a settlement was reached over the future of the company, and that Lewis purchased his brother's share in the management.

As sole proprietor and manager of a thriving and successful company, Lewis undoubtedly planned to give performances in the main ports of the West Indies; but soon after arriving in those islands, he fell ill and died.

DAVID DOUGLASS (?-1786) AND THE AMERICAN COMPANY

Little is known of David Douglass' early days except that he was by descent and education a gentleman. He was touring with a theatrical company in the West Indies, where in 1758 he met the widowed Mrs. Hallam. The meeting blossomed into marriage and Douglass formed a new company which he called the American Company.

He brought Mrs. Hallam, her children, and some members of his original company to New York where he built a temporary theatre on Cruger's Wharf, the old Nassau Street theatre having been demolished. His application to the authorities for the customary license to perform was, however, met with a blank refusal. He used his theatre as an "histrionic academy" in which he gave dissertations on subjects which were "moral, instructive and entertaining," while a further appeal was being made to the authorities. The City fathers relented to the extent of permitting thirteen performances.

The American Company opened with *Jane Shire*. Lewis Hallam, Jr., now a handsome youth of eighteen, delivered Singleton's former

LEWIS HALLAM, JR. (1740?-1808)   One of the youngest members of the famed Hallam Company, the first professional troupe of players from England to try the New World, Lewis Hallam, Jr., appeared on September 15, 1752, as Portia's page. Though he had only one line to deliver, according to a well-known story, the 12-year-old actor suffered a severe case of stagefright and ran from the stage. Despite this unsteady beginning, Hallam at 18 had become the leading man of the newly organized American Company. His reputation grew as actor-manager of the company, until in 1799, internal squabbles led him to give up the troupe's leadership. He remained active on the boards, however, until 1806, two years before his death. This portrait is from a miniature by an unknown artist.

prologue. The success of this short season established the reputation of the new company and Douglass continued with a long series of tours to Philadelphia, Newport, Williamsburg, and Annapolis, returning eventually to New York. He proved to be a very efficient manager—building new theatres, dealing skillfully with the authorities, always giving a special performance at the close of a season for the benefit of the poor, and obtaining a testimonial from the authori-

THE JOHN STREET THEATRE   The first permanent playhouse in New York, built by Douglass as the home of the American Company, opened on December 17, 1767 with George Farquhar's "The Beau Strategem." Lewis Hallam played Archer. Like its counterpart, The Southwark, it was built principally of wood, and was painted red. The pit was occupied by gentlemen only, the side areas being reserved for the ladies. (The woman

shown in the pit is there only because of an imaginative error on the part of the engraver.) Two proscenium doors, a feature of the English Restoration theatre, are seen in the foreground. The openings above the proscenium doors are presumably balconies for spectators and actors alike. The row of reflectors at the front of the stage indicates that footlights were then in use; but since the date of this engraving by S. Hollyer is unknown, the actual date of the introduction of footlights is uncertain.

ties as to the character and ability of the players.

The American Company prospered. The company was further strengthened by the addition of players such as John Henry and Thomas Wignell recruited from England.

The first plays by American authors were performed, including Thomas Godfrey's *The Prince of Parthia,* and Colonel Thomas Forrest's *The Disappointment, or The Force of Credulity,* but these works were generally not too successful, and the latest plays from London remained the main draw.

Overcoming all difficulties, the company had firmly established the theatre in America. Mrs. Douglass died in 1773. Douglass played a last season at Charleston in 1774, then returned to New York to prepare for a new season there. But in October of that year Congress passed a resolution forbidding all public amusements, so the company packed their trunks and sailed for the more dependable West Indies. Here they stayed throughout the years of the Revolutionary War. Douglass eventually retired from management and became a judge.

THE REVOLUTIONARY WAR

During the war, some theatrical activity continued. The troops on both sides felt the need for the relaxation offered by the stage. The occupation of Boston by General John Burgoyne was enlivened by many productions, for Burgoyne was himself a playwright and is reputed to have acted on the stage.

A performance of his farce, *The Blockade of Boston,* was interrupted by a sergeant who came on the stage with the news that "the rebels have attacked the lines," and the soldier was applauded for his very natural acting. It was only after some time that it was discovered that the man who made the announcement was not in fact part of the cast but was a real sergeant who had brought the news of the beginning of the triumphal action that led to Burgoyne's surrender at Saratoga.

In New York in 1777, British troops under General Howe also

MRS. LEWIS HALLAM, SR. (? -1773)   One of the earliest
American actresses, Mrs. Hallam is depicted here in the role of
Marianne. This engraving by Tiebout is after a drawing by William
Dunlap.

THE SOUTHWARK THEATRE   *The first permanent theatre in America was built in Philadelphia in 1766 by David Douglass, manager of the American Company. This drawing by Edwin F. Durang is a reconstruction of that historic building. Contemporary journalists described it as ugly but substantial. The lower portion was constructed of brick, the upper section of wood, and the entire structure was painted red. Oil lamps lit the stage. The smoke considerably obscured the view of the stage, as did the huge wooden pillars which supported the balcony and roof. The Southwark remained in use until May 9, 1821 when it was partially destroyed by fire. Subsequently rebuilt, it was converted into a brewery, and was finally demolished in 1912.*

found time to perform a number of plays at the John Street Theatre, now renamed the Theatre Royal. The acting, scenery, and direction were handled by officers, with an occasional professional, a civilian actor, assisting. Major André, later to become notorious as a spy behind the American lines, was one of the actors. The bills advertised that the performances were given for charity, for the benefit of widows and orphans of fallen soldiers.

In January, 1778, a military company gave the first performance of Horne's *Douglas* which was received with great applause. Richard Cumberland's *West Indian* was also performed in America for the first time.

A good deal of money was spent by these military companies on costumes and properties. At first, the female parts were taken by men; but later, the wives of the officers were persuaded to appear in the roles. Among the plays produced were *Tom Thumb, Othello, Douglas,* and *The Rivals.* The performances were open to the public, to the joy of the young William Dunlap who later became a playwright and manager of the American Company, and the first historian of the American stage.

During the long wait at Valley Forge, Washington's troops performed the inevitable *Cato.* The military companies were fortunate in having at their disposal the military bands which were used as orchestras. The productions were excellent in many ways. Though the scenery in general was poor, the costumes were elegant; and the performances, lively though unskilled, won a sympathetic reception.

When the British occupied Philadelphia, they took over the Southwark Street Theatre, and British officers took charge of the stage. However, the playacting enthusiasm of the military gradually slackened; and after 1781, no more performances were given.

THE POSTWAR PERIOD

After the surrender of the British in 1783, professional players began to return to the stage. Philadelphia was chosen by Hallam for his opening in 1785, but Hallam's full company was not used, as this debut was something by way of a trial to test the feeling of the townspeople. The company was successful during a short season, and performed the customary benefits for the poor.

Now Hallam was sufficiently encouraged to open with his full company in New York, led by himself and his partner, John Henry. On January 16, 1786, Hallam played Hamlet, which is probably the first time the tragedy was performed in America. The reception was polite, applause accorded more for the pleasure of seeing a favorite again than for the play itself. Hamlet was generally considered a difficult role to sustain; and although, in England, Thomas Betterton had been outstanding in the part, and David Garrick (in his more realistic rendering) made a great impression, Shakespeare's great tragedy was rarely attempted in early American days.

During that season, Richard Sheridan's *The School for Scandal* and *The Duenna* were also played for the first time in America. John O'Keeffe's farces and light operas were also produced; the most successful among which were *The Poor Soldier* and *Wild Oats.*

Hallam and Henry also built a theatre in Baltimore, now a rapidly growing city, and opened their playhouse in 1786. The company traveled from Baltimore to Richmond, now the leading city of Virginia, and from thence to Philadelphia, and finally came back to New York.

In Philadelphia, where the Quakers were still petitioning strongly for the closure of the theatre, musical pieces and pantomime predominated. The old Southwark Street Theatre was renamed the Opera House. Plays were disguised under the euphemistic description of "moral lectures." For instance, the billing for Goldsmith's *She Stoops to Conquer* was "Lecture on the Disadvantages of Improper Education, Exemplified in the History of Tony Lumpkin." Eventually, the more liberal members of the population prevailed on the Legislature to permit the theatre to be opened "by Authority."

AMERICAN PLAYWRIGHTS

The American theatre was in the doldrums at this time. During this period, new American authors were tried out by the Company. In 1787, the first American comedy, *The Contrast* by Royall Tyler was performed in New York with some success. This encouraged the management to accept a farce by the same author, entitled *Mayday or New York in an Uproar,* which was performed for the benefit of

FATHER OF THE AMERICAN DRAMA   A major force in the growth of the American theatre, William Dunlap (1766-1839), dramatist, manager, theatre historian, is credited with having written 53 plays, 29 of which were original. The others were adaptations of foreign plays. One of the best of his original plays, "André," an historical tragedy produced in 1798, utilized for the first time a native American event, a spying incident growing out of the War of Independence. His pioneering work "A History of the American Theatre," published in 1832, is an invaluable source of reference for the early years of the American Theatre.

Thomas Wignell, now the most popular comedian of the Company. Wignall played in what William Dunlap termed a "Yankee dialect." Generally, however, the home-written play was not too popular; and these pieces, although occasionally performed, were not often repeated. A tragedy in blank verse by Barnaby Bidwell entitled *The Mercenary Match* was performed by students of Yale, and was greeted with roars of laughter which must have been most dismaying to the author.

WILLIAM DUNLAP (1766-1839)

William Dunlap acquired his taste for the theatre after seeing the military performers in New York during the Revolutionary War. His interest in the drama had been further strengthened by a three-year sojourn in London, where his father had sent him in 1784 to study painting, and where he spent much of his time attending performances by most of the leading players of the time, including John Philip Kemble and Mrs. Siddons.

After his return to the Colonies in 1787, Dunlap wrote his first play, a comedy in five acts with the title of *The Modest Soldier, or Love in New York*. The author read it to Hallam and Henry who accepted it. However, as there were no suitable parts for either John Henry or Mrs. Henry, the play failed to achieve production.

Dunlap was nevertheless encouraged to write another comedy with parts suited to both Henry and his wife. *The Father of an Only Child* received its first performance in 1789, and was well received, the piece playing for six further performances. Hallam, Henry, and Mrs. Henry were excellent in the serious or pathetic parts, and Wignell added to his reputation as a comedian in the part of Tattle, the family physician.

In November of that year, Dunlap provided Wignell with another occasion for triumph; his comic sketch, *Darby's Return,* based on a popular character in O'Keeffe's *The Poor Soldier* was performed for a benefit. Dunlap had included some references to topical matters; and President Washington, who was in the audience, was well pleased with the complimentary allusions to his inauguration.

REORGANIZATION OF THE AMERICAN COMPANY

Due to the continued hostility of Henry, Wignell seceded from the old American Company at the close of the season in 1791, and took some of the company with him. Joining forces with Alexander Reinagle, a prominent musician, Wignell formed a new company and set about raising funds for the erection of a new theatre in Chestnut Street. In the meantime, the actor-manager sailed to England to recruit more experienced players. Henry had sailed to Britain earlier in the year on a similar mission.

Some competition was also felt from a smaller company, the New

American Company, which was led by Mr. and Mrs. Kenna, formerly members of the Hallam and Henry Company. This little group played in New York at a small wooden theatre in Front Street.

The old American Company was joined by a troupe of dancers and pantomimists led by Mr. and Mrs. Placide from France, who had begun performances at Charleston and later moved to New York. Inevitably, the old Company was weakened by the loss of its mainstays, and by the shift from acting to spectacle.

In 1792, the American Company was completely reorganized. Many of the older performers left to seek their fortunes elsewhere. The new players, brought by Henry from England, greatly strengthened and revitalized the company, the chief acquisition being John Hodgkinson (1767-1805), a brilliant actor of twenty-six. Hodgkinson was extremely versatile; he had such a wide range and had such a lively manner that he eventually became known as the "provincial Garrick." He was described by Dunlap as some five feet, ten inches tall, rather thickset, and with his hair worn in the old fashion— powdered and with his side curls ending in a black queue.

Hodgkinson's wife was an excellent actress, particularly good in comedy, playing hoydenish girls with great spirit. She was also very moving in tragedy, especially in the role of Ophelia. She had the advantage of having been trained as a singer by her father who had been a performer at both Covent Garden and the Haymarket. Dunlap records that her voice was both powerful and sweet.

The new company made its debut in Philadelphia at the end of September, 1792, and enjoyed a successful short season before returning to New York for the New Year. In the years following, Hodgkinson became a performer of increasing popularity, while Henry and Hallam enjoyed less appeal. This led to much ill feeling; and eventually, to downright hostility from Henry, when Hodgkinson claimed a share in the management to which he felt entitled, since he was supporting the leading roles in comedy and tragedy.

DUNLAP'S MANAGEMENT OF THE AMERICAN COMPANY

After Henry's death in 1795, the American Company was led by Hodgkinson. At this point, Hallam was no longer a partner, but a salaried actor.

The company successfully produced Dunlap's play *André,* based on an incident in the War of Independence. Hodgkinson played the main part of Major André, and Thomas Abthorpe played the character of Bland, the young American officer, whom André had befriended. *André* represents the first native American tragedy.

After this season, Hodgkinson continued as an actor but retired from management. Dunlap took over in 1796. He produced a large number of his own plays, based on or adapted from foreign originals. His first important success was with *The Stranger,* a comedy adapted from the German dramatist Kotzebue, which had originally been entitled *Menschenhass und Reue.*

At this time, August Friedrich Ferdinand von Kotzebue (1761-1819) was turning out play after play and submitting them to most of the leading playhouses of Europe. The English playwright Sheridan adapted one of Kotzebue's dramas which subsequently proved very popular under the title *Pizarro.* A letter from Kotzebue to Dunlap offered several of his plays for use, payment to depend on what the house would take. The letter noted that the manager of Covent Garden had paid £100 for each play. Kotzebue's works were of little lasting merit: they were nothing more than sensational melodramas; but Kotzebue's plays were enormously popular with the audiences of his day and provided many excellent acting parts. Hodgkinson was continually successful in the Kotzebue plays, the best of which, according to Dunlap, were *The Stranger, False Shame, Lovers' Vows, The Force of Calumny,* and *The Death of Rolla,* from which Sheridan had adapted *Pizarro.*

Hodgkinson had strengthened the American Company by the addition of Mrs. Melmoth, famous for her great success in tragic roles in Dublin and Edinburgh. He also obtained the services of Mrs. Merry of Covent Garden, and Mrs. Pownall who was celebrated in London for roles in both comedy and opera.

Greater attention was now paid to the quality of the scenery. The Company now acquired the valuable services of Charles Ciceri as scene painter and machinist. Ciceri had received his early training in France and London, and was particularly good at architectural effects and detail.

Hitherto, little attention had been paid to settings; and many early critics of the theatre in America had made reference to the poor "dirty canvas" scenes. The staging of that day utilized a backcloth and side wings. The backcloth unrolled to depict an interior or exterior scene, while the side wings rolled in grooves on the floor and could be changed. The actors made their entrances and exits either through the stage doors situated on either side of the front of the stage, or entered or exited through the wings. Gradually, changes were introduced; more curtains were used, and elaborate chandeliers provided better illumination to a more elegant house.

Strife created by recurrent disagreements among the actors and the disruption caused by fever epidemics of yellow fever eventually caused Dunlap to go bankrupt. He retired from the theatre in 1805; but came back to work as a stage manager when Cooper took over the Park Theatre.

THE FEDERAL STREET THEATRE IN BOSTON

In 1792, attempts were made to found a theatre in Boston. A number of actors from England, together with two former members of the American Company, Harper and Wools, gained the support of some prominent citizens and started a subscription fund for the erection of a theatre. Much opposition was met with from other sections of the community, but a temporary theatre was built in 1792 called the New Exhibition Room. It was opened in August of that year with a mixed entertainment of music, ballets, and pantomimes performed by the Placide troupe. By the end of September, the management was sufficiently emboldened to present standard plays. But the law was invoked by the opposition; and on December 5, a sheriff interrupted the performance and, despite loud protest from the audience, arrested Harper, then acting as manager.

The theatre was permanently closed; but a good many citizens had enjoyed the performances and developed a taste for the drama. When Harper was released the following day, an association of interested parties was formed to save the theatre by a repeal of the law. This was achieved the following year. Plans for a first-class theatre were made; and Powell, one of the leading players, departed for England to recruit members for the company.

In 1794, the Federal Street Theatre was built and became firmly established, even surviving a disastrous fire in 1798. It continued to be the leading theatre in Boston for the next thirty years. Another playhouse, the Haymarket, was built in 1796; and for some years offered alternative fare, but it could not compete successfully with the Federal Street Theatre, and was closed in 1803.

WIGNELL AND REINAGLE'S COMPANY IN PHILADELPHIA

In Philadelphia, Wignell and Reinagle built a fine new theatre on Chestnut Street, based largely on the design of the Theatre Royal at Bath. The auditorium was semicircular. There were two tiers of boxes and a gallery. Wignell brought Milbourne, an excellent scene painter, from England who decorated the house and who produced stage settings better than anything that had been seen in America.

The new company included Mrs. Oldmixon, the celebrated singer from Covent Garden and the Haymarket, who played the leading roles in light opera, and who also appeared in straight plays. The other members too, were experienced players of the first rank. For many years, Wignell and Reinagle's company eclipsed the American Company in the standard of its productions.

THOMAS ABTHORPE COOPER (1776-1849)

Thomas Abthorpe Cooper, brought from England by Wignell, first appeared at the Park Theatre in New York as Hamlet, a role in which he achieved immediate success. The son of a surgeon, Cooper had been trained by Stephen Kemble, a member of the famous theatrical family. Cooper made his debut at Edinburgh in 1792. Three years later, at twenty, he played leading roles at Covent Garden, including Hamlet and Macbeth. He was a handsome young man with a fine, eloquent voice, and he had great dignity. Cooper was soon to become the most popular tragedian in America.

After quarreling with Wignell, Cooper joined Dunlap's American Company, at the new Park Theatre in New York. However, the inevitable quarrel with the management over salary led to his return to England, where he enjoyed a brilliant triumph playing Othello with George Frederick Cooke and Charles Kemble at Drury Lane. This acclaim hastened his return to America, where he was immediately re-engaged by Dunlap at a much increased salary.

After Dunlap's failure and bankruptcy in 1805, Cooper took over the management of the Park Theatre with Stephen Price, later employing Dunlap as stage manager.

Cooper appeared in most of the tragic Shakespearean leads; his Macbeth was particularly notable. He also appeared in such popular roles as Jaffier in *Venice Preserved*. He is renowned as one of the first and finest of the English actors to have settled permanently in America.

In 1815, the partnership with Price was dissolved, and Cooper took to touring the country. In the early years of the 19th century, the touring star—not always with adequate support—was to epitomize the theatre to the inhabitants of many of the smaller towns in America.

GEORGE FREDERICK COOKE (1756-1812)

In 1810, the brilliant though erratic George Frederick Cooke came to the Park Theatre in New York to spend the last two years of his life in America. Cooke was a powerful actor, generally playing villainous parts. After many years of touring the provinces in England, Cooke came in 1786 to play with Mrs. Siddons and John Kemble at Covent Garden. He gained immediate acclaim in the role of Richard III and remained at Covent Garden for 10 years. When with great passion he

CHESTNUT STREET THEATRE   Modelled after the Theatre
Royal at Bath which was opened on February 17, 1794, this lavish
structure was the leading house in America for a quarter of a century.
Its raked stage, deep apron, proscenium doors and proscenium boxes
—familiar features in English theatre—were then still unknown in
America. Because of its prominence in American Theatre history, the
playhouse was sometimes dubbed "Old Drury." The Chestnut Street
Theatre in Philadelphia assembled together a superior acting company, mostly recruited from England.

played the villainous roles of Richard III, Iago, Stukely, and Sir Pertinax MacSycophant, his lack of grace was no disability. His strong, dark appearance, long hooked nose, and powerfully deep voice enhanced his charcterizations. He was, however, an inveterate drinker and was utterly undependable.

Cooke enjoyed an enthusiastic reception at the Park Theatre during his first season there. However, during his second season—when his appearances became increasingly uncertain—his popularity dwindled. He toured America and by his powerful acting created a sensation in Boston, Philadelphia, Baltimore, and Providence. He died in 1811 and was buried in St. Paul's Church in New York. Edmund Kean, who admired Cooke's powerfully intuitive, although undisciplined, skill, erected a monument to his memory in the churchyard.

THE EARLY NINETEENTH CENTURY

The first half of the nineteenth century saw a spurt in the development of the theatre in America. The major capitals of the drama were New York, Philadelphia, Boston, and Charleston. New theatres were being built in these cities. The secondary circuit was Baltimore, Washington, Richmond, Savannah, and other towns along the Atlantic seaboard in which theatres had been erected. Later, even the frontier towns further west offered opportunities for touring companies. In order to draw full houses, the old stock theatres with their permanent companies and their repertory of standard plays found it necessary to support the performances of visiting players of great fame and reputation.

GEORGE FREDERICK COOKE (1756-1812)   Brought to America in 1810 by Cooper and Price, managers of the Park Theatre, George Frederick Cooke, a luminary of the London stage, took America by storm. His debut performance as Richard III, perhaps his greatest role, was played without the conventional hump back or crooked legs of the English monarch.

Generally, the plays were familiar, and the audiences went to see vivid performances and new interpretations of well-known parts. New plays were infrequent; few were of lasting merit. It was a period of great acting, and of great partisanship among the audience. It was not the play which was discussed by theatregoers, but the performance of one actor as compared with that of another.

At this time, the theatres in England were being rebuilt to house vast audiences, and were becoming increasingly difficult to fill. An American tour was looked upon by an English actor as a means of adding to his reputation, and as a happy relief from the search for a new vehicle at home. But in time, similar tendencies overtook the American theatre, and the English stars were not always successful in filling American theatres either.

AMERICA'S FIRST ACTING FAMILIES

A number of English actors settled permanently in America. Some of these actors founded families of players. Such a one was Junius Brutus Booth (1796-1852), whose successful appearance at the newly rebuilt Park Theatre in New York in 1821 in the role of Richard III led to a long and popular career in America. His three sons—Edwin Thomas (1833-1893) eventually to become America's greatest tragedian of the age; Junius Brutus, Jr., (1821-1883), a popular supporting player and manager; and John Wilkes (1839-1865), later to achieve notoriety as the assassinator of Lincoln at a performance of *Our American Cousin* at Ford's Theatre on April 14, 1865—carried on their father's acting tradition through the middle of the century.

Another acting family was established in America by William Warren (1767-1832) who joined Wignell's Philadelphia company in 1796. After the death of Wignell in 1803, Warren became co-manager with William B. Wood (1779-1861) of the Chestnut Street Theatre in Philadelphia. Warren was noted for his portrayals of older men. He and Wood strengthened their company by recruiting such fine actors as Edwin Forrest, William Twaits, and Joseph Jefferson. Warren and Wood were in control of no less than four theatres in Philadelphia, Baltimore, Alexandria, and Washington. Having been thrice married, Warren contributed six children to the theatre. His daughters married actors or managers, and his son William achieved a most respected reputation as an actor.

Another acting family to be established was that of the Wallacks. James William Wallack (1791-1864) was recruited from England for the Park Theatre, making his debut in Macbeth in 1818. His brother, Henry John (1790-1870), made his debut in America the following year. They were to become two of America's leading actor-managers. James's son, Lester, and various nephews and nieces continued to keep the Wallack name prominent in the theatre for the rest of the century.

JUNIUS BRUTUS BOOTH (1796-1852)
The founder of the famous American acting family is seen here as Sir Giles Overreach in Massinger's "A New Way to Pay Old Debts." Failing to outshine Edmund Kean, Booth emigrated to the United States and opened as Richard III at the Park Theatre in 1821.

EXPANSION OF THE THEATRE IN AMERICA

As the country expanded, theatrical companies began to explore hitherto untried territories. Luke Usher and Noah M. Ludlow went up the Allegheny River to Pittsburgh and established a theatre there. They then pushed on to Frankfort on the Ohio River, traveling partly by wagon and partly by boat. Ludlow's company continued down the Mississippi to Nashville and Cincinnati, and eventually founded the first English-speaking theatre in New Orleans, where already a French theatre was giving performances of Racine, Molière, and Beaumarchais. An excellent actor himself, Ludlow traveled a great deal, and was often the first actor to perform in certain towns of the South and the West. Other theatres were founded in Alabama and St. Louis.

American actors were also beginning to achieve star status. John Howard Payne (1791-1852), who was to make his name as playwright and composer as well as actor, and James Henry Hackett (1800-1871) both achieved sufficient reputation to enable them to play leading roles in England.

THEATRE FIRES

During this period, when some of the leading playhouses were inexplicably burned to the ground, the theatre suffered reverses. In 1798, the Federal Street Theatre in Boston was seriously damaged by fire and had to be rebuilt. At Richmond in 1811, during a play produced by the Placide Company, the scenery caught fire and the blaze spread to the auditorium. Though it was the ensuing panic which was largely responsible for the deaths of seventy-one members of the audience, the reaction of the Richmond authorities was to prohibit stage plays for four years. The news of the Richmond fire spread throughout the country, and must have had a deleterious effect on the theatre by frightening away some of the audiences.

In 1820, on the night of May 24, the Park Theatre, long the most fashionable and popular of the several theatres now established in

New York, burned to the ground. Fortunately, the flames took their toll after the audience had left.

In April, 1820, the Chestnut Street Theatre in Philadelphia caught fire, and its scenery, costumes, properties, library, and new gas works which had introduced gas lighting to the theatre in 1816, were all severely damaged and had to be rebuilt. Forty years later, in 1856, this theatre was completely demolished by fire. In 1820, the theatre of Warren and Wood in Washington went up in smoke.

In spite of these setbacks, public interest in theatregoing continued, and new and enlarged theatres immediately sprang up on the sites of the smoldering ruins.

EDMUND KEAN (1787?-1833) IN AMERICA

In 1820, before the fire-damaged Park Theatre was rebuilt and when the company was temporarily established at the small Anthony Street Theatre, a most notable event occurred: the guest appearance of Drury Lane's leading star Edmund Kean. Up until then, George Frederick Cooke had been the greatest attraction to come from England. His brilliant but erratic performances were now completely eclipsed by the greatest actor of the day whose passionate style captivated all who saw him.

When Kean made his American debut in Richard III, he received a guarantee of £50 per performance plus a share of the profits. He also appeared in *Hamlet, Othello, The Merchant of Venice,* and Payne's *Brutus.* His short season was well attended by enthusiastic audiences. Kean was wont to build emotional effects by interpolating additional lines into the script of a play, a privilege commonly allowed leading players of those times.

Kean continued his triumphal tour in Philadelphia and Boston, met with great success, and then returned to New York. An ill-judged attempt at a return engagement in Boston as late in the season as May, was met by poor attendance. On the third night, seeing only about twenty in the audience, Kean walked out of the theatre and

IRA ALDRIDGE   *He is shown in the traditional costume of Othello.*

refused to play. This enraged the people of Boston; the newspapers gave Kean a bad press, and his reputation suffered as the news spread to other theatres. Although Kean courageously issued a public apology and tried to make good his relations with the townspeople, he was never forgiven or ever allowed to play in Boston again.

In 1825 Kean essayed another American tour, after his conduct in London—his frequent non-appearances, as well as his scandalous involvement with the wife of Alderman Cox—had turned his audiences there against him. His appearance at the Park Theatre on November 24 in *Richard III* was greeted with such abuse and showering of the stage with missiles that nothing of his performance could be heard. He refused to retire, however, and completed his performance entirely by miming. After another contrite public apology, Kean was allowed to give eight more performances in different roles, which to some extent helped him regain the favor of his audiences. But his attempt to play in Boston was completely frustrated by a mob which gathered outside the playhouse breaking the doors and windows of the theatre and causing the audience to riot. Kean managed to escape, and left the town immediately—in tears, it is said. The theatre was badly damaged, but no one was hurt.

IRA ALDRIDGE (1804-1867)

During Kean's first tour of America, he had as a valet a young Negro named Ira Aldridge, a native of Bel Air, Maryland, who was inspired by his employer to essay the stage. Aldridge traveled to England with Kean; and in 1826, Aldridge made a successful debut as Othello at the Royalty Theatre in London. Known as the African Roscius, he went on tour with a good company. At one time, Aldridge had Charles Kean as his Iago.

WILLIAM MACREADY (1793-1873) The celebrated English actor, whose feud with Edwin Forrest culminated in the fatal Astor Place Riot, is pictured here as Shylock, one of the roles which brought him fame during his American tours. A cerebral actor, whose manner differed markedly from Kean's passionate style of acting, Macready was one of a number of English actors imported to infuse excitement in the nascent American theatre. In 1849, his triumphant tours came to an ill-fated end when the Astor Place Riot brought him into disfavor.

The favorable reception accorded him as Othello led Aldridge to play Lear, Macbeth, and many other roles, including the West Indian slave, Merugo, in the comedy *The Padlock*. He eventually came to be regarded as one of the leading actors of his time. Aldridge settled in England, became naturalized, and extended his tours to the Continent, where he was even more popular. He played in Russia, and was very well liked in Germany, where he played in English while his supporting cast played in German. Aldridge continued acting in England and on the Continent until his death in 1867.

WILLIAM CHARLES MACREADY (1793-1873) IN AMERICA

When he appeared in America at the Park Theatre in October, 1826, William Charles Macready had already achieved enormous stature in England. Roles in which Macready was justifiably famous were Virginius, Macbeth, Lear, and Hamlet. Giving more time to rehearsals than was customary, his portrayals were consistently intelligent.

Macready restored the original Shakespeare texts, discarding the tamperings of Nahum Tate and others, which were universally accepted at that time. His further appearances in America in 1843, 1848, and 1849 terminated when he was caught up in a regrettable feud with Edwin Forrest which culminated in the Astor Place riot in New York.

THE SUPPORTING CASTS

When there was a "guest" performance, the supporting players were the members of the permanent theatre company. Many of these supporting actors had been recruits from the London stage; although sufficiently proficient, they must have suffered by comparison with the visiting star.

There was no question of ensemble playing. Rehearsals were perfunctory, and the entire success of the play's performance was de-

THE NEW PARK THEATRE   Opened in September, 1821,
*this house was built on the site of its predecessor which was destroyed
the previous year by fire. The new theatre still had proscenium doors,
but proscenium boxes were eliminated, and the stage apron was much
more shallow.*

pendent on the acting of the leading players. Actor rivaled actor to win the playgoer's allegiance. That individual stars reached great emotional heights moving the audience deeply is attested by the violent passions which split audiences into rival groups and made attendance at the theatre an occasion for bitter warfare.

EDWIN FORREST (1806-1872)

In November, 1820, Edwin Forrest, perhaps the finest American tragic actor of the 19th century, made his debut at the Walnut Street Theatre in Philadelphia, then the rival of the Chestnut Street Theatre. Success did not come easily to Forrest; and in his early days, he suffered much hardship. But his ambition carried him along, and he gradually matured his own style, influenced perhaps by Cooke and Cooper. Forrest also benefited from seeing Edmund Kean perform.

Forrest was a slow-moving, ponderous giant of a man with a magnificent voice which he used to good advantage. He gave an impression of immense strength subdued under a much admired dignity. His repose had been painstakingly acquired after flashes of fierce emotion accompanied by snorts, groans, and roaring had led critics in his early days to accuse him of ranting. But his performances were always remarkably effective, and sometimes reached the heights of greatness. In the physical aspects of the characters he portrayed, he was unequaled; it was in the spiritual and poetic aspects of certain roles that he was less convincing.

Forrest appeared successfully in the standard tragic roles of Othello, Lear, Macbeth, and Richelieu; but it was in his portrayal of Spartacus in *The Gladiator*—a play he inspired Montgomery Bird to write—that he achieved his greatest success.

Through his encouragement, several other Philadelphia writers began to write plays. These new dramatists included Richard Penn Smith, Robert T. Conrad, and G. H. Miles. John Augustus Stone was awarded a prize by Forrest for writing the best tragedy in five

EDWIN FORREST (1806–1870)   The leading native American tragic actor of the 19th century, Forrest was hailed for his powerful voice and form. In 1826, after a long and difficult apprenticeship, he was established as an actor of note. Although his repertory included the classical roles of the day, it was in native American drama that he excelled. Among his most popular portrayals were Spartacus in "The Gladiator," and the title role in "Metamora," characters particularly suited to Forrest's bombastic style.

WALNUT ST. THEATRE

N. E. CORNER OF NINTH AND WALNUT STREETS, PHIL'A.

LAST NIGHT BUT 1

OF MR.

EDWIN FORREST

Dr. Bird's Celebrated Tragedy, in 5 Acts, of THE

GLADIATOR!

SPARTACUS, - Mr. EDWIN FORREST.

PHASARIUS, ... MR. BARTON HILL
JULIA, ... MISS LILLIE

Thursday Evening, Nov'r 14th, 1867,

Overture—"Yelva," . . . . Reissiger

After will be performed the Celebrated Tragedy in 5 Acts, written by Dr. Bird for MR. FORREST, entitled

GLADIATOR

Spartacus, a Thracian,   Mr Edwin Forrest

Phasarius, his Brother	Barton Hill
Marcus Lucinius Crassus, Roman Proctor	Jas. Taylor
Lucius Gellius, a Consul	Aug. Pitou
Schropha, a Questor	M. Slevin
Jovius, a Centurion	W. H. Bailey
Baliatus Lentulus, a Capuan Lanista	G. W. Johnson
Bracchius a Roman Lanista	W. L. Street
Florus, Son to Lentulus	E. A. Emerson
Enomaus, a Gaul	D. E. Reiny
Crixus, a German	M. Neville
Child, Son to Spartacus	Mast. Reed
Julia, Niece to Crassus	Miss Lillie
Senona, Wife to Spartacus	Miss Alice Gray

Citizens, Soldiers, Gladiators, Slaves, Women, &c.

During the Evening the Orchestra, under the direction of Simon Hassler, will perform the following Programme—

March—"Eroica,"	.	Keller
Introduction and Waltzes—"Pesther,"	.	Lanner
Goethe's Poem—"The Erl King,"	.	Schubert
Operatic Selection—"Norma,"	.	Bellini

Friday, Shakspere's Sublime Tragedy in 5 Acts, of

HAMLET.

HAMLET, ... MR. EDWIN FORREST

SATURDAY NIGHT, Victor Hugo's Historical Drama of

LA TOUR DE NESI

And the Beautiful Drama of

WALLACE, THE HERO OF SCOTI

Business Manager and Treasurer
Stage Manager,
Musical Director.

SPARTACUS PLAYBILL "The Gladiator," a play written in 1831 especially for Forrest, was so well received that the actor made it a permanent part of his repertory, and selected it for his London debut in 1836 at the Drury Lane. The character of Spartacus, the rebel fighting overwhelming odds, made the role a particularly effective vehicle for this muscular actor.

acts in which the hero or principal character was an American. Forrest successfully performed this play for many years, although he subsequently commissioned Bird to rewrite it.

In 1836, Forrest visited London appearing as Spartacus. Although the *Times* noted his spirited acting, his reception was very mixed. On this first tour to England, Forrest also played Othello at Drury Lane, just after Macready had played the part at Covent Garden. Macready and Forrest had met in New York in 1826, when Macready played at the Park. Forrest was then playing at the large new Bowery Theatre which, although never to achieve the fashionable popularity of the Park, was nevertheless playing to large audiences. Forrest, then only twenty-one, played Mark Anthony in *Julius Caesar*. Macready's reaction was encouraging, although he remained doubtful of the young player's powers of self discipline, so necessary in a first-class actor.

Although the two actors met off stage with friendliness, the press tended to whip up a rivalry between them that neither desired. On his later tour of America in 1843, Macready renewed the acquaintanceship on friendly terms. He attended Forrest's Lear in Philadelphia, and felt that the performance, powerful in its rage, lacked grandeur and pathos. Although warm and charming under normal conditions, both actors displayed ungovernable tempers when upset.

THE FORREST-MACREADY FEUD AND THE ASTOR PLACE RIOT

When Forrest returned to tour Britain in 1846, he met with much opposition from the critics. It was then that the trouble between him and Macready really began. Forrest believed that Macready's influence with the press was responsible for his bad notices.

When Macready was playing Hamlet in Edinburgh, at one point he made some extravagant gesture with a handkerchief. A long sustained hiss emanated from the upper side box. Everyone turned to the source of the interruption, and recognized the somber dark figure of Edwin Forrest sitting motionless with arms folded. He glared at the audience, and then got up and left. Much was made of this by the press; and a few days later, Forrest justified himself by a statement that he sometimes applauded actors and had an equal right to hiss them.

In 1848, Macready set out on another American tour. Although successful in New York, he met opposition in Philadelphia where Forrest had fanned the flames with a denunciation of Macready's supposed intrigues with the press in London.

Macready returned to New York the following year. No sooner had he stepped out on stage at the Astor Place Opera House on May 7 to do Macbeth, then pandemonium broke loose. One section of the audience was obviously set on howling him off stage, while another group applauded him with cheers. Macready walked forward to address the audience, but was drowned out. Rotten eggs and other missiles were thrown at him. Determined to continue, Macready played out two acts in dumb show. The audience grew increasingly hostile, and chairs were flung from the gallery. At this, without showing either fear or bravado, Macready bowed to the audience, withdrew, and left the theatre.

That same evening, Forrest also played Macbeth at the Broadway Theatre, and was received with great enthusiasm.

Macready had contracted to play again three days later. Despite contrary advice, he decided to appear. This time, police were in the theatre to quell opposition, and the first three scenes were played through without any disturbance. But during the fourth scene, the police were obliged to close in on the rioters, and bundled a number of them out of the pit and onto the street. There the unruly were joined by others who had gathered in anticipation of trouble. The angry crowd snatched up loose paving stones and smashed the windows of the theatre; and soon missiles began to fall inside the theatre itself. The roar from the outside increased, and the players began to lose nerve. But Macready refused to give up, and the performance dragged on to its end, when he was cheered by his faithful followers among the much-depleted audience who were seeking shelter wherever they could.

THE ASTOR PLACE RIOT (1849)   The international feud between Macready and Forrest over Macready's alleged mistreatment of the American actor during his London appearance in 1845, culminated in the fatal Astor Place Riot, illustrated here by an engraving from the Illustrated London News, of June 2, 1849. Because of this incident, Forrest lost favor with the theatre aristocracy, but retained the loyalty of the masses who saw him as a champion against English tyranny.

The mob outside increased, and it began to storm the theatre. The police, sensing a sizable riot, had sent for the military, and soon, more than two hundred troops arrived at the theatre. Their presence, however, incensed the mob, now increased to many thousands more. Stones and brickbats flew, and the troops were ordered to fire above the heads of the crowd. In the noise and confusion, some of the soldiers misheard the order and fired into the mob. The crowd, believing the troops were using only blanks, pressed forward and received the full force of a second round of musket fire. Several men fell. Now another charge by the mob was met with further fire, causing many casualties. Only the appearance of two brass cannon loaded with grapeshot finally broke up the crowd.

Macready escaped from the mob by disguising himself and mingling with the remnants of the theatregoers as they left the playhouse. But he dared not return to his hotel, as he knew a crowd awaited him there; so he spent some hours at the house of a friend, and left New York for good in a covered phaeton at four in the morning.

Seventeen people had been killed in the riot and many others injured. At the inquest, the authorities were vindicated, although it was adjudgd that more police instead of military might have prevented loss of life.

As a result of this unhappy affair, Forrest lost many supporters among the thinking, sober citizens. Although he remained the idol of the masses, he experienced failure and bitterness in his later years. The rise of the young Edwin Booth, and the inevitable comparison of their performances to Forrest's detriment, clouded the last years of his life. He made his last appearance in Boston in 1872 in the role of Richelieu. He died the same year, ending his life as it had begun, in misery and penury.

CHARLOTTE CUSHMAN (1816-1876)

The first great actress to arise in America, Charlotte Cushman began her career in 1835 at the age of nineteen in Boston as Countess Almaviva in Mozart's opera *The Marriage of Figaro*. When she lost her fine contralto voice, she turned to the legitimate stage and appeared at the Bowery Theatre as Lady Macbeth. Her success was immediate; and she embarked on a long and brilliant career in America and England, playing opposite both Forrest and Macready.

A tall and commanding figure, Miss Cushman possessed a strong and definite style, imparting to her roles a grandeur which no one could resist. Her Lady Macbeth was unequaled in her time, but the sympathetic qualities of Queen Katherine in *Henry VIII* made it her

CHARLOTTE CUSHMAN (1816-1876)   The leading native American tragedienne, "Our Charlotte," as she was known to her partisans, first played Lady Macbeth, the role illustrated here, on September 12, 1836. Not until 1839, however, when she played Nancy Sykes in "Oliver Twist," was her potential recognized. Encouraged by Macready, who noted in his diary that she had "mind and sympathy," Miss Cushman made her London debut on February 13, 1845 as Lady Macbeth, which with Nancy Sykes and Meg Merrilies in "Guy Mannering," were parts to which she returned frequently in her long and distinguished career.

favorite role. Her third great characterization was her most popular, that of Meg Merrilees in Scott's *Guy Mannering*. In this role which she first created at the age of twenty-one, the imaginative power with which she portrayed romance, pathos, and grief rendered her performance moving beyond belief. Her power to stir audiences, to embrace their sympathy and to compel their applause, equaled at supreme moments that of the great tragic actors. Some critics wrote that she lacked femininity, perhaps because she also essayed male roles such as Romeo to her sister Susan's Juliet. She also played the part of Hamlet, Claude Melnotte in Bulwer-Lytton's *The Lady of Lyons*

"JUMP JIM CROW"   *Thomas D. Rice plays Jim Crow at the American Theatre on the Bowery, New York City in 1833. Play had a sensational run.*

FATHER OF AMERICAN MIN-STRELS   In 1828, while playing Ludlow and Smith's Southern Theatre in Louisville, Kentucky, Thomas D. Rice, an itinerant actor, created his famous "Jim Crow" routine with which he was permanently identified. The song-and-dance patter was allegedly inspired by an old Negro who sang, as he limped about his job currying horses, the refrain: "Turn about and wheel about/ An do jis so/ And ebery time I wheel about/ I jump Jim Crow." A curious dance step called "rocking de heel" was added. This routine caught the public's imagination and paved the way for the American minstrel show.

and—almost unimaginably—Cardinal Wolsey. In her last years, Miss Cushman acted only occasionally, devoting much of her time to very successful readings of Shakespeare.

THOMAS D. RICE (1808-1860)

The American Negro was first popularized on the stage by Thomas D. Rice. His act was first produced in Louisville, Kentucky as an interlude between the acts of a play. He appeared in the blackface part of Jim Crow, singing and dancing in the supposed manner of the Negro slave. This turn caught the fancy of the audience, and immediately Rice was in much demand all over the United States.

MECHANICS' HALL!

NO. 472 BROADWAY, BETWEEN GRAND AND BROOME STREETS.

OPEN EVERY NIGHT DURING THE WEEK

CHRISTY'S

G. N. CHRISTY, W. PORTER, E. P. CHRISTY, T. VAUGHN, J. RAYNOR, E. H. PIERCE.

MINSTRELS

ORGANIZED, 1842.

THE OLDEST ESTABLISHED COMPANY IN THE WORLD

The First to Harmonize Negro Melodies, and originators of the present popular style of Ethiopian Entertainments, whose success in this City during the past THREE YEARS, is without Precedent in the annals of Public Amusements in this Great Metropolis; convincing evidence of their Superior Merit and Attractiveness.

The Company,

UNDER THE DIRECTION AND MANAGEMENT OF E. P. CHRISTY,

WENESDAY EV'ING, Sept. 19, 1849,

PROGRAMME—PART I.

Medley Overture ....Full Band
Dinah's Wedding Day, from the Opera of Leonora ....Company
Come with me, my Dinah dear..................................E. P. Christy
Stop that knocking, introduced with Happy and Light, from the Bohemian Girl . Company
Julius's Bride...George Christy
Rosa Lee, or don't be foolish Joe................................E. P. Christy
    yrolean Solo, displaying a flexibility and volume of voice truly astonishing and
    hitherto unknown...Christian
Phantom Chorus, or the Darkey's Apparition, from La Sonnambula ....Company
Masquerade Waltz, with Street Organ and Automaton Imitations ....Company

PART II.

The Original Burlesque, entitled

VOYAGE MUSICAL

Commencing "Somewhere" and ending "When 'tis done;" comprising a variety of AIRS for the occasion. To give full effect to this most Stupendous Work,

The Celebrated and DISTIN-guished performers on the

SIX-HORNS

Will perform a grand POT POURRI &c.

For a Due appreciation of the above INCOMPREHENSIBLE MUSICAL COMBINATION, much and a little more is depending on the imagination of the audience.

After which, the Celebrated RONDO from the Finale of

"LINDA DI CHAMOUNI,"

Composed by MARETZEK, and sung by Mme. LABORDE, will be "Executed," by the

Prima Donna of the Troupe..M. Zorer
Musical Director & Conductor...Signor Johnsonio

ACCORDEON SOLO..H. DONNELLY
MISS LUCY LONG..GEORGE CHRISTY
ETHIOPIAN POLKA BURLESQUE..........................T. VAUGHN & GEORGE CHRISTY
HUNGRY-ARIAN DUET, with Echo, "Burlesque,"...............Christian & Zorer

G. N. CHRISTY, AS LUCY LONG.

POLKA, BY T. VAUGHN, & G.N.CHRISTY.

PART III. Representing the peculiar Characteristics of the Southern or Plantation Negroes
Characteristic Banjo Song ....E. Peirce
Banjo Duet..E. Peirce & T. Vaughn
That Good Old Coon, Quartette .... Vaughn, Raynor, Upson & George Christy
Sugar Cane Reel ....E. Peirce
Life by the Galley Fire ....E. P. Christy
The Skeeters do bite...Company
Burlesque Lecture on Mesmerism.............W. Porter & George Christy
Down in Carolina, introducing Specimens of Ethiopian
    Statuary..............................Geo. Christy and E. Pe

ADMISSION 25 CENTS.

Doors open at 7.   To commence at 8 o'clock precisely.

AN AFTERNOON CONCERT EVERY SATURDAY,

COMMENCING AT 3 O'CLOCK.

Herald Print.

MINSTREL PLAYBILL This is a program of one of the most famous blackface troupes, the Christy Minstrels, who are credited with having introduced the two-act minstrel show, thus providing a full evening's entertainment.

In Washington, on his benefit night, he appeared carrying a sack which he carefully placed on the stage while he went through his act. At the conclusion, he opened the sack and out rolled the four-year-old Joseph Jefferson, in a similar costume and makeup. To the great delight of the audience, Rice and the child prodigy proceeded to sing and dance together as a finale.

Rice's solo turn was so popular that he was often more highly paid than the leading player in the drama. Audiences at the Bowery Theatre adored him, and he appeared in several shows especially written to perpetuate the character he had created. His *Bone Squash* and *The Virginia Mummy* were perhaps the forerunners of the Negro minstrel shows which swept the United States and England in the 1840's.

THE MINSTREL SHOW

The first regular minstrel troupe consisting of a quartet led by Daniel Emmett, composer of *Dixie,* appeared on the stage in 1843. Wearing bright, gala costumes, with faces blacked with burnt cork, they performed with fiddle, banjo, and tambourine, telling jokes, singing songs, and ending with a dance and engaging promenade. Very soon, larger troupes were formed, among which The Kentucky Minstrels and The Original Christy Minstrels were the best known. Stephen Foster wrote many of his best loved songs for the latter.

The performances followed a basic pattern. The curtain rose on a semicircle of blackfaced players, with a single whitefaced man in the center, known as Mr. Interlocutor. Always dignified and correct, Mr. Interlocutor played the straight man, supplying the feed to the two end men, the chief comedians, who were known as Mr. Bones and Mr. Tambo. Quips and conundrums, jokes and wisecracks, interpolated with comic and sentimental songs by various members of the company, comprised the first part of the show, which concluded with a chorus and parade.

The second part of the performance was chiefly individual variety

LEW DOCKSTADER'S MINSTRELS *Here is one of the*

most famous 19th century companies of black-face comedians.

— dances, instrumental offerings, and songs — concluding with a "breakdown" in which all joined.

The show concluded with a burlesque or farce much in the nature of an afterpiece, winding up with a parade by all of the troupe.

The Minstrel Show brought to the stage the simple folk humor and catchphrase, the popular song and dance of the time. In the hands of expert performers it had much appeal, and never failed to attract an appreciative audience. Even in today's times, although in a form far removed from its original pattern, "The Black and White Minstrel Show" was popular on the London stage for four years, after great success on television.

"UNCLE TOM'S CABIN"

Rice also appeared in a dramatization of Harriet Beecher Stowe's *Uncle Tom's Cabin*. The immediate success of the book made its transposition to the stage inevitable, although Mrs. Stowe's religious beliefs forbade her from being connected in any way with the theatre. Within six months of the first appearance of the book, two versions of the novel were presented in the New York theatre, and the play soon swept the country. Touring companies soon brought to every little town the "Tom Show" as it was known in stage circles. It is claimed the play continuously performed without a break right up to the early 1930's.

Even in England, the popularity of *Uncle Tom's Cabin* was immense. In 1878, no fewer than five London theatres were presenting the drama concurrently.

The best-known version was that of George L. Aiken, who capitalized heavily on the sentimentality of the story, and used techniques borrowed from the minstrel shows. The staging of Eliza crossing the ice became a theatrical sensation. Large, fierce hounds were especially bred and trained to appear in the shows, and contributed much to the spectacle.

Many first-rate American actors received their apprenticeship in the theatre by joining one of the many Tom road companies.

Because of the lack of copyright laws, Mrs. Stowe failed to benefit from the immense sums taken in by these performances.

GROWTH OF THE AMERICAN THEATRE

After the middle of the 19th century, the theatre enjoyed a period of rapid growth, following the opening of new frontiers and the remarkable expansion of major cities. By 1850, New York was a city of half a million inhabitants and could support six theatres which presented legitimate drama: the Park, the Broadway, Burton's, the Bowery, the National, and Brougham's Lyceum, later known as Wallack's. In addition, several other houses — Barnum's American Museum, the Astor Place Opera House, Niblo's Garden, Castle Garden, and Tripler's—scheduled concerts, ballet, variety shows, and an occasional play.

The Gold Rush of 1849 established theatres on the Pacific Coast at San Francisco, Stockton, and Sacramento. During this era, the floating theatre, or showboat, was born.

SETTINGS AND LIGHTING

The theatres by this time were also much bigger; the Bowery, for instance, had a capacity of over nearly thirty-five hundred. In such large houses, the emphasis was on spectacle, and much greater attention was devoted to making the settings more effective and to achieving greater realism. The stage retreated somewhat behind the proscenium. Actors rarely used the forestage which gradually dwindled. Creating a stage picture and illusion became increasingly important. Actors no longer made their entrances and exits from open wings, but used doors and windows built in architectural unity with the setting.

By now, most theatres were using gas lighting, which through ease of control, allowed for diverse effects. The larger theatres, of course, required more light on the stage; this was achieved by placing gas battens at various positions over the stage which were concealed

"THE WORLD'S GREATEST HIT"   *Dramatizations of Harriet Beecher Stowe's famous novel, popular originally because of the anti-slavery sentiments expressed, were later produced as melodrama and pure spectacle. The famous escape scene, illustrated*

in this 19th century lithograph, typical of the sensational melodramas of the time, shows Eliza floating down the Ohio River pursued by bloodhounds. Henchmen of the arch-villains, Haley and Lawyer Marks, hover in the background.

DION BOUCICAULT (1822-1890)
The prolific actor-dramatist, Dion Bouci-
cault, who appeared in many of his own
plays, is seen here as Conn from "The
Shaughraun," one of the best of his Irish
plays, produced in 1874. Although he was
considered a "cold" actor, Boucicault
achieved considerable success with his
portrayals of Irish characters, types he
knew well from his own background.
His reputation rests principally on his
adaptation of "Rip Van Winkle," com-
missioned by Joseph Jefferson, and on his
serious treatment of the Negro in "The
Octoroon."

by borders. Burners were arranged like rungs of a ladder in the side wings. Footlights increased illumination. Flexible tubing and tempo- rary pieces of apparatus were moved to wherever extra lighting was required. The control of all the illumination was centered at the prompter's desk, where a number of handles could be manipulated to throw light on any part of the stage. A complete blackout could be achieved by moving one switch; by the same maneuver, every burner could be instantly relit.

In addition to gas lighting, limelight, perfected by Drummond in 1816, imparted a brilliant white light which was much used to create the effect of sunlight or moonlight shining through windows and doors. Limelight was also used for spotlighting and for following an actor about on the stage.

Thus, in the larger theatres, while the players had retreated be- hind the proscenium and were much farther from the audience than they had ever been, this disadvantage was somewhat offset by the much greater brilliance of lighting and its easy control. A necessary change of atmosphere could be more easily accomplished.

When the electric arc lamp made its appearance, it proved to be much more brilliant than the limelight; but the noise of its operation and the flickering which occasionally attended its functioning limited its use. The complete lighting of the stage had to await the perfection of the filament lamp. In 1879, Thomas Alva Edison personally supervised the installation of overhead stage lighting for Steele MacKaye at the Madison Square Theatre.

DION BOUCICAULT (1822-1890)

Having begun his career on the London stage, Dionysius Boucicault became one of the most important figures of the American theatre during the third quarter of the 19th century. He achieved an instant hit when his first play, *London Assurance,* opened in London at Covent Garden in 1841 with Charles Mathews, Madame Vestris, and William Warren. Boucicault was then only nineteen years old. His subsequent plays, although of no great literary merit, were very much in tune with the taste of the time, provided many good acting parts, and were very popular among the stars of his day.

Boucicault was born of Irish parents. He spent four years in France where he became acquainted with the French drama from which he translated and adapted many of his own versions.

Boucicault acted in many of his own plays, as did his putative second wife, Agnes Robertson, the adopted daughter of Charles Kean. They first came to America in 1853, and they appeared together with many of the leading companies. The first outstanding play he wrote in America was *Grimaldi, or the Life of an Actress,* produced in New Orleans in 1855, which satirized society's attitudes toward women taking up the stage as a career. He turned to domestic drama in *The Sidewalks of New York,* and to low life in *Ten Nights in a Bar Room.* But his most successful plays, *The Colleen Bawn, Arragh-na-Pogue,* and *The Shaughraun,* were aimed at America's large Irish immigrant population.

In 1859, Boucicault took over the management of New York's Burton's Theatre, renamed the Winter Garden. The opening play was his version of a French piece which, unbeknownst to him, was based on Dickens' *The Cricket on the Hearth*. When he discovered the original source, he rewrote the play under the title *Dot*. The same year he wrote *The Octoroon, or Life in Louisiana,* a strong treatment of the subject of slavery.

The pirating of plays was then very common, and Boucicault joined with his colleagues in petitioning for legal action to limit plagiarism.

Consistent with the tradition of the time, Boucicault's involvement with the theatre was total; he was a prolific writer, actor, producer and manager. He organized touring companies which spread his work throughout the country. He and his wife appeared with Laura Keene's company, where Miss Robertson achieved great popularity as Jeanie Deans in a dramatization of *The Heart of Midlothian*.

As an actor, Boucicault was best in comedy and character parts. As a producer, he introduced many ingenious stage effects. His plays were generally a mixture of domestic scenes, heightened with occasional melodramatic passages. These plays had great appeal.

JOSEPH JEFFERSON (1829-1905)

The son and grandson of actors of the same name, Joseph Jefferson was the most talented member of this acting family. Having made his stage debut in a minstrel show at the age of four, he was later to become one of the most outstanding figures of the American theatre.

After a difficult apprenticeship and years as a strolling player, in 1857 he joined Laura Keene's company and achieved distinction in roles such as Caleb Plummer in *Cricket on the Hearth* and Dr. Pangloss in *Heir-at-Law*.

He then joined Boucicault at the Winter Garden and appeared in Boucicault's *Dot,* creating the role of Caleb Plummer. Essentially a comedian, Jefferson was persuaded to attempt the more serious character role much against his own belief in his powers to sustain such parts. He insisted that he should appear in a farcical afterpiece in which he could display his talent for comedy. Much to his surprise, his success as Caleb Plummer on opening night made the farce an anticlimax, so it was immediately dropped.

Jefferson's most famous part with which he is always identified was Rip Van Winkle. He had his own version of the Washington Irving story, and he also appeared in Boucicault's version which he altered over the years to forge his own characterization.

Like his father, Jefferson was something of a painter, with an eye for visual effects. He built up his great part of Rip with a host of small details; and his acting of a long silent passage in the play was much enjoyed by the audience, and regarded by his fellow actors with great respect. He did not aspire to a wide range of parts, but he was also notable as Salem Scudder in *The Octoroon,* and as a less boorish Bob Acres alongside Mrs. John Drew's Mrs. Malaprop in *The Rivals.*

Jefferson succeeded Booth as President of the Players' Club in 1893, establishing his major status in his profession. He retired in 1904 after a long and brilliant stage career. His work typified the growing tendency toward naturalistic acting and greater realism in the theatre.

LAURA KEENE'S (?-1873) COMPANY

Born in England, Laura Keene became one of the leading actresses in America during the 19th century, playing at her best in light comedy roles.

In 1856, she opened her own theatre, becoming the first female theatre manager. It was under her direction that Tom Taylor's *Our American Cousin* was first produced in America, with E. A. Sothern (1826-1881) very successfully creating the character of Lord Dundreary. At rehearsals of the play, Sothern was disappointed in what he considered a very dull part, and at first could make little of it.

JOSEPH JEFFERSON III (1829-1905)
"I think I have played 'Rip Van Winkle'
2,500 times," Jefferson wrote to a friend
in 1881. Eulogized after his death in 1905
as "the one-part actor par excellence,"
Jefferson is seen as Rip Van Winkle, a
role he played intermittently for 40 years.

Jefferson, who was also in the play as Asa Trenchard, recalls that after playing a week or so, Sothern, in desperation, introduced some dramatic business—skipping about the stage, sneezing, stammering, and generally behaving extravagantly. To the surprise of the cast, the audience received this with delight, and by gradually building up the character, Sothern achieved a record run of five months in New York. It was this play that Laura Keene's company gave at Ford's Theatre, Washington, on the fateful night of April 14, 1865, when Lincoln, while watching the performance, was shot dead by John Wilkes Booth.

ACADEMY OF MUSIC

C. B. JEFFERSON • • • • • • • MANAGER.

Six Nights Only

COMMENCING

MONDAY, MAY 11, 1874.

MR. JOSEPH

JEFFERSON!

◄►— AS —◄►

RIP VAN

WINKLE

ACT I.

Rip Van Winkle, Mr. Joseph Jefferson

Derrick,	Mr. M. J. Jordan
Cockles,	Mr. W. J. Gilbert
Vedder,	Mr. R. Johnston
Stine,	Mr. S. Phillips
Clausen	Mr. R. Armond
Gretchen,	Miss Jennie Anderson
Little Meenie,	Miss Cohen
Little Hendrick	Master Julian Reed

ACT II.

Rip Van Winkle, Mr. Joseph Jefferson

Dwarf,	Master Julian
Hudson,	Mr. O. B. Jones

ACT III.

Rip Van Winkle, Mr. Joseph Jefferson

Derrick,	Mr. M. J. Jordan
Cockles,	Mr. W. J. Gilbert
Hendrick,	Mr. Charles Burke
S... b,	Mr. M. Lerone
...tchen,	Miss Jennie Anderson
...nie,	Miss Annie Moston
...hen,	Miss K. Johnston

RIP VAN WINKLE

MATINEE!

Saturday, at 2 o'clock.

"RIP VAN WINKLE" PLAYBILL   In 1859, Joseph Jefferson attempted a stage version of Washington Irving's tale. Here is a playbill of Jefferson's famous role dated fifteen years later.

LAURA KEENE (? -1873) One year after she settled in the country in 1855, Laura Keene, an English actress of some distinction, opened her New York Theatre on Bowery and Houston Street. She offered good classical and native dramatic fare, avoided the use of foreign stars, and developed a strong stock company.

JUNIUS BRUTUS BOOTH (1796-1852)

The Booths were, perhaps, the most important family in the American theatre for much of the 19th century. Junius Brutus Booth was the first member of his family to take to the stage. An erratic and temperamental disposition, with a hint of mental instability, drove him from his father's law office after he had received a sound classical education.

Junius joined a small stock theatre at Deptford, then a suburb of London, making his debut in 1813. Within a few years, he was playing leading roles. After touring the English provinces, he deputized for Edmund Kean as Sir Giles Overreach and was then invited to appear at Covent Garden as Richard III. At this time, Kean was at Drury Lane.

Although his style was similar to that of Kean—indeed one of the critics noted the resemblance as "surely one of nature's duplicates"—

Booth began to offer such serious competition that the Drury Lane management approached him with a contract at a much greater salary than Covent Garden was paying him. Accepting with great alacrity, Booth joined the rival house, and then found that he was playing Iago to Kean's Othello. To his further dismay, he was advised he would not be permitted to play any part that Kean performed. In high dudgeon he returned to Covent Garden where audiences received him badly, deeming he was part of a conspiracy against Kean. So Booth once again returned to touring the provinces.

In 1821, Junius came to America at the age of twenty-five, making his debut in Richmond, Virginia, as Richard III. His passionate, eloquent acting ensured him a popularity in America which was to last for thirty years or more, although his erratic behavior and the gradual increase in his bouts of heavy drinking clouded his later years.

Booth bought some farming land near Baltimore and moved a log cabin to this property. Here his large family were born and grew up in a completely free environment. Richard Booth, Junius's father, joined them from England to farm the land. Junius was a strict vegetarian on humanitarian grounds, and was intensely moved at the death of his pony Peacock, seeking for him a burial by clergy.

The eldest son, Junius Brutus, Jr. (1821-1883) acted with his father; but being of a reliable and settled temperament, he was attracted more to the management side, and followed a reputable career as producer and manager.

After the Gold Rush and the opening of the Pacific Coast, Junius Brutus, Jr., arranged in 1852 to take over management of one of the theatres in San Francisco, with his father and his brother Edwin, doing standard plays for a season. This proved financially successful, and encouraged them to move on to Sacramento where, however, they failed. On the long return journey, Junius fell ill while aboard a Mississippi steamer and died. He was buried in Baltimore.

Junius Brutus, Jr., continued in management at the small theatre in San Francisco where he presented burlesques and farces with his brother Edwin playing a host of small roles.

EDWIN BOOTH AS HAMLET   Member of a distinguished acting family, America's leading tragedian opened in "Hamlet" at the Winter Garden in New York on November 26, 1865. The production ran for 100 performances the longest run of any Shakespearean play up to that time. Booth developed his great talent playing minor roles while touring throughout the West with his father, Junius Brutus Booth.

EDWIN BOOTH (1833-1893)

Edwin Booth, named after Edwin Forrest with whom his father Junius had acted and who was a great friend, displayed a close and sympathetic attachment to his father. Often when Junius was called upon to tour, he would take Edwin with him. As the boy grew up, he acquired a knowledge of the theatre which stood him in better stead than his irregular attendance at school.

Edwin served as dresser to his father, and eventually appeared in small parts in the plays in which his father was performing. He remained with his father until his death, all the while acquiring a mastery of acting technique.

Under his brother's management, he first played Petruchio, and then Richard III. The favorable reception he received moved Junius to cast him in other great Shakespearean parts. Shylock and Macbeth and Hamlet followed. All met with great success.

In 1854, Edwin undertook a tour of Australia under the management of Laura Keene, and achieved a great success with Shylock in Sydney. However, his reception in Melbourne was not as good, and he decided to part company with the management and took ship for San Francisco. On the way back, he stopped at Honolulu for two months, playing *Richard III* and *The Lady of Lyons*. In San Francisco, Edwin successfully played Benedick in *Much Ado About Nothing* at the Metropolitan Theatre; and in 1856, he played Lear for the first time.

By now he had sufficient experience and reputation to return to the East. After completing successful tours of Baltimore, Washington, Richmond, New Orleans, Mobile and Memphis, Edwin Booth scored brilliant triumphs in Boston and New York.

Edwin was described at this time as a young man of extraordinary personal grace with a magnetic personality, full of the fire of youthful genius, vigorous but without the overpowering robustness of Forrest, and the most sensitive and imaginative interpreter of Shakespeare that had yet appeared in America. He was of slight build, with an extremely mobile and expressive face, and luminous dark eyes. His voice had great beauty; his elocutionary skill was remarkable; and he was able to impart psychological depths to the characters he played.

In contrast to Forrest who built up his roles by external effects and techniques, Edwin Booth penetrated below the surface of the character. Using his intelligence and matchless theatrical skill, Booth brought new light to the familiar tragedies of Shakespeare. He also received critical applause for his melodramatic acting in such parts as Overreach and Richelieu, probably because he brought new insights to the interpretation of these familiar roles.

In 1861, when America was torn by the strife of war, theatres continued to operate in America, but under stress of having to select offerings that would provide relaxation for an anxious audience. There was also a shortage of actors, since many had flocked to the colors. During that year, Booth was on tour in England. In 1862, he returned to New York.

In March of the same year, his brother John Wilkes appeared at Wallack's old theatre playing Richard III, Hamlet, and Macbeth. Inevitably, the critics made comparisons between John, his father Junius, and his brother Edwin. They pronounced John's Richard a notable performance.

In 1863, Edwin entered management at the Winter Garden Theatre, where he produced such pieces as *East Lynne,* a successful dramatization of the popular novel starring Lucille Westen, and *The Ticket of Leave Man,* a new play by Tom Taylor in which Mr. and Mrs. W. J. Florence were outstanding.

On November 25, 1864, an event occurred which would have given the elder Booth deep satisfaction: his three sons played in a benefit performance of *Julius Caesar* to commemorate the tercentenary of Shakespeare by the erection of a memorial statue in Central Park. Junius Brutus, Jr., played Cassius, Edwin played Brutus, and John Wilkes played Mark Anthony. This was the only occasion on which the three Booths appeared together.

BOOTH PLAYBILL   *Built by Edwin Booth and Richard A. Robertson a Boston businessman at a cost of $1,000,000, Booth's lavish theatre opened on February 3, 1869, with an opulent production of "Romeo and Juliet," a production in which Booth and Mary McVicker, later his second wife, starred. Important technical innovations in theatre design were the presence of a loft of flies above the stage in which to house scenery for quick changes, as well as stage elevators to lower entire box sets to the basement.*

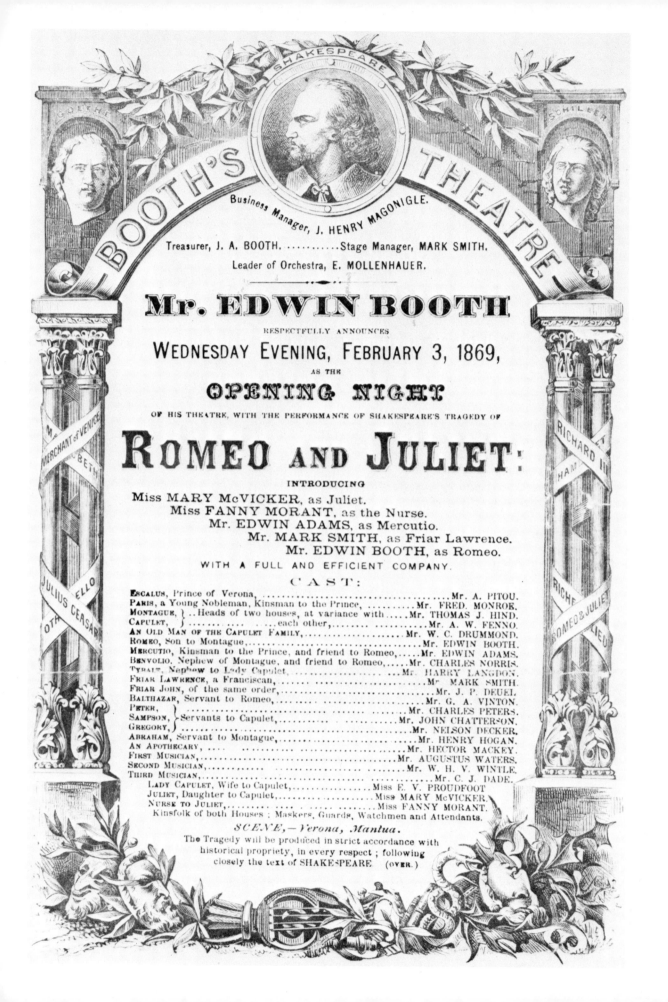

BOOTH'S THEATRE

Business Manager, J. HENRY MAGONIGLE.

Treasurer, J. A. BOOTH. ....Stage Manager, MARK SMITH.

Leader of Orchestra, E. MOLLENHAUER.

Mr. EDWIN BOOTH

RESPECTFULLY ANNOUNCES

WEDNESDAY EVENING, FEBRUARY 3, 1869,

AS THE

OPENING NIGHT

OF HIS THEATRE, WITH THE PERFORMANCE OF SHAKESPEARE'S TRAGEDY OF

ROMEO AND JULIET:

INTRODUCING

Miss MARY McVICKER, as Juliet.

Miss FANNY MORANT, as the Nurse.

Mr. EDWIN ADAMS, as Mercutio.

Mr. MARK SMITH, as Friar Lawrence.

Mr. EDWIN BOOTH, as Romeo.

WITH A FULL AND EFFICIENT COMPANY.

CAST:

ESCALUS, Prince of Verona, ...Mr. A. PITOU.
PARIS, a Young Nobleman, Kinsman to the Prince, ...Mr. FRED. MONROE.
MONTAGUE, } ..Heads of two houses, at variance with.....Mr. THOMAS J. HIND.
CAPULET, } ....each other,........ ....Mr. A. W. FENNO.
AN OLD MAN OF THE CAPULET FAMILY,.....................Mr. W. C. DRUMMOND.
ROMEO, Son to Montague,..Mr. EDWIN BOOTH.
MERCUTIO, Kinsman to the Prince, and friend to Romeo,.....Mr. EDWIN ADAMS.
BENVOLIO, Nephew of Montague, and friend to Romeo,.....Mr. CHARLES NORRIS.
TYBALT, Nephew to Lady Capulet, ...Mr. HARRY LANGDON.
FRIAR LAWRENCE, a Franciscan,........................Mr. MARK SMITH.
FRIAR JOHN, of the same order,.............................Mr. J. P. DEUEL.
BALTHAZAR, Servant to Romeo,..............................Mr. G. A. VINTON.
PETER, } ....Mr. CHARLES PETERS.
SAMPSON, }Servants to Capulet,.......................Mr. JOHN CHATTERSON.
GREGORY, } ....Mr. NELSON DECKER.
ABRAHAM, Servant to Montague,...........................Mr. HENRY HOGAN.
AN APOTHECARY, ...Mr. HECTOR MACKEY.
FIRST MUSICIAN,..Mr. AUGUSTUS WATERS.
SECOND MUSICIAN,...Mr. W. H. V. WINTLE.
THIRD MUSICIAN,..Mr. C. J. DADE.
LADY CAPULET, Wife to Capulet,..................Miss E. V. PROUDFOOT.
JULIET, Daughter to Capulet,.......................Miss MARY McVICKER.
NURSE TO JULIET,.......... ....Miss FANNY MORANT.
Kinsfolk of both Houses ; Maskers, Guards, Watchmen and Attendants.

SCENE,—Verona, Mantua.

The Tragedy will be produced in strict accordance with
historical propriety, in every respect ; following
closely the text of SHAKESPEARE. (OVER.)

"SALVATION NELL"   *Minnie Maddern Fiske (1865-1932), shown here in Edward Sheldon's first successful drama of city low-life, starred in the realistic plays of the early 20th century. An Ibsenite, she nurtured realism in the theatre in the face of puritanical opposition. Miss Fiske was among the first American actresses to look at life realistically, and to consider the new science of psychology for guidance in acting. In Sheldon's "Salvation Nell," a contemporary account noted, "as the scrub woman in the barroom, she sat holding her drunken lover's head in her lap for fully ten minutes without a word. . .(till) one became absorbed in the pathos of that dumb, sitting figure."*

MAUDE ADAMS (1872-1953)   From 1892 to 1896, under the Frohman aegis, Maude Adams was John Drew's leading lady. But it was not until the 1905 premiere of "Peter Pan," the most popular of Barrie's fantasies, that the actress was elevated to stardom. Her long association with the Scottish playwright, with whom she was identified as the "Barrie heroine," afforded the elfin actress some of her major roles. These included Phoebe in "Quality Street," Maggie in "What Every Woman Knows," and Babbie in "The Little Minister," perhaps her most famous role.

The next evening, Edwin played Hamlet in a production which ran for one hundred nights, the longest run ever achieved in America in the 19th century. Edwin reached new heights in this role; the critics were universal in their praise, proclaiming the performance as one of the noblest pieces of dramatic art ever seen, and acclaimed Edwin as an actor who had no living equal.

On the fateful night of April 14, 1865, John Wilkes Booth walked casually through the stage door of Ford's Theatre in Washington where he was well known, having played there. He proceeded through the wings behind the stage where Laura Keene's company was giving *Our American Cousin;* went through the pass door to the auditorium; slipped quietly into the first box; and at 10:22 p.m., drew a revolver, aimed it at President Lincoln and shot him point blank in the back of the head. He then climbed over the front of the box, and jumped onto the stage. In so doing, he misjudged the jutting cornice and broke his leg. He landed on his feet, however, on the stage. He could not resist declaiming from Julius Caesar, "Liberty! Freedom! Tyranny is dead." John Wilkes then ran through the wings and out of the theatre, and disappeared into the night.

By mutual agreement, the theatres of New York remained closed for two weeks in mourning. Edwin Booth, intensely shocked on learning of his brother's unbelievable deed, immediately went into retirement from the stage. On April 26, the body of John Wilkes Booth was found in a barn in Virginia. He had died of a shot through the head, probably self-inflicted. Edwin's tortured thoughts must have revolved about the strain of mental instability which had manifested itself in both his father and his grandfather, and now was so patent in the actions of his younger brother.

For months Edwin lived in a private hell, which was finally interrupted when a faithful following persuaded him to return to the stage early in 1866. He opened at the Winter Garden in *Hamlet,* then performed in *Ruy Blas,* followed by a long run in *Richelieu.*

The next years saw many lavish and beautiful productions. Booth was acknowledged by all as the leading actor in America. When the

Winter Garden burned down in 1868, he built his own theatre on Sixth Avenue. Booth's Theatre was large and impressive and equipped with the last word in stage equipment: hydraulic lifts for moving entire settings from below, and a great stage loft for flying solid backdrops and other scenery. There was no forestage and no proscenium doors, and the side boxes were situated in the auditorium.

Unfortunately, Edwin Booth's talent lay in acting and not in managing. He failed financially as a manager, gave up his theatre, and in 1873 embarked on a long series of successful road tours throughout America. He performed in England from 1880 to 1882, and also in Germany with continued success. He appeared at the Lyceum in London with Henry Irving; and by agreement, they alternated the parts of Othello and Iago. Many critics considered his characterization of Iago, in which he revealed depths of a subtle, malignant evil beneath the outward show of friendliness, his finest performance.

Upon his death, Edwin Booth bequeathed his residence in Gramercy Park, New York City, to the Players' Club.

NEW THEATRICAL DEVELOPMENTS FROM 1870 TO 1900

The last thirty years of the 19th century witnessed many new developments in the theatre. A new audience was created by the increase in travel due to the building of new railways, continued improvement in education, the growth of the cities, immigration, and the doubling of the total population of the country. It was an era in which entertainment was paramount; and to provide it in the theatre, a new group rose to importance.

The old style actor-manager who played the chief roles and also governed his company both in a metropolitan theatre and on tour was generally unable to cope with the greatly increased financial risk incurred in running the new, large theatres and organizing the extensive touring companies. There was now a vast amount of money to be gained or lost in theatrical enterprises, and the business manager emerged as an important figure. He treated the stage as one would

any other business enterprise; he was concerned with capital invest-
ment, running costs, and returns. He chose his plays with great care,
used the emergent arts of publicity to advertise them, and created the
star system. The most successful business managers controlled several
theatres; organized circuits for touring their productions; contracted
prominent actors exclusively to their own organizations; and employed playwrights to write for them. Their organizations serviced the
whole country, and some spread their dominion to England, taking
over the management of some London theatres.

REALISM ON THE AMERICAN STAGE

While the great actors of England and Europe were still frequently
seen in America, it was the native product who developed chiefly in
this period. New plays by American writers were being performed by
American actors whose character and ability were uniquely suited to
the tempo and climate of the age. Audiences were now responding to
plays dealing with themes and experiences reflecting the richness and
variety of American life. The development of realism in the theatre,
made possible by new technical machinery and lighting, required a
change in acting style if the actor was to hold "a mirror up to nature."
Many of the new plays were domestic dramas, sometimes rather
melodramatic, but often the action would involve great events of a
nationwide significance.

The striving for realism did not precipitate an immediate or complete overthrow of the long tradition of stage technique which actors
had assiduously cultivated over the years. Theatricality persisted, and
a complete synthesis of stage realism was not achieved until the 20th
century. Playwrights too, although drawing their themes from life,
were still dependent on the soliloquy or the stage aside directed to the
audience and other traditional methods of ensuring continuity of plot.

*ITALIAN OTHELLO   Tommaso Salvini (1829-1916), Italian tragedian, celebrated
for his interpretation of "Othello," first visited America in 1880. Although he played
Shakespeare in his native tongue, the actor astounded American audiences with his
emotional range. As a guest artist in 1886, he again played Othello, opposite Edwin
Booth's Iago.*

ELEONORA DUSE (1858-1924)   Born to a family of poor Italian strolling players, Eleonora Duse first appeared on stage at the age of four, and played Juliet at fourteen. She became a legend in her own lifetime. Playing "Camille" before an American audience in 1893, during her first tour of the country, she scored one of her greatest triumphs. Noted for its simplicity and naturalism, her unique interpretation of this role became the hallmark of her art. On subsequent visits to America, she presented her repertory of D'Annunzio plays: "La Gioconda," "La Città Morta," and "Francesca da Rimini," elevating through her genius the florid works of the celebrated poet to art. Duse left the theatre in 1914 only to be forced out of retirement by straitened circumstances. She died in Pittsburgh in 1924 on her last tour of America.

America saw many fine actors from Europe during this period: Tommaso Salvini and Adelaide Ristori from Italy; Gabrielle-Charlotte Réjane, Sarah Bernhardt, and Coquelin from Paris; Henry Irving, Ellen Terry, William and Madge Kendall, and many others from the London stage—all welcomed with the warmth traditionally shown distinguished visitors. America's own leading players undoubtedly gained much from witnessing the superb technique of these overseas luminaries, but the portrayals basically followed traditional acting styles.

THE "ROYAL FAMILY OF BROADWAY"

Mrs. John Drew (1820-1897), for over thirty years an indefatigable manageress of the Arch Street Theatre in Philadelphia, was a fine actress in her own right. She started in the theatre as a young child, and was later noted for her performances as Lady Macbeth and Mrs. Malaprop. Her children were all involved in acting and writing for the theatre. Her son, John Drew (1853-1927), became one of the best romantic actors of light comedy, particularly excelling as Major Pendennis in a dramatization of Thackeray's novel, and in Pinero's *Trelawney of the Wells.*

When her daughter, Georgiana, married Maurice Barrymore, the "Royal Family of Broadway" was founded. Their three gifted children—Lionel, Ethel, and John—were each to make his own contribution to the theatre in the 20th century.

SARAH BERNHARDT (1844-1923) The "Divine Sarah" toured America nine times between 1880 and 1917. So many of her later engagements were "farewell tours," that the use of the term caused considerable merriment in theatrical circles. Intermittently associated with the Comédie Française from her 1862 debut until her permanent break in 1880, Bernhardt built a repertory of heroines—Phèdre, Camille, La Tosca, Fedora, Theodora, and Adrienne Lecouvreur—which dazzled American audiences. She is seen here in the character of Theodora.

JOHN DREW (1853-1927)   *This distinguished actor, member of the noted family of performers, excelled in playing sophisticated comedy. After years of barnstorming and playing support to Edwin Booth and Fanny Davenport, he joined Augustin Daly's Company in 1879, where with Ada Rehan as his leading lady, he became part of one of the most brilliant comedy teams in American theatre history.*

OTHER LEADING PERFORMERS

Among other leading actors of the time were Otis Skinner (1858-1942), who appeared in many Shakespearean roles, but is also noted for his later successes in contemporary plays. Booth Tarkington wrote *Your Humble Servant* and *Mr. Antonio* for him.

Edwin Hugh Sothern (1859-1933) was the talented son of E. A. Sothern, whose name is always associated with the role of Lord Dundreary. Although Edward played much in Shakespeare along with Julia Marlowe, and was also successful in tragedy, his skills were better suited to light comedy and romance and he was immensely popular as a romantic hero in *The Prisoner of Zenda*.

Richard Mansfield (1854-1907) made his reputation in roles such as Cyrano de Bergerac and Monsieur Beaucaire, and in Clyde Fitch's *Beau Brummell*, a play especially written for him. He appeared as Peer Gynt in the first English production of Ibsen's play and also first introduced the plays of Bernard Shaw to America, appearing

JOHN BARRYMORE (1882-1942)   *On November 20, 1922, Arthur Hopkins and Robert Edmund Jones presented John Barrymore, a young actor from a notable acting family in the great Shakespearean tragedy. There had been no great American Hamlet since Edwin Booth. The performance broke Edwin Booth's record of 100 consecutive performances in New York, and then repeated that success in London. John Barrymore had been established as one of the leading actors of the English-speaking stage.*

OTIS SKINNER (1858-1942) *Although he played a wide variety of roles in his long and distinguished career, the versatile actor is remembered for his performance as Hajj, in the oriental fantasy "Kismet," produced in 1911. The play had a two-year run, and was revived frequently on tour.*

RICHARD MANSFIELD (1854-1907) *This British-born actor is chiefly remembered for his Shakespearean performances, and for introducing G. B. Shaw to American audiences. Here he is seen as Dick Dudgeon in Shaw's "The Devil's Disciple," a play given its premiere performance on October 4, 1897.*

with success in *Arms and the Man* and *The Devil's Disciple*.

Henry Miller (1860-1926) appeared in many contemporary plays in the early twentieth century. In 1916, he opened his own theatre in New York.

James O'Neill, the father of one of America's greatest dramatists of the twentieth century, Eugene O'Neill, was well known as a romantic actor.

Of the many actresses, both foreign and native, to become prominent on the American stage are: Helen Modjeska (1840-1909), Annie Russell (1864-1936), Lillian Russell (1861-1922), Ada Rehan (1860-1916), Julia Marlowe (1866-1950) Maude Adams (1872-1953), Fanny Davenport (1850-1898) and Minnie Fiske (1865-1932). Many of them played leading roles well into the 20th century.

JULIA MARLOWE (1866-1950) Seen here as "Barbara Frietchie," the title role of Clyde Fitch's historical play, Miss Marlowe's portrayal of 1899 catapulted her to fame. Identified primarily with Shakespearean repertory, she and her actor-husband, E. H. Sothern, barnstormed throughout the country for much of their later years.

"THE AUTOCRAT OF THE STAGE"   Theatre manager, producer, dramatist and critic, Augustin Daly (1839-1899) was a titan in the age of melodrama. He wrote "Under the Gaslight" in 1867, a sensational drama which nevertheless revealed touches of realism.

AUGUSTIN DALY (1839-1899)

The new trends in the American theatre were well exemplified in the presentations of Augustin Daly, one of the most successful managers of the period. His somewhat lurid melodrama, *Under the Gaslight,* produced at the New York Theatre in 1867, had a sensational climax in which the chief character, bound hand and foot to a railway line in the path of a thundering locomotive, is rescued just in time by the heroine—a situation much employed some years later in the first movies. For this production, Daly devised many ingenious stage effects which he was able to patent.

Daly made many adaptations from successful English novels by Wilkie Collins, Anthony Trollope, and Florence Marryat; from the French writers, Sardou, Dumas, Meilhac, and Halevy; and from the contemporary German writings of Gustav von Moser and Julius Rosen. But he also encouraged Americans to write for the stage, including Bronson Howard, who became one of the most important dramatists of the period.

Daly operated one or more theatres in New York and organized touring companies with steady success. In 1879, he took over Wood's Museum and remodelled and renamed it Daly's Theatre. Here he

THE FOYER OF THE DALY'S THEATRE   *When Augustin Daly leased the Fifth Avenue Theatre in 1869 from James Fisk, he launched one of the most notable director-manager careers in the history of the American theatre. With unsparing energy he refurbished the house, and assembled an acting company which he managed with autocratic zeal. The theatre was destroyed by fire on New Year's Day, 1873. But Daly immediately leased the dilapidated New York Theatre and remodelled it within three short weeks, dubbing it Daly's Broadway Theatre. This print reveals the meticulous attention to detail characteristic of the great régiseur.*

*LAST-MINUTE RESCUE   This illustration of a scene from
Augustin Daly's "Under the Gaslight," is typical of the melodrama*

rampant in the very early 20th century. This kind of incident drew audiences.

gathered some of the most brilliant actors of the time, including James Lewis, Mrs. Gilbert, Clara Morris, Fanny Davenport, Ada Rehan, and John Drew. He concentrated on comedy, including much of Shakespeare, with occasional farces and melodramas.

In 1884, Daly took a company to England and the Continent. He received such a warm reception in London that he decided to establish himself there; and in 1893, with George Edwardes, opened his own theatre, known as Daly's.

Some of his outstanding successes were *Frou-Frou* from Meilhac and Halevy, and *Our Boys* with Maurice Barrymore and Fanny Davenport. Daly also successfully presented some of Shakespeare's comedies, as well as Colley Cibber's *She Would and She Would Not*. He also produced Garrick's expurgated version of Wycherley's *The Country Wife* in which Ada Rehan and John Drew were very popular. Ada Rehan won considerable acclaim in Daly's Shakespearean productions.

Daly exercised close control over his productions, setting a high standard of presentation, and eliciting skillful, elegant acting. He occasionally produced native works, such as Bronson Howard's satirical comedy *Saratoga,* and his own play *Horizon,* a frontier drama of great realism.

LESTER WALLACK (1820-1888)

Lester Wallack, the son of James William Wallack, the English actor, operated a fine stock company for over twenty years, taking roles in and producing brilliant comedies and romantic pieces. He employed some of the finest actors, including E. L. Davenport, Charles and Rose Coghlan, Maurice Barrymore, John Brougham, Steele MacKaye, and H. J. Montague. His long career in the theatre was crowned by a magnificent production of *Hamlet* with Edwin Booth and Helen Modjeska as Hamlet and Ophelia, John Gilbert as Polonius, Joseph Jefferson and W. J. Florence as the gravediggers, and many other notable stars walking on stage in small parts and as supers.

LESTER WALLACK (1820-1888) A *member of the noted Wallack theatre family, John Johnstone Lester Wallack was an actor, stage manager, producer, and playwright. He successfully managed the Wallack Theatre for many years, staging many English plays and acting in many of his productions. He wrote, produced and acted in a dramatization of a novel* ROSEDALE *(1863).*

STEELE MACKAYE (?-1894)

Steele MacKaye, an erratic but versatile and inventive man, was an actor-manager-writer in the classic tradition. He became interested in acting when he was in Paris, where he had gone to study painting. In Paris, he prepared for the stage under François Delsarte and Régnier of the Comédie Francaise.

His first venture into management at the St. James Theatre, New York, in 1872, ended in failure. He then returned to France where he played Hamlet in French in Paris, and he also played the part in London. In 1874, he returned once again to America where he devoted himself for some years to writing plays, inventing new stage effects and machinery, occasional acting or stage managing, and giving lectures.

In 1879, he obtained control of the Madison Square Theatre and rebuilt the stage with elevators and overhead electrical lighting. Steele also remodeled the auditorium, installing folding seats and a modern system of ventilation. The following year, he opened the theatre with his own play *Hazel Kirke,* a domestic drama realistically presented. It achieved the distinction of a record run of 486 performances. A second cast took the play on tour at the same time.

In 1885, Steele joined Daniel Frohman and installed new equip-

BRONSON HOWARD (1842-1908)
Primarily a writer of comedy and farce,
Howard nevertheless holds an important
place in the history of the American
theatre as one of the first playwrights to
use native material effectively. His "Sara-
toga" (1870) had a long run in New
York, and was also produced in London
under the title of "Brighton." Written in
a more serious vein, "Young Mrs. Win-
throp" (1882) is probably Howard's most
important work.

ment in the Lyceum Theatre. Many of his new ideas were gradually assimilated into general theatrical practice. MacKaye's career adumbrates the emergence of a new figure in the theatre—the director with a knowledge of both acting and the management of all stage techniques. The role of this type of technician was to become much more important in the 20th century.

BRONSON HOWARD (1842-1908)

Important as one of the first native American playwrights to successfully use native scenes and themes, Bronson Howard's biggest success was probably *Shenandoah*, a drama which skillfully interwove plot and character against a Civil War background. Other important plays by Howard were *The Young Mrs. Winthrop*, a social drama, and *Henrietta*, a satirical play especially written for Stuart Robson and William H. Crane, actors of the Union Square Company.

Howard was instrumental in getting the copyright laws amended to protect playwrights from piracy. In 1891, he founded the American Dramatists' Club which eventually became the Dramatists' Guild, a society which still functions today to protect playwrights from exploitation.

THE FROHMANS

The two Frohmans, Daniel (1851-1940) and Charles (1860-1915) were entrepreneurs who began in the theatre on the management side. Neither was trained as an actor. Their success in the field of theatre depended on their flair for anticipating public taste.

Daniel worked as the business manager of the Madison Square Theatre before he took over the management of the Lyceum in New York. He established a strong stock company with E. H. Sothern, Frank Mayo, Henry Miller, James K. Hackett, Mrs. Whiffen, Effie Shannon, and May Robson.

Charles Frohman shared his brother's love for the theatre. He worked, at first, as a tour manager; then took over the Star Theatre in New York and produced Bronson Howard's *Shenandoah* which became a great success and earned him a fortune.

STAR MAKER   From 1900 to 1910, Charles Frohman (1860-1915), producer, star maker, theatre builder and financial wizard, controlled the destiny of the American theatre. Before his death on the ill-fated Lusitania, Frohman owned theatres in London and New York worth $5 million, paid $35 million in salaries to 10,000 employees, and spent over half a million annually on advertising.

At the height of his career, Charles Frohman operated five theatres in New York and one in London. He also controlled the bookings of many theatres throughout America. He made stars of Maude Adams, Ethel Barrymore, May Robson, Arthur Byron, Henry Miller, John Drew, William Gillette, Julia Marlowe, Blanche Bates, and William Faversham. Frohman produced popular plays by the American writers David Belasco, William Gillette, and Clyde Fitch, particularly at the Twenty-third Street Theatre and at his new playhouse, the Empire Theatre. He many not have been a great innovator, but he organized and rationalized much theatre practice, and he was well-loved in theatrical circles in both London and New York.

DAVID BELASCO (1859-1931) Playwright, actor-manager, and great impresario of the very early twenties, Belasco produced plays ranging from Shakespeare to "East Lynne." He is best remembered for his lavish stage settings replete with realistic details.

DAVID BELASCO (1859-1931)

David Belasco, noted theatre showman, was born in San Francisco of a father who had played a clown in London theatres. Starting from the age of twelve, Belasco had a long and rich association with the theater. At fourteen, he played the young Duke of York in the Charles Kean production of *Richard III* at Victoria, British Columbia. During the 1870's, he continually acted in California and Nevada, meeting most of the important figures in the theatre at that time. He became assistant to Dion Boucicault who taught him stage management and the difficult art of play writing. In 1882, Belasco became stage manager to Daniel Frohman at the Madison Square.

Belasco collaborated with Henry C. de Mille to produce such popular successes as *The Wife, Lord Chumley, The Charity Ball,* and *Men and Women.* His plays possess no great literary merit, but were efficient vehicles for stars, with fine acting parts, simple themes, and strong dramatic climaxes. More than one player owed his success to Belasco. He made a leading lady of Mrs. Leslie Carter, a divorceé from Chicago society who had charm, looks, but no stage training. She proved successful in Belasco's *The Heart of Maryland, Zaza,* and *Andrea.*

Another of his stars, Blanche Bates, appeared in *Madame Butterfly,* a one-act play he wrote with John Luther Long. This was later used by Puccini as the scenario for his well-known opera. His *The Girl of the Golden West,* produced as a starring vehicle for Blanche Bates in 1905, was presented as an opera at the Metropolitan Opera House with Caruso and Emmy Destinn in 1910.

Belasco also made a star of David Warfield, a Jewish comedian whom he found in vaudeville, presenting him in a number of dramatic roles in *The Auctioneer, The Music Master, A Grand Army Man, The Return of Peter Grimm,* and *The Merchant of Venice.* Other luminaries developed by Belasco were Henrietta Crosman, Frances Starr, and Beth Merrill. Many of his leading players eventually also became stars of the movies; George Arliss, Lillian Gish, Mary Pickford, and Henry Hull all appeared in Belasco productions before starting their film careers.

Belasco directed his productions with great attention to detail and invented many realistic stage effects which were much admired. For one of his plays, he went so far as to reproduce on stage a replica of a Child's restaurant. He also made many improvements in the practical matters of scenery construction, and he worked out imaginative uses of stage lighting.

In 1890, Belasco left the Frohmans and became an independent producer. He found it difficult to get his productions launched because of the monopoly control of the Frohmans and of other theatre managers and booking agents in New York and Philadelphia; so in 1902, he took over the Republic Theatre in New York, which he renamed the Belasco. He continued in opposition to the syndicate, supported by many of the leading actors. Eventually, the monopoly was broken by a rival organization of theatre managers run by the three Shubert brothers, who in time became the leading producing and booking company throughout America.

Spectacular and flamboyant though he may have been, Belasco gave much sympathetic handling to his players and got the most out of them in his productions, often training young actresses from scratch and building their reputations by promoting them in increasingly important and dramatic roles. His use of advanced technique displayed an imaginative and artistic sensibility. He had a sure grasp of what the public wanted, and he rarely experienced anything but financial success, producing plays successfully until well into the 1920's.

LATE NINETEENTH CENTURY PLAYWRIGHTS

Other Amercian playwrights of the late 19th century were Edward Harrigan, William Dean Howells, James A. Herne, William Gillette, Charles Hoyt, Augustus Thomas, and the prolific Clyde Fitch. These writers wrote drama based mostly on themes taken from American life. Although perhaps not reaching the stature of the European work of the time, they laid the foundation of American drama which was to blossom profusely in the second quarter of the 20th century.

"FATHER OF AMERICAN REALISM"   Though the reputation of William Dean Howells (1837-1920) rests principally on his novels, his 12 one-act farces, called the Roberts-Campbells plays, furthered the development of realism in the American theatre. Howell's witty dialogue accurately captured the foibles of Boston's Back Bay gentry.

JAMES A. HERNE (1839-1901)

James A. Herne toured the country as an actor. He learned much about play writing by collaborating with David Belasco. His early attempts at writing were adaptations from English originals, *Marriage by Moonlight* and *Chums*. The latter, retitled *Hearts of Oak* (and, still later, *Sag Harbor*), became a hit in Chicago and New York. Herne and his wife toured in this play for many years.

Herne's first original works were *Drifting Apart,* a drama woven around the lives of fishermen, and *Shore Acres,* a simple melodrama of farm life with excellent characterization. After a slow start, this play brought him recognition and fortune when it ran for a whole season at Daly's in 1893. Herne and his wife played *Shore Acres* on tour and in stock with constant success.

Some of Herne's best plays, such as *Margaret Fleming,* a social drama, and *The Reverend Griffith Davenport,* a Civil War drama

AUGUSTUS THOMAS (1857-1934)   Noted for his well-made melodramas, Thomas added to the tide of realism with a strong infusion of local color in his plays. His dramas, such as "Arizona," which was written in 1899, were distinctive. The settings in which Thomas' characters acted out his melodramatic plots were quite authentic.

with a principal character cast as a Southerner who opposed slavery, ended in failure and considerable financial loss, perhaps because they were ahead of their time. His characterizations of the simple life were perhaps sentimental, but were written with a profound understanding of his subjects.

WILLIAM GILLETTE (1855-1937)

William Gillette was another actor who turned to the writing of plays, many of which he appeared in with great acclaim. His first play, *The Professor,* a light comedy in which he took the title role, was presented at the Madison Square Theatre in 1881 where it had a fair success. His second was an adaptation from a story by Frances Hodgson Burnett, *Esmeralda,* which ran for a whole year at the same theatre.

In his original work, he turned to melodrama. It was in action-packed drama which Gillette presented realistically and effectively on the stage that he was to make his name. *Held by the Enemy,* a Civil War melodrama with conflicts and heroism behind the lines, enjoyed a long run in 1886 at the Madison Square. He also wrote three farces based on foreign sources: *All the Comforts of Home, Mr. Wilkinson's Widows,* and *Too Much Johnson,* in which he appeared with great popularity as a philandering plantation owner.

His two last great successes were *Secret Service* (1895) with a Civil War spy theme, and *Sherlock Holmes* (1899). Playing the title role in this play which was based on the Conan Doyle stories with much original material added, he was enthusiastically received in both America and England for over twenty years. Although the success of the play was partly a reflection of the popularity of the immortal character, Gillette was the first actor to achieve the complete embodiment of the masteur sleuth on the stage.

AUGUSTUS THOMAS (1857-1934)

Augustus Thomas grew up in the theatre his father managed in New Orleans. He began writing in his teens; and by his early twenties, he was touring the Midwest with farces. The favorable reception of *The Burglar* in Boston and New York in 1889 encouraged Thomas to continue writing; and during the next thirty years or so, he produced about fifty plays. These were mostly serious pieces based on American themes.

Thomas explored many controversial subjects. He was particularly interested in depicting the struggle of the individual for freedom against local pressures.

His plays, with their regional settings, were received with great interest. *Alabama,* produced by A. H. Palmer at the Madison Square Theatre in 1891, touched on the aftermath of the Civil War at a time when the bitterness of the South was patent. In *The Witching*

Hour, Thomas dealt imaginatively with telepathy. In *As a Man Thinks,* he dealt with faith healing.

CHARLES HOYT (1860-1900)

Charles Hoyt, a writer of well-constructed farces, was adept at the creation of character roles. A keen sense of lively fun perfused his popular pieces, the first of note being *A Bunch of Keys,* which was produced in 1882. *The Texas Steer,* written in 1890, was a tilt at the antics of Congressmen in Washington. But Hoyt's greatest success was *A Trip to Chinatown* (1891), a play set in San Francisco. It ran for 650 performances; and, in 1894, it ran still longer. Later, the play had a favorable reception in London.

CLYDE FITCH (1865-1909)

One of the most prolific writers of the period was Clyde Fitch. After graduating from Amherst, Fitch went to New York intending to write for the stage. In 1889 he was commissioned by Richard Mansfield to write a play suited to the actor's considerable talents. Fitch's *Beau Brummell* was successfully produced at the Madison Square Theatre in 1890, and the drama was subsequently played by Richard Mansfield throughout his career.

Fitch wrote with facility and produced over forty plays. While some of these were adaptations, his work covers a wide range of style. Otis Skinner appeared as Charles II in *His Grace of Graumont,* a comedy of manners. *Nathan Hale* and *Barbara Frietchie* were based on American history. His melodramas—*The Moth and the Flame* (1898) and *The Cowboy and the Lady* (1899)—brought Fitch further success. In 1901 came *The Climbers,* an acidly written social satire of New York society which enjoyed a long run. In *Captain Jinks of the Horse Marines,* the young Ethel Barrymore became a star under Charles Frohman's management.

CLYDE FITCH (1865-1909) One of the most prolific and successful American playwrights of the 19th century, Fitch was the first American dramatist to gain international fame.

Many of Fitch's plays were written for particular stars, in the prevailing fashion of the time. Fitch's excellent depiction of contemporary life was somewhat weakened by his overriding wish to provide the melodrama the public wanted. His work, therefore, never quite reached its early promise, although his comedy, *The Truth* which opened inauspiciously in New York in 1907, a study of a congenital liar, did receive international acclaim.

Fitch's last play, *The City,* written the year he died, is an excellent study of a small-town family suffering under the stresses of life in a big city. His characters were drawn with understanding and sympathy; and it is for this fine play that he is best remembered.

Without doubt, Fitch's plays were excellent vehicles for the luminaries of his day, but his work as a serious dramatist might have reached greater heights had he sought less to accommodate to the taste of his audience.

WILLIAM VAUGHAN MOODY (1869-1910)

Although he didn't live to see his major plays produced, Vaughan Moody did much to promote the craft of playwriting. A scholar,

teacher, and poet, Moody's early verse plays were not produced in the commercial theatre.

However, *The Great Divide,* produced and acted by Henry Miller and Margaret Anglin in 1906, became a popular success. The play dealt with the marriage of a sensitive girl reared in an Eastern state, to a crude character from the Rocky Mountains who had violated her. This strong drama, well written and excellently constructed, treated fundamental matters in an honest and dignified manner. It pointed the way to the deeper exploration of psychological and social problems on the stage.

Moody wrote only one other play, *The Faith Healer,* before his early death in 1910.

THE THEATRE BOOM

During the early years of the 20th century, many new theatres were built, audiences increased their support for stars of their choice, and many managers, actors, and playwrights made fortunes. Failures there were, but there were also great opportunities for new ventures in the theatre; and the great over-all economic expansion in the country was reflected in an unprecedented boom in the American theatre.

"THE GREAT DIVIDE" (1906)   The stalwart figure on the left is Henry Miller, who played the lead in this famous melodrama as Stephen Ghent, the contending Westerner. Although flawed by mawkish sentiment, W. V. Moody's drama was a sincere exposition of two conflicting cultural traditions: the open spirit of the West and the conservative attitudes of the East.

The Russian Theatre

THE STAGE IS SET

Toward the end of the 19th century, a feeling of dissatisfaction with the state of things in the theatre arose in Europe, which manifested itself in the formation, in many countries, of small groups of individuals who joined together with the common purpose of encouraging writers and directors of serious contemporary plays that would be unlikely to receive production in the established theatres. The staginess of the acting and the commercial manager system, with its emphasis on starring roles, proved to be a disappointment. The new plays produced, although excellent vehicles for the star players, were usually without any great literary merit and did not arouse much serious thought in their audiences, being primarily intended to entertain or amuse.

The time was ripe for a change—and the most profoundly influential of the new theatres was to arise in Russia: The Moscow Art Theatre.

CONSTANTIN SERGEYE-VICH STANISLAVSKY (1865-1938)   Actor, director, teacher, major theorist of the 20th century, Stanislavsky was co-founder of the Moscow Art Theatre, a revolutionary theatre group noted for its naturalistic style of acting and for its incomparable ensemble playing. The "Stanislavsky System," known in America as "The Method," was given formal expression in Stanislavsky's famous book, AN ACTOR PREPARES, published in America in 1926. Essentially, the "Method" stresses the inner life and psychology (underlying motivations) of the character being portrayed. The ideas promulgated by Stanislavsky were disseminated in America primarily through the teaching and directing of Lee Strasberg, Harold Clurman, and Stella Adler, members of the Group Theatre and confirmed believers in Stanislavsky's concepts.

THE FOUNDING OF THE MOSCOW ART THEATRE

In 1897, two men met at a restaurant in Moscow to discuss the formation of a new theatre. They were Vladimir Ivanovich Nemirovich-Danchenko (1859-1943) and Constantin Stanislavsky (1863-1938). Danchenko, a playwright, critic, and producer, was at the time director of one of the two dramatic academies in Moscow, the Philharmonic. Stanislavsky was a well-to-do merchant of thirty-four, who some years previously had organized a group of actors, all ama-

VLADIMIR NEMIROVITCH-DANCHENKO (1859-1943)   *Co-founder and director of the famed MAT, Nemirovitch-Danchenko was one of the leading figures in the Russian theatre. Dissatisfied with theatre conditions under the Tsar, he undertook many reforms. At a meeting with Stanislavsky on October 4, 1897, in a cafe in Moscow, the MAT's foundations were laid during the course of a legendary 15-hour conversation.* AT RIGHT, *MAT CO-FOUNDER   Vladimir Nemirovitch-Danchenko as he looked in 1898 at the age of 39.*

teurs, in order to produce interesting and unusual plays. Both men were dissatisfied with the current state of the theatre; both had new ideas about the ways in which plays should be produced, and—with Danchenko's students and Stanislavsky's amateurs—together they had the nucleus of actors necessary to form a permanent new company.

Having agreed on the organization of the new group, what they now needed was money and a theatre. This was difficult to come by until a sympathetic millionaire merchant named Sava Morozov provided them with the greater part of the money required. They then acquired a small theatre in Moscow and called it the Moscow Art Theatre.

ART THEATRE'S FIRST HOME   This was the first rehearsal studio of the Moscow Art Theatre company, in Pushkino, near Moscow. In this simple shed, Stanislavsky made his introductory speech to the newly-formed company.

At the outset of the undertaking, it was agreed that Stanislavsky was to have charge of the artistic policy and actual direction of the productions, while Danchenko was to choose the plays and control the administration of the theatre. A whole year was spent in preparation for the opening—time spent in welding the two groups of actors into a single, trained unit, and in rehearsing a repertoire of several plays.

The policy of the new theatre was to produce plays of distinction by Russian and foreign writers, to subordinate individual acting to the idea of the play itself, to pay great attention to detail and characterization, and to avoid completely the conventional staginess current in the theatre of the time.

Stanislavsky was himself a fine actor, and he appeared in many leading parts; he was also a great director, with a will of iron. With infinite patience, he worked at rehearsals throughout the summer of 1898.

REHEARSAL METHODS

The method of rehearsal of plays which prevailed generally in the theatre at that time was one of the things Stanislavsky was most eager to reform. The usual rehearsal procedure of the time went like this: the actors would arrive on the stage for the first rehearsal, be presented with copies of their parts, and would immediately begin to read their lines and walk about the stage, taking up various "effective" positions. The whole play would be gone through at each rehearsal until the actors were word-perfect, at which time the play would be considered ready for the first performance. The producer suggested the actors' movements on the stage which, if found convenient, were adopted without thought being given to their dramatic significance. Often the stars would disagree with the producer, whose authority was little higher than that of a stage manager. On these occasions, the producer would have to give way.

Stanislavsky's methods were quite different. In the first place, there were no stars in the Moscow Art Theatre; instead, all the players were submitted to the rigid discipline of the director. The rehearsal of a new play would begin, not on the stage, but in the comfort of a private room. Actual rehearsal was preceded by discussion: the director and the whole cast would thrash out their ideas of the play and how the various parts should be played. Sometimes the discussion would take place with the author present to explain his ideas of the play. Not until the play had been read and thoroughly understood by everyone in the cast did actual rehearsals begin.

Stanislavsky would rehearse only a small part of the play at one rehearsal—perhaps only one scene. This material would be gone over several times until the actors found just the right cadence of voice or just the right stage movements for the characterization. Thus, by rehearsing one scene at a time, or even a fragment of a scene at one time, the whole play would be built up by a concentration of effort on minute detail, and by virtue of an underlying conception of just how the characters would have acted in real life.

In the other theatres of the time, a dress rehearsal was not con-

FIRST READING   Members of the Moscow Art
Theatre listen to a reading by Anton Chekhov of his
play, "The Seagull," which had failed when first produced at the Alexandrinsky Theatre in 1896. "The
Seagull's" successful revival in 1899 brought lasting
fame to the newly-established theatre and to its re-
juvenated author. Stanislavsky is seated at Chekhov's
right; Nemirovitch-Danchenko, a long-time friend
of the playwright, is standing far left.

sidered necessary. The players had their own wardrobes and wore
what they pleased, often without even consulting the director. By
mutual arrangement, the actresses decided what gowns to wear so
that there should not be a clash of color. Stanislavsky, by contrast,

held five or six dress rehearsals of the entire play, and many more of the fragments of the play, with leading actors in costume and makeup and with the appropriate scenery. These dress rehearsals of parts of the play took place two months before the final dress rehearsals.

STAGE SETTING

Another principle of the Moscow Art Theatre was that each play should have its own setting, especially designed to suit the theme and mood of the play. Today, this does not seem an outrageous demand, but in those times the theatres usually had a stock of scenery—a drawing-room set, a forest set, and so on—and whatever the setting of the play, the scenery which was on hand was used. The management of these theatres having never conceived the idea of attracting artists into the theatre to design the settings, the scenery was painted by a "decorator," a kind of superior stagehand.

By contrast, the Moscow Art Theatre, brought in an artist, Simov, to design the settings. A painter of the Russian realistic school, Simov took to his task with great enthusiasm, and produced outstanding results. Danchenko, in his book *My Life in the Russian Theatre,* writes of a child in the audience at a performance of *The Seagull* who turned to his parent and said, "Mother, let's go into the garden for a walk."

The Moscow Art Theatre also developed a more naturalistic method of lighting. It used a much greater variation in light intensity than had been thought possible up to that time; at times, even choosing to illuminate the stage so weakly that the actors were hardly visible.

THE DEBUT OF THE MOSCOW ART THEATRE

The Moscow Art Theatre opened in October, 1898, with a performance of Tolstoy's *Tsar Feodor.* Productions of Shakespeare's *Merchant of Venice,* Hauptmann's *The Sunken Bell,* Sophocles's *Antigone,* Ibsen's *Hedda Gabler* and Chekhov's *The Seagull* followed. These plays became part of the permanent repertory as they were presented, and were repeated alternately from time to time. The actors were thus spared the boring task of playing the same part every night. Instead, each had a variety of parts; and occasionally no part, which ensured one or two free evenings for every player during the week.

SPIRITUAL COMRADES   In 1900, in the Crimea, Tolstoy (at left) with Maxim Gorki shared with his young compatriot a concern over the degradation of the lower classes. His play, "The Power of Darkness," is considered the greatest portrayal of peasant life.

KINDRED SPIRITS   In Yalta in the summer of 1900, Anton Chekhov (seated at left) was confined to his home by illness. Here, shown with Maxim Gorki, he entertained members of the MAT then touring the Crimea. It was this chance encounter between Gorki and the MAT that led to their production during the following season of two of Gorki's plays, "Smug Citizens" and "The Lower Depths."

"UNCLE VANYA"   Based on "The Wood Demon," one of Anton Chekhov's earlier plays, "Uncle Vanya" continued the creative union of playwright and acting company until the dramatist's untimely death in 1904. Here Stanislavsky, who appeared in and directed all of Chekhov's plays at the MAT, is seen (third from right) as Astrov and Olga Knipper-Chekhova appears as Y. Andreyvna (seated on the swing).

At its debut, the new theatre received an appreciative response from public and press, but the audiences fell off after the opening. Only the production of Chekhov's *The Seagull* ensured the ultimate success of the company.

ANTON CHEKHOV (1860-1904)

If Chekhov rescued the Moscow Art Theatre, the Moscow Art Theatre can also be said to have rescued Chekhov—at least Chekhov, the playwright.

A medical doctor who had taken to writing short stories of Russian life, Chekhov had won fame and literary distinction, culminating in the award of an Academy prize. He then wrote two one-act farces, vaudeville pieces as he called them—*The Bear* and *The Proposal*—which were successful everywhere. These were followed by *Ivanov*, which achieved only moderate success at a performance in a private theatre.

Chekhov represented human beings as he observed them in life; and his training as a doctor made his characterizations extremely

COSTUME FOR THE CHARAC-TER OF "BREAD"   This costume was used in the Moscow Art Theatre's production of "The Blue Bird" by Maeterlinck.

DEBUT PERFORMANCE   Olga Knipper-Chekhova (Mrs. Anton Chekhov) and Ivan Moskvin were charter members of the MAT. Here they are seen as the Tsarina Irina and the Tsar in Alexei Tolstoy's tragedy, "Tsar Feodor," in the debut production of the MAT on October 14, 1898. Both performers, former members of Danchenko's student company, moved with him to the MAT, and were soon hailed as major talents. The striving for realistic detail is evident in the authenticity of the costumes.

penetrating. His characters are inseparable from their particular surroundings, and his plays are full of atmosphere; merged with his dialogue are the sounds of neighbors arriving at the house, the samovar, the rain, and the soft playing of guitar or piano. It can be understood that the actors of the old school, with their staginess of technique and their conventional style, could not hope to portray the author's conception of character and mood.

The Seagull was Chekhov's first great play. Nevertheless, its first production, at one of the Imperial theatres in St. Petersburg, was a complete failure. Although Chekhov attended the rehearsals in St. Petersburg, the actors could make nothing of his play.

Chekhov subsequently offered the play to the Moscow Small Theatre, the most advanced of the established theatres; but Lensky,

STAGE SETTING   A sketch for the ACT IV setting of "The Three Sisters," designed by V. Dmitriev for the 1940 MAT production.

SETTING FOR CHEKHOV'S "THE THREE SISTERS"   This realistic set was typical of the Moscow Art Theatre's early naturalistic productions.

A SLICE OF LIFE IN THE LOWER DEPTHS   The MAT won its
loudest acclaim with the 1902 debut of Gorki's "The Lower Depths." To reproduce the seedy life of a lodging house, the company made frequent field

the leading actor, returned the play, advising Chekhov to give up
writing for the stage. Chekhov was discouraged and resolved to
write no more for the theatre. Fortunately for theatrical history, this
was not to be the end of the story. Two years after the failure of *The*

trips, examining at firsthand the squalid Khitrov Market flophouse and its inhabitants. Stanislavsky (standing at the far left) is shown here in a scene from the original production.

Seagull, Danchenko persuaded Chekhov to let the Moscow Art Theatre produce the play.

In Stanislavsky, Chekhov at last found the director his work required. Stanislavsky, by his rejection of the old conventional style of acting, and his concentration on deep exploration of the feelings of the individual characters, gave Chekhov competent interpretation. Only with naturalistic acting can Chekhov's plays be convincing; in the old-fashioned declamatory style of acting, the dialogue seems ridiculous.

Stanislavsky had not Chekhov's knowledge of the provincial Russian intelligentsia of the time, with its loves, its tears, its envies, and its quarrels, but he successfully reproduced the milieu on the stage. The greatness of Chekhov lies in the lyrical qualities of his plays, which always emerge through the everyday realities of his provincial households. The Moscow Art Theatre's production of *The Seagull* was an instant success, establishing the theatrical reputation of both the company and the playwright overnight.

THE MOSCOW ART THEATRE'S EARLY YEARS

Stanislavsky's productions were always theatrical. While it was real life he reproduced on the stage, it was reality enlarged. In historical plays, for instance, if high hats had been worn in the period presented, the characters' hats were made even higher; if long sleeves were worn, they would be so long that they had to be tucked in; if a door was to be small, it was made so small that the actors had to bend double to pass through.

Although the first season showed a loss, the enthusiastic Morozov made it good and the other shareholders followed suit, so the theatre was safe for the next season. The following season other plays by Hauptmann, Tolstoy, and Shakespeare, together with Chekhov's *Uncle Vanya,* were added to the repertory. The Moscow Art Theatre now gained a considerable reputation and began to make its influence felt in other theatres.

In 1901, Chekhov's *The Three Sisters,* which had been especially written for the actors at the Moscow Art Theatre, was produced there. This play was considered their finest production. *The Cherry Orchard* was produced in the spring of 1904. In the summer of that year, while on a holiday in Germany, Chekhov died.

Another great writer whose work was produced at the Moscow Art Theatre was Maxim Gorky (1868-1936). In plays such as *The Lower Depths* (1902), Gorky presented a starkly realistic picture of low life in the vast interior of Russia. In those days, such a play could only have been produced at the Moscow Art Theatre.

However, the Moscow Art Theatre was not confined entirely to naturalistic productions; and in such productions as Maurice Maeterlinck's (1862-1949) *The Blue Bird,* the naturalistic element was entirely subordinated to a spirit of pure fantasy.

STANISLAVSKY'S INFLUENCE ON ACTING AND THE ACTOR

Stanislavsky was the pre-eminent teacher of acting in modern times. He was the first to codify the art. His books *An Actor Prepares, My Life in Art, Stanislavsky Rehearses Othello* and *Building a Character,* have instructed generations of actors and acting teachers. In America, the Stanislavsky method of acting became so well-established that it is now just known as The Method.

Stanislavsky believed in fine acting, but he did not believe in stars. One of his finest achievements was the establishment of ensemble acting at the Moscow Art Theatre. In that theatre where no one was a star, everyone was a star.

ACTORS OF THE MOSCOW ART THEATRE

Among the actors, the names of Katchalov, Luzhsky, Gribunin, and Moskvin are particularly memorable. Outstanding among the actresses were Olga Knipper, who married Chekhov; Stanislavsky's wife, Marie Lilina; Germanova, Zhdanova, and Butova.

GORDON CRAIG (1872-1966)

In 1911, Gordon Craig produced *Hamlet* for the Moscow Art

STANISLAVSKY (1863-1938)   The gifted actor-director is shown on the left here as Vershinin in "The Three Sisters," Chekhov's nostalgic play about Russian provincials whose lives drift idly by, as they dream of going to Moscow. ABOVE RIGHT. On the right, the noted director Stanislavsky appears as Famusov in Alexander Griboyedov's satire of Moscow society, "Woe from Wit," written in 1823. Banned during the playwright's lifetime, the complete text was not available until 1869. This brilliant indictment of society was produced by the MAT in 1906.

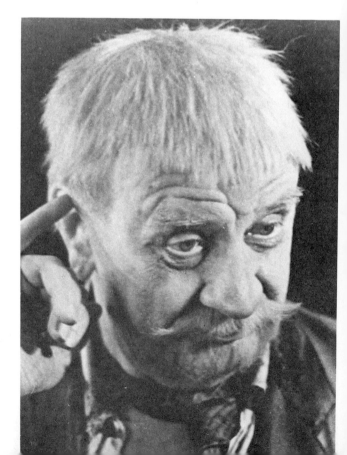

AT RIGHT THE LOWER DEPTHS Vassily Kachloff, one of the foremost actors of the MAT, portrays the Baron in the first performance of Gorki's play in 1902. His career, which spans the transition from imperial to Soviet theatre, was marked by great success in such roles as "Hamlet" (Gordon Craig's 1912 production), Ibsen's "Brand," and Vershinin in "The Armoured Train 14-69." In a 1938 revival of "Woe from Wit," he played Chatsky, a part he had first performed in the 1906 MAT premier production of Griboyedev's masterpiece.

V. F. GRIBUNIN   This fine actor, who is noted for his limning of odd characters, is shown here as Chebutykin, retired army doctor and Irina's tiresome wooer, in the 1916 MAT production of Chekhov's "The Three Sisters."

V. V. LUZHSKY   This actor was an original member of the MAT and was recognized as a character actor of great range. He appears here as Andrei in MAT's 1901 debut of Chekhov's "The Three Sisters."

IVAN MOSKVIN (1874-1946)   He played the lead in the MAT's premiere production, "Tsar Feodor," and is remembered for his memorable portrayals of Luka in "The Lower Depths." He appears here as Epihodov in "The Cherry Orchard."

Theatre, but in his own unique style. Craig, the son of Ellen Terry, had begun his career acting in Irving's company. After two or three years, deciding that he could no longer continue as part of a system for which he had no sympathy, he resigned from a well-paid position in order to formulate his own conception of what a production group should be and the way a theatre should be organized. Craig evolved ideas which were so revolutionary at that time that he could find no outlet for his work; and in order to make a living, he was compelled to write and publish his ideas and to make designs for settings, chiefly through the medium of woodcuts.

His chief objection to contemporary staging lay in the fact that on the stage the actors were three-dimensional flesh-and-blood characters who reproduced the story of the play, while the scenery merely served as a background and was largely two-dimensional. Craig conceived a bigger function for the setting; he believed that, like the actors, scenery, too, should be three-dimensional, and should play an integral part in the telling of the story or the communication of the mood of the play. In other words, the scenery should be designed to act in co-ordination with the players in creating a dramatic effect.

CRAIG'S STAGE SETS

Craig designed settings composed chiefly of simple abstract forms—stairways, rostrums, blocks, and cubes—the whole effect presenting a great variety of planes. By throwing various kinds of colored lighting on the surfaces of these planes and arranging the lighting to come from different angles, Craig was able to achieve an appearance of change and movement, although the actual setting remained static. The actors' positions on the stage were worked out as a part of the complete setting, so that actors and scenery, both three-dimensional, formed an integral whole.

VSEVOLOD MEYERHOLD This outstanding director was an innovator devoted to the idea of a non-realistic theatre. His experiments led to a system of actor-training called Bio mechanics. However, not until the 1920's did he score his most notable successes, chiefly with "The Bed Bug" and "The Bath House." In 1938, he was accused of "Formalism," and his theatre was closed.

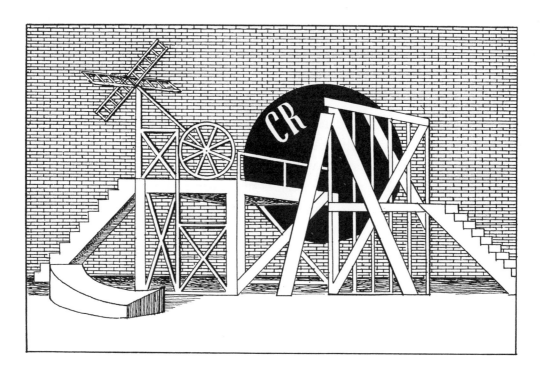

CONSTRUCTIVISM   *This early constructivist set was designed for a Meyerhold production.*

The scene painter, trained to represent a three-dimensional effect in two dimensions, was rejected by Craig as an anachronism. Craig's settings were usually painted in a neutral color, lighting alone being used to produce the effect of color. Craig was the first man to understand the tremendous value of shadows in producing dramatic effect.

Craig's method meant, of course, the complete subordination of the actor to the will of the director; the latter was to conceive the dramatic idea of the play, design the setting, arrange the lighting, and dictate the movement and speech of the actors. In those days in England, when the actor-manager was supreme, Craig found no enthusiasm for his ideas, and he was never able to run a theatre in England.

He went to live in Italy, where he had an opportunity to study the theatre of the past and to develop his ideas further. For many years, he published a periodical called *The Mask* in order to propagate his ideas and to earn a living. He started a dramatic school which unfortunately came to an end during the First World War. His writing and woodcut designs, however, found their way all over Europe, and his influence was great, particularly in Germany. In Germany, Adolphe Appia developed along similar lines to Craig, and was particularly noted for his staging of Wagner's operas. But he had little influence in England, being regarded there primarily as a scenic designer and secondly as a graphic artist.

In his formal production of *Hamlet* at the MAT, Craig used a series of screens which could be placed in a variety of positions. He was thus able to create a complete change in the shape of a scene with very little actual movement. His work there, however, was considered to be little more than a novelty. What Craig's system and Stanislavsky's had in common was insistence on a unity of the various elements of production imposed by the director, who exercised a strict discipline over actors and technicians of the theatre.

SPECIAL COSTUMING   *The above illustration depicts a costume for a Meyerhold constructivist production. The drawing at the right is of a costume for "La Princesse Brambille" at the Kamerny Theatre.*

MEYERHOLD AND THE REVOLT AGAINST NATURALISM

Stimulated by Stanislavsky, other theatres began to revolutionize their productions, sometimes in an entirely new direction. Vsevolod Meyerhold (1874-1943) was probably the first and most important director to break away from the Art Theatre's naturalism. He was originally one of the most promising students at Danchenko's dramatic academy, the Philharmonic; and when the Art Theatre was founded, he played in the early productions, notably as Treplef in *The Seagull* and the Baron in *The Three Sisters*.

Although an accomplished actor, Meyerhold's ambition was to direct. After a few years with the Art Theatre, he left to direct productions at the theatre of Vera Komisarjevskaya, a noted actress of the time. After a short period at this theatre, Meyerhold became director at the two Imperial theatres in St. Petersburg, the Alexandrinsky and the Marinsky.

Meyerhold was never satisfied with the intimate atmosphere of the Art Theatre, nor with its policy of naturalistic representation. In a way, his ideals were more in keeping with the Elizabethan stage. He rejected the conventional stage picture seen by the audience through the "picture frame" of the proscenium arch; he wanted the audience to be much closer to the actors and to play more than the passive part of merely watching the performance. Meyerhold regarded the audience as an integral part of the performance.

At first, he swept away the footlights and curtain in the large Imperial theatres, and brought back the apron stage. Scenery was largely dispensed with, the bare wall at the back of the stage becoming visible to the audience. Ramps were constructed to lead from the stage to the auditorium.

CONSTRUCTIVE SCENERY

Immediately after the revolution, a further development in abstract scenery came about which has come to be known as *constructivism*. This was, as Komisarjevsky points out, partly thrust upon the theatres

of the revolution by the shortage of canvas in the early days of the
Soviet state. A constructivist setting was non-naturalistic, and consisted of an arrangement of wooden platforms, ladders, steps, and
gangways, built as a unit, which gave the actors a great variety of
levels, angles, and positions from which they could perform.

ABSTRACT SETTINGS
Meyerhold's abstract scenery was an attempt to break away from the
conventional painted scenery which presented a flat background to

SETTING DESIGNED BY FERNAND LEGER FOR A BALLET
This set shows the influence of abstract painting.

SETTING FOR "ROMEO AND JULIET"   *Presented at the Kamerny Theatre and designed by Alexander Exter, this set shows cubist influence.*

the solid figures of the actors. Like Craig, he designed his settings in three dimensions, with the actors serving as an integral part of the design.

The plays presented were chiefly the classics, but the scripts were completely re-edited by Meyerhold, who adopted a kind of film technique in cutting them up into a series of short episodes. After the Revolution, when there were more contemporary plays dealing with the recent upheaval of social forces, Meyerhold introduced crowd scenes, in which the actors, in ordinary day clothes and without makeup, were indistinguishable from the audience.

In one play, Meyerhold used only the wooden framework of a house, for his set; while in others, considerable ingenuity was displayed in arranging the various platforms, ladders, and gangways into a pleasing geometrical design. Other theatres also used constructivist settings at this time, necessity becoming the mother of a new and exciting method of staging.

EFFECTS OF STAGING INNOVATIONS

It is obvious that the actors' style had to be modified to conform to these new surroundings. Among these settings, naturalistic acting would have appeared ridiculous, and a more stylized acting style— somewhat acrobatic and staccato—came into use.

As conditions became easier, naturalistic presentation again became the norm. But the abstract and constructivist period had a lasting effect. It cleared away many outmoded and conventional ideas, and it made possible a new and more balanced conception of the values of the various elements in the theatre, emphasizing the need for a more elastic use of the stage.

TAIROV AND THE KAMERNY THEATRE

Another of Russia's experimental theatres was the Kamerny Theatre, founded in 1914. Under its director, Alexander Yakovlevich Tairov (1885-1950), the Kamerny produced drama, comedy, pantomime,

ALEXANDER TAIROV Founder of the Kamerny Theatre in 1914, Tairov was a theorist and practitioner of non-realistic stage techniques. Though he weathered the Revolution, his 1934 production of "The Optimistic Tragedy" brought charges of "Formalism." Forced to work thereafter under a "management committee," he was restored to favor in 1939 with a production of "Madame Bovary." His work, however, never again achieved its former eminence.

and light opera. The Kamerny's style of presentation was frankly artificial compared with the Moscow Art Theatre's realism. At the Kamerny, each production had a setting particularly suited to it, and the general tendency was in the direction of abstract staging.

The revolution affected all the theatres, which either had to find new plays by revolutionary writers or to produce the classics in a style acceptable to the new times. Tairov produced several of Eugene O'Neill's plays, using a formal, non-abstract style, with settings designed in a naturalistic but simple fashion. The shapes and forms were severe and usually monochromatic. While returning somewhat to the ideas of the Art Theatre, Tairov did not go so far as to adopt naturalistic representation, and the performances were rather stylized, making much use of pantomime.

EUGENE VAKHTANGOV (1883-1922)

Eugene Vakhtangov, who died in 1922 at an early age, was a director who, although influenced by the Moscow Art Theatre, developed acting technique in a different direction. He felt that there was a danger of exaggeration in Stanislavsky's policy of basing characterization on a deep psychological exploration of inner motivations. He felt this might easily develop into a series of emotional experiences too psychological to be "good theatre." Thus, where the actors of the Moscow Art Theatre built their characterizations on their conceptions of the inner mind of a character, Vakhtangov's actors based their interpretations on their conceptions of the actions of a character.

Vakhtangov's best-known production was *Princess Turandot*, a formal production that employed an abstract setting. His production methods, like Meyerhold's, made necessary the drastic editing or rewriting of the plays.

INFLUENCE OF THE RUSSIAN THEATRE

The importance of the Moscow Art Theatre and its various offshoots lies in their profound effect on the theatre of the 20th century. Their

"THE BEDBUG" *Vladimir Mayakovsky's (1894-1930) play "The Bedbug," written in 1929, was a satire set in a futuristic Soviet society in which the only survivors from the old world are a pre-revolutionary bourgeois and a bedbug.*

SOVIET PLAY   *The bell tower scene in V. Ivanov's play*

innovations in acting technique and production, coupled with their uncompromising dedication to the highest standards of theatrical art, brought a renewed standard of excellence and provided a fresh source of inspiration.

The style of acting and method of preparation and production which prevailed before the day of the Russians would be unthinkable

"Armored Train 14-69" presented at the MAT in 1927.

today. The concept of a unified production in which sets, costumes, lighting, acting, and direction are all organized to produce a single effect is one which we owe to the experimental theatre of early 20th century Russia. We take this approach so much for granted today that it is hard to realize that not so very long ago such a concept would have been considered bizarre.

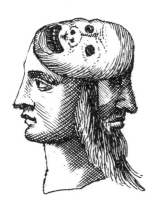

The English Theatre
of the 20th Century

THE INFLUENCE OF IBSEN (1828-1906)

Toward the end of the 19th century, dissatisfaction with the theatre led to the formation of small groups who hoped to stage drama that would evoke serious thought. In London, such a group was formed by J. T. Grein to produce, at semiprivate performances, certain Continental and British plays which were not likely to be produced on the popular stage. Ibsen had written *Ghosts* in 1881. But *Ghosts* an off-beat play at that time, was first produced in England in 1891 in a private production by Grein's Independent Theatre Group, later to become the Stage Society.

One cannot overestimate the great importance Ibsen has had on dramatists of the 20th century. The first great modern playwright to delve below the surface of polite behavior, Ibsen sought to delineate fundamental urges. His cleverly constructed plays, set in the matter-of-fact surroundings of provincial towns, spoke of man's strivings and failings in simple everyday language. Although slow to take effect, ultimately the impact of the Norwegian dramatist was tremendous.

Ghosts was censored by the Lord Chamberlain, who to this day can prevent a work from receiving public performance in Britain. His powers of veto, however, do not extend to plays produced for members of a club or association; and this is how *Ghosts* received its first English presentation.

When first produced in Ibsen's native Norway, the play received much adverse criticism; and at first, it fared no better in London. This powerful play about the sham of an arranged marriage, about venereal disease, insanity, and euthanasia was undoubtedly too daring in dealing with subjects which could hardly be mentioned in polite society at that time. A storm of controversy was aroused by this story about a woman who remains faithful to her dissolute husband to find in later life that her son is doomed to insanity through congenital venereal disease.

Ghosts is an immensely actable play. Mrs. Alving, the central character, was played in later productions by such outstanding stars as Mrs. Patrick Campbell, Sybil Thorndike, and Flora Robson.

Ibsen implied certain truths by raising questions to which he provided no answer. This device was carried further by many later playwrights, notably Strindberg, Shaw, Galsworthy, and Chekhov.

Ibsen's early plays had been in the main poetical and historical works, such as *The Vikings of Helgeland* and *The Pretenders*. *Brand* (1864), his first major poetical drama of contemporary Norwegian life, dealt with the grim tragedy of a poor minister who refuses to compromise in his struggles against the forces of a materialistic society. *Peer Gynt*, written in 1867, is perhaps the greatest of his early verse plays, portraying the fascinating, highly irresponsible, character of Peer in long passages of lyrical beauty. It was his last play in verse.

Ibsen wrote his first prose work, *The League of Youth* in 1869, a satire on the politics of the time. The dramatist then harked back to the days of early Christianity, and took for his theme in *Emperor and Galilean* the character of the Emperor Julian. This play was completed in 1873.

HENRIK IBSEN (1826-1906)   Regarded as the father of the modern drama, Henrik
Ibsen had a profound effect on contemporary playwrights, particularly on George Bernard Shaw, Ibsen's protagonist in England.

It is Ibsen's subsequent plays, written between 1875 and 1882, which have had the greatest influence on the drama of our time. These are realistic dramas of small-town life. In these powerful pieces the playwright has limned and exposed the hypocrisy, the lies, and the meanness of parochial society. *The Pillars of Society, A Doll's House, Ghosts,* and *An Enemy of the People* are plays which have a universal validity.

The Wild Duck, written in 1884, remains perhaps his most appealing and beautiful work. In this play and in *Rosmersholm* (1886) and *The Lady from the Sea* (1888) Ibsen reveals an individual searching within himself for a self identity and a valid value system.

HEDDA GABLER (1890)

Hedda Gabler is a study of an emotional woman whose bitter envy for what she does not possess leads to tragedy. The role has attracted some of the greatest actresses of the times. In England, Mrs. Patrick Campbell, Laura Cowie, Jean Forbes-Robertson, and Peggy Ashcroft have played the part with great distinction; while in America Mrs. Fiske, Nazimova, and Eva LeGallienne have also won laurels in the role.

IBSEN'S LAST PLAYS

In *The Master Builder* (1892), and in all his last plays—*Little Eyolf, John Gabriel Borkman,* and *When We Dead Awaken*—written between 1894 and 1899—Ibsen makes use of symbolism as he explores universal human themes: youth and age, the artist in society, ways of loving.

Ibsen's stature as a foremost dramatist derives not only from his fearless tackling of monumental themes, but also from his skilled and often poetic treatment of character, plot, and dialogue. As a craftsman, Ibsen observed the unities of time and place. To reveal the thoughts of a character, he avoided the artificiality of the soli-

"AN ENEMY OF THE PEOPLE" (1950)   *In Arthur Miller's adaptation of Ibsen's polemical play, Frederic March as Dr. Stockmann exhorts the townspeople to resist the continued pollution of their water. This play embodied Miller's precept that "the stage is the place for ideas, for philosophies, for the most intense discussion of man's fate."*

loquy. His dialogue in everyday language is so strong that it carries with it all the needed implication to perfectly delineate his characters and give his work substance. He sees the evils, the follies, the stupidities of life, and he reveals the weaknesses and the strengths of his characters as they grapple with the mores and rules of a materialistic society. Yet the playwright offers no solution to the problems inherent in his exposition. Ibsen offers no way out, only a plea for understanding.

"HEDDA GABLER"   Minnie Maddern Fiske is seen here in the title role of a 1903
New York production of Henrik Ibsen's drama *"Hedda Gabler."* With her, as Judge
Brock, is George Arliss, who joined the company in 1904. One of the earliest champions

of Ibsen in the United States, Minnie Fiske performed many of the major roles in the Ibsen repertory including Nora Helmer in "A Doll's House," Rebecca West in "Rosmersholm," and Laura Hessel in "Pillars of Society."

OSCAR WILDE (1854-1900)   Irish dramatist and noted wit, Wilde wrote what is considered the most outstanding polished light comedy since the Restoration. "The Importance of Being Earnest," written in 1895, is an outstanding example of his elegance and wit.

THE COMEDY OF MANNERS

Though some dramatists were now beginning to portray a more serious view of life in writing for the stage—as illustrated in the problem plays of John Galsworthy—this seriousness was offset to some degree by a revival of the comedy of manners in the witty, satirical plays of Oscar Wilde, and by the fantasy and humor in the works of James Barrie.

OSCAR WILDE (1854-1900)

The first important success of Oscar Wilde, *Lady Windermere's Fan*, was staged in 1892 at St. James's Theatre by Sir George Alexander, a leading actor-manger. Wilde's epigrams and the brilliance of his dialogue, with its sharp satire and wit, brought him great popularity.

"THE IMPORTANCE OF BEING EARNEST" (1939)   *Gwen Ffrangcon-Davies, John Gielgud, and Edith Evans as they appeared in Sir John Gielgud's production of Oscar Wilde's play.*

A Woman of No Importance was produced by Tree at the Haymarket in 1893. It was a success, although it is the weakest of Wilde's plays. In 1895, Wilde wrote his two best plays: the first, *An Ideal Husband,* was a play involving political intrigue; the second, *The Importance of Being Earnest,* was a lighthearted gallop. This clever and hilarious picture of a grand lady of Victorian society choosing suitable marriage partners for her daughter and nephew is the play most often revived.

Oscar Wilde wrote one other play, *Salome,* in French, for Sarah Bernhardt, although she never undertook the part when it was produced in Paris. A poetic fantasy on the biblical theme, it was censored in England, but was later converted by Richard Strauss into an opera.

Wilde's career came to an untimely end when in 1895, he was sent to prison for two years for a homosexual offense. His spirit broken, he died soon afterwards.

JAMES M. BARRIE (1860-1937)

Before turning to the theatre, James M. Barrie had already made a reputation as a novelist. In 1897, his dramatization of his novel *The Little Minister* was a great financial success. *Quality Street,* in 1902, gave a well-considered picture of a bygone age. *The Admirable Crichton,* written the same year, is a delightful comedy in which a shipwrecked upperclass family is rescued from helplessness when their butler and maid assert a natural leadership, which is swiftly relinquished when the family is rescued and returns to its old home. Underlying the topsyturveydom of the escapade is delicious social satire.

Peter Pan (1904), perhaps the best known and most continually successful of Barrie's fantasies, was written for children and its royalties were donated to a London children's hospital. This story of the boy who never grew up is performed every year at Christmas time in London. *Peter Pan* became a popular musical in New York, and continues to be a perpetual delight to both children and adults.

What Every Woman Knows (1908) is a well-constructed comedy disclosing the unseen power of woman over her man. *Dear Brutus* (1917) and *Mary Rose* (1920) are fantasies in which a real and an imagined world are delightfully blended. Barrie's last work, *The Boy David*, was an attempt to present the well-known Bible story in contemporary terms. It was played in 1936 by Elizabeth Bergner for whom it had originally been written, but it was considered too lighthearted a piece for the subject matter and did not prove to be a success.

Barrie displayed a masterful handling of stage effect. Although his impish delight in underlining the fact that things are never what they seem leads him at times to sentimentality, his fanciful and kindly humor give his works a timelessness which enables them to be constantly revived.

JOHN GALSWORTHY (1867-1933)

John Galsworthy, like Barrie, made a reputation as a novelist before writing for the theatre. His great novel of late Victorian society, THE FORSYTE SAGA aptly describes the changing social patterns of his time through characters created with consummate skill and understanding.

The Silver Box, his first play, was written for Granville-Barker and produced at the Court Theatre in 1906. In this, as in many of his plays, Galsworthy was concerned with the social injustice of one law for the rich and another law for the poor.

Galsworthy's characters are drawn from his own acute observation of life. There are no heroes and no true villains. His plays are realistically written in simple language, with no false heroics or artificial devices. What makes his dramas so effective is that Galsworthy has selected profound social themes which depict humanity in conflict with the conventions of society, and the playwright has

*JOHN GALSWORTHY (1867-
1933)   Born into a family of means
and educated at Oxford University,
Galsworthy was a stalwart exponent
of social justice. He is best known
for his massive novel "The Forsyte
Saga" which depicts Victorian society with penetrating accuracy.
Galsworthy produced many dramas
dealing with the social and political
problems of his time.*

convincingly given his subject matter pulsating life through everyday dialogue.

In *Strife* (1906) conflict between labor and management in a
tinplate works leads to a strike which ends in purposeless tragedy.
In *Justice* (1910), Galsworthy drew on his experience as a barrister
to realistically portray what takes place in a solicitor's office, in a
court of justice, and in a prison. The first production of this play at
the Duke of York's Theatre in 1910 received distinguished performances by many fine actors, including Dion Boucicault, Edmond
Gwenn, Charles Maude, and Lewis Casson.

Galsworthy's dramatic power lies in his serious questioning of
the cruelty, ugliness, poverty, and inequity that pervade the circumstances in which the individual finds himself imprisoned. His plays
however lack the depth and breadth of life portrayed in his novels,
and his dramas lack enough humor and optimism to leaven the
heavy social outlook.

GEORGE BERNARD SHAW (1856-1950)

Perhaps the most outstanding playwright of his time was G. B. Shaw. Shaw learned much from Ibsen; yet in his fifty plays, Shaw expressed his ideas with an aptness, a logic, and a whimsical speculation that have made him one of the great dramatists of our time. He approaches Wilde in wit, excels Barrie in fantasy, and in implication, his themes are deeper than those of Galsworthy. Above all, Shaw is eloquent. His plays were published with extremely detailed stage directions. Even today his prefaces on social and political reform are read independently as masterpieces of prose.

In contrast with Ibsen, Shaw seeks an answer to the problems inherent in the world in which he lives. The evils of slum landlords, and of prostitution—the cant of the medical profession—the hypocrisy of certain aspects of religious belief—the needless tragedy of war—and the economic power of the great industrialists—all came under his questioning, rational scrutiny. Yet Shaw did not employ the stage merely as a platform to air his theories of reform. He used his craft as a dramatist to exert his extraordinary power of stimulating thought by creating fresh individual characters and having them speak in deliciously sprightly dialogue. Despite a paucity of action, Shaw's plays were easily as entertaining as the old love and sex dramas and farces. Little happens in a Shaw play except talk. But *what* talk! What eloquence! There is a continuous rain of paradox and satire, a shattering of established beliefs, an exposing of false ideals, a questioning of every social convention. And all is leavened with a riotous humor and a sparkling wit which hold his audience spellbound. Shaw's power of language, the breadth and depth of his knowledge and intellect, the clearness of his vision, brought to the theatre a distinctive and thoughtful urbanity unequaled in this century. Shaw can justly be called the father of the theatre of ideas.

After years of functioning as a novelist and as a critic of books, music, art, and drama, Shaw started late in life as a dramatist. Shaw was persuaded by J. T. Grein to write something for the Independent Theatre Group after their production of Ibsen's *Ghosts.*

Widowers' Houses, begun some years earlier during a period of collaboration with William Archer, was completed and received its first production in 1892. The play was received with mixed feelings by the audience. The younger, more liberal elements applauded its attack on the vested interests, while the more conservative minded regarded Shaw as subversive and objected to the injection of political matters which they considered outside the sphere of the theatre.

Nevertheless, the encouragement Shaw gained from seeing his work on the stage set him to writing plays in earnest. The following year saw *The Philanderer,* a lighthearted comedy on a subject Shaw generally eschewed—sexual attraction. Then followed *Mrs. Warren's Profession,* a serious play dealing with prostitution. The latter was produced in 1902 by the Stage Society, and did not come to public performance until the Lord Chamberlain's veto was relaxed in 1920.

When the play was first produced in New York by Arnold Daly during a two-month season of Shaw's plays, the police arrested Daly, Mary Shaw, his leading actress, and other members of the cast, as a result of complaints by the more shocked members of the audience. The judge, who had the advantage of knowing neither the author nor the play, suspended proceedings while he took a week to read the play, and then returned to acquit the company, with the pronouncement that, as far as he was concerned, there was nothing wrong with the play.

America has always made Shaw welcome on its stages; and no fewer than nine of his plays were first produced in the United States, chiefly by the Theatre Guild. Indeed, The Devil's Disciple was played in America with Richard Mansfield as Dick Dudgeon, two years before it received its first London production.

The last three mentioned dramatic works, along with *Arms and the Man, Candida,* and *The Man of Destiny* were published together in 1898 as *Plays, Pleasant and Unpleasant,* with prefaces and very detailed descriptions of the characters and stage directions. *Arms and the Man,* an anti-romantic view of Balkan cloak-and-

GEORGE BERNARD SHAW (1856-1950)   With "Widowers'
Houses," written in 1895, Shaw embarked on a career that was to make
him the most important playwright of his time. In the bulk of his plays,
the noted dramatist-critic dealt with social issues such as prostitution
and slum landlordism—subjects that had not previously been introduced on the stage. As a critic, Shaw is remembered for his "The
Quintessence of Ibsenism (1891), and the famed prefaces to his plays.

dagger warfare, was remarkably advanced in its concept that military operations can be conducted in as businesslike and efficient a manner as a Swiss hotel. *Candida* is a domestic play with a strong title role. A woman has to make a choice between an adoring youthful poet and her idealistic and philanthropic middle-aged clergyman husband. *The Man of Destiny* is a short play that yields an unconventional picture of Napoleon.

Before the 1890's, dramatists in England were wary of publishing their plays because of the laxity of the copyright laws in America; but in 1891 an agreement afforded playwrights the opportunity to publish with full protection. Thus the works of the important writers for the theatre rapidly began to enjoy wide interest; and in many cases, yielded not only literary fame but royalties through worldwide production by both repertory theatres and amateur groups.

In the years following, Shaw continued to pour out plays. *You Never Can Tell* (1896) was an amusing light comedy, as "commercial" as any seen in the theatre at that time. *The Devil's Disciple*, a melodrama, set in the time of the American Revolutionary War, followed that same year. *Caesar and Cleopatra* was written in 1897 for Shaw's favorite actor, Forbes-Robertson; and *Captain Brassbound's Conversion*, a tilt at imperialism, was especially written for Ellen Terry. In 1900, Shaw wrote *The Admirable Bashville*, based on an earlier unsuccessful novel.

Man and Superman, written in 1901, may be briefly described as a parable of love and life. Romantic and realistic, this drama contains a complete play within a play. The third act presents Don Juan in Hades. The main characters reappear in different roles to engage in a long and amusing discussion on heaven and hell. This third act is often omitted from the play's presentation.

"TOO TRUE TO BE GOOD"   *Lillian Gish and Sir Cedric Hardwicke appear in the 1963 Broadway production of Shaw's 1932 play. The all-star cast also included Eileen Heckert, David Wayne and Ray Middleton. In this play about a preacher who has lost his faith and a wealthy girl turned thief, Shaw displayed his despair about mankind's will to save itself from a dying civilization.*

Shaw's Irish origin and his friendship with W. B. Yeats encouraged him in 1904 to write *John Bull's Other Island* for the Abbey Theatre in Dublin. The play failed, although the dramatization of English and Irish characters and attitudes was wonderfully apt and is still basically valid.

Major Barbara, produced in 1905, was an attack on the power of the great munitions manufacturers, and also offers a glimpse of the work of the Salvation Army in its fight against the evils of poverty and drink.

The following year came *The Doctor's Dilemma,* a tragicomedy in which the medical profession, almost the bitterest of Shaw's detestations, is mercilessly exposed. *Misalliance* (1910) considers religion and eugenics; *Fanny's First Play* (1911), attacks suburbs and drama critics. Trotter, for instance, was a recognizable portrait of A. B. Walkley, the Times critic of the day.

Shaw chose the Roman period of early Christianity for *Androcles and the Lion,* written in 1912. That same year, he produced one of his best plays, *Pygmalion,* for Mrs. Patrick Campbell whom he much admired and who played brilliantly in the role of Eliza. This play has become more widely known through its film version and through its musical version, *My Fair Lady,* one of the fabulous successes of our time.

The next few years cover the period of the First World War, when the time was not ripe for the performance of serious works. But during this period Shaw began writing *Heartbreak House,* which saw completion in 1919, a comedy with a Chekhovian flavor which must be ranked with his best plays.

His next great work, *Back to Methuselah,* a collection of five plays, speculates about the consequences of an enormous increase in longevity; the last part of the play is set 30,000 years in the future. This work was first produced in America by the Theatre Guild.

Shaw's interpretation of medieval history in *Saint Joan* (1923) starred Sybil Thorndike in the London production. In 1930, Cedric Hardwicke gave an excellent performance in *The Apple Cart* as

SIR JAMES M. BARRIE (1860-1937)   This Scottish novelist and dramatist is beloved by generations of readers and theatregoers, for producing works which, though appealingly warm and whimsical, escape sentimentality through the exercise of sure wit and craftsmanship. Who of us does not cherish memories of proclaiming our belief in fairies to keep Tinker Bell alive and Peter Pan eternally young?

the wily and intelligent King Magnus, manipulating the weaknesses of his ministers. *Too True to be Good,* a fantasy completed in 1931, introduced Private Meek, based on Shaw's own friend, T. E. Lawrence. *The Millionairess* followed in 1936, with a dynamic, bossy woman as the main character, which provided a wonderful role for many fine actresses, including Ellen Pollock and Katherine Hepburn.

The rise of fascism in Europe brought forth *Geneva,* written in 1938, whose caricatures of Mussolini and Hitler prove too lighthearted in view of the enormity of the event.

Shaw was never completely popular with London audiences until J. E. Vedreune and Harley Granville-Barker introduced a repertory season at the Court Theatre in Sloane Square between 1904 and 1907. Eleven of Shaw's plays were put on, as well as other fine productions by Euripides, Maeterlinck, Hauptmann, Yeats, Masefield, Galsworthy, and Granville-Barker.

Shaw took an active interest in the production of his plays, attending many rehearsals and going over the plays in every detail, explaining and demonstrating how each character should speak. Whenever Shaw found himself conveniently near a production of any of his plays, he would descend on the theatre during rehearsals to give the actors first-hand knowledge of his intentions in writing the piece.

Shaw's last play, *In Good King Charles's Golden Days,* was written when he was eighty-three, and gives a picture of a sympathetic and intelligent monarch in the days of the Restoration. Shaw wrote on a wide range of topics, until the ripe age of ninety-five when he died.

SHAW AT THE MALVERN FESTIVAL

In his later years, Shaw had the pleasure of seeing his plays performed at the Malvern Festival. Founded in 1929 by Sir Barry Jackson of the famous Birmingham Repertory Theatre, the festival ran for a month each summer. Plays were presented by such dramatists as Sheridan, Fielding, Dion Boucicault, James Bridie, J. B. Priestley, C. K. Munro, and Lord Dunsany.

Shaw was always strongly represented. Indeed, during its first season, the repertory was confined to Shaw's works: *The Apple Cart, Back to Methuselah, Caesar and Cleopatra,* and *Heartbreak House.* Seven of Shaw's plays received their first performance at the Festival, to be transferred later to London.

Lectures and discussions on the theatre were given during the

Festival, which attracted a large number of interested parties—critics from London, writers, producers, actors, and good enthusiastic audiences.

CURRENT INTEREST IN SHAW

Interest in Shaw's plays had slackened in England in the last decade or so, but there have been periodic revivals. Very successful productions have recently been staged in London: *Fanny's First Play, Too True to be Good, Man and Superman,* and *Captain Brassbound's Conversion.*

HARLEY GRANVILLE-BARKER (1877-1946)

Granville Barker was a fine combination of a scholar and a theatrical craftsman of artistic sensibility. In addition to his plays, the chief of which are *The Voysey Inheritance* and *The Madras House* he published prefaces to Shakespeare, the fruit of his notable productions of Shakespeare at the Savoy Theatre in 1912, and his researches and studies. He was responsible for a new attitude toward stage presentation, using simplified settings in contrast with the elaborated stage pictures of the customary West End production.

Barker was an indefatigable worker for the institution of a subsidized National Theatre in England, which Shaw also ardently and actively supported. Neither saw its eventual birth and extraordinary success at the Old Vic in 1962.

THE ABBEY THEATRE

During the early years of the century, the rising Nationalist movement in Ireland found expression in Dublin's Abbey Theatre, founded by the poet W. B. Yeats (1865-1939) and Lady Gregory (1852-1932) in 1904 for the purpose of presenting works on Irish

JOHN SYNGE (1871-1909)
A leading figure in the Irish Dramatic Movement, he is considered by many as Eire's greatest playwright. His fame rests principally on his poetic one-act play "Riders to the Sea" (1904) and his ironic comedy "The Playboy of the Western World" (1907).

themes by native dramatists. Within a few years, the Abbey had gained a worldwide reputation as a repertory theatre. Its plays were presented in a simple but lively manner and dealt with every aspect of Irish life. Other Irish writers were attracted to it, including J. M. Synge, A. E. (George William Russell), Lennox Robinson, Padraic Colum, and St. John Ervine.

Lady Gregory and J. M. Synge wrote plays in the idiom of the country people of Western Ireland, using authentic dialect. This practice of using the living "language of the folk" was adopted by other Irish dramatists; and the richness of Irish poetic fantasy and of Irish speech projected in the fine acting of the Abbey players made the Abbey a theatre of distinction.

The Abbey continues to the present time, and of the later writers associated with it the most important are Denis Johnston, Paul

SEAN O'CASEY (1880-1964)
Known as "The dramatist of the
Dublin slums," this Irish play-
wright came into prominence with
his first play "Shadow of a Gunman"
(1920), a melodrama dealing with
the Anglo-Irish wars. Thereafter
his plays turned increasingly to-
ward symbolism. O'Casey's reputa-
tion rests on his too realistic master-
works "Juno and the Paycock"
(1924) and "The Plough and the
Stars" (1926).

Vincent Carroll, and Sean O'Casey. These playwrights have also been widely produced in England and America.

SEAN O'CASEY (1880-1964)

Sean O'Casey wrote some extremely powerful dramas of the Dublin slum life which he knew so well. Despite the grim realism of his works, his dramas possess an essentially poetic quality. In *Juno and the Paycock* and *Shadow of a Gunman* the bitter strife of the years between 1915 and 1922 in Ireland is the background for laughter and tears. *The Plough and the Stars*, an even stronger tragic play about the Easter uprising of 1916, caused a riot when it opened in Dublin in 1926. His antiwar play, *The Silver Tassie*, with its skillful blending of naturalism and symbolism, is considered by some critics the greatest expression of his deeply spiritual, if somewhat bitter, view of life.

THE DUBLIN GATE THEATRE

The Gate Theatre was started in Dublin in 1928 by Hilton Edwards and Micheal MacLiammoir to give superior productions to great plays from all periods and all countries, and to encourage works by Irish writers different in style and subject from those produced at the Abbey. The plays of Shakespeare, Ibsen, Strindberg, Chekhov, Shaw, Eugene O'Neill, and Elmer Rice have been acted at the Gate, as were plays written by such contemporary Irish writers as Denis Johnston, Mary Manning, David Sears.

IRISH ACTORS

The Irish theatre has had great significance in both England and America. Moreover it has produced some notable actors such as Sara Allgood and her sister Maire O'Neill, Dudley Digges, Barry Fitzgerald, Siobhan McKenna, and Micheal MacLiammoir.

SOMERSET MAUGHAM (1874-1965)   Noted for the sardonic humor and epigrammatic wit of his polished comedies of manners, Somerset Maugham turned later to more serious social comedies. However, with the failure in 1933 of his bitter comedy "Sheppy," Maugham gave up writing for the theatre.

WILLIAM SOMERSET MAUGHAM (1874-1965)

In the period between the two wars, a group of plays were presented on the English stage which can be broadly described as the social comedy of manners. This genre, established by Oscar Wilde in the 1890's, depends for its success on brilliance of wit, excellent characterization, and dexterity of stage craftsmanship.

Without doubt, the greatest of the dramatists in this style is Somerset Maugham, who wrote over thirty plays between 1896 and 1933. He was a superb storyteller who could create characters and situations with implications far more profound than is at first apparent in the dialogue. The performance of his plays by such stylish actors as Marie Lohr, Irene Ranbrugh, Constance Collier, C. Aubrey Smith, Reginald Owen, and A. E. Matthews contributed much to their great success.

Presenting a somewhat sardonic view of humanity, Maugham does not preach and never ingratiates. He draws a picture of people as they are in life, neither good nor bad, and exposes the clash of personalities in unforeseen situations. In many ways, he is the modern embodiment of the Restoration playwrights, and represents a stage of transition, between the grim realism of his time and avant garde experimentalism.

Typical examples of his work are *The Constant Wife* and *Our Betters,* plays about idle members of society whose main preoccupation is with illicit love. The clinical analysis of character in these plays is greater in depth than it is in his other works which present an acutely accurate, but general, picture of the frivolous society of the 1920's. His last play, *Sheppey,* written in 1933, is entirely different in character; it is a kind of Everyman morality play set in a working-class milieu. In the London production, Ralph Richardson played the title role with great distinction.

Having left a body of highly polished works which entertained a generation of playgoers, Maugham retired from the theatre to resume the writing of novels, short stories, and memoirs.

FREDERICK LONSDALE (1881-1954)

Writing drawing room comedy and satirizing social manners with sharp wit was Frederick Lonsdale, whose not unworthy aim was to be entertaining. *The Last of Mrs. Cheyney, On Approval,* and *Canaries Sometimes Sing,* successes of the 1920's, are popular perennials with repertory companies since their amusing plots and witty dialogue offer opportunities for sophisticated, stylish acting.

NOEL COWARD (1899-   )

A consummate man of the theatre—actor, director, playwright, and composer—is the urbane Noel Coward. His early plays, written and produced in the 1920's, are witty and accurate reflections of trends in society of that epoch. Coward reflects the growing freedom in thought and behavior, coupled with a paradoxical disillusionment.

Noel Coward appeared with Lillian Braithwaite in 1924 with considerable success in *The Vortex,* his first notable achievement. The following year, *Hay Fever* and *Fallen Angels* added to his rise to fame. He wrote most of the sketches and composed the music and lyrics for *Charlot's Revue* (1924), *On With the Dance* (1925), and *This Year of Grace* (1927). There was a break in his good fortune with *Sirocco* in 1927; but he returned in triumph in 1929 with the brilliant musical play *Bittersweet.* In this play set in the Victorian age, Coward accurately gauged the public's desire for sentiment and romance, sated with years of enjoying brittle, matter-of-fact pieces. *Bittersweet* was followed by his spectacular, patriotic evocation of the Edwardian age in *Cavalcade* (1931), presented at Drury Lane with considerable success.

Private Lives, a witty and amusing battle of the sexes involving two ill-assorted couples, well merits its periodic revivals. In 1932, Coward wrote *Design for Living* for Alfred Lunt and Lynn Fontanne, and appeared with them as the third member of the menage a trois. Next, there was *Tonight at 8:30,* a program of nine one-act plays.

NOEL COWARD (1899-   )
The tradition of English high comedy in the manner of Congreve and Wilde found its foremost contemporary exponent in Noel Coward. He has won distinction as an actor, a composer, and as a writer of musical comedies and farces noted for their witty dialogue and polish.

With *This Happy Breed* he abandoned the typical Coward bohemian locale to create a suburban setting for his sympathetically treated everyday family. During the war, he wrote *Blithe Spirit* (1941) a gay and amusing fantasy on the subject of spiritualism, which enjoyed a record run, and was later made into a musical. In *Present Laughter* (1942), Coward returned to his successful formula, and wrote a comedy of theatrical life.

Though his more recent works have not been great successes, his older works are constantly revived on and off the major circuits.

Coward's plays, with their witty, laconic dialogue, rely for their success on expert timing and technique, attributes well evidenced in his own distinguished performances. Lately, Coward has appeared in films; he is currently readying a bill of new plays for a London presentation.

DAME EDITH EVANS
(1888-   )   *The actress
appeared at the Globe Theatre, London, in 1939, as Lady
Bracknell in Oscar Wilde's
"The Importance of Being
Earnest."*

TERENCE RATTIGAN (1911-   )

Master of the deft light comedy, Terence Rattigan's first success
was the long-running farce *French Without Tears* (1939). The
Lunts played *Love in Idleness* (1944) very successfully in London,
retitled *O Mistress Mine* in New York.

Rattigan plumbed a deeper vein in his prize-winning *The Winslow Boy* (1946). Based on a cause célèbre of Edwardian days, the

"DESIGN FOR LIVING"   *Noel Coward's sprightly comedy about a ménage à trois opened in 1932 to the consternation of some critics. This humorous dig at conventional marriage was delightfully portrayed by Alfred Lunt and Lynn Fontanne. Author Noel Coward is seen at the right.*

Archer-Shee case, the play deals with the struggle of the family of a young naval cadet to vindicate a lad wrongly accused of theft.

Adventure Story (1949), an attempt at an historical drama which presents Alexander of Macedon as a brash fascist dictator, had touching moments, but was a failure.

In *The Browning Version* (1948), Rattigan created a memorable character in the sensitive, aging schoolmaster, married to a rapacious, vulgar woman. *The Deep Blue Sea* (1952) provided Peggy Ashcroft with a wonderful full-length role which she played magnificently in the London production of a woman whose deep, unsatisfied love for a ne'er-do-well drives her to an unsuccessful attempt at suicide. *The Sleeping Prince* (1953) was a return to the light-hearted comedy of manners about European aristocracy in the Edwardian age; Laurence Olivier and Vivien Leigh appeared in the London production.

In 1954 came *Separate Tables,* with its unusual construction. The piece consists of two separate plays sharing a common setting, a genteel residential hotel. The play delineates two sets of main characters, completely different but sharing human experiences that have in common the perpetual torment of introspection and loneliness. The couples, drawn together by sympathy for their respective weaknesses, fall in love. In London, these double parts were played with great feeling and distinction by Margaret Leighton and Eric Portman.

Rattigan has provided the West End theatre with a series of successes by courting the middle-class audience with a demonstration of respect for their intelligence. His plays, skillfully entertaining, show a depth of thought and feeling.

OTHER WRITERS OF COMEDIES OF MANNERS

Other dramatists who produced works of social comedy were Dodie Smith, whose *Autumn Crocus, Dear Octopus,* and *Call it a Day* were among the successes of the 1930's; John Van Druten (1901-

TERENCE RATTIGAN (1911-) Highly regarded for their excellent craftsmanship, Terence Rattigan's light comedies—typified by the Lunt's vehicle "O Mistress Mine" (1944) and the comic operatic romance "The Sleeping Prince" (1953)—overshadowed his plays with more serious themes. He was especially successful with "The Winslow Boy" (1946), a drama which won considerable acclaim both in England and the U.S.

1957), who wrote light comedies such as *Young Woodley, There's Always Juliet, After All,* and *The Voice of the Turtle;* and W. Chetham Strode. The last named wrote *The Guinea Pig,* a comedy of class distinctions in a famous public school, and *The Gleam* which portrays doctors in the National Health Service.

More recently, Hugh Williams, in collaboration with his wife Margaret, concocted light comedies such as *The Grass is Greener, The Plaintiff in a Pretty Hat, The Happy Man,* and *Past Imperfect.*

William Douglas Home, whose brother relinquished his peerage to become Prime Minister, uses his familiarity with politics to create comedies such as *Chiltern Hundreds, The Reluctant Debutante,* and *The Reluctant Peer.*

JOHN DRINKWATER (1882-1937)

Before he turned to drama, John Drinkwater had been a poet but he also had worked in the Birmingham Repertory Theatre as an actor, director, and manager. His subjects were chosen from the past, but his theme was eternal: the impact of circumstances on strong moral purpose. His early verse plays include *Rebellion,* set in Victorian times and written in 1914. *X=O : A Night of the Trojan War* was an antiwar play.

Drinkwater later turned to prose and was a dramatist of power and integrity. His most important work is *Abraham Lincoln* which had a successful run in 1919 of over a year at the Lyric Theatre, Hammersmith, under the enterprising management of Nigel Playfair. The play utilizes two chroniclers who explain and comment in verse.

Oliver Cromwell was written in 1920 but was not produced until two years later. Although it is a rare incursion into a strangely neglected period of English history, it was not a success. Two more well-wrought but not too successful historical dramas were *Robert E. Lee* (1923) and *Mary Stuart* (1922).

In complete contrast, Drinkwater wrote a delightful modern comedy, *Bird in Hand,* which opened the 1927 season at the Birmingham Repertory Theatre and later had a successful run in London.

RUDOLF BESIER (1878-1942)

Rudolf Besier wrote a play in verse, *The Virgin Goddess,* and some run-of-the-mill comedies before he produced *The Barretts of Wimpole Street,* for which he is chiefly known. This poignant story of the merciful escape of Elizabeth Barrett Browning from her tyrannical Victorian father through the love of Robert Browning was a great success in London where Cedric Hardwicke and Gwen Ffrangcon-Davies played the main parts with great distinction. The play was later made into a successful film with Charles Laughton; and then, into the musical *Robert and Elizabeth.*

JAMES BRIDIE (1888-1951)

The Scottish dramatist James Bridie started life as O. H. Mavor, a doctor, serving as an Army surgeon in both World Wars. He joined the Scottish National Players and began turning out play after play in quick succession. He found his themes in the Bible, as in *Tobias and the Angel, Jonah and the Whale,* and *Susannah and the Elders;* in medical history, as in *The Anatomist;* and in Scottish Calvinism, as in *The Devil and Mr. Bolfry.* He also wrote many imaginative plays based on affairs of the day, such as *The King of Nowhere,* and satirical comedies such as *It Depends What You Mean, What Say They, The Black Eye, Dr. Angelus,* and *A Sleeping Clergyman.*

His plays are written with a facility for witty dialogue which reminds us of Shaw; but Bridie does not always possess the force to bring his plays to successful resolution.

Bridie divided the major part of his life between medicine and the theatre. He rejoined the Medical Corps when World War II broke out; and when he returned to civilian life, he played a leading part in establishing the Glasgow Citizens Theatre, the most important of the few repertory theatres in Scotland.

R. C. SHERRIFF (1896-   )

R. C. Sherriff is known chiefly for his first play, *Journey's End,* which had a memorable impact on the London audience in 1929. The play deals with the horrors of trench warfare in France during the First World War. A moving and dramatic story, it tells of a small group of officers waiting to carry out a futile order to attack the enemy in the face of insurmountable odds. It has been played all over the world, and remains one of the most powerful anti-war pleas in the modern theatre. The fine playing of Colin Clive, Maurice Evans, and Robert Speaight contributed to the long success of the London production.

Sherriff wrote other plays, none of which possesses the underlying seriousness of his first play, but many of them have been successful. These include *Badger's Green* (1930), a comedy about a village cricket match, *St. Helena* (1935), about Napoleon's last years, splendidly played in the Old Vic production by Kenneth Kent and Ian Swinley, *Miss Mabel* (1948), *Home at Seven* (1950), a study of a victim of amnesia, provided an excellent part for Ralph Richardson.

Sherriff's recent work has a more imaginative quality, as evidenced by *The Long Sunset,* a drama about the closing years of the Roman occupation of Britain, which has many moments of beauty and pathos.

J. B. PRIESTLEY (1894-   )

A dramatist who ranges far and wide in the world of ideas is J. B. Priestley, who was first known as the author of a very successful novel THE GOOD COMPANIONS (1929). In collaboration with Edward Knoblock, this story was adapted for the stage and produced in 1931 with John Gielgud in the leading role. Its success inspired Priestley to write for the theatre, and he has produced well over twenty plays. These differ widely in scope and purpose, but most of them are serious in their implications. Priestley has also evidenced the ability to provide sheer entertainment with such lighthearted comedies such as *When We Are Married* (1938), *Ever Since Paradise,* and *Are They the Same at Home.*

Dangerous Corner, Priestley's first play, produced at the Lyric Theatre in 1932, embeds its criticism of the middle class in an ingenious plot. The first part of the drama brings its characters into unnerving conflict, spurred by a chance remark. Then the play begins all over again. This time, the chance remark is not made, and the play ends with the characters in full control of their thoughts and emotions. We realize that what we have witnessed is only what might have been.

Priestley's interest in J. W. Dunne's theories of time was given dramatic expression in *Time and the Conways* and *I Have Been Here Before,* both produced in 1937. During the war, Priestley's themes became topical, and his *Desert Highway* reflects the soldier's thoughts in a questioning mood. *Are They the Same at Home?* depicts life in evacuated Britain as a comedy of muddling through. *They Came to a City* (1942), a vision of a new life and existence set in the future, reflected thoughts and dreams cherished by a people at war.

The Linden Tree was written after the war, in 1947, during the difficult period of adjustment to spiritual needs and material short-comings. A popular play of the post-war period was Priestley's 1945 work, *An Inspector Calls*. The inspector, a mysterious figure investigating the death of a poor girl, questions all the characters in the play who have in some way been responsible for the tragedy. The inspector—an outsider and the symbol of conscience—is skill-fully integrated with the characters drawn from real life.

Priestley later collaborated with his wife, Jaquetta Hawkes, on two successful productions, *Dragon's Mouth* (1952) and *The White Countess* (1954). An amusing comedy on love, *The Severed Head*, written in collaboration with the novelist Iris Murdoch, has settled down in London for a long run.

EMLYN WILLIAMS (1905-   )

Emlyn Williams, equally known as an actor and dramatist, met success with his thriller *Night Must Fall* (1935), in which he

EMLYN WILLIAMS (1905-   ) This noted Welsh producer, author, and actor drew on his own background for his auto-biographical "The Corn is Green," in which he played the young Welsh miner. Williams became known all over the world for his one-man reading of selections from Dickens. He did a similar reading from the works of Dylan Thomas which he called "A Boy Growing Up."

played the main character, a psychopathic killer. Then, drawing on his own upbringing in a Welsh mining village, he wrote *The Corn is Green* (1938), a study of a woman teacher with the absorbing desire to give one of her pupils, a young miner, the chance to compete for an Oxford scholarship. Emlyn Williams played the part of the young student to a magnificent performance by Sybil Thorndike as the teacher. *The Wind of Heaven,* produced in 1945, which again takes place in a Welsh village—this time in Victorian times—is an ambitious play based on the theme of the Second Coming. Although it may be claimed that he borders on sentimentality at times, Williams' work is extremely effective on the stage.

W. C. HUNTER

W. C. Hunter's plays are somewhat reminiscent of the mood of Chekhov. *Waters of the Moon, A Day by the Sea,* and *The Tulip Tree* have been successfully presented in London, partly due to the fine opportunities they gave for the sensitive playing of some of England's greatest actors such as Sybil Thorndike, Edith Evans, John Gielgud, and Ralph Richardson.

CHARLES MORGAN (1894-1958)

Charles Morgan was primarily a writer of novels and essays but he wrote three plays that are distinguished by their craftsmanlike writing and unusual themes. *The Flashing Stream* (1938) deals with the painful decision of a man and woman engaged in important and secret mathematical calculations. They conclude that their respective duties, in view of the coming war, are more important than their own personal relationships. *River Line* (1952) and *The Burning Glass* (1954) represent Morgan's other attempts on serious themes, but his characterization in these is somewhat less well realized than his basic ideas.

PETER USTINOV (1921-   )

Peter Ustinov is probably more widely known for his work in films, radio, and television than for his work in the theatre. Nevertheless, this actor-author and director of broadly comic creations has produced some serious work as a playwright.

Graduating as an actor from the Drama School of Michel St. Denis in 1939, Ustinov began writing plays almost as soon as he made his debut as a performer. During the war he served almost five years in the Army where he performed occasionally in satirical revues. His first successful play, *House of Regrets,* produced in 1942 was a sensitive study of aged emigrés from Eastern Europe living in a seedy London boarding house, where they relive their earlier lives through their memories, and fail to come to grips with their new circumstances. Ustinov's preoccupation with the problems of life is mitigated by a richly comic vein.

In 1943, the Old Vic Company presented *Blow Your Own Trumpet.* This was not successful. The following year, *The Banbury Nose* enjoyed a long run. In this play, members of a military family encompass several generations of struggle with Army traditions. Ustinov skillfully presents the inability of a conventional people to understand the changing values of their children.

With *The Love of Four Colonels* (1951), Ustinov had another great success. This delightful satire of the well-contrasted national characteristics of the four colonels—American, English, French, and Russian—in occupied Austria just after the war, is written with great wit and understanding.

Possibly Ustinov's most impressive play is *The Moment of Truth,* produced in 1951. This drama is set in the recent past and concerns a European country defeated in war. A very old and ailing Marshal is made the nominal head of the unoccupied part of the country as he is the only one to have retained the respect of the people. Although he is manipulated by the wily Prime Minister and is unaware of the puppet nature of his position, he fulfills his duty to

his country. After some years, the invaders are routed and the Army of Resistance takes over. The Marshall and his daughter, who has looked after him throughout the war, are imprisoned as collaborators. She dies in his arms, and he has a momentary vision of clarity in which he becomes aware of the tragic train of events in which he has been trapped. At the beginning, one is reminded of Pétain and Laval, which does not diminish the play's universality as a powerful argument against war, in which none are victors and all are vanquished.

In *Romanoff and Juliet* (1956), a lighthearted comedy, Ustinov sets the scene in a mythical European country of minute size which is nevertheless strategically important to both East and West. The American and Russian embassies face each other across the town square. The Prime Minister plays one country against the other; but love inevitably crosses national boundaries, and the fun begins when the son of the Russian Ambassador falls in love with the American Ambassador's daughter. The Prime Minister becomes a go-between for the two families. Ustinov's humor and satire are riotously triumphant throughout.

In *Photo Finish,* an eighty-year-old author confined to his bed, relives his past life through imaginary conversations with himself, first as a young man, then a middle-aged man, and finally an elderly man. Ustinov immensely enjoyed playing the main part when the play was first produced in London in 1962.

While Ustinov has successfully produced serious drama from time to time, he excels in the creation of pure satirical comedy.

"JUNO AND THE PAYCOCK"   Colin Blakely is seen here as Cap'n Boyle and Frank Finlay as Joxer Daly in Laurence Olivier's 1966 production at the National Theatre of Sean O'Casey's moving tragedy.

GRAHAM GREENE (1904-   )
Known as a distinguished novelist,
Graham Greene achieved distinc-
tion with a series of plays devoted
to moral questions. All of his
dramas bear the strong impress of
his Roman Catholic religious be-
liefs.

GRAHAM GREENE (1904-   )

This well-known novelist turned to the theatre as a forum for his strongly held Roman Catholic beliefs. He has written four original plays: *The Living Room* (1953), *The Potting Shed* (1958), *The Complaisant Lover* (1959), and *Carving a Statue*. These dramas have all seen production in London during the last decade, with varying degrees of success. His novels, BRIGHTON ROCK, THE POWER AND THE GLORY and THE END OF THE AFFAIR, have also been dramatized.

Graham Greene's view of life is uncompromising and pessimistic. His characters struggle nobly, but rarely come to terms with their world. Unable to effect a sensible compromise with life in order to survive the human condition, they take to infidelity, suicide, and emotional breakdown. Greene is concerned with the battle between material and spiritual values and man's search for the redemption of his soul—themes which inhere in all great drama.

POETIC DRAMA

Periodically in England there is a spurt in the development of poetic drama. The plays of W. B. Yeats, John Masefield, and John Drinkwater combined a poetic form with contemporary language. This worked well with historical subjects, but was less effective in plays of contemporary life. An attempt to resolve this problem was made by W. H. Auden and Christopher Isherwood who collaborated on *The Ascent of F.6* (1936) and *The Dog Beneath the Skin* (1935), plays with serious contemporary themes written in the form of satirical verse.

T. S. ELIOT (1888-1965)

The master of the modern verse play was T. S. Eliot. Of American birth, Eliot chose British citizenship and spent most of his life in England. He achieved a reputation as the foremost poet of our time with the publication of THE WASTE LAND (1922) and FOUR QUARTETS (1943). His first attempts at writing for the theatre were *Sweeney Agonistes,* a short experimental piece based on an ancient Greek drama, and *The Rock,* a pageant play in which he used a chorus of voices to explain the action.

His first major poetic drama, *Murder in the Cathedral* (1935) about Thomas à Becket was very fittingly first performed at Canterbury Cathedral, the very place where eight hundred years previous Becket had been murdered. This play, written for a Canterbury festival, was later produced in London with great success. Eliot, who was a practicing member of the Church of England, was sensitive to the importance of ritual, and skillfully interwove it with his dramatic narrative. He also used a chorus of women who chant their comments and intensify the sense of ritual.

The Family Reunion, in 1939, was set in modern times; but the underlying theme was taken from the classical story of Orestes pursued by the Furies. The play is set in the country home of a dowager, where there is a family reunion to welcome back her

T. S. ELIOT (1888-1965) "Murder in the Cathedral," the first play in verse written by the eminent poet-dramatist, initiated a brief revival of poetic drama in England in the mid-30's. Thereafter, using contemporary themes with metaphysical overtones, Eliot attempted to create a viable poetic form for the stage.

son after his absence of eight years. He is suffering from a guilt complex, as he believes himself responsible for his wife's death. After much probing and somewhat mystical discussion by the various members of the family, he is finally convinced that it is only in his imagination that he killed his wife. Freed of his guilt and no longer feeling himself a pursued man, he decides to leave. It is at this point that his mother dies. The play explores many deep religious and psychological meanings, using the language of blank verse as an attempt to arrive at a poetic form of everyday speech. The uncles and aunts chant as a chorus, which makes for a strong sense of ritual but reduces the play's contemporaneity.

In *The Cocktail Party*, written in 1949 in blank verse, Eliot again directs himself to the redemption of the soul and the revaluation of spiritual needs. In the 20th century materialistic postwar world, the psychiatrist has become a universal father confessor.

Eliot's last two plays, *The Confidential Clerk* (1953) and *The Elder Statesman* (1958), continue in blank verse form, but there is

"MURDER IN THE CATHEDRAL"   *Robert Donat as Becket is seen with William Squire playing as the Fourth Tempter in Robert Helpmann's production of T. S. Eliot's verse play, presented at the Old Vic Theatre.*

a greater attempt at characterization and at simplification of meaning.

Eliot may not have resolved the problem of using dramatic verse in writing modern plays, but he used his powers as a poet and his strongly held Catholic beliefs to underline the need for a greater sense of spiritual values in the contemporary theatre, and he pointed the way to the use of a language of heightened style.

CHRISTOPHER FRY (1907-   )

The importance of linguistic style is strongly evident in the plays of Christopher Fry. His plays have been extremely popular, with their fecundity of imagery, witty phraseology, and his almost Elizabethan ability to play with words. While his meaning is sometimes obscure, his humor is delicious; and the facility of his poetic fancy and his ornamentation of language provide a delightful change from the laconic, matter-of-fact ordinariness of much contemporary dialogue.

His first play, the one act *A Phoenix Too Frequent,* was produced in London in 1946. *Venus Observed* (1950) was a charming vehicle for Laurence Olivier. In the same year, Fry wrote *Ring Round the Moon,* adapted from the French of Anouilh. He also wrote some religious dramas in verse and an historical play, *Curtmantle.*

Of recent years, Fry has been chiefly occupied in writing for films. He has also written *The Dark is Light Enough, The Lark* (also adapted from Anouilh), and two adaptations from Giraudoux, *Tiger at the Gates* and *Duel of Angels.*

Fry's happiest creation, *The Lady's Not for Burning,* is set in the early 15th century. Riotously comic, the play involves a young woman who is being held as a suspected witch and is reputed to have turned a tinker into a dog. A young man insists that he should be hanged for the murder of the rascally tinker who has disappeared. The young woman and the young man fall in love.

CHRISTOPHER FRY (1907-   )   *The verse plays of this poet-dramatist enjoyed considerable vogue in the 1940s and early 1950s, but when the trend moved away from highly verbal, romantic, verse drama, Fry virtually abandoned the theatre, except for a historical play "Curtmantle" which he wrote in 1961, and the summer comedy "A Yard of Sun" penned in 1970.*

The tinker turns up after waking from his long drunken sleep in a ditch, and all ends happily and merrily.

Fry can create a mood with felicity. His heightened use of words stirs the audience to share his sensibilities and his perpetual wonder at life.

THE NEW YOUNG PLAYWRIGHTS: SOCIAL REALISM

During the last decade, England has seen a number of new plays by younger men who have, with great vitality, broken away from almost all accepted conventions of the West End theatre. They have been chiefly associated with two theatres in London, both outside the West End: The Royal Court Theatre of the early Granville-Barker regime, home of the English Stage Company directed by George Devine; and the Theatre Royal, Stratford, in East London, occupied by Joan Littlewood's Theatre Workshop. Many of the original productions at these two theatres were eventually transferred to the West End where they were very successful.

JOHN OSBORNE (1929-   )

Generally acknowledged to be the spark which ignited this explosion in the English theatre is *Look Back in Anger,* by John Osborne, first produced at the Royal Court in 1956. Returning to realistic language, often of a blunt and savage character, the play gives voice to the despairs and frustrations of contemporary life as experienced by a younger generation eager to rebel but without any clear convictions or causes.

The chief character, Jimmy Porter, is an egotistic anti-hero who reviles the conventions of the society in which he lives—class, the Church, the Press—and behaves with cruelty first to his wife, who leaves him, and then with like cruelty to her friend who replaces her. Although Porter has had a university background, he ekes out an existence by running a stall in a street market with another young man, who also shares his flat. The play has little action and a sordid setting; but the vociferous, challenging Jimmy Porter holds his audience in spellbound suspense at the prospect of his gaining fulfillment. But little happens. The wife returns after the friend has duly left the husband, and we begin all over again.

Osborne has succeeded in creating a theatrically convincing, although unlikeable character, and in using powerfully effective

*JOHN OSBORNE (1929-   )
Chief spokesman of the post World
War II "angry generation," John
Osborne's landmark drama "Look
Back in Anger" was produced in
1956. Subsequent work won varied
critical response; but "The Entertainer" (1957), "Luther" (1961) and
"Inadmissible Evidence" (1964)
were acclaimed as brilliant vehicles
for Laurence Olivier, Albert Finney, and Nicol Williamson in the
lead roles.*

language. The bad manners, the crudities, and the sordid nature of
this play did not inhibit its long run.

Osborne followed this play with *The Entertainer* (1957), a picture of a seedy vaudeville comic, Archie Rice, a third-rate peformer
in a dying profession. Again the milieu is a sordid provincial
household. The chief character, an utter failure in his profession
and in his life, remains unconvinced of his inability to rise above
either his audience or the problems of his home life. The playwright
juxtaposes Archie's patter of vulgarities, jokes, and songs, with
scenes from his home life with his drunken wife; and with Rice's
old father, a variety performer in the Edwardian heyday, still living
in the past; and also with Rice's grownup children. Laurence
Olivier's memorable performance as Archie Rice evoked great
feeling for the tragedy behind the mask.

"LOOK BACK IN ANGER" (1956)   John Osborne's drama *marked the playwright as the spokesman for the "angry generation." Here Kenneth Haigh and Mary Ure are seen as Jimmy Porter and his wife Allison at the Royal Court Theatre.*

Osborne's *Luther* (1961), written for the Royal Shakespeare Company, was an attempt to see the implications of the Reformation through the character of its chief protagonist. The title role provided a magnificent part for Albert Finney, one of the rising stars of a new generation of actors.

With *Inadmissible Evidence* (1964) Osborne created another study in the despair and dissolution of a main character, this time a solicitor. This difficult part was played with great distinction by Nicol Williamson both in London and in New York.

ARNOLD WESKER (1932-   )

Another young playwright whose work has been almost universally praised is Arnold Wesker. *Chicken Soup with Barley* (1958) is the first play of his trilogy about a Jewish family, the Kahns, and their friends in the East End of London. Set in 1936, during the time of the Moseley marches, the play displays an unerring ear for the nuances of working-class language, and captures the poignancy of socialist striving for a better life.

In the second play of the trilogy, *Roots* (1959), the setting is shifted to the deep country of Norfolk and a different set of characters appear. However, the main character, Beatie, has become engaged to the idealistic Ronnie Kahn, who has aroused in her new visions and strivings. She grows increasingly aware and articulate about the stifling circumstances in her working class environment. Joan Plowright's touching performance as Beatie enhanced the Court production.

In the third play, *I'm Talking About Jerusalem* (1960), we witness the daughter and her husband's attempts to build a better life in the country. Their efforts to build a happy life emulating the teachings of William Morris by making fine furniture by hand are doomed to failure, and the close of the play sees the family packing to return to the city.

Of Wesker's other plays—*The Kitchen* (1959), *The Four Seasons*

ARNOLD WESKER (1932-   )
A writer of realistic plays, Arnold Wesker is noted principally for his trilogy "Chicken Soup with Barley" (1958), "Roots" (1959), and "I'm Talking about Jerusalem" (1960)—three plays which chronicle the life of an East End Jewish family. His most successful play "Chips with Everything" (1962) describes life in the armed services.

(1965), and *Chips with Everything* (1962)—only the last became popular and enjoyed a long run. In that play, an all-male cast reveals their various reactions to the rigors and discipline of army service with humor and camaraderie. Wesker's talent for characterization and his ear for authentic dialogue are manifest.

WILLIS HALL

Another remarkable play of wartime service life, also with an all-male cast, is Willis Hall's *The Long and the Short and the Tall*, produced at the Court in 1959. The play is concerned with the treatment of a captured Japanese soldier by an infantry patrol cut off in the Malayan jungle. It is, in its own terms, an antiwar play as potent as *Journey's End*.

ENID BAGNOLD

Enid Bagnold is the author of two plays with a somewhat mystical turn: *The Chalk Garden* and *The Chinese Prime Minister*. The latter was distinguished by the presence of Edith Evans in one of her rather rare appearances in a contemporary play. In a more popular vein was the stage adaptation of Bagnold's novel.

"CHIPS WITH EVERYTHING" (1962) *The barracks setting, in which a group of proletarian servicemen react differently to an upper class addition in their midst has been viewed as "a microcosm of the world outside." This scene shows Alan Dobie as Corporal Hill, Terence Taplin as Seaford, John Noakes as Richardson, and John Levitt as Cohen.*

THE THEATRE OF THE ABSURD

Social realism is only one of the directions in which the younger writers have been turning; the other main trend is toward the realm of fantasy and surrealism, currently known as the Theatre of the Absurd. Here the inspiration comes from the work of Pirandello, Ionesco, and Samuel Beckett.

Other Continental writers in the same vein—such as Adamov, Genet, Arrau, and Arrabal—have been published and occasionally performed in England, too. This movement departs from the theatre of ideas, and from the probing of psychological and metaphysical truth to assert, instead, the absurdity of life and the non-communicativeness of language.

Ionesco's *Rhinoceros* (1960) was produced in London and New York with considerable success. In this play in which the characters change into rhinoceroses, the varied degrees of opposition and acceptance of this metamorphosis are explored. Other plays by Ionesco which have been produced in England and influenced the theatre public there have been *The Chairs, The Lesson, The Bald Prima Donna,* and *Amédeé.*

SAMUEL BECKETT (1906-   )

Beckett's *Waiting for Godot* (1955) is perhaps the greatest triumph of this particular school. The central characters, two tramps, who wait endlessly and ineffectually for help which never comes, epitomize Beckett's philosophy of the senselessness of life in a world in which mankind rushes uncontrollably to its own destruction. It is considered by some people as a parable of life, an eternal question with no answer. Others prefer to regard it simply as a comedy fantasy.

Beckett's *Endgame* and *Krapp's Last Tape,* present production difficulties, but offer excellent acting opportunities. In order to demonstrate the agony of man's helplessness and loss of moral

"THE CHAIRS" (1952)   Ionesco's one-act tragic farce peoples the stage
with invisible guests and empty chairs, in celebration of an aged man's imaginary triumph. As the old man and his wife, played by John Harding and
Mary Carver, totter about, it becomes apparent they are living an illusion.
This play, produced by the Theatre Group is one of the most representative
works in the canon of the Theatre of the Absurd.

choice or freedom, the plays are practically devoid of action or
movement.

Beckett is an Irishman who lives in Paris, and his plays were
first written and produced in French.

HAROLD PINTER (1930-   )

The most outstanding young English playwright in the tradition
of Beckett and Ionesco is Harold Pinter. His plays are set in dingy
working-class households. Although the characters are richly drawn,
their behavior toward each other is quite unaccountable. Pinter has

HAROLD PINTER (1930-   )   *Foremost English representative*
of the "Theatre of the Absurd," Harold Pinter was recognized as a
promising playwright with his early one-act plays. Not until the "ab-
surdist" genre won broader audience approval, however, did Pinter
come into prominence. "The Caretaker" (1960), his first full-length
play, won acclaim on both sides of the Atlantic.

an unerring gift for dialogue which endows his plays with an intelli-
gibility that is more illusory than real. There is always an air of
mystery, and even horror hovering over the action, as in *The Birthday Party* (1958).

The Caretaker (1960) is involved with two brothers and an
elderly tramp who has been invited to stay in the house. The
meaning is obscure, but it could be taken as an expression of the

"THE CARETAKER"   Donald Pleasance appears here as the tramp in Pinter's provocative play produced at the Duchess Theatre in 1960. The other two parts were played by Alan Bates and Peter Woodthorpe. In the New York production at the Lyceum in 1961 Donald Pleasance and Alan Bates again appeared, this time with Ronald Shaw.

complete inability of people to communicate once the social conventions are dispensed with.

The Homecoming (1965), in which a son brings his wife home to meet his father and brothers but leaves her there for good when he returns to the States, gave some leading stars, including Paul Rogers and Vivien Merchant (Pinter's wife), provocative roles in the 1965 London season.

"WAITING FOR GODOT"   In the 1955 production of Samuel Beckett's "Waiting for Godot," produced at the Arts Theatre, Peter Hall directed (left to right) Peter Bull, Paul Daneman, Peter Woodthorpe, and Timothy Bateson in the decade's most influential play.

THE OLD VIC   *The famous Old Vic Theatre building is currently the home of the National Theatre Company. Permanent quarters for the Old Vic are being completed on the south bank of the Thames.*

PLAYWRIGHTS IN THE THEATRE GROUPS

Many of the younger dramatists in England have been closely connected with the theatre as actors or directors. They have thus acquired a working knowledge of theatre, which may explain the presence of rich acting opportunities in their plays. It sometimes happens in the theatre today that the acting is far superior to the play itself. Shelagh Delaney, whose *A Taste of Honey* brought her fame, worked closely with Joan Littlewood's Theatre Workshop and has acknowledged her debt to this experience. Pinter has both acted and directed.

HISTORY OF THE OLD VIC

With the passing of the old actor-managers' stock companies early in the century, the production of classics fell into decline. The West

End theatres of London were generally concerned with modern plays; and these were usually well produced with players of expert skill.

Today, the West End, like Broadway, is composed of many theatres owned by people who never have a hand in the production of plays, who are merely landlords, leasing their buildings to producing companies. In some cases, the theatres are further sublet by producing companies to other companies who wish to present a particular play. The money required to put on a play is usually very considerable; there is very likely a gamble involved, especially in the case of a new and untried play. Actors are engaged for the particular play; and when the production comes to an end, the play closes and the cast is dispersed.

The idea of a repertory theatre in London, in which the classics could be performed and a company of actors could be employed for a whole season seemed desirable to people on both sides of the footlights. This came into being early in the century at an old playhouse just south of the Thames known as the Old Vic.

When the Old Vic was built in 1818, there were other theatres nearby—Astley's and the Surrey—although the area was largely rural. The outer walls and the horseshoe plan of the interior and much of the original structure of the Old Vic remain today. In the 19th century, this playhouse had seen some great figures. Its first manager was William Barrymore, an ancestor of the famous Broadway family. Junius Brutus Booth, Samuel Phelps, Macready, Edmund Kean, Grimaldi, Charles Mathews, and Madame Vestris had all performed in that building.

But in time, the neighborhood deteriorated into a slum; and the theatre, first known as the Royal Coburg and then as the Royal Victoria, declined as well. A program of crude melodrama and variety was presented; until eventually, even this fare became unprofitable.

In 1879, the management passed to Miss Emma Cons, an alderman and a well-to-do lady of middle age, much interested in social welfare. She had an idea that the theatre might be used as a means of education. Universal primary education had only just been legally enacted, and there was even less provision for further education among the masses of the working people. Miss Cons's intention must have been to enlarge the leisure life of the poor.

She opened with a mixed program of lectures, recitals, and music hall turns, abolished the sale of liquor, and began to attract a young audience, anxious to benefit from serious cultural opportunities.

Miss Cons employed managers to attend to the day-to-day running of the theatre, one of whom was young William Poel. He began to experiment with his own ideas of staging plays, and was later to become instrumental in causing a return to the original text of Shakespeare.

Soon evening classes on a variety of topics were being held in the various rooms behind the auditorium. Eventually, this part of the theatre's activities was moved to its own building nearby, where it has flourished ever since as Morley College.

LILLIAN BAYLISS' (1874-1937) MANAGEMENT AT THE OLD VIC

In 1898, Miss Cons introduced her niece, Lillian Bayliss, to the theatre as an assistant manager. Miss Bayliss had been a music teacher and had danced in South Africa. Like her aunt, she was deeply religious, but she developed a burning enthusiasm for the theatre; and when her aunt died in 1912, Miss Bayliss took over the management.

By now the presentations included opera recitals, and a small permanent theatre orchestra was built up under Charles Corri. Films were shown, and occasional single performances of Shakespeare were given. These must have been successful because in 1914, Miss Bayliss began the productions of Shakespeare's plays which were to become the Old Vic's lasting glory during the next forty years. She had the help of some experienced actor-managers:

LILLIAN BAYLISS (1874-1937)
Theatre manager and founder of
the Old Vic and the Sadler's Wells
companies, Lillian Bayliss is remem-
bered for her single-minded devo-
tion to the production of good
drama at the Old Vic. Between
1914 and 1923, all the plays of
Shakespeare were presented.
Though occasionally the work of
some other playwright was offered,
the Old Vic came to be regarded as
the home of Shakespeare.

Matheson Lang who also played in *The Merchant of Venice, The Taming of the Shrew,* and *Hamlet;* and Ben Greet and Andrew Leigh.

Many well-known actors played at the Old Vic during these early years, often for a nominal fee, pleased to be able to help in establishing the theatre. Lillian Braithwaite, Angela Baddeley, Florence Saunders, Estelle Stead, Nancy Price, Hermione Gingold, Sybil Thorndike, her sister Eileen, her brother Russell, Robert Atkins, Basil Sydney, Ernest Milton, and Malcolm Keen were some of the players who appeared in those early years.

Miss Bayliss was emphatic in her policy of low admission prices. The gallery was twopence, and a stall seat was two shillings. This was the only income of the theatre, out of which production expenses and actors salaries had to be paid. From time to time, appeals were made to the public for development funds.

The old theatre equipment was still in use; the scenery consisted mainly of painted flats in grooves; and the principal stage lighting was still by gas. In spite of all the practical difficulties—which in some ways were a blessing, paucity of props often leading to ingenuity in staging—the enthusiasm of the players, and the invincible character of Miss Bayliss, succeeded in establishing the Old Vic as the London home of Shakespeare and opera.

A permanent and faithful audience was gradually built up, enlarged occasionally by parties of school children. This became a permanent feature when the London County Council took over the whole theatre for special school matinees. An Old Vic magazine was instituted; and two theatre clubs were formed to foster interest in the theatre, the players, and the productions; occasional lectures were given to members.

A special annual event was Shakespeare's birthday celebration. The evening's program was made up of short excerpts from Shakespeare's plays. Well-known players, many of them currently appearing in the West End theatres, would appear with members of the resident company. Such stars as Ellen Terry and Lady Forbes-Robertson were seen in these revels.

By 1923, the Old Vic became the first theatre to have presented the complete cycle of Shakespeare's plays. Other plays produced were Sheridan's and Goldsmith's comedies; Marlowe's *Dr. Faustus;* *Everyman,* the medieval morality play; Ibsen's *Peer Gynt;* and occasionally the work of contemporary writers, such as Barrie's *Pantaloon,* Lawrence Binyon's *King Arthur,* and Gordon Bottomley's *Britain's Daughter.* Except for a month or so in the summer, the Old Vic was open throughout the year, and the plays alternated every week with opera.

During the 1920's, greater attention was given to standards of production, and the pioneer work of Robert Atkins (1886-   ) as director made a lasting contribution to the Old Vic's success. Influenced by William Poel's theory that the Elizabethan stage made for a much quicker development of the action, Atkins created a kind of apron stage by erecting a false proscenium behind the existing one, but in front of the stage curtain. An entrance door on either side enabled actors to play in front of the curtain, behind which another scene could be erected at the same time. The old system of stage grooves was discarded, and the scenery was now especially designed for each production. The stage lighting was modernized with electricity.

Another innovation was the establishment of a permanent wardrobe for the theatre; hitherto costumes had been hired.

Atkins, a fine actor, played in most of the productions along with such actors as George Hayes, Francis L. Sullivan, Russell Thorndike, Marie Ney, Florence Buckton, Jane Bacon, and Florence Saunders.

Robert Atkins left the Old Vic in 1925 to take his own company on tour, eventually becoming a producer at the Stratford-on-Avon Memorial Theatre, and during the summer, he operated at the Open Air Theatre in London's Regent's Park. His place as director of the Old Vic was taken by Andrew Leigh.

The company had the good fortune to have two brilliant new players, Baliol Holloway and Edith Evans; and for a season saw the return of Sybil Thorndike with her husband, Lewis Casson. Edith Evans in comedy, and Sybil Thorndike in tragedy became the particular favorites of the Old Vic audiences. Both these fine actresses returned from time to time throughout their long and successful careers.

In the 1920's, Harcourt Williams, Henry Cass, and Tyrone Guthrie were the directors. The cast included almost all the distinguished leading actors presently performing on the English stage.

JOHN GIELGUD (1904-   )

John Gielgud played his first Hamlet at the Old Vic in 1929, and soon established himself as a rising favorite, playing Romeo, Richard II, Macbeth, and many other parts. His fine stage presence, magnificent voice, and sensitive poetic reading have earned him a

SIR JOHN GIELGUD (1904-   )   *Ranked by many as the outstanding actor on the English stage of our time, Gielgud has a long
record of stellar performances in Shakespearean, classic, and modern
parts. His intelligent and masterful reading brings new insights and
nuances of meaning to the widely divergent roles he has created.
Gielgud is also outstanding as a producer.*

reputation as one of the foremost actors in the contemporary theatre.

Gielgud's performance in *Hamlet* enjoyed long runs in London and New York. His interpretation is considered by many critics to be the finest on the current stage.

Although he is probably at his best in Shakespeare, Gielgud has given excellent performances in classic and modern plays, such as *Love for Love, The Importance of Being Earnest, Noah, The Lady's Not for Burning, Ivanov, The Potting Shed, Tiny Alice, Home.* He has also done much directing of plays, and produced seasons of repertory at the Haymarket toward the end of the war.

Gielgud has arranged a solo reading of selected passages from Shakespeare which he calls *Ages of Man.* This reading has been enormously successful, and he has toured many parts of the world in it.

RALPH RICHARDSON (1902-   )

Another of England's leading actors, Ralph Richardson, made his reputation at the Old Vic in the 1930 season along with John Gielgud. Richardson had been a member of the Birmingham Repertory Company and was playing a small part in *Othello* at the Savoy Theatre—the production with Paul Robeson and Peggy Ashcroft—when he was offered the opportunity of a season at the Old Vic under Harcourt Williams' direction. He has played a wide range of roles including Bolingbroke, Sir Toby Belch, Prince Hal, Henry V, Iago, Caliban, with much success. A solid actor, Richardson has appeared in many classic and contemporary plays: *The Heiress, Uncle Vanya,* Bluntschli in Shaw's *Arms and the Man, Peer Gynt, Home.* In his rendering of the main roles in J. B. Priestley's *Johnson over Jordan* and in Somerset Maugham's *Sheppey,* he vividly created the universal man struggling against his destiny with humility and resignation.

With superb gifts as a character actor, Richardson is a favorite both in England and the United States.

RALPH RICHARDSON (1902-   ) *The eminent actor is shown here as Bluntschli,*
in George Bernard Shaw's "Arms and the Man." Margaret Leighton plays Raina.

LAURENCE OLIVIER (1907-   )   *Laurence Olivier is seen here playing Justice*
Shallow in "Henry IV."

THE BEGINNINGS OF THE ROYAL BALLET

The Old Vic was firmly established in the 1930's. Now Miss Bayliss enlarged her sphere of activities by engaging Ninette de Valois to form a small ballet company to perform short ballets in the opera. Further expansion came with the chance to take over the old Sadler's Wells Theatre at Islington, then being rebuilt with publicly raised funds. For some two or three years, the Old Vic Company would repeat their performances at Sadler's Wells, alternating with the opera. Eventually it was decided to concentrate the plays at the Old Vic, and Sadler's Wells became the home of the opera. The ballet then developed into a spearate entity, and eventually, some evenings were devoted entirely to ballet performances. After the war, the ballet moved to Covent Garden, still under Ninette de Valois, and became the famous Royal Ballet of today.

CHARLES LAUGHTON AT THE OLD VIC

During the 1930's, the artistic standards of the Old Vic rose consistently. By bringing in established stars, the company attracted audiences from all parts of London. This practice was instituted by Tyrone Guthrie, who began directing in 1933. He initiated the star custom with Charles Laughton and his wife, Elsa Lanchester. Laughton had already made a reputation in the West End in modern plays in parts such as the gangster Perelli in *On the Spot,* and as the respectable suburban murderer in *Payment Deferred.* Laughton had also become universally known for his performance in the film *The Private Life of Henry VIII.* He stayed the entire season of 1933-1934 at the Old Vic and played a wide range of parts, including Prospero and Macbeth. Laughton was memorable as Lopakhin in *The Cherry Orchard.*

Laughton attempted to repeat his film success on the stage, playing *Henry VIII* with Flora Robson as Katherine, but although it was beautifully played and the production notably designed by Charles Ricketts, it was anticlimactic after the film. He played a

RALPH RICHARDSON (1902-   )   A highly intelligent and con-
sistently fine actor, Ralph Richardson has given subtle performances in a
wide range of roles. Having made his reputation in the 1930 season at the
Old Vic, he has performed with them continuously, memorably portraying
Peer Gynt, Sir John Falstaff, and Timon.

dignified Prospero to Elsa Lanchester's sprite Ariel in *The Tempest.*
Perhaps his happiest creation was Tattle in *Love for Love,* with
Athene Seyler as Mrs. Frail.

Unquestionably, Laughton is best known for his film performances in a wide range of comic and dramatic roles, bringing to
this medium the same standards of excellence that prevailed on
the stage.

MAURICE EVANS (1901-   ) AT THE OLD VIC

Maurice Evans joined the Old Vic Company in 1934 under the
directorship of Henry Cass, and distinguished himself in Shakes-
perean roles. His magnificent voice and lively, intelligent interpretation were much admired in *Richard II* and in *Hamlet* played in
its entirety. But he was perhaps more at home in comedy, as in his

LAURENCE OLIVIER (1907-   )   *Sir Laurence Olivier, considered by many to be the finest actor of the English speaking theatre, is seen here in two Shakespearean roles: as Othello (below), and as Hotspur in "Henry IV" (right).*

Benedict to Mary Newcombe's Beatrice in *Much Ado About Nothing*. Evans lives now in America and has become a citizen of the United States.

THE 1936 SEASON AT THE OLD VIC

Tyrone Guthrie returned as director in 1936 and remained for the next twelve years. His most brilliant production of 1936 was, without a doubt, Wycherley's *The Country Wife*. This was presented in the original unexpurgated version; and his fine cast played it with all the wit and sparkle that one imagines was characteristic of the Restoration theatre. The title role was played by Ruth Gordon, the American actress, and the cast included Edith Evans and Michael Redgrave. The costumes and settings were designed by Oliver Messel, England's leading designer, who without slavishly reproducing the period, aptly caught its spirit.

The 1936 season also saw the Old Vic debut of Laurence Olivier (1907-   ), who had by then played in many productions in the West End and in films. He made an agile, quicksilver Hamlet, a riotous Sir Toby Belch to the Aguecheek of Alec Guinness, and a noble Henry V with Jessica Tandy as the French princess. He won his audiences completely.

Edith Evans (1888-   ) had played many roles at the Old Vic in the 1925 season. She returned in 1936 to play a memorable Rosalind to Michael Redgrave's Orlando in a production of *As You Like It* set in Watteauesque costumes and decor. A scintillating season of talent!

LILLIAN BAYLISS' CONTRIBUTIONS TO THE OLD VIC

The theatre sustained a great loss in 1937 with the death of Miss Bayliss, who had been ailing for some time. This remarkable woman of tremendous character had the ability to bring unexpected talent to the surface. She was eccentric in some ways, but was beloved by her players and staff. She had steered the Old Vic through a period of some forty years, years of great change and development, and she was responsible for the auspicious beginnings of opera and ballet at Sadler's Wells.

ACTORS AND PRODUCTIONS AT THE OLD VIC

Old Vic audiences were widely drawn from all classes of the community, and particularly from among the young. The roster of players during the next few seasons reads like a Theatrical Hall of Fame and includes Laurence Olivier, Ralph Richardson, Roger Livesey, Alec Guinness, John Mills, Robert Morley, Anthony Quayle, Robert Helpmann (who had hitherto been seen in ballet), Esme Percy, Morland Graham, Angela Baddeley, Pamela Brown, Jean Cadell, Freda Jackson, Ursula Jeans, Agnes Laughlan, Vivien Leigh, Marie Ney, Veronica Turleigh, and Sybil Thorndike.

Some of the notable productions were *Coriolanus,* in which Laurence Olivier extended his range to tragedy, with Sybil Thorndike; *Hamlet* in modern dress with Alec Guinness; a lively revival of *Trelawney of the Wells*; Ibsen's *An Enemy of the People*; a production of *A Midsummer Night's Dream* charmingly reminiscent of early Victorian prints, with the music of Mendelsohn; and *The Taming of the Shrew,* produced in the manner of the Commedia dell'Arte.

THE OLD VIC DURING THE WAR

During the war years, the Old Vic Company went on tour, performing sometimes in remote parts of England and Wales, and established a headquarters at the Victoria Theatre in Burnley in the North of England.

Early in 1940, the Old Vic Theatre opened a season with a fine *Lear* by John Gielgud, in which Jack Hawkins, Nicolas Hannen, Andrew Cruickshank, Fay Compton, Jessica Tandy, and Cathleen Nesbitt achieved much distinction. Lewis Casson and Harley Granville-Barker directed. This was followed by a remarkable production by George Devine and Marius Goring of *The Tempest,* with Gielgud as Prospero, and settings and costumes beautifully designed by Oliver Messel. This was the last production at the Old Vic Theatre until it reopened long after the war.

During 1943, the Playhouse Theatre in London was taken over as a temporary home for the Old Vic, but it failed to attract the restless wartime public. Three plays were produced: Drinkwater's *Abraham Lincoln,* in which Herbert Lomas gave a fine interpretation of the title role; *The Russians,* an English version of a topical play by Konstantin Simonov about life among the Russian partisans, and Peter Ustinov's *Blow Your Own Trumpet.*

REPERTORY AT THE OLD VIC

Then, in the autumn of 1944, the Old Vic Company was re-formed at the New Theatre to present plays in repertory. The new company was headed by Tyrone Guthrie, Laurence Olivier, Ralph Richardson, and John Burrell. The new plan was to rehearse three plays, which would be given alternately; then gradually to add more plays. Hitherto, each play at the Old Vic had run for three weeks, or occasionally for four, and was then abandoned for the next production. The new form of repertory is the form that exists on the Continent; it implies a permanent company in which the actors play a variety of parts during the week.

The opening plays were Ibsen's *Peer Gynt,* Shaw's *Arms and the Man,* and Shakespeare's *Richard III.* Chekhov's *Uncle Vanya* was added later in the year. Laurence Olivier and Ralph Richardson played leading roles. The excellent casts included Sybil Thorndike,

Margaret Leighton, Joyce Redman, Nicolas Hannen, George Relph, Michael Warre, and Harcourt Williams.

Peer Gynt was the opening piece and Ralph Richardson was magnificent as the willful, erratic, and hapless Peer, portraying the change from youth to old age with remarkable skill. Sybil Thorndike was extremely moving as Ase; Olivier took the small part of the buttonmoulder; and the whole cast played together with an ease and ability that promised well for the future of the company. Tyrone Guthrie directed.

The decor was the work of a young designer, Reece Pemberton, who made interesting use of semitransparent settings on which various cutout shadows were projected, facilitating a rapid change of scene. The production was received with rapturous applause.

In *Arms and The Man,* the two leading parts of Sergius and Bluntschli were taken by Olivier and Richardson, and Nicolas Hannen played Petkoff. Joyce Redman, Margaret Leighton, and Sybil Thorndike contributed to make it a gay romp. John Burrell directed this and the following plays of the season with great attention to movement, action, and ensemble playing, which the company so successfully achieved.

Richard III was a triumph for Olivier, whose interpretation minimized the passion of previous players, but enhanced the logic of satanic evil. In *Uncle Vanya,* Richardson shone as a tragic but wholly human failure of a man.

In the summer of 1945, the company toured the Continent, appearing with great success in Antwerp, Brussels, Hamburg, and finally at the Comédie Française in Paris.

The first season which presented brilliant playing in productions of standard plays on an alternating repertory basis was wholly successful both financially and artistically, despite the fact that at the time London was being bombarded with flying bombs and rockets. The leading players added further distinction to their already considerable reputations, and the repertory system of playing was firmly established.

"A FLEA IN HER EAR" (1966)   The Georges Feydeau farce has become a staple
of the National Theatre repertory. This scene from the Jacques Charon production
discovers Robert Land as Poche, Anthony Hopkins as Etienne, Kenneth Macintosh as
Dr. Finache, and Geraldine McEwan as Raymond.

For the next four years, The Old Vic Company continued operations at the New Theatre, during which time more distinguished players joined the company, including Alec Guinness, Baliol Holloway, Miles Malleson, John Clements, Trevor Howard, Edith Evans, Pamela Brown, Celia Johnson, and Rosalind Atkinson.

The Old Vic Company made some notable tours abroad; in 1946, to America and Paris; in 1948, to Australia; and later, to South Africa, and to various countries on the Continent, including Russia.

THE BRISTOL OLD VIC

A branch of the Old Vic was established at Bristol in the beautiful Georgian Theatre Royal, and became known as the Bristol Old Vic. This company, however, was autonomous, with its own productions and players.

THE POSTWAR OLD VIC

In 1950, the Old Vic Theatre in Waterloo Road reopened, refurbished, its war damage repaired, and ready for business with a new generation of players and directors. Olivier, Richardson, and Guthrie departed from the company to their own individual activities in the West End and elsewhere. The new system of repertory was retained and the new directors, Hugh Hunt and Michael Benthall, worked steadily through the Shakespeare cycle of plays, completing it in 1958.

THE NATIONAL THEATRE

In 1962, the Old Vic became the National Theatre under the directorship of Laurence Olivier, with financial backing by the Government. It continues at the old theatre at present until an entirely new building, already designed, will be constructed on the South Bank. The National Theatre's policy is to provide a home for Shakespeare and the classics, and also to produce new plays. The plays are performed in repertory.

"BLACK COMEDY"   *Peter Shaffer's comedy featured Derek Jacobi as Brin, and Maggie Smith as Clea. Graham Crowden who plays Colonel Melkett stands in the background. This National Theatre show was produced in 1966.*

THE ENGLISH STAGE COMPANY

The English Stage Company at the Court Theatre, now the Royal Court, which was established under the direction of George Devine 1910-1965) in 1950, has also been a major influence, particularly in its encouragement of plays by new writers. These have generally been plays of serious purpose, often iconoclastic works such as John Osborne's *Look Back in Anger*. Devine also produces established works, mostly Continental or American, and even Shakespeare sees occasional production. In addition to Devine, who has given some outstanding performances, some fine players have been associated with the Royal Court, including Robert Shaw, Ronald Fraser, Alfred Lynch, and Peter O'Toole.

THE ROYAL SHAKESPEARE COMPANY

Another important influence on the English theatre is the Royal Shakespeare Company, whose home is the Memorial Theatre at Stratford-on-Avon. Built in 1930, for some years it housed only a summer festival of Shakespeare's plays. Many distinguished players and directors made the journey from London for the short season.

The company was not fully developed, however, until after the war when Anthony Quayle, as director, lengthened the season from early spring to late autumn. Quayle concentrated chiefly on presenting Shakespeare in a fresh, vital manner.

"ARMSTRONG'S LAST GOODNIGHT" (1965)   Albert Finney in the role of Johnny Armstrong of Gilnockie in the Chichester production of the John Arden work.

"KING LEAR" (1962)   The Peter Brook version, presented by the Royal Shake-speare Company, was considered revolutionary in concept. Based on ideas from SHAKE-SPEARE OUR CONTEMPORARY by Polish critic Jan Kott, the production featured Paul Scofield as King Lear in one of the most significant performances of that role. Here Lear is seated on a small throne in a setting of white flats, on which are hung sheets of rusted metal. The noted cast included Irene Worth as Goneril, Alex McCowan as the Fool, John Laurie as Gloucester, Diana Rigg as Cordelia and Ian Richardson as Edmund.

This policy was continued by Peter Hall, who extended the activities of the company by taking over the Aldwych Theatre in London. Contemporary plays have been introduced into the repertory at the company's London home, and some present day dramatists have been commissioned to write plays for the company. Plays are presented in alternating repertory at Stratford and London.

VISITING FOREIGN COMPANIES

During the summer months, when the emphasis is on Shakespeare at Stratford, the company relinquishes the Aldwych Theatre to a season of visiting companies from Continental theatres. Companies from France, Poland, Greece, Italy, and elsewhere on the Continent have performed their repertory in their own languages, with modern electronic devices providing simultaneous translation at the option of individual members of the audience. Lee Strasberg's Actors' Studio Theatre from New York has also performed here. The Moscow Art Theatre Company has made two visits to London, with their great productions of Chekhov and other Russian works. A wide range of theatrical experience has thus been available in London, and much has been learned of methods of staging and production.

THE BERLINER ENSEMBLE COMPANY IN ENGLAND

The Berliner Ensemble Company of Bertold Brecht (1898-1956) has also had two London seasons; in 1956, at the Palace Theatre; and in 1965, at the Old Vic. Their unique methods of presentation created widespread interest, although their propaganda for a Marxist view of history has been less well received.

"LOVE FOR LOVE"   This Restoration comedy by William Congreve was produced by Peter Wood at the National Theatre, London, in 1965. Joyce Redman appears here as Mrs. Frail, and Colin Blakely as Ben, the plain-spoken seafaring son who is brought back into polite society by his plotting father.

The meticulousness of their productions in all their detail, and their facility in blending divergent approaches into a rapid and continuous unfolding of the main theme has been admired and extensively imitated. Sometimes in an expressionist manner, often in a formal symbolic mode, and at other times quite realistically, actors play short scenes. The lights fade, and the minimal scenery changes are made for the next part of the action. During such short pauses, a screen is lowered on which is projected a commentary on the action or on the political background. The acting is often brilliant in the broad—but to English ears—rather old fashioned, Continental manner.

Brecht's aim was to create audience participation in his productions. To this end, no curtain is used; the stage is open from the beginning to the end; and the climax is obtained by an extremely skillful building up of theatrical effects, using all the technical resources of the modern theatre in lighting, and through electronically produced sounds and music. Actors sometimes address the audience directly. Occasionally they actually appear among the audience.

Some actors and directors consider the use of the stage as a political platform as anti-theatrical; others have been deeply impressed by the originality of the methods and by the vitality of the performances of the Berlin Troupe. Joan Littlewood, in her Theatre Workshop production of *The Hostage* by Brendan Behan, adopted some of the Berliner Ensemble's methods to bring the audience closer to a play. She found the interpolation of songs and dances into the action, and the minimal use of scenery effective techniques in moving the drama along rapidly.

THE MERMAID THEATRE

Another center of theatrical activity was created with the opening of the Mermaid Theatre on the banks of the Thames in the City of

ROYAL SHAKESPEARE THEATRE, STRATFORD-UPON-AVON   *Summer home of the Royal Shakespeare Company, this is the scene of a yearly festival devoted to the presentation of a repertory of Shakespeare's plays. The theatre, second on the site, opened April 23, 1932 with "Henry IV."*

MERMAID THEATRE   *This was the first theatre to be built on the North Bank of the Thames in 400 years. It opened in 1959 near Blackfriar's Bridge, London.*

London in 1959. The first theatre to be located in the center of trade and commerce in some four hundred years, the Mermaid arose on the bomb-blasted but solid walls of a Victorian warehouse. Its inception was largely the work of its director, the fine character actor Bernard Miles.

It is a simple theatre, with a rectangular racked auditorium sloping directly into a wide-open stage without a proscenium. A large revolve is built into the stage and is used in much of the action.

The opening production was a musical play based on a comedy about London in 1730 by Henry Fielding, retitled *Lock Up Your Daughters.* The performers had the vitality of a new company anxious to show their paces and even without any great stars, the offering became a smash hit, which ran for several months and firmly

INTERIOR OF THE MERMAID THEATRE   *The auditorium shows the sharply raked open stage without footlights, the absence of a proscenium, and the seats leading directly to the stage.*

established the new theatre.

Since then, the policy has been to present a varied program of classical plays other than Shakespeare's, as well as contemporary plays by English, American, and Continental playwrights. Among the plays presented have been *Galileo* by Bertold Brecht, Pirandello's *Right You Are*, Maxwell Anderson's adaptation of Alan Paton's novel *Cry the Beloved Country*, Dekker's *The Shoemaker's Holiday*, Gogol's *The Marriage Brokers*, the Oedipus plays of Sophocles, and Beaumont and Fletcher's *The Maid's Tragedy*.

Links with the off-Broadway theatre in New York were forged when the Living Theatre Company visited the United States during the early summer of 1965 with their production of *The Brig* by Kenneth H. Brown.

PETER BROOK (1925-   )   As a stage director, Peter Brook made his London debut at age eighteen with his 1943 production of "Dr. Faustus" at the Torch Theatre. Later experimental productions, remarkable for their inventiveness, brought him increasing distinction. In 1962, he became a co-director of the Royal Shakespeare Company directing that company in some of their most notable productions: "King Lear" with Paul Scofield in 1962, "Marat/Sade," also in 1962, and his much acclaimed version of "Midsummer Night's Dream" in 1971.

REAL ESTATE PROBLEMS

The West End theatres suffer occasional onslaughts by real estate companies. As in New York, the theatres are chiefly housed in old buildings sitting on land which has increased enormously in value.

Since London's authorities have removed the building height limit, and office towers are becoming a familiar feature of the city, the St.

James's Theatre and the Stoll Theatre, among others, have been demolished. There are, however, still some forty theatres which are open most of the year. Some of these, such as Drury Lane, are too large for anything but musicals, which are chiefly imported from the United States. The longest-running productions—excluding the phenomenal thriller *The Mousetrap* by Agatha Christie, now in its fourteenth year at a small theatre, the Ambassadors—have been musicals and farces such as those Brian Rix has provided at the Whitehall Theatre for the last twenty years.

JOAN LITTLEWOOD (1914-   )   Director, manager, and found of the Theatre Workshop, Miss Littlewood has been acclaimed for her experimental productions. She is noted mainly, however, for her pioneering efforts to advance the work of promising young playwrights. Among the plays for which her workshop provided a premier showcase were: Brandon Behan's "The Quare Fellow" (1956), Shelagh Delaney's "A Taste of Honey" (1958), Frank Norman's "Fings Ain't Wot They Used T'Be" (1959), and the musical satire "Oh What a Lovely War!" (   ).

THE CHICHESTER FESTIVAL THEATRE

Some new theatres have been established outside London, the most notable being the Chichester Festival Theatre, a summer repertory theatre which has been under the directorship of Laurence Olivier. Many of their productions were subsequently absorbed into the repertory of the National Theatre at the Old Vic, including Peter Shaffer's *The Royal Hunt of the Sun* and *Black Comedy*, and Strindberg's *Miss Julie*.

PROVINCIAL THEATRES

Other new theatres of note in the provinces are the Nottingham Playhouse, the Belgrade Theatre in Coventry, the new Shakespeare Theatre in Liverpool, and the latest, *The Arnaud*—a delightful theatre in the country outskirts of Guildford. This theatre, named after Yvonne Arnaud, the well-known West End actress, opened with a fine production of *A Month in the Country* with Michael Redgrave and Ingrid Bergman. The production was later transferred to the West End. In addition, well-established repertory companies at Birmingham, Manchester, Liverpool, Glasgow, and other cities, continue to provide the drama of today and the classics of the past to avid audiences.

THE ADVANCE IN ACTING TECHNIQUE

Acting in England has perhaps seen the greatest advance in many decades, probably due to the establishment of the repertory system. The wide variety of contemporary and classical drama being constantly produced has broadened the actors' range of experience. The English actor of today must be prepared to speak the verses of Shakespeare and the prose of his contemporaries, to move in the affected manner of the Restoration beau, speak in the Cockney accent of an East End character. He must be something of an acrobat and dancer, and he must also be prepared to endure playing his part completely immobile, as in *Endgame*.

THE CHICHESTER FESTIVAL THEATRE   *Founded in 1962 by Leslie Evershed-Martin, the Chichester Theatre was inspired by the Shakespeare Theatre in Ontario, Canada. The open stage with its two playing areas is surrounded on three sides by the audience. No seat is more than 66 feet from the stage. A gallery encircling the top of the auditorium can be used as a third playing area.*

"HOME"   *Sir John Gielgud (left) and Sir Ralph Richardson provided one of the highlights of the 1970 London season by appearing together in David Storey's play "Home," in which they portrayed two old men in an old age home.*

The older English actor grounded in Shakespeare and in the classics, is used to portraying an infinite range of characters, conveying fine shades of meaning, and transmitting a sure sense of period. Many of today's younger actors, without this very sound background, have nevertheless been highly successful in roles of the contemporary plays of social realism. These actors may be more limited in their range, but they have developed a naturalistic style well suited to the demands of the modern play.

STAGING

Outside of some minor Brechtian influences, there have been few advances in the staging of plays in England. It is possible that the old theatres do not lend themselves to experimentation in this field. New theatres in the United States have an arena stage or a thrust stage which brings audiences into much closer contact with the actors. Yet the new dramatists have achieved a naturalistic setting within the traditional stage picture. It remains to be seen whether experimentation with new forms and idioms will bring in its wake transformation in stage design.

The American Theatre
of the 20th Century

NEW TRENDS IN THE AMERICAN THEATRE

While the theatre prospered materially in the early years of the 20th century, what with its large new theatres and growing audiences and productions of great technical skill, the plays were chosen mainly for their entertainment value. The theatre was indeed Big Business now. Yet the great dramas, in which leading actors could extend the range of their interpretation, were still largely the works of the past, or the works of foreign dramatists.

It is the work of the newer writers of the century that changed the look of the theatre and brought the American theatre international acclaim. In an age of great material advancement, there has also been great reassessment of spiritual values; and in the work of its younger dramatists, the American theatre has reflected this turmoil of thought. There was a natural reaction against what had gone before—the well-worked-out plot, the spectacular climax, and the sacrifice of realism to theatrical effect. In the new plays the trend has been away from the pat formula to more vital themes, to less contrived stories, to the essentials of true character portrayal.

New American writers had to learn the business of stagecraft and its importance to dramatic form. In the early years of the century, small groups of individuals interested in serious writing for the theatre put on semiprivate performances in order to see their work in practice. The actors were amateurs, as were the directors and designers. What was lacking in technical skill was partly replaced by an infectious enthusiasm which gradually improved skills, and ultimately raised the standard of the drama.

Eventually, some of these groups made the difficult crossing into the professional theatre, becoming in the 1920's, the most potent force in the American theatrical world. They had to learn their craft from scratch, and in so doing were fortunate to avoid the influence of traditional theatricality. The result, expressive of the new generation, was something fresh and vital.

GEORGE PIERCE BAKER (1866-1935)

George Pierce Baker, a professor of English Literature at Harvard, was probably one of the most important single influences in this upsurge of the American theatre. Although he was never able to persuade the Governing Board to upgrade his drama course to full academic acceptance, he was able in 1912 to organize his "47 Workshop." Here students actually produced their own plays. In the process, they learned acting, directing, costuming, scenic designing, lighting, and the many practical aspects of staging. He continued this work for nearly twenty years at Harvard.

In 1925, Baker moved to Yale, where he became chairman of a newly created Department of Drama, with a new university theatre. The study of drama was raised to graduate status. Baker remained at Yale directing his department until shortly before his death in 1935.

Many of Baker's students became major figures in the American theatre of this century. Among the playwrights who emerged from this group were Edward Sheldon, Eugene O'Neill, S. N. Behrman,

Sidney Howard, Philip Barry, Percy MacKaye, Edward Knoblock, George Abbott, Hubert Osborne, and Thomas Wolfe. Some other Baker students who became producers and directors were Winthrop Ames, Alexander Dean, Sam Hume, Irving Pichel, and Theresa Helburn. Some of the Baker students who became critics are John Mason Brown, Robert Benchley, Heywood Broun, Walter Prichard Eaton, and Kenneth Macgowan. Three of his students became leading designers: Robert Edmond Jones (who was also a director), Lee Simonson, and Donald Oenslager. Two others became well-known actors: Mary Morris and Osgood Perkins.

Professor Baker must have exuded an extraordinarily contagious enthusiasm and great ability as a teacher to inspire so many of his students to go on to great accomplishments. These young people brought to the American theatre an integrity in human and artistic values which has caused the American Theatre to become important internationally.

Since Baker, colleges and universities throughout the country have offered degrees in drama and have been active in mounting public performances. It is in the colleges that many new experimental ideas are tried out.

EUGENE O'NEILL (1888-1953)

The most outstanding of the new dramatists, without doubt, was Eugene O'Neill. Born in 1888, the son of a well-known actor, James O'Neill, Eugene spent much of his early life accompanying his father on tour. He must have acquired a taste for, and a knowledge of, the theatre at a very early age.

After a varied education, including a year at Princeton University, O'Neill drifted into many occupations: he prospected for gold, worked in business, and served in the Merchant Navy on many voyages to the various ports of the Atlantic. He began his writing career as a newspaper reporter; but in 1913 he was discovered to be suffering from tuberculosis and spent six months in a sanitarium. It

was during this time that he first began to write for the theatre. In 1914-15, he was a student with Professor Baker at Harvard.

THE PROVINCETOWN PLAYERS

In the summer of 1916, the Provincetown Players, an experimental theatre group of actors and playwrights, was founded in Provincetown, Massachusetts, by a small group of writers, O'Neill himself being one of them. Among the original members were Susan Glaspell, John Reed, and Robert Edmond Jones. Many other talented people were attracted to the company as writers, directors, designers, and actors, including Floyd Dell, Lawrence Langner, Mary Morris, Henry O'Neill, Walter Huston, Otto Kruger, Donald Oenslager, and Kenneth Macgowan.

In 1916, the Provincetown Players produced two of O'Neill's short plays, *Bound East for Cardiff* and *Thirst*. The following winter, the company moved to a small playhouse in Greenwich Village. Here they functioned intermittently, producing many other works by O'Neill. The depression of 1929 finally forced the group to close down.

In 1917-1918, O'Neill wrote several more one-act plays—*In the Zone, The Long Voyage Home,* and *The Moon of the Caribees*—drawing on his experience at sea. These plays expressed O'Neill's views of humanity with a realism hitherto unknown in the American theatre. He soon began to be noticed by the critics as a promising dramatist; and during the next few years O'Neill developed broader themes and a more ambitious means of expression.

His early work shows his wonderful grasp of the essentials of character, and his deep sympathy for a humanity caught in the coils of circumstance. There is an intensity in his work which brings a

EUGENE O'NEILL (1888-1953)   The towering figure of American drama of the 20th century, Eugene O'Neill first became known for his one-act sea plays "S.S. Glencairn" and "The Long Voyage Home" (1916-1918). Four of his plays were produced posthumously: "Long Day's Journey Into Night" (1956), "A Moon for the Misbegotten" (1957), "A Touch of a Poet" (1958), and "More Stately Mansions" (1957).

sweep to his drama. The inexorable gloom of the tragic situations he creates is occasionally lit by flashes of real humor.

O'Neill was fortunate in having so much of his early work produced by the Provincetown Players who were exploring various experimental means of presenting new plays. In his search for a means of expressing his ideas in an atmosphere of untrammeled freedom, O'Neill learned much of value from his association with Robert Edmond Jones and Kenneth Macgowan.

O'NEILL'S EARLY PLAYS

O'Neill was first presented on Broadway in 1920. *Beyond the Horizon* was an immediate success, and won a Pulitzer Prize for the best play of the year. This bitter tragedy of a man who longs for the sea but is tied to life on a farm in which he is unsuccessful established O'Neill in the commercial theatre. In the following years, O'Neill became a prolific and ever-questing writer who was rapidly accepted as the leading American dramatist.

The Emperor Jones, also produced in 1920, has remained one of O'Neill's best known and most often produced plays. It is a study of primeval fear, effectively suggested by the constant background of tom-toms. The main role in the drama was played by the magnificent Paul Robeson.

The following year came *Anna Christie,* a second version of an earlier work formerly entitled *Chris Christopherson.* This story of romantic and venal love, played against a background of the sea, earned O'Neill a second Pulitzer Prize.

In 1921, O'Neill wrote *The Straw* and *The First Man.* Although minor works, they provide very actable parts.

THE HAIRY APE

Produced by the Provincetown Players in 1922, Eugene O'Neill's symbolic, experimental play posed the problem of a man no longer in harmony with himself or with nature who, in his need to belong, moves inexorably towards self-destruction. O'Neill's use of expressionistic techniques effectively dramatized the gradual disintegration of Yank, a steamship stoker, who is seen not wholly as a person but as a symbol for a whole aspect of life.

Although the profanity of the crew in the stokehole shocked some of the audience, the realism and the novelty of the setting and its characters were enormously effective.

DESIRE UNDER THE ELMS

O'Neill's next important work was *Desire Under the Elms*, produced in 1924. This tragedy of an elderly New England farmer of the 1850's whose young wife falls passionately in love with her stepson, bears his child, and then in desperation kills it and is led away to be tried for murder, created much discussion. Walter Huston was memorable in the part of the puritanical old farmer, Ephraim Cabot; Mary Morris played the tragic young wife, Abbie, with an extraordinary sense of warmth and humanity. The play was also a triumph for Robert Edmond Jones, both for his sensitive direction, and for his unique farmhouse setting in which the various rooms and the action taking place in them were seen simultaneously by the audience.

In 1926, O'Neill experimented further with symbolism in *The Great God Brown*. In this play, the characters wear masks to denote how they appear to others, and they remove their masks to reveal their true selves. The play excited much interest as an experimental work. Today, it is no longer considered one of O'Neill's most important efforts.

The following year came *Lazarus Laughed*, in which O'Neill reworked the Biblical tale of the resurrection of Lazarus from the dead.

MARCO MILLIONS

The presentation of Marco Polo as a brash young business go-getter

"DESIRE UNDER THE ELMS"   This early O'Neill play, first presented by the Provincetown Players in 1924, is considered by a number of critics to be "the first great American tragedy." The bleak character of the drama, admirably caught by Robert Edmond Jones' set, imparted a sense of intolerable closeness and impending doom.

was produced in 1928. The cast included Alfred Lunt, Morris Carnovsky, Ernest Cossart, Dudley Digges, Baliol Holloway, and Mary Blair. The play has little of enduring value.

DYNAMO

Produced in 1929, *Dynamo* was not one of O'Neill's outstanding dramas, even though the theme—the failure of modern science to provide a valid foundation for spiritual values— was an interesting one. The first production, presented by the Theatre Guild at the Martin Beck Theatre, was directed by Philip Moeller with striking constructivist settings by Lee Simonson. The cast included Claudette Colbert, George Gaul, Helen Westley, Glenn Anders, Ross Forrester, Edgar Kent, and Dudley Digges.

STRANGE INTERLUDE

Produced in 1928, *Strange Interlude,* an extremely long play of nine acts, tells the tragic story of a neurotic woman, extremely possessive by nature, and of the men who are alternately attracted to and repelled by her. In this play, O'Neill again contrasts the outer and the inner man. The characters punctuate their conversations with soliloquies to the audience, which voice their innermost thoughts.

O'Neill's massive drama, with its Freudian overtones, sought to reveal the sources of his characters' motivation. Dealing with such unconventional themes as sexual repression and abortion, the play— considered revolutionary in 1928—was banned before its Boston opening, and was forced to premier in Quincy, Massachusetts. The resulting notoriety added much to the drama's outstanding success.

In the Theatre Guild production in New York, O'Neill reached a high point of success with a run of more than 432 performances, followed by a long road tour.

Strange Interlude was shown in the John Golden Theatre in New York City. The play was directed by Philip Moeller. The sets were

"STRANGE INTERLUDE"   *This scene, from the original production, shows Nina Leeds (Lynn Fontanne) surrounded by the men in her life, who are arrested momentarily as they speak their revealing asides.*

designed by Jo Mielziner, who today is considered one of the country's leading stage designers. The cast included Lynn Fontanne, Tom Powers, Earle Larrimore, and Helen Westley.

THE MOURNING BECOMES ELECTRA TRILOGY

For the next two years, O'Neill was busy on his trilogy, *Mourning Becomes Electra,* which became his most widely acclaimed work. First produced by the Theatre Guild in 1931 at the Martin Beck Theatre with Philip Moeller directing and with magnificent settings by Robert Edmond Jones, the trilogy became an immediate success. In a presentation of six hours, O'Neill unfolds a modern version of the Orestean tragedy, set in a New England mansion at the time of the Civil War.

The first play, *The Homecoming,* depicts the return from the war of Ezra Mannon (Agamemnon) and his son Orin (Orestes); the murder of Ezra by his wife, Christine (Clytemnestra), and her lover, Captain Brant (Aegisthus).

In *The Hunted,* Lavinia (Electra), moved by the deep love she had for her father and her hatred of her mother, persuades Orin to avenge the crime. He confronts Brant and shoots him in the presence of Christine, who then commits suicide.

In the final play, *The Haunted,* Orin, overcome by remorse at the death of his mother whom he loved, and beset by fears of madness, takes his own life. Lavinia's fate is to be left to live out her life alone in the gaunt Mannon house, haunted by the consequences of hate and passion.

There are great pyschological overtones in the play, profound in their implications and subtly revealed in the dialogue. In spite of its length, the story is gripping; considerable suspense is built up. O'Neill's attempt to parallel in modern psychological drama the old Greek sense of fate is carried out with consummate skill. To many critics, however, the characters were not full drawn and were sub-servient to the theme—the reverse, if anything, of the normal O'Neill approach.

OTHER O'NEILL PLAYS

Mourning Becomes Electra was followed in 1933 by the comedy *Ah, Wilderness!* in which small-town life in the early years of the century is aptly caught. George M. Cohan played the father with all the whimsical geniality for which he was so well loved, and Will Rogers took the play on the road.

Days Without End, written in 1934, is a study of the religious faith of a split personality. Two actors were used to interpret the main character. The play had a mixed reception in New York, although it was well received when produced at the Abbey Theatre in Dublin.

During the next twelve years, O'Neill retired from active participation in the theatre and settled down to writing a long cycle of plays which were to represent American life in the present century. O'Neill's intention was that none of these plays would be produced until all were completed.

In 1936, O'Neill was awarded the Nobel Prize for literature but he remained in retirement. He completed many plays, some of which were inordinately long; but he destroyed some first drafts being unable, because of illness, to complete their revision. In spite of failing health, O'Neill achieved new heights of dramatic insight in his last works.

THE ICEMAN COMETH

New York saw the production in 1946 of *The Iceman Cometh,* which enjoyed a long run, despite its mixed reception. *The Iceman Cometh* was the first of a series of dramas, all of which are permeated with a gloomy despair of life. The setting is a cheap saloon in 1912. The characters are drunks who spend their days living in the past or in pipe dreams. Attempts are made by one of the characters to rouse his cronies from the depths of their despair, but he, too, succumbs in the end, and confesses to the murder of his deeply loved wife through his inability to control his cravings. And the gloom descends still deeper. In this long play, O'Neill returned to the naturalism of

*"THE ICEMAN COMETH"   In 1956, the highly acclaimed revival of O'Neill's
philosophical drama, "The Iceman Cometh," by Circle-in-the-Square, added luster to
the company that had spearheaded the Off-Broadway theatre movement and developed
renewed interest in O'Neill's work. A then unknown actor, Jason Robards, brilliantly*

his early works, and conveyed the atmosphere of the sleazy bar with
consummate skill.

O'NEILL'S LAST PLAYS
His later plays—*Long Day's Journey into Night, A Moon for the*

recreated the role of Hickey, the itinerant salesman. In this characteristic moment, Hickey in his jaunty straw hat is seated among the habitués of Harry Hope's saloon and attempts to rouse his companions to action and to talk them out of their life-sustaining illusions.

Misbegotten, and *A Touch of the Poet*—were not produced in New York until some years after his death in 1953, partly because of wishes expressed in his will. The two last named dramas did not have the expected O'Neill impact.

LONG DAY'S JOURNEY INTO NIGHT

On November 7, 1956, with the opening of Eugene O'Neill's masterpiece, the American theatre was treated to a drama of gigantic stature. "In some curious way," it was said of this grimly obsessive autobiographical play, "the agony that O'Neill felt, whenever he contemplated his own beginnings . . . [was] . . . exorcised, washed away, leaving in its place an undefined . . . agreed upon peace." Written in 1941, the manuscript was brought by O'Neill some years later to his publisher Bennett Cerf, with the stipulation that the sealed envelope containing the manuscript "not be opened till 25 years after my death." However, Mrs. O'Neill, as executrix of the estate, countermanded her husband's wishes and had the play published three years after his death.

O'NEILL'S INFLUENCE

O'Neill's life in the theatre spanned a period of great development. During this time, many other dramatists produced work which, although never reaching the heights of O'Neill's achievements, nevertheless added considerably to the stature of American drama. Generally speaking, these dramatists reacted more closely than did O'Neill to the affairs of the day, or to periods of history wherein the main theme had a parallel validity.

O'Neill is now regarded as the towering figure of the 20th-century American drama.

MAXWELL ANDERSON (1888-1959)

Maxwell Anderson, who was born in the same year as O'Neill, wrote plays on many varied subjects and in many different styles; his poetic imagination colors most of them.

Anderson's earliest success, written in collaboration with Laurence Stallings, was the popular *What Price Glory?* (1924), a realistic presentation of the American soldier in World War I.

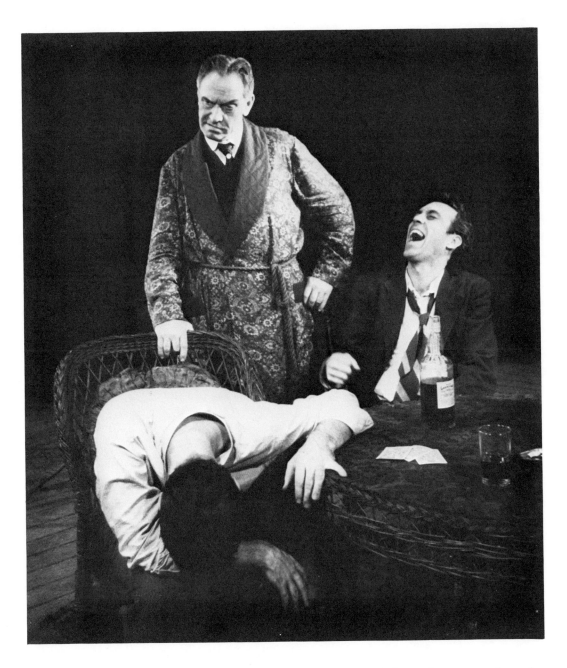

"LONG DAY'S JOURNEY INTO NIGHT"   This play was given its
world premiere at the Royal Dramatic Theatre in Sweden in 1956. Nine
months later, the play premiered in New York City, under the aegis of Circle-
in-the-Square's producers Leigh Connell, Jose Quintero, and Ted Mann.

MAXWELL ANDERSON (1888-1959)   The foremost American exponent of poetic drama, Anderson held that "without great poetry, there is no great drama." This principle was most successfully applied in his historical plays. WINTERSET (1935), a contemporary drama based on the execution of Sacco and Vanzetti, was a notable exception. ELIZABETH THE QUEEN (1930), NIGHT OVER TAOS (1932), MARY OF SCOTLAND (1933), and WINGLESS VICTORY (1936) are generally considered to be Anderson's best historical verse plays.

This work was followed by *Saturday's Children* (1927), the playwright's first popular success done entirely by his own hand. A realistic comedy of young love and marriage, but with serious implications, the play was an outstanding success.

Gypsy, another realistic play, is a tragedy of city life in which a young girl, disappointed at passing from one man to another without finding love, commits suicide.

Anderson experimented with verse drama. In *Elizabeth, the Queen* (1930), he produced a moving dramatic play, written with considerable beauty.

In 1933, he continued this trend with *Mary of Scotland* in which he took artistic license by making Mary and Elizabeth meet.

"MARY OF SCOTLAND"   In this famous confrontation scene just before her execution, Mary mocks Elizabeth (Helen Menken) for not having lived as full a life as she.

MARY OF SCOTLAND

Maxwell Anderson's verse play about the struggle for power between Elizabeth I and Mary Queen of Scots brought to the theatre "a certain lordly dignity that it seldom attained." The 1933 Theatre Guild production presented Helen Hayes as the impetuous Mary in a milestone performance, noted as a turning point in her career. From being a player in light comedies, she enjoyed her first acclaim as a serious actress.

OTHER ANDERSON PLAYS

Other historical plays were *Valley Forge,* a dramatization of the life of Washington and his struggles with Congress; *The Masque of Kings,* the tragedy of Crown Prince Rudolf and Maria Vetsera; *Night Over Taos; Joan of Lorraine,* in which Ingrid Bergman was memorable as Joan of Arc; *Anne of the Thousand Days;* and *Knickerbocker Holiday,* with music by Kurt Weill, in which Walter Huston splendidly characterized old Peter Stuyvesant.

Anderson turned to political satire in *Both Your Houses,* a play which earned him a Pulitzer Prize in 1933. However, his best play is considered to be *Winterset* (1935), a verse tragedy about injustice which bore strong echoes of the Sacco and Vanzetti case, without being a literal transcription of that episode. *Winterset* received a memorable production in New York with Burgess Meredith as the young man who sacrifices his life to vindicate a father unjustly executed for murder. The setting by Jo Mielziner with the Brooklyn Bridge in the background admirably expressed the inexorable march of fate.

Other Anderson plays, in different styles, are: *Key Largo; The Star Wagon; Truckline Cafe; The Wingless Victory; High Tor; The Bad Seed;* and *Journey to Jerusalem.* Anderson's plays display a practical understanding of the theatre, and however tragic his theme may be, this fine craftsman never loses sight of the basic need to entertain.

ELMER RICE (1892-1967)

Trained as a lawyer, Elmer Rice became a well-known director and a dramatist. His first play, *On Trial* (1914), an outstanding success, was the first American play to use the flashback, a technique much employed by later dramatists.

In *The Adding Machine,* in 1923, Rice employed the expressionist technique then being used by German dramatists. This satire of the machine-age man, symbolized as Mr. Zero, was well staged by the Theatre Guild. Dudley Digges, Helen Westley, and Margaret Wycherley were in the cast.

Many consider *Street Scene* Rice's best play. Produced in 1929, this realistic treatment of life in a New York tenement was awarded the Pulitzer Prize. *Counsellor-at-Law* (1931) gave Paul Muni an excellent role as a Jewish attorney and drew on Rice's own expert knowledge of the law. In *Judgment Day* (1934), Rice wrote a powerful dramatization of the Reichstag Fire trial.

During the 1930's, Rice's allegiance to the underdog was manifested in his work for the Federal Theatre Project. His idea of providing employment for the growing numbers of unemployed actors crystallized in the "Living Newspaper," a dramatization of current events presenting many short scenes using different actors and rapid changes. Rice's interest in social problems was also expressed in *We, the People* (1933) in which the theatre turns into a political meeting.

Between Two Worlds (1934) was a failure. It was a serious attempt to dramatize the differences between the American and the Russian ways of life.

Two on an Island (1940) is a romantic and charming Manhattan comedy. In *Flight to the West* (1940), Rice deals with Nazi madness and introduces an element of melodrama. Two years later, Rice wrote *A New Life,* a slight work of youthful idealism and its conflict with conventionality. *Dream Girl* (1945) gave Betty Field a good role as a very imaginative girl discovering romance in the least expected place.

"STREET SCENE"   Although critically rebuked by one journalist as "point-less realism" for having "an actual garbage can on stage," the play won popular

success as a slice of life. Frank Maurrant (Robert Kelly), having just slain his wife and her lover, holds a curious crowd at bay.

GEORGE S. KAUFMAN (1889-1961)

Known as "The Great Collaborator," George S. Kaufman was also one of the best directors of farce and comedy. He had a keen sense of satire. Kaufman wrote many plays with Edna Ferber, including *The Royal Family* (1927), *Dinner at Eight* (1932), and *Stage Door* (1936).

His other chief collaboration was with Moss Hart, which produced *Once in a Lifetime,* a 1930 satire on Hollywood; *Merrily We Roll Along* (1934); and *You Can't Take It With You,* which won a Pulitzer Prize in 1936. With Moss Hart, Kaufman also painted a hilarious portrait of Alexander Woollcott in *The Man Who Came to Dinner* (1939). [He had previously collaborated with Woollcott on *The Channel Road* [1929] and *The Dark Tower* [1933].] All these were extremely successful farcical comedies, witty, and with an underlying feeling for humanity.

Kaufman also collaborated with Marc Connelly on several plays, including *Beggar on Horseback* (1924). His most important solo effort was *The Butter and Egg Man* (1925), a farce of theatrical life.

YOU CAN'T TAKE IT WITH YOU

When this zany comedy won the Pulitzer Prize in 1936, some of the critics grumbled. Although it was called a "perfectly swell hit show" by the New York Daily News, the eminent critic, John Mason Brown, felt that in a season offering Maxwell Anderson's *High Tor* and Paul Green's *Johnny Johnson,* the prize might have gone elsewhere. Nonetheless, Kaufman's and Hart's lovable family of eccentrics caught the fancy of the American public. Frequently revived, the play has become a favorite of American audiences.

MOSS HART (1904-1961)

In early collaborative efforts, Hart contributed not only straight plays but the books for some of the theatre's outstanding musicals: *Strike Up the Band* (1930), *Of Thee I Sing* (1931), and *I'd Rather Be*

ELMER RICE (1892-1967)   *The playwright is seen here on the set of* STREET SCENE.

"YOU CAN'T TAKE IT WITH YOU"   *In this scene, each member of the Sycamore family is seen doing his "own quirky thing." Josephine Hull, poised at an easel, draws inspiration from her model who is posing as "The Discus Thrower."*

Right (1937). Called by Alexander Woollcott "the first wit of his time," Hart's quips were legendary: "I saw the show under unfortunate circumstances: the curtain was up."

On his own, Hart also contributed notable books for eminent musicals. In 1933, he wrote his first libretto for *Face the Music,* the Irving Berlin tunefest. In 1941, he wrote a classic book for *Lady in the Dark.*

The names and the plays of Kaufman and Hart are synonymous with one of the brightest epochs in the history of the American theatre.

ROBERT E. SHERWOOD (1896-1955)

A critic before he served in World War I and was gassed and wounded, Sherwood became a distinguished dramatist between the two World Wars, creating both comedy and serious plays. His first success, in 1927, was a satirical farce about Hannibal, *The Road to Rome,* in which he debunked the glory of the ancient Carthaginian general's march. The play had fine roles for Philip Merivale, Barry Jones, and Jane Cowl. The following year, *The Queen's Husband* gave Roland Young an amusing opportunity as the henpecked king of a Central European country.

London found *Waterloo Bridge* (1930), a melodrama of World War I, more acceptable than did New York. Its story of a street-walker and an American soldier in London was suffused with a deep human sympathy.

A very successful excursion into high romantic comedy followed in 1931 with *Reunion in Vienna,* in which the Lunts appeared brilliantly in both New York and London.

In 1935, came *The Petrified Forest,* a popular melodrama about a disillusioned young writer who chooses death at the hand of an escaping gangster in preference to the negative, empty life in which he felt himself to be drifting. The memorable performances of Leslie Howard and Humphrey Bogart in the stage production of *Petrified Forest* were repeated for universal enjoyment in the film version.

Tovarich (1936) was an adaptation from the French of Jacques Deval's amusing comedy of Russian emigré life in America.

Sherwood's awareness of the coming storm in Europe was evidenced in *Idiot's Delight,* in which his earlier pacifism was superseded by a positive protest against fascism. It earned him the Pulitzer Prize in 1936.

In 1939, Sherwood wrote *There Shall Be No Night,* a drama of a pacifist scientist who turns to war during the Russian invasion of Finland (changed, in the London version, to Germany's invasion of Greece).

Abe Lincoln in Illinois was directed by Elmer Rice in 1938; Ray-

ROBERT E. SHERWOOD (1896-1955)   At his best, Sherwood wrote delightful high comedy like "Reunion in Vienna" (1931), such satiric war drama as "Idiot's Delight" (1935), and a straightforward biographical study "Abe Lincoln in Illinois" (1938). Many consider "The Petrified Forest" (1935)—a romantic portrayal of the lost generation—to be his best play.

mond Massey brought distinction to this story of the great man's formative years.

Sherwood wrote no more plays until 1945, when *The Rugged Path,* a philosophical account of the motives of soldiers and journalists during World War II, was successfully produced with Spencer Tracy.

"REUNION IN VIENNA"   Robert Sherwood's romantic comedy, produced by the Theatre Guild in 1931, was another vehicle in the long line of glittering successes for the Lunts. Their first Guild performance was in Ferenc Molnar's "The Guardsman" in 1924. Thirty-four years later, they played the leads in Friedrich Durranmatt's "The Visit." During this stretch, the famed husband-and-wife acting team dominated Theatre Guild history. In this scene, Alfred Lunt, as an expatriate Hapsburg Prince reduced to driving a taxicab in Nice, returns to Vienna for one night to resume an affair that was interrupted ten years earlier. Lynn Fontanne is his former mistress.

THE GREEN PASTURES

The most famous entrance line in Broadway history is heard in Marc Connelly's classic folk play of 1930: "Gangway!" called the angel Gabriel, "Gangway for de Lawd God Jehovah." Out stepped a man who had never been on stage in his life—66-year-old Richard B. Harrison, son of fugitive slaves, a one-time newsboy, bellhop, and railroad worker. Based on Roark Bradford's short stories, OL' MAN ADAM AN' HIS CHILLUN, Connelly's episodic folk play charmed audiences with the simplicity of its Old Testament tales, told much as an old Negro preacher might have spoken them. The part of de Lawd was so closely identified with Harrison that, after his death in 1935, it was felt that the play could not be revived without him. He performed the role 1,659 consecutive times.

THORNTON WILDER (1897-   )

Thornton Wilder is known chiefly for two plays, *Our Town* (1938) and *The Skin of Our Teeth* (1945), both of them experimental in form and unusual in production technique.

Our Town was an attempt at a close-up view of some of the inhabitants of a small New England town. The town itself, and the various settings in which the action takes place, are left to the imagination of the audience, as the whole play takes place on a bare stage. Except for a few chairs and rostrums, there is no scenery.

A citizen of the town acts as a stage manager and sets each short scene by his description and introduction of the characters. In spite of this apparent lack of realism, the behavior of the characters—in their daily lives, in falling in love, and in dying—is played out in a naturalistic style; there is an imaginative use of lighting. The play is extremely effective and moving.

The Skin of Our Teeth is a rather rambling play, lacking the unity of *Our Town,* but it does set out to embrace the whole of human history, depicting the indomitable courage and ingenuity of man in his struggles to make a comfortable and meaningful life despite the various disasters he has been faced with since the Ice Age. The action is not presented in historic sequence, but episodically. The play uses devices from the expressionistic technique developed by Brecht. Wilder, however, unlike Brecht, has no axe to grind, and the play conveys its story as a kind of modern morality play with many light-hearted moments of humor.

Wilder's other plays are more conventional in form. *The Matchmaker* (1954), a reworking of his earlier *The Merchant of Yonkers* (1938), is perhaps his best known work. This farce about a designing widow, set in the early years of the century, provided an excellent part for Ruth Gordon. *The Matchmaker* was later made into the highly successful musical comedy *Hello Dolly* (1965).

S. N. BEHRMAN (1893-   )

Noted for his social comedies, which appeared regularly throughout the 20's and 30's, Samuel Nathan Behrman provided sprightly vehicles for such stylish players as the Lunts, Ruth Gordon, Constance Collier, and Henry Daniell. Among these plays were: *The Second Man* (1927), *Serena Blandish* (1929), *Brief Moment* (1931), *No Time for Comedy* (1939), and *Amphitryon 38* (1937).

AMPHITRYON 38

Adapted by S.N. Behrman from an original play by Jean Giraudoux, the title *Amphitryon 38* was based on the French playwright's wry assumption that there had been 37 versions of the Jupiter-Alcmene legend since the Roman diversion *Amphitruo* was penned by Plautus in 186 B.C. Behrman's turn at this burlesque of a God's way with a lady revealed a deft comic touch.

LILLIAN HELLMAN (1905-   )

Lillian Hellman's plays exhibit great dramatic force and an impres-

THORNTON WILDER (1897-   )   Two plays of enduring quality—"Our Town" (1938), a rueful and tender portrait of small-town America, and "Skin of Our Teeth" (1942), a study of an indomitable family escaping from one disaster after another through aeons of history—mark Thornton Wilder as a major figure of the contemporary American theatre.

sive command of the stage. Her first play, *The Children's Hour,* produced in 1934, was set in a private school and deals with the slander of two women teachers by a schoolgirl, which once set in motion, relentlessly pursues its evil path to final tragedy. The subject of homosexuality was dealt with both delicately and powerfully, and with a sure dramatic touch. The play had a successful run for two years.

Her next play, *Days to Come* (1936), about a labor strike, was not successful, but *The Little Foxes* (1939), a biting play which takes its title from the biblical reference to the foxes that destroy the vines, was a hit. Her other notable works have been *Watch on the Rhine* (1941), a study of fascism; *Another Part of the Forest* (1946), a bitter comedy about the earlier connivings of the characters in *The Little Foxes; The Autumn Garden* (1951) about loneliness; and

"THE LITTLE FOXES" (1939)   *Members of the Hubbard clan gather round the dining table in Lillian Hellman's penetrating study of a family racked by greed. Tallulah*

Bankhead scored her greatest stage triumph as the voracious Regina Giddens.

"THE CHILDREN'S HOUR"   *A tense moment from Lillian Hellman's first play which opened November 20, 1934, at the Maxine Elliott Theatre shows Mary Tilford, a spoiled neurotic child, played by Florence McGee and her troubled teachers, Anne Revere and Katherine Emery, whose lives she is destroying.*

Toys in the Attic (1959), a penetrating study of a weak possessive woman.

Lillian Hellman always chose strong themes to write about, and she wrote strong dramas about the evil that is bred in the human character by social forces. Born in New Orleans, she is particularly strong in her portrayal of the Southern character and the Southern scene.

THE LITTLE FOXES

The moral degeneracy of the Hubbards, a rapacious Southern family, was mercilessly chronicled in Lillian Hellman's realistic drama produced in 1939. Distinguished by the triumphant performance of Tallulah Bankhead as Regina Giddens, the most vicious vixen in the litter, the play heralded the entry of Lillian Hellman to the front rank of American dramatists.

REGIONAL WRITERS

Lynn Riggs has written both tragedies and comedies depicting life in the South and Southwest. His best-known play is the comedy *Green Grow the Lilacs* in which Franchot Tone made his name in 1930. This story became much more widely known when it was adapted as a musical comedy by Oscar Hammerstein II and Richard Rodgers, to become the record-breaking *Oklahoma!* Other plays by Riggs are *Russet Mantle, Roadside,* and *The Cream in the Well,* a fine tragedy of farm life which unfortunately appeared on Broadway when war threatened.

DuBose Heyward, collaborating with his wife, wrote sympathetically of the southern Negro. *Porgy,* produced in 1927, provided perhaps for the first time in the theatre, a serious view of the Negro.. Previously, the Negro had been treated largely as a figure of fun on the stage. The play also provided fine acting opportunities for its Negro cast. Some years later, Heyward reworked this play for

LILLIAN HELLMAN (1905–) Calling herself a "moral writer" Miss Hellman in all her plays is concerned principally with social ills, and with their degenerative effects on individuals. Her dramas are noted especially for their superior craftsmanship and their well-knit plots.

"OUR TOWN"   Thornton Wilder's elegiac chronicle of life and death in a small New England town was universally admired for its mixture of sentiment and simple truth. The play was produced in 1938. Employing unconventional

stage techniques, the drama captured, in the author's words, his affection "for those little white towns in the hills." This photograph of the poignant funeral scene indicates the non-realistic style of this American classic.

George Gershwin, and it became the folk opera *Porgy and Bess,* produced with great success in 1935.

Mamba's Daughters (1938), also written with Mr. Heyward, provided a fine character part in which Ethel Waters of revue fame came to be regarded for the first time as a serious actress.

PAUL GREEN (1894-   )

Virtually unknown in 1927, Paul Green, poet and dramatist, burst on the theatrical scene with a full-length play, *In Abraham's Bosom,* which won the Pulitzer Prize.

This was followed, in 1931, by his brooding Chekhovian drama of the decadent South, *The House of Connelly,* presented by the Group Theatre as its first production. In 1936, at the Group Theatre's request, he and Kurt Weill reworked *The Good Soldier Schweik* to produce the jeering anti-war play *Johnny Johnson.* In this play, bittersweet melodies of Weill form an acrid counterpoint to Green's satirical episodic drama.

Disillusioned by the theatre's commercialism, Green returned to his native North Carolina in 1937 where he devoted himself to folk drama and pageants. These include: *The Lost Colony,* performed annually on Roanoke Island, and *The Highland Call,* played at Fayetteville. Among his better plays are the powerful chain gang drama *Hymn to the Rising Sun* and a dramatization of Richard Wright's novel NATIVE SON.

THE GROUP THEATRE

The Group Theatre was formed by Harold Clurman, Cheryl Crawford, and Lee Strasberg, with a group of people who had been associated in various ways with the Theatre Guild. This company was to become a powerful influence during the 1930's, due to its demonstration of extraordinarily fine ensemble acting by a troupe with no stars. The success of the Group Theatre also derived from the originality

THE GROUP THEATRE   This photograph, taken about 1938, shows some of the future luminaries of the stage and the motion picture world: (Left to right, back row) Art Smith, Walter Fried, Sanford Meisner, Ruth Nelson, Lee J. Cobb, Leif Ericson, Roman Bohnen, Morris Carnovsky, Kermit Bloomgarden. (Below in a group of three) Luther Adler, Phoebe Brand, and Harold Clurman. (Below, front) Irwin Shaw, Eleanor Lynn, Frances Farmer, Robert Lewis, and Elia Kazan.

of the work of the dramatists within the group. The major focus was on the social, political, and economic problems of the times, and on the conflicts of the individual in his struggle for a better life.

The Group Theatre established itself with Paul Green's *The House of Connelly,* but its next productions met with failure. The play *1931,* was an attempt by Claire and Paul Sifton to dramatize the great economic depression. *Night Over Taos* by Maxwell Anderson

was a poetic drama of the Mexican War. Toward the end of 1932, *Success Story* by John Howard Lawson had a run of 121 performances; but this success was followed by another failure—*Big Night* based on Dawn Powell's *The Party*. In some measure, all these were plays of social consciousness.

MEN IN WHITE

The next production, *Men in White* by Sidney Kingsley, was a melodrama about hospital interns. This play included a scene in an operating room which was played completely in pantomime. In this drama, the actors of the Group Theatre reached a new level of excellence, and the production was a great success. Two years of hard work, with a mixed bag of failures and near successes, now culminated in this finished and unified presentation. Lee Strasberg directed.

GROUP THEATRE FOUNDERS   In 1931, Harold Clurman, *Cheryl Crawford and Lee Strasberg, with other youthful members of the Theatre Guild, left their parent company to form the Group Theatre. From 1931 to 1941, during its brief but illustrious history, the Group produced plays of social consciousness, developed native American playwrights like Clifford Odets, and promulgated a naturalistic style of acting based on the Stanislavski System.*

The quiet, simple settings of Mordecai Gorelik, who created so many of the Group's designs, served admirably to enhance the mood and atmosphere. The play won the Pulitzer Prize for 1934, and enjoyed a run of nearly a year, putting the company's finances on a firm basis for the first time.

PHILIP BARRY (1896-1949)

Philip Barry was a student of Professor Baker's "47 Workshop" at Harvard, where he won the Prize Play contest in 1922 with *You and I,* an inherently serious play which has a surface polish of witty comedy. This quality was to permeate most of Barry's plays. *The Youngest* (1924), a satire of social pretensions, was followed by *In a Garden,* an obscure play which was memorable largely for Laurette Taylor's performance. *White Wings* (1926) proved a failure with the public, although it was well received by the critics for its satire and symbolism.

Other comedies of manners followed; they included *Paris Bound, Holiday,* and *The Animal Kingdom.* Perhaps the best of his comedies is *The Philadelphia Story,* written in 1939, which is brilliantly witty and is remembered for Katharine Hepburn's sparkling performance.

In *Tomorrow and Tomorrow* (1931), Barry addressed the more serious theme of married happiness and sexual passion. *Hotel Universe* (1930) was a serious psychological drama in which a revelation is made to a group of troubled individuals of the naked truth within them, which results in a symbolic expiation for their sins. This was probably Barry's most ambitious work, but it proved to be too obscure for its audience.

In *The Joyous Season* (1934), Barry attempted to deal with the underlying importance of religious faith in coloring the impulses and actions of individuals. Although a sincere and moving play, it failed with the public, as did *Bright Star* in 1935. *Here Come the Clowns* was more successful in 1938, with Eddie Dowling giving a fine performance.

Barry later contributed *Liberty Jones* (1941), *Without Love* (1942), and *Foolish Notion* (1945), thus leaving a body of writings that embraced comedy, fantasy, and serious drama and covered a provocative range of subjects.

THE PHILADELPHIA STORY

Philip Barry's mastery of the comedy of manners was most elegantly

"THE PHILADELPHIA STORY" *Katharine Hepburn as* Tracy
Lord is lording it over her amused husband-to-be Frank Fenton.

"AMPHITRYON 38"   *In this scene from the 1938 Theatre Guild production, Alfred Lunt as the amorous Jupiter is shown with Richard Whorf as Mercury. They plot the seduction of a mortal woman. According to Behrman, Gods in pursuit of the fair sex behave just as men do: foolishly and passionately.*

displayed in *The Philadelphia Story* (1939). In the Theatre Guild production, a stellar cast, including Joseph Cotten, Van Heflin, Shirley Booth, Lenore Lonergan, Dan Tobin, Vera Allen and Nicholas Joy, among others, was sparked by the presence of Katherine

Hepburn, whose return to the stage marked an upturn in the Theatre Guild's fortunes, then at a particularly low ebb. As the spoiled debutante Tracy Lord, daughter of a Philadelphia Main Line family, Miss Hepburn proved in the words of a journalist, "the essential humility of a fashionable snob." Her smashing triumph in this role—the most memorable in her stage career—affirmed her position as one of the finest actresses not only in films but on stage, and led to a continued association with the Theatre Guild in such plays as Barry's *Without Love* (1942), Shakespeare's *As You Like It* (1950), and Shaw's *The Millionairess* (1952).

TOBACCO ROAD

Jack Kirkland's play, *Tobacco Road,* based on the Erskine Caldwell novel, was a study of the lives and lusts of a southern white trash family in decline. Produced in 1933, it ran for seven and a half years, probably because its earthy realism severely jolted the bourgeoisie of that day, and they considered the play a shocker.

MARC CONNELLY (1890-   )

Marc Connelly often collaborated with other writers, particularly with George S. Kaufman. Their partnership proved to be most successful, and included *Dulcy,* in which Lynn Fontanne established her reputation as a star in 1921; *To the Ladies,* a comedy of the astute young wife behind her not-so-ambitious husband; *The 49-ers; Merton of the Movies,* a hilarious satire of Hollywood from the original novel of Harry Leon Wilson; *Beggar on Horseback;* and *Be Yourself.*

Connelly then parted company with Kaufman and wrote *The Wisdom Tooth* (1926), following this with his masterpiece, *The Green Pastures.* This retelling of the Bible stories in terms of the Negro spiritual greatly impressed the public with its reverence, its humor, and its deep and sympathetic understanding. Connelly himself directed the New York production in 1930, with Robert Edmond

"THE GREEN PASTURES"   *The celestial fish fry delights a covey of angels.*

Jones designing the settings. It had a successful run of nearly two years, won the Pulitzer Prize, and continued for three years on the road.

In 1934, Connelly began a collaboration with Frank B. Elser that resulted in a moderate success with *The Farmer Takes a Wife*, a comedy of canal life in New York State in which Henry Fonda and June Walker gave fine performances. Other plays on which he has collaborated with various authors have been *Having a Wonderful Time, The Two Bouquets, Everywhere I Roam, The Flowers of Virtue,* and *A Story for Strangers.*

ACTING IN THE GROUP THEATRE

The actors of the Group Theatre—unknown in their day—would today read like a roster of stars: Stella Adler, Luther Adler, Clifford Odets, Franchot Tone, Morris Carnovsky, Elia Kazan, Frances Farmer, J. Edward Bromberg, Mary Morris, John Garfield, Russell Collins, and Lee J. Cobb.

Lee Strasberg, the director, developed a new system of rehearsal for the Group Theatre, inspired by Stanislavsky of the Moscow Art Theatre. Each production was preceded by a good deal of discussion of the true meaning of the play, and of how each actor might contribute to that deeper meaning through his acting. To develop the actor's powers of projection, scenes were improvised *outside* the action of the play; but these scenes would have an emotional relationship to the drama under discussion. Also, scenes of the play were run through without using the actual dialogue; an actor would be made to improvise his own speeches so that he would get to feel the part that he was trying to project.

All this was intended to achieve the Group's goal of a theatre based on real life, with natural spontaneous acting working from the inside outward.

However, such naturalism, appropriate in realistic productions, doesn't quite hold in poetic drama where an approach more sympathetic to the lyricism of the language may be more suitable.

CLIFFORD ODETS (1906-1963)

A Group actor, Clifford Odets also tried his hand at playwriting. His first work, *Waiting for Lefty,* was produced in 1935 at a Sunday night performance. This violent one-act play, based on a taxi drivers' strike of the previous year, was effectively performed by the Group and well received by the audience. Odets became the voice of "revolutionary drama."

Till the Day I Die, a one-act anti-Nazi piece, and *Waiting for Lefty* were quickly snatched up by the many new theatre societies being formed all over the country, and so both these works were widely performed.

WAITING FOR LEFTY

In his chronicle of the Group Theatre *The Fervent Years,* Harold Clurman recalls the historic opening on January 5, 1935, of Clifford Odets' proletarian play. "When the audience, at the end of the play, responded to the militant question from the stage: 'Well, what's the answer?' with a spontaneous roar of 'Strike! Strike!' it was something more than a tribute to the play's effectiveness. It was the birth cry of the thirties." The play, as part of a double bill with another Odets one-acter *Till the Day I Die,* became "the thing to see for all who wished to remain abreast of the times."

AWAKE AND SING

Odets' first full-length play *Awake and Sing* expressed the hopes and disappointments of a Bronx family during the depression of 1932.

"Boychick, wake up," says the grandfather to Ralphie, "take the world in your two hands and make it like new. Go and fight so life

CLIFFORD ODETS   *"Boychik, wake up," says the grandfather to Ralphie in "Awake and Sing." "Take the world in your two hands and make it like new. Go and fight so life shouldn't be printed on dollar bills." This affecting speech illustrates the idealism that informs the best plays of Clifford Odets.*

shouldn't be printed on dollar bills." This affecting speech illustrates the idealism that pervades the best plays of Clifford Odets.

Although not a great financial success, *Awake and Sing* established Odets in theatrical circles outside the radical elements associated with the activities of the Group Theatre. Odets was offered lucrative employment as a Hollywood writer, which he accepted; for some years he alternated between writing for the movies and writing plays for the Group.

PARADISE LOST

In 1935, Odets' next play *Paradise Lost* was produced by the Group Theatre. The drama was a study of the effect of bankruptcy on a middle-class family. This Odets play was accorded a mixed reception, and ran for only two months.

GOLDEN BOY

Produced in 1937 at the Belasco Theatre, *Golden Boy* was a major success—the biggest money-maker in the history of the Group Theatre. The profits were so great that the company earned enough money to sustain it for the next two seasons. And road companies were formed which took the play to London, and on tour through the United States. *Golden Boy* ran in New York for a record 250 performances. The film version made Odets, the ardent idealist, a rich man.

Golden Boy is a romantic drama of a violinist turned pugilist, having been tempted to become a prizefighter because of the great financial rewards offered by the ring. The hero wants to help his family, and therefore turns to what, in a deep sense, he considers a sordid employment. In doing so, he ruins his hands; and his violin playing is foreclosed forever.

"WAITING FOR LEFTY"   *In a potentially explosive moment, company men, bent on disrupting a meeting, confront the angry workers.*

"GOLDEN BOY"   *In this picture of the original production, Luther Adler, as the future champion, Joe Bonaparte, renounces music for the almighty dollar. Joe Bonaparte, a promising young fighter, accepts the bitter knowledge that life*

Written with great sympathy and conviction, the play did not deal with any political issue of the times. Perhaps because of this non-political stance, *Golden Boy* attracted a wide audience among a public that was now saturated with political debate.

offers "success and fame, or just a lousy living." Seen on stage with the central
character are Lee J. Cobb, Phoebe Brand, John Garfield, Luther Adler, Morris
Carnovsky, and Frances Farmer.

Luther Adler played the title role magnificently. The rest of the
cast included such stalwarts as Jules Garfield, Frances Farmer, Lee
J. Cobb, Morris Carnovsky, Elia Kazan, Howard Da Silva, and Karl
Malden.

OTHER ODETS PLAYS

Odets' subsequent plays were *Rocket to the Moon* (1938), a psychological study of an elderly dentist, his wife, and his insane young mistress; *Night Music* (1940), a lyrical fantasy of a boy searching for a home in the big city; *Clash by Night* (1941), a drama of despair set on Staten Island. None of these plays had the clarity and power of his earlier works.

OTHER GROUP THEATRE PRODUCTIONS

During the ten years of its existence, the Group Theatre produced plays by many new authors. Irwin Shaw, whose grim anti-war play *Bury the Dead* was a notable production of the short-lived American Repertory Theatre, wrote *The Gentle People* for the Group, a comedy which tells how some honest and practical souls do away with a racketeer. Irwin Shaw later wrote *Sons and Soldiers* and *The Assassin* which were not successful on Broadway.

Robert Ardrey's *Thunder Rock* was produced by the Group Theatre in 1939. It was a moving fantasy of how a writer's attempt to isolate himself from world affairs is frustrated when the characters he has created persuade him to return to the darkening world. This play was successfully presented with Michael Redgrave in London in 1940, where it sounded a note of optimism amid the perils of the first year of war. Ardrey later wrote *Jeb*, a notable play of Negro life.

WILLIAM SAROYAN (1908-   )

In 1939 the Group Theatre also produced *My Heart's in the Highlands,* a lyrical one-act play about a poet's struggle against an encroaching materialism.

His first full-length play *The Time of Your Life* was produced by the Theatre Guild and won both the Pulitzer Prize and the Drama Critics' Award of 1939. Set in a San Francisco honky-tonk, the play is a whimsical fantasy in which an assortment of motley characters has gathered to seek refuge from loneliness. Saroyan's admonition to "live" is expressed by Joe, the central character. Loving and living are Saroyan's message; and though he plays on the emotions, what Saroyan really offers is honest sentiment. "A sort of cosmic vaudeville show," "a prose poem in ragtime" were two journalistic hosannahs greeting William Saroyan's tender fable of the small people in 1939.

In his work, Saroyan established himself as a master of fantasy. "I believe in dreams, sooner than statistics," says Joe. Throughout *Love's Old Sweet Song* (1940), *The Beautiful People* (1941), and *The Cave Dwellers* (1957) runs Saroyan's prevailing faith in the goodness of little people.

VISITS BY FOREIGN COMPANIES

The appearance on Broadway of a large number of European plays in the 20's and 30's proved to be a potent force in the development of theatre technique in America. These dramas were sometimes presented by foreign companies; more frequently, they were offered in translation by American companies. Enterprising management brought in works which had been long known in literary circles, but had never received production in the United States.

This trend began with a visit by Jacques Copeau and his Vieux-Columbier Company between 1917 and 1919 at the Garrick Theatre. In 1921, the Chauve-Souris Company from Moscow presented a season of musical revue. The following year, the Moscow Art The-

WILLIAM SAROYAN (1908-   )   Principal American bard of the "little people," in all his plays Saroyan trumpets the invincibility of the poetic spirit and the triumph of goodness in a materialistic world. The author's faith in the essential beneficence of man is movingly illustrated in his gallery of unique characters: The poet-father in "My Heart's in the Highlands" (1939), the philosophical Joe in "The Time of Your Life" (1939), and the head of the household in "The Beautiful People" (1941).

atre presented a season of repertory, which included Chekhov's *The Cherry Orchard* and Chekhov's *The Three Sisters,* Turgenev's *The Lady from the Provinces,* and Gorky's *The Lower Depths.*

With Stanislavsky came the great players Katchalov, Moskvin, Knipper-Chekhova, and Maria Ouspenskaya. Ouspenskaya and two other members of the Moscow company, Leo Bulgakov and Richard Boleslavski, decided to remain in America. Ouspenskaya and Boleslavski set up as teachers of the Stanislavsky system of acting; and it was with them that Lee Strasberg studied between 1923 and 1926, later utilizing what he learned in his work with the Group Theatre. Also in 1926, from Moscow came the Habimah players with a repertory of Hebrew plays, including their renowned production of *The Dybbuk.*

Max Reinhardt staged his production of *The Miracle* in 1923. Four years later, his Berlin company came to the States for a season, doing such works as Büchner's *Danton's Death,* Von Hofmannsthal's version of *Everyman,* and Shakespeare's *A Midsummer Night's Dream.* From Freiburg came a German company to do the *Passion Play.*

Such Continental stars as Eleanora Duse and Sacha Guitry appeared with their companies; and the Spanish Art Theatre came with a repertory of modern Spanish plays. There were, of course, a large number of productions with English players transferred from London; and there were periodic seasons by the Abbey Theatre of Dublin.

THE THEATRE GUILD AND THE WASHINGTON SQUARE PLAYERS

In the production of foreign plays with American actors, the most important organization was the Theatre Guild. This was primarily an organization of actors and directors which had grown out of an earlier group, the Washington Square Players. From 1914 until their dis-

"THE TIME OF YOUR LIFE"   *Seated in Nick's Pacific Street saloon is Joe (Eddie Dowling), the philosophical central character of the play, who lends moral support to Kitty Duval (Julie Haydon), the ingenuous prostitute. With the production of this lyrical play in 1939 which won both the Drama Critics' Award and the Pulitzer Prize, Saroyan emerged as a dramatist of significance.*

banding in 1918, the Washington Square Players gave performances of musical and noncommercial plays at the little Band Box Theatre, and later at the Comedy Theatre, in New York. Their primary interest was in acting and staging plays which would not normally be seen on Broadway, but which had artistic merit. They encouraged their members to write plays—usually of one act—which they staged with other short pieces.

At first the actors were unpaid, and only two performances a week were given; but as they became established, the Washington Square Players increased the number of plays to seven, and paid both actors and staff a small wage.

In 1917, having outgrown the tiny Band Box, they moved to the Comedy, where they put on some full-length plays, including Ibsen's *Ghosts,* Andreyev's *The Life of Man,* Shaw's *Mrs. Warren's Profession,* and O'Neill's *In the Zone.*

The leaders of the company were Edward Goodman and Lawrence Langner, both of whom wrote plays and directed. Among the talented members of the casts were Katharine Cornell, Roland Young, Rollo Peters, Jose Ruben, Frank Conroy, Margaret Mower, Glen Hunter, and Marjory Vonnegut.

Lee Simonson began his career as a designer with the Washington Square Players. Other members who later designed and directed for the Theatre Guild were Rollo Peters, Robert Edmond Jones, and Philip Moeller.

In 1919, the Theatre Guild was established by Lawrence Langner and other members of the Washinton Square Players with the intention of producing plays of merit, staged with the highest artistic standards. The group took over the small Garrick Theatre, and began a scheme of selling tickets by subscription for the entire season. This proved to be an extremely successful way of financing; to this day, it is used by the more important repertory companies in the country.

However, the Theatre Guild did not build up a permanent company, and it engaged actors for each production. Some of the more notable players—Dudley Digges, Helen Westley, Henry Travers, and

Erskine Sanford—of course, were constantly employed. Perhaps the most consistent players in leading roles were the great team of Alfred Lunt and Lynn Fontanne.

By 1925, the Theatre Guild was flourishing sufficiently to build its own 1,000-seat theatre. Their audiences numbered no less than 15,000 regular subscribers. Eventually, this figure was doubled in New York City alone.

The majority of the plays that were given were by European authors, although the American offerings included a number of O'Neill's plays: *Marco Millions; Strange Interlude, Dynamo,* and *Mourning Becomes Electra.* Also presented were: Elmer's Rice's *The Adding Machine;* Dorothy and DuBose Heyward's *Porgy;* Sidney Howard's *The Silver Cord* and Sidney Howard's *They Knew What They Wanted.*

Among the British dramatists, Shaw was the chief contributor; the Guild Theatre became his main platform in America and produced: *Heartbreak House, The Devil's Disciple, Saint Joan, Caesar and Cleopatra, Arms and the Man, Pygmalion, Androcles and the Lion, The Doctor's Dilemma, Major Barbara, The Millionairess,* and *Back to Methuselah.* This last-named play was presented in three parts, each part played in a successive week.

FOREIGN PLAYS PRODUCED BY THE THEATRE GUILD

The Guild produced the works of many foreign dramatists. German plays included those of Georg Kaiser, Stefan Zweig, Ernst Toller, and Franz Werfel. From France came the plays of Claudel, Courteline, Giraudoux, and Anouilh. From further East came works by Capek, Molnar, Vajda, Andreyev, and Evreinoff. From Scandinavia came Ibsen and Strindberg.

The Theatre Guild extended its activities to cities as far as the Pacific Coast. As time went on the Guild became more of a backing organization for plays they had not originated; in consequence, there were times when their early high standards of artistic merit faltered to some degree.

THE CIVIC REPERTORY THEATRE

Another venture in New York which operated through a difficult time and was finally closed by the depression of 1932 was the Civic Repertory Theatre which was started in 1926 by the actress Eva Le Gallienne.

Miss Le Gallienne had played leading roles in some of the Guild Theatre's productions, notably Julie in Molnar's *Liliom.* She later became the leading interpreter of Ibsen in America, and is remembered particularly for her Hilda Wangel in *The Master Builder,* Ella Renthein in *John Gabriel Borkman,* and Mrs. Alving in *Ghosts.*

Recruiting some keen young players, Miss Le Gallienne established a company which performed a large number of European plays to an audience which was attracted by intelligent drama at low admission prices; the best seats were sold for less than two dollars.

The choice of plays was of an exceptional standard and included works by Molière, Goldoni, Ibsen, Chekhov, Schnitzler, Dumas, Benavente, the Quinteros, and occasionally Shakespeare. Miss Le Gallienne not only directed but acted in most of her productions. Had times been more favorable, Miss Le Gallienne's company might easily have developed into something like London's Old Vic, with an analogous importance to the American theatre as a whole.

THE FEDERAL THEATRE PROJECT

During the difficult depression times of the mid-thirties, much good work was done by Hallie Flanagan, previously a teacher of drama at Vassar, who directed the Federal Theatre Project in its many enterprises throughout the country. She organized countless productions —often in towns where there was no theatre—converting movie houses and lecture halls. Miss Flanagan's activities kept many actors employed at low but regular salaries.

The low prices of admission to these productions brought new audiences into the theatre; and an enormous market for serious repertory theatre was brought into being. But during World War II, much of this ground was lost when despite the boom in attendance, public taste veered largely to light entertainment.

A.N.T.A.

The American National Theatre and Academy, known popularly as A.N.T.A., was chartered by Congress in 1935, as a nonprofit corporation whose purpose was to present theatrical productions of the highest type and to advance the public interest in the drama. While the government provided the charter, it did not provide any funds for the new corporation; these were to be raised independently by A.N.T.A.

Nothing much came of this until after the war. In 1946, a new board of officers including Vinton Freedley, Robert E. Sherwood, Gilbert Miller, and Rosamund Gilder began a vigorous campaign to acquire a nationwide membership for A.N.T.A. Through subscription and benefit performances, A.N.T.A. built up funds for a long-range program. Much of A.N.T.A.'s work has been in the educational field; but the organization has served generally in an advisory capacity and has sponsored various experimental performances.

In 1950, A.N.T.A. took over the Guild Theatre. A.N.T.A. then began to sponsor a series of interesting American and foreign plays. Later, A.N.T.A. established its own theatre in Washington Square, New York, where the Lincoln Center Repertory Company held its first two seasons. Now the Vivian Beaumont Theatre in Lincoln Center has become the permanent home of A.N.T.A.'s repertory company.

ORSON WELLES (1915-   ) AND THE MERCURY THEATRE

Another product of the Federal Theater Project, Orson Welles is recognized as a directorial genius. While still extremely young,

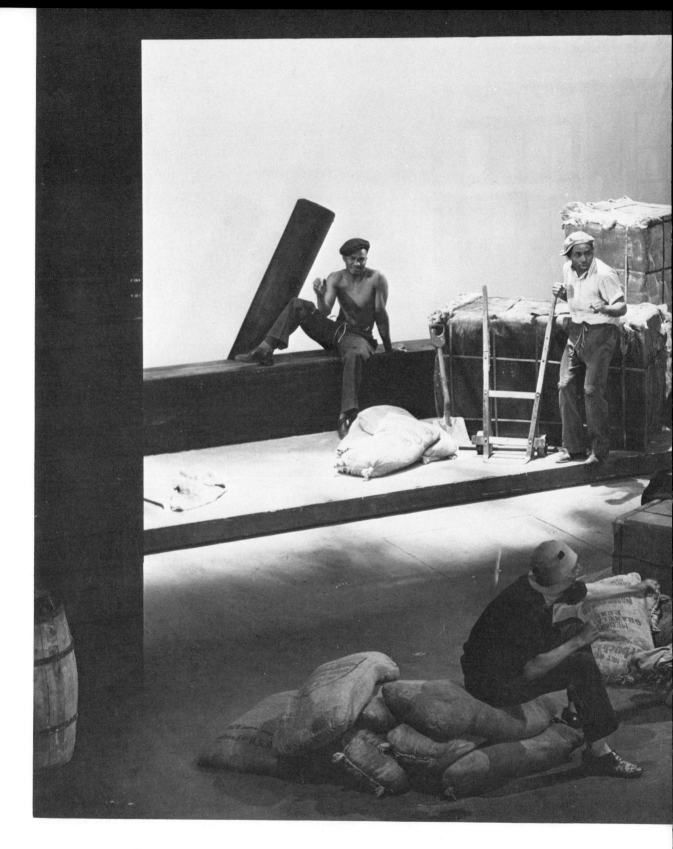

CIVIC REPERTORY THEATRE   In 1926, Eva Le Gallienne
opened her Civic Repertory Theatre in a huge barnlike theatre on New
York's West 14th Street with a shimmering production of Chekhov's
"The Cherry Orchard." For six fulfilling years until the depression

forced the theatre to close, the company presented native plays of merit as well as outstanding works of world drama. One of Repertory's highlights was its 1933 production of "Stevedore" by Paul Peters and George Sklar.

TENNESSEE WILLIAMS One
of the most eminent of contempo-
rary dramatists, Tennessee Williams
has been extolled as an alchemist of
the stage. His earliest success, "The
Glass Menagerie" (1945), was a
touching portrait of a southern
family clinging to illusions of gen-
tility. Later, in his more strident
plays, Williams exhibits a passionate
regard for the lonely people in a
brutal world, a concern which pre-
vails throughout his work.

Welles had produced many revivals for the Project, including Marlowe's *Dr. Faustus.*

After the demise of the Federal Theatre Project, Welles and John
Houseman formed the Mercury Theatre, where they produced many
striking revivals in a new and original manner, presenting modern-
dress productions of *Julius Caesar* and Dekker's *Shoemaker's Holiday.*

Departing from the more usual revivals, in 1937, the Mercury presented Marc Blitzstein's memorable *The Cradle Will Rock,* performed without scenery.

However, the Mercury Theatre is probably best remembered for
its celebrated and frighteningly realistic radio performance of H. G.

Wells's *War of the Worlds* which, in 1938, caused panic in many places.

Welles later went on to produce, direct, and star in the film *Citizen Kane* which is now regarded as a classic.

TENNESSEE WILLIAMS (1914-   ) AND ARTHUR MILLER (1915-   )

Arthur Miller and Tennessee Williams are today's deans of the theatre. Both are sensitive interpreters of American life; and though they differ markedly in underlying ideas, each presents his unique vision of the world.

Miller, like the great dramatists before him, is concerned with morality, with social corruption, and with man's search for truth. The integrity, insight, and power of his work are beyond cabal. Along with Tennessee Williams, he is regarded as one of the two preeminent dramatists of the contemporary American theatre. In strong prose, Miller affirms the dignity of man. On the other hand, Williams, using a supple, poetic diction, offers us man brutalized and irretrievably lost. Violence and loneliness set the tone of Williams' plays; yet his romantic vision and his compassion for his victimized heroes have forged a body of work unsurpassed for sheer theatricality.

TENNESSEE WILLIAMS

Winner of a Theatre Guild award in 1939, the aspiring dramatist began to attract attention with the publication of four, one-act plays *The American Blues*. His first full-length play *Battle of Angels* (1940) failed to reach Broadway, but rewritten as *Orpheus Decending,* was subsequently produced in 1957.

THE GLASS MENAGERIE

Williams' wrote his first great success *The Glass Menagerie* in 1945 which was distinguished by the presence of Laurette Taylor in the

role of Amanda. Like many of his plays, *The Glass Menagerie* is set in the American South. Its central character, Amanda, unable to cope with the realities of her life, takes refuge in illusions of gentility; her gentle, crippled daughter, Laura, also retreats into a private world of her own, which is centered on a collection of tiny glass animals which she constantly rearranges. The action of the play arises from the confrontation with reality which Amanda unwittingly brings on herself and her daughter by having her son, Tom, bring home a friend, "a gentleman caller," to meet Laura.

The Glass Menagerie contains many passages of sheer beauty. Williams expresses great feeling for his characters. The play was staged with dim lighting and transparent scenery. Areas of the stage were illuminated from time to time with shafts of light, not always focusing on the chief action but used symbolically.

SUMMER AND SMOKE

Written in 1948, *Summer and Smoke* is a play in which Williams explores the forces of spiritual and physical love. As in *The Glass Menagerie,* the settings are intended to be fragmentary, with most of the mood and atmosphere achieved by lighting.

A STREETCAR NAMED DESIRE

With the opening of *A Streetcar Named Desire* on December 3, 1947, Tennessee Williams was established as a dramatist of the first magnitude. Called a "touching study of feminine decay along the Mississippi," the play portrayed with great compassion the destruction of its faded heroine Blanche Dubois, a woman who tried to come to terms with a life she was never fitted to meet. Blanche Dubois and her sister Stella are the last members of an old Southern family which

"A STREETCAR NAMED DESIRE" This scene shows the brutal encounter between Blanche Dubois, played by Jessica Tandy, and Stanley Kowalski, played by Marlon Brando—a confrontation which leads to her violation and ultimate collapse.

has fallen on hard times. Although Blanche has become a school-teacher and clings to her old respectability, an unfortunate experience in an early marriage turns her toward drink and promiscuous sexuality. She leaves her teaching post and eventually drifts into prostitution.

At the beginning of the play Blanche, a once attractive woman now prematurely aging and losing her looks, visits her young sister, who is married to Stanley, an uncouth, passionate, vigorous young man, entirely without sensitivity. Stella finds completeness with her brother-in-law through the bonds of sexuality. The visit gradually lengthens and begins to look as though it may become permanent, much to the opposition of the young husband, who recognizes Blanche's dissolute character.

For a time, Blanche has hopes of marriage with a friend of Stanley's, a sensitive and quiet man, unlike Stanley in character. But Stanley sets out to unearth something of Blanche's past; and when he passes on his knowledge of her profession, his friend's reaction is to break away from her. This final disappointment eventually leads Blanche to a complete breakdown.

The conflict of personalities is very revealing. Blanche cannot face the harsh reality of life, nor Stanley's contempt for her. Rarely allowing herself to be seen in daylight, Blanche shields the lamps with Chinese shades; a naked bulb seems to her to be like a vulgar word. She seems continually about to take, or to be coming from, a bath.

Stanley's drunken poker parties and Stella's attempts to reconcile her love for her sister and her love for her low-down husband build up the tension.

The power and sensitivity of Elia Kazan's direction, the drab but evocative set of Jo Mielziner, the interminable poker game, the drunken brawls, and the rape of Blanche in the last act became the elements of a masterpiece.

Marlon Brando played the part of Stanley Kowalski, Blanche's brutish brother-in-law. He was then a virtually unknown young actor. The role catapulted him to fame. Startlingly magnetic in an earlier Broadway appearance in *Truckline Cafe,* Brando's overwhelming stage presence soon brought him to the attention of the film world;

and he was quickly snatched away from the legitimate stage.

THE ROSE TATTOO

In *The Rose Tattoo,* Williams again explores the realms of physical love. A Sicilian immigrant widow seeks a lover in the likeness of her former husband, in spite of her knowledge that her husband had been unfaithful to her.

Williams wrote this drama for the Italian film actress Anna Magnani, who did not appear in the stage production, but made a memorable Serafina in the film.

CAMINO REAL

To date, perhaps Williams' most controversial play is *Camino Real,* a fantasy which takes place in a kind of limbo in which Don Quixote, Lord Byron, Casanova, Marguerite Gautier, and many characters appear. The scene is set in a mythical Central American town full of decadence, violence, and cruelty. There is no clear story, but much action, some of which startlingly takes place in the auditorium. Most of the characters are waiting to pass through to somewhere else— although it is not clear where—and in the waiting, they meet, talk, and part. There are crowds, and a fiesta with a mock fertility ritual. Some critics found this work hard to understand; others regarded it as a splendid and original piece of theatre.

CAT ON A HOT TIN ROOF

This drama is about a wealthy Southern family headed by "Big Daddy," who is dying of cancer. His son Brick is an alcoholic who sleeps apart from his wife, Maggie, whose frustrated sexuality explains the title. Other members of the family are scheming to get control of the estate. Maggie tries to resolve the situation by announcing that she is pregnant. The play ends with Brick rejoining his wife to make good the claim.

"CAT ON A HOT TIN ROOF" (1955)   *Maggie (Barbara Bel Geddes) is comforted by her father-in-law Big Daddy (Burl Ives), in Tennessee William's Pulitzer Prize winner about alcoholism, greed and latent homosexuality. Accused of writing obscurely, Williams declared that his intention was to capture "that interplay of live human beings in a . . . common crisis."*

The play starkly reveals the emotional lies of conventionality. Williams has drawn a portrait of much bitterness, cruelty, and passion.

NIGHT OF THE IGUANA

In what Williams announced as his last play for Broadway, he returns to the quieter searchings of the inner soul. The story concerns Shannon, an unfrocked minister whose fall has been due to his unorthodox beliefs and to his passionate sexuality which has led him into behavior irreconcilable with his calling. He now makes a living as a tourist guide in Mexico, and carries on a more or less permanent affair with the proprietress of the Costa Verde Hotel, the seedy surroundings of which form the setting of the play.

Into his life comes a New England spinster, traveling the country with an old blind grandfather, who was once a minor poet and now ekes out an existence reciting his works. They seek room in the hotel but are refused by the proprietress. Shannon persuades the proprietress to take them in. After a violent fit to which he is periodically prone, Shannon and the spinster—a wise, sympathetic and virginal person—reach an understanding, despite the difference in their personalities. They seem to be about to fall in love; but their very disparity allows nothing more than a brief moment of sympathy for each other. The spinster and her grandfather move on to their next engagement, and Shannon returns to his sex-ridden existence.

WILLIAMS' OTHER PLAYS

Some of the later plays of Williams may be considered too sensational in their nightmarish stories of sex, violence, and physical mutilation; surely the view of life expressed in them is an abnormal one. In his plays, emotions are charged to an explosive degree. His dialogue is always convincing, even when the characterization and the action appear to be contrived. His plays include: *Suddenly Last Summer* (1958), produced initially as part of a twin-bill called *Garden Dis-*

ARTHUR MILLER (1915-   )   The foremost contemporary American dramatist, Miller is considered by many second only to Eugene O'Neill.

trict; *Sweet Bird of Youth* (1959); Williams' one comedy *Period of Adjustment* (1960); *The Milk Train Doesn't Stop Here Anymore,* two versions (1963, 1964); *Slapstick Tragedy* (1966); *The Seven Descents of Myrtle* (1968).

Although Williams' later work lacks the dramatic power and coherence of his best plays, this sensitive playwright continues to probe the human heart for agonizing truths.

ARTHUR MILLER (1915-   )

While a student at the University of Michigan, Arthur Miller won several drama prizes. In 1939, he won the Theatre Guild Award, sharing honors with Tennessee Williams.

Arthur Miller began his career with *The Man Who Had All the Luck,* which was produced on Broadway in 1944 but achieved only four performances. From this play, he elaborated the theme of the relationship of two sons with their father which was presented in two further plays, although they dealt with different characters.

ALL MY SONS

All My Sons, which Elia Kazan staged in 1947, deals with Joe Keller, a war profiteer whose partner is in jail, unjustly taking the consequences of Keller's criminal actions. One of Keller's sons has been killed in action during the war; the other, Chris, is haunted by feelings of guilt at having survived a combat action in which all the men under his command were killed. Chris wants to marry Ann, his dead brother's fiancée. Ann also happens to be the daughter of his father's jailed business partner. Ann agrees to marry Chris.

The tension mounts when Ann's brother arrives at the Keller house. The brother has just visited his father in prison, and is now convinced that Keller is the guilty party. Once certain of the truth, he passes on his knowledge to Chris.

There follows a dramatic scene in which Chris confronts his father with this accusation. Keller admits his criminal responsibility, but tries to excuse his action by saying he did what he did in order to help his family.

Chris is completely stunned; his love for his father is shattered. Ann then produces a letter from her brother, written just before he took off on a mission. The letter indicates he knew of his father's disgrace, and was so moved, he couldn't bear to live anymore.

This finally drives Keller to seek the only way out. He leaves the room quietly; shortly after, a shot is heard which brings the play to an end. Although the ending is somewhat melodramatic, this is a play with solid characterization, and simple, effective dialogue.

DEATH OF A SALESMAN

Miller's next play, *Death of a Salesman,* is considered his most successful work. It is a strong drama about a weak personality, for whom Miller arouses our sympathy throughout. Willy Loman, a middle-aged traveling salesman, is a complete failure in life: in his job, in the bringing up of his two sons, and in his inability to realize the great strength of his wife's love for him. Loman lives partly in a dream world.

Some of the characters in the play exist only in that world, and there is a constant shift from the present to scenes of the past. This is so skillfully done by Miller that there is a continuous flow of the narrative.

Emotions are given full rein, and the drama is particularly taut when exposing the relationship between Willy and his elder son, Biff, whom he has always idealized.

Although the boy has had his moments of popularity at high school where he was a football star, he fails to graduate, drifts from one job to another, and sinks to stealing. Unbeknown to his father, Biff has spent three months in jail.

Biff has also surprised his father on one of the latter's selling trips, and discovered Willy in a hotel room with a woman.

In spite of his exaggerated ideas of his powers of salesmanship, Willy finally loses his job. He tries to make a success of his son's life; but the climax of the play arrives when Biff, who knows that he can never be anything but a failure, forces his father to accept the truth, revealing his prison sentence. This finally breaks Willy, and his love now turns to hatred. Unable to face life without his dreams, Willy drives off in his car to a fatal crash.

The tragedy's most poignant figure is Willy's wife, Linda, who has all along borne with his salesman's exaggerations, his massive dreams, and his occasional cruelties and infidelities, and has given the pitiful Willy her deep love and understanding.

Death of a Salesman stunned audiences with its unrelenting portrayal of the downfall of an ordinary man. In the words of playwright Arthur Miller: the tragedy of Willy Loman "is the tragedy of a man who gave his life, or sold it" in pursuit of a corrupt vision of the American dream. "He was the classic American figure—the chump who believed in the slogans and all the banalities."

Basically a decent man, his tragedy represents the end of a man no longer useful to the system he believed in. A salesman should be "out there in the blue, riding on a smile and a shoeshine." But Willy, believing in the public relations image and the puffery of sales promotion, has grown too old to sell, and is discarded.

The single-unit setting by Jo Mielziner allowed the mood to alter without the impediment of shifting the sets, while the pace and fluidity of Elia Kazan's direction allowed the play to soar.

Lee J. Cobb as Willy Loman gave what most opinion holds to be the greatest performance of his career. His shuffling gait, his weariness, and his irascibility etched an unforgettable portrait in the annals American theatre.

Death of a Salesman was a great success on Broadway, where it had a run of 742 performances and gained Miller the Pulitzer Prize for 1949. It also had a long run in London, with Paul Muni and Katherine Alexander in the leading roles.

THE CRUCIBLE

Miller's next play, *The Crucible,* was written in 1953. Here Miller has obviously sought an historical parallel with the hysteria of the Salem witchcraft trials of the 17th century. In this play, Miller creates an intensely dramatic atmosphere. As he has explained, he does not attempt to treat his characters in depth, but rather presents them as personifications of injustice.

Miller's moral purpose is conveyed in writing of great force; and the playwright aptly reproduces the rhythms and cadences of the speech of the period.

The Crucible was produced at the Martin Beck Theatre in 1953, but had only a modest run. It is, however, a popular addition to the repertory of London's National Theatre Company. A film was made from the play in France.

"THE CRUCIBLE" (1952)   *Arthur Miller's powerful drama about bigotry and mass hysteria, based on an historical event—the Salem witchcraft trials—had inescapable contemporary implications. This scene from the original New York production had*

Arthur Kennedy as John Proctor and Jenny Egan as the accused witch. "Crucible" was also performed in London at the Court by the English Stage Company in 1956.

A VIEW FROM THE BRIDGE

Originally a one-act play in its first New York production, *A View from the Bridge* was offered with another short piece, *A Memory of Two Mondays*. Later, the play was lengthened to two acts, and was presented by itself.

Miller sets his story of a longshoreman in a slum near the docks of Brooklyn in the shadow of the Brooklyn Bridge. With Eddie Carbone and his wife Beatrice lives Catherine, the seventeen-year-old daughter of his wife's dead sister. Eddie has gradually and unconsciously fallen in love with Catherine who is just leaving school to start work as a stenographer.

The arrival of two Italian immigrant brothers who have entered the country illegally, and the interest which Catherine shows in Rodolpho, the younger of the two, causes Eddie to realize the depth of his passion. He determines to use any means to stop the two young people from forming an alliance. He tries to persuade Catherine that Rodolpho is interested in marriage only because it would legalize his illegal position and give him a right to stay in the country. When Catherine refuses to accept this interpretation, Eddie tries to humiliate Rodolpho before her by claiming that Rodolpho is a homosexual. Catherine won't credit this accusation and is quite unshaken. Eddie then decides to inform on the two brothers to the immigration authorities. They are duly taken away, but are released on bail while awaiting a court hearing. Marco, the older brother, shattered by the sudden end of his chance for a new life, returns to denounce Eddie to the neighbors. Although Eddie tries to bluster his way out, a fight with Marco ensues in which Eddie draws a knife. In the struggle, he is killed.

As in his earlier plays, Miller sees his main character in depth. An outline of the plot can only hint at the forceful sweep of this overwhelming tragedy which befalls a common man.

AFTER THE FALL

There was an interval of nine years before Miller's next play was produced. *After the Fall* became the first production of the new Lincoln Center Repertory Company, in January of 1964, at their temporary home, the A.N.T.A. Washington Square Theatre. Later in the same year, another of Miller's plays *Incident at Vichy,* was produced by the same company.

After the Fall is a memory play, at the beginning of which Quentin, a writer, addresses the audience and tells of the high moments of his life. The narrator reveals his past with an intense self-searching, and a somewhat fearful contemplation of the future. In the background stand the key figures of his past. During the play, the characters come forward and enact various scenes of Quentin's life.

The play was imaginatively directed by Elia Kazan on the bare thrust stage of the A.N.T.A. Theatre with an absolute minimum of setting and properties. The changing moods of the story were well created by Jason Robards, Jr., abetted by an able cast.

In this work, Miller poses the question of whether, in the eternal chaos of life, it is possible to find a stable basis for the future. At the end, the playwright arrives at a quiet but affirmative answer.

After the Fall had a mixed reception, some critics regarding it as Miller's most mature work, others seeing in it certain autobiographical material which they felt weakened its objectivity.

INCIDENT AT VICHY

This play about Nazi barbarity toward Jews during the Second World War is involved with a major moral issue—the playwright sought to uncover the tragedy of the indifference of men to the fate of others.

A group of individuals are brought by the Gestapo for questioning. The contrast of the prisoners in their reactions to their unknown fate and to each other forms the development of this drama. One of the characters is a temperamental painter who is unable to control his fright. Another is a businessman; others are a Communist electrician; a young waiter; a flamboyant and confident actor; a proud and sensisive doctor; an aged and silent bearded man; and an Austrian prince

"DEATH OF A SALESMAN" *In this scene, Willy's sons, Biff (Arthur Kennedy) and Happy (Cameron Mitchell), overhear to their dis-*

may another painful moment of their father's disintegration. Lee J. Cobb
as Willy is comforted by his wife Linda, played by Mildred Dunnock.

who is a homosexual, humane and sensitive, but weary of life. He is the only Gentile among the arrested.

While the rounded-up are waiting to be interrogated, the doctor questions them as to what their behavior is likely to be when the dreaded call comes. The actor sees himself as a hero in a dramatic climax, outwitting his enemies by sheer force of self-confidence. The electrician asserts that he will be upheld by his conviction of the ultimate triumph of Marxism. Others exhibit a paralyzed fear at the realization they are doomed. A long discussion on the inexplicable evil that has entered their world follows. As the characters are taken off one by one, the Austrian prince makes the ultimate sacrifice by exchanging his identity papers with those of the doctor.

This play did not receive the critical acclaim of Miller's earlier works. In London, although the play benefited by a distinguished cast headed by Alec Guiness and Anthony Quayle, it did not win popular success.

MILLER'S OTHER PLAYS

Miller's later works are: *A Memory of Two Mondays; An Enemy of the People,* an adaptation of the Ibsen classic; and *The Price.* Although his literary output of recent years has been limited, his stature as a man of letters is undiminished.

Miller's future plays will be awaited with eager interest for his vision, his depth of human understanding (in spite of his obsessions and pessimism), and his ability to create characters with a language rooted in life.

ARCHIBALD MACLEISH (1892-   )

Archibald MacLeish is a poet who has written many plays for stage and radio since the 1930's, including the sensational *The Fall of the City* (1937).

It is, however, with *J. B.*, produced in 1958, that MacLeish has made his mark on the contemporary theatre. In *J. B.* he recreates the story of the Old Testament Job in terms of contemporary American life. It is the fantasy of a play within a play. There is no curtain, and the setting is suggestive of a vast circus tent, old and battered after unsuccessful years on the road. Various employees wander on, depressed by their failure to attract an audience. In pantomime, they decide to perform a play for their own entertainment. They pick the story of Job.

Using the props of the circus, an old actor and a popcorn vendor don masks. One plays God; the other, the Devil. A disembodied voice recites the play's introduction.

Job is represented as J. B., a successful businessman whose fear of God and love for his family is beset by the tribulations of our times: the failure of his business, disasters befalling each member of his family, war and the atom bomb. J. B. does not know if he is being punished for past sins. In a long debate on the question of justice in the world, his friends and his wife fail to persuade him to "curse God and die." Finally, his wife leaves him. But J. B. has withstood his test of faith, and as in the Old Testament tale, his wife returns to him and they begin life together again.

The play was directed by Elia Kazan with great imagination and creative skill. Raymond Massey as God, Christopher Plummer as Satan, Pat Hingle and Nan Martin as J. B. and his wife—all contributed much to the success of a play that gained MacLeish the Pulitzer Prize for 1958.

EDWARD ALBEE (1928-   )

Edward Albee began by writing some short plays in the vein of Ionesco: *The Zoo Story, The American Dream,* and *The Death of Bessie Smith*. These proved to be popular off-Broadway offerings

In 1962 he wrote *Who's Afraid of Virginia Woolf*, his first full-

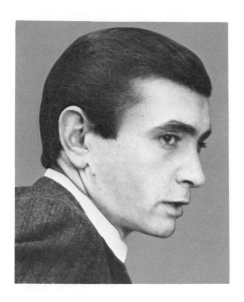

EDWARD ALBEE (1928-   )
With his Off-Broadway drama
"The Zoo Story" in 1961, Edward Albee was recognized as an
important dramatist. His corrosive portrait of a monstrous marriage "Who's Afraid of Virginia
Wolff?", produced in 1962, exhibited his flair for incisive dialogue. In "All Over," produced
in 1971, his somber reflection on
mortality confirmed his superior
craftsmanship. Albee is regarded
as the most important American
dramatist of the 60's.

"WHO'S AFRAID OF VIRGINIA WOOLF?"   In this scene from the
1962 production of Edward Albee's brilliantly corrosive drama about a marital misalliance, visiting Professor George Grizzard restrains Uta Hagen. After
having scored a point, Arthur Hill, playing the victimized husband, presses
the attack.

length play. In this acerbic drama, two couples engage in a revealing interplay which unbares with a quite savage wit much of their inner personalities, their hopes, and their despairs.

His more recent *Tiny Alice,* described by its author as two mysteries in one—metaphysical and conventional—did not repeat his earlier Broadway triumph. The play enjoyed a most distinguished cast. Irene Worth played Miss Alice, the richest woman in the world. John Gielgud played Brother Julian.

A Delicate Balance was presented in the fall of 1966. Considered by some critics to be Albee's best play, in it the playwright exhibits more compassion for humanity than he had in his earlier works.

Albee's more recent work includes adaptations, notably *The Ballad of the Sad Cafe* (1963), based on a Carson McCullers story; *Everybody in the Garden;* and *Malcolm* (1965), from a novel by James Purdy.

A one-act play *Box—Ma—Box* was well received when it opened in Buffalo, but it did not survive the move to New York from that regional theatre.

Despite its unevenness, Albee's body of work, with its intensity, its grappling with modern themes, and its experiments in form represents a major contribution to the American theatre.

ARTHUR LAURENTS (1918-   )

The work of Arthur Laurents is infused with a strong social consciousness. His plays are concerned with the dignity of the individual. In his first play *Home of the Brave* (1945), Laurents makes a study of the baleful effects of religious prejudice on a psychotic soldier. *The Bird Cage* (1950), *The Time of the Cuckoo* (1952), *A Clearing in the Woods* (1957), and *Invitation to a March* (1960) explore the individual's struggle for autonomy and love. The latter two plays were experimental in form, and broke new ground for the playwright.

WILLIAM INGE   Noted for his superior craftsmanship, William Inge depicts with compassion and warmth the lives of ordinary folk in the smal towns of heartland America. In the best of his plays, "Come Back Little Sheba" (1950), "Picnic" (1953) and "Dark at the Top of the Stairs" (1957), the playwright mingles sex and sentiment in portraying the tribulations of little people.

WILLIAM INGE (1913-   )

Other significant postwar dramatists are William Inge, Arthur Laurents, and Paddy Chayefsky. Inge's plays focus on the loneliness and spiritual desolation of little people. Although he shares with Arthur Miller and Tennessee Williams an empathy for the unhappiness of lower-middle class characters, he lacks Miller's force and the poetic suppleness of Williams. His earlier works, *Picnic* (1935), a study of repressed women in small-town America, *Bus Stop* (1955), which focuses on various attitudes toward love, and *The Dark at the Top of the Stairs* (1957), an examination of a family's struggle for understanding and love, are marked by superior craftsmanship.

PADDY CHAYEFSKY (1923-   )

Paddy Chayefsky, originally a TV writer, is noted for *Middle of the Night* (1956), a study of a May-December romance; *The Tenth Man* (1959), a comedy-drama based on the medieval Jewish legend of the dybbuk; *Gideon* (1961), a humorous dialogue between man and God; *The Passion of Joseph D.* (1964), about Stalin; and most recently, *The Latent Heterosexual* (1969).

SIGNIFICANT COMMERCIAL PLAYS OF RECENT DAYS

During the last thirty years, Broadway has not been in its golden age. Although jolted each season by an exciting production imported from abroad, or stirred occasionally by an outstanding American play, the New York commercial theatre has been, as one critic has put it, "a midway for entertainment." Most seasons have been desultory. Few dramas of great stature have been presented.

Among the most interesting plays have been Lillian Hellman's *Autumn Garden;* the early post-war plays *I Am a Camera* and *The Diary of Anne Frank;* two sensitive works by William Gibson: *Two for the Seesaw* and *The Miracle Worker; A Raisin in the Sun,* the affecting play of Negro life penned by Lorraine Hansberry; and Howard Sackler's excellent drama about Jack Johnson entitled *The Great White Hope.*

During this period, two productions of special significance were presented. In 1955 Samuel Beckett's masterpiece *Waiting for Godot* set off a wide reaction of plays in the genre of Theatre of the Absurd.

Despite all the critical furore in 1955 over Samuel Beckett's masterpiece, the play has become a landmark drama of the decade and the most pervasive influence on contemporary playwrights. Poetic, pithy, and pitiless in its existential view of man's condition, *Waiting for Godot,* though a low-gear drama pared down to bare-stage simplicity, was performed in high style by the master clown Bert Lahr playing Estragon.

In 1966 *Marat-Sade,* brilliantly staged by Peter Brook, set the tone

"DARK AT THE TOP OF THE STAIRS"   Considered by many to be William Inge's finest play, "Dark at the Top of the Stairs" was a modest success in 1957. A sensitive portrayal of a troubled family, it evoked the need for compassion and understanding among members of a typical middleclass family. In this scene, Pat Hingle, as the father, Judith Robinson as the daughter, and Teresa Wright thrash out a family dispute.

"LAST OF THE RED HOT LOVERS"   Neil Simon's comedy triumph featured James Coco, as Barney Cashman, the fat and fortyish seafood restaurateur who bumbled unsuccessfully through sexual games with three willing women. The play marked yet another hit chalked up by Broadway's perennial winner Neil Simon, and brought Coco to stardom as a gifted comic actor. In the hilarious "pot-smoking" scene, Barney soars to a new high as the light-witted lady, played by Marcia Rodd, puffs coolly on.

NEIL SIMON   Once a gag-writer for TV, Neil Simon followed his first Broadway comedy hit, "Come Blow Your Horn" (1962), with a string of successes that have made him a legend in his lifetime. "Barefoot in the Park," "The Odd Couple," "Plaza Suite," and "Last of the Red Hot Lovers" are but a few of the plays in his incredible bag of hits.

for the devotees of the theatre of cruelty and the theatre of nudity. With the emergence of Marat naked on stage, a wave of nudity began. *Ché, Sweet Eros, Futz,* and *Oh! Calcutta!* are only a few of the plays that did not observe any inhibitions.

NEIL SIMON

Undoubtedly the most spectacular success story of the sixties is that of playwright Neil Simon. Beginning as a TV script writer, he moved to a position of prominence on Broadway with his first comedy *Come Blow Your Horn.* Thereafter, he annually entered the Broadway lists. *Barefoot in the Park, The Odd Couple, Plaza Suite, Promises, Promises, The Last of the Red Hot Lovers*—these constitute an unbroken series of successes. At one time Simon had three plays running simultaneously on Broadway. His annual income from royalties alone was said to be in the neighborhood of $2,000,000.

THE OFF-BROADWAY THEATRE

The phenomenon of the Off-Broadway theatre, forged by a thrust of creative ideas from a number of venturesome playwrights and producers who could not find a congenial home in the commercial theatre, found a welcome in Greenwich Village and the East Side. In old movie-houses, churches, and cellars, the "little theatre" movement

"NEXT"   In 1968, the Off-Broadway comedy hit "Next"—part of a double bill called Adaptation/Next—was adroitly directed by Elaine May. This short piece spotlighted the emerging talent of dramatist Terence McNally who had earlier been represented off Broadway by the trenchant one-acter "Witness" and the black comedy "Noon." The fine performance of James Coco, who was hailed as a comic actor in the tradition of the Comédie-Française, rocketed that actor to stardom. In this scene, the plight of army inductee Coco, stripped of his clothes and dignity, is ignored by the efficient examining non-com, Elaine Shor.

"SWEET EROS"   *Typical of the dramas that featured sex and nudity during the Off-Broadway ferment of the 60's was Terence McNally's "Sweet Eros." This one-acter produced off Broadway in 1968 depicts a young woman held captive by an alienated and loveless young man. Tied to a chair and silent throughout, she is systematically stripped of her clothes. Gradually, during the course of a lengthy monologue, in a virtuoso performance by Robert Drivas as the Young Man, she is stripped of her ego defenses as well. Ultimately, a compliant victim, Sally Kirkland as the Young Woman shares bed and board with Robert Drivas, her Svengali.*

flourished as it had in the days of the Provincetown Players and the Washington Square Players. At first, audiences were limited, for hard benches, cramped halls, and poorly equipped stages deterred even the hardiest theatregoer. But with recognition, a wider audience was attracted; new playwrights were encouraged; and that "fabulous invalid," the ailing theatre, was infused with new vigor.

"RHINOCEROS"   *In 1961, Eugene Ionesco, most notable exponent of the Drama of the Absurd, was represented on Broadway by "Rhinoceros." In this symbolic play about conformity, a town's inhabitants are systematically transformed into rhinoceroses, as each in turn succumbs to the urge to be like the others. Here the incomparable Zero Mostel is undergoing a transformation from man to rhino, while the town's only non-conformist, Berenger, played by Eli Wallach, looks on in dismay.*

CIRCLE-IN-THE-SQUARE

One of the earliest groups formed was the famous Circle-in-the-Square. In 1950 under the aegis of director Jose Quintero, a group of actors, organized the previous season to present summer stock in Woodstock, New York, revived *Dark of the Moon* in an old Greenwich Village cabaret.

"WAITING FOR GODOT"   *With Vladimir, his inseparable companion, Bert Lahr as Estragon is one of two tramps awaiting Godot, an unseen figure thought to represent God. Alvin Epstein (left) acted Lucky, Pozzo's servant, a symbol of degraded humanity. Kurt Kazner (second from right) played Pozzo, the symbol of power, and E. G. Marshall took the role of Vladimir. Bert Lahr—whose illustrious career as the country's greatest comic actor extended from his earliest success in musical comedies such as "Hold Everything" (1928) to an occasional venture into classics as Bottom in "Midsummer Night's Dream"—brings his inimitable style to the era's most controversial and influential play.*

Their fortunes teetered precariously until a revival of Williams' *Summer and Smoke* in which the then unknown actress Geraldine Page appeared. Word of her extraordinary performance and of the group's excellence filtered uptown, and the company's reputation was established.

In the years that followed, though the Circle was forced to move from its first home in Sheridan Square to an old opera house on Bleecker Street, it produced revivals and noted avant-garde plays, including *Cradle Song, Our Town,* and Edwin Justis Mayer's *Children of Darkness.*

Equally important, the group received acclaim as an interpreter of O'Neill plays. *The Iceman Cometh* catapulted Jason Robards to fame, and led to a warm tie between Quintero and O'Neill's widow. In turn, that alliance led to productions in later years of *More Stately Mansions, A Touch of the Poet,* and O'Neill's masterpiece *Long Day's Journey into Night.*

PHOENIX THEATRE

In 1964 the Phoenix Theatre, which had begun on Second Avenue in 1953, joined forces with Ellis Rabb's repertory company. Rabb, back in 1960, had assembled a touring troupe which called itself The Association of Producing Artists. The Phoenix, presided over from its inception by T. Edward Hambleton, an indomitable spirit who had devoted himself to the development of a company which would produce low-cost dramatic fare, found that it shared a common goal with Ellis Rabb. The new company, called the Phoenix-APA, settled into the Lyceum Theatre on Broadway in 1968.

A series of brilliant productions followed—plays not commonly seen in the commercial theatre: *Dr. Faustus, Pantagleuze, School for Scandal,* Tolstoy's *War and Peace.* These were all well received. But it was the revivals of such plays as *You Can't Take It With You* and *The Show Off* that the audiences supported.

"THE CONNECTION"   *A group of addicts waiting for a "con-nection"—their supplier of drugs—engages the audience in conversation while they wait. Having gotten his fix, the addict seen mainlining here is intent on his "high" soon to follow. Produced in 1958 by the Living Theatre, Gelber's play was a forerunner of the Absurd genre in America.*

Beset by financial problems, and their difficulties apparently exacerbated by internal differences between the two groups, Ellis Rabb withdrew. In 1970 the company disbanded, and the theatre reverted to the banner of T. Edward Hambleton.

In February, 1970, the undaunted manager-director mounted an excellent revival of *Harvey*, Mary Chase's fable about an invisible rabbit, in which Helen Hayes and James Stewart co-starred. Later, in 1971, Hambleton presented an outstanding version of Molière's *School for Wives*. This was an adaptation of the text by the poet Richard Wilbur, who rendered Molière into English rhymed verse. In this production the English actor Brian Bedford won the Antoinette Perry Award for his portrayal of Arnolphe.

THE LIVING THEATRE

In 1947 an enterprising husband-and-wife team, Julian Beck and Judith Malina, devoted themselves primarily to the production of plays written by young American playwrights. However, they did present works by older, established playwrights. *Many Loves* by William Carlos Williams and *Tonight We Improvise* by Luigi Pirandello were among the foremost offerings.

But it was with their first attempt in the Theatre of the Absurd that they established themselves as a significant repertory company. *The Connection,* a play about a group of junkies waiting for a fix, written by Jack Gelber, was presented in 1959, and was highly successful. As the actors conversed among themselves and talked to the audience improvisationally, there was a studied attempt to simulate reality by merging the action of the play with the real audience.

The Apple, produced in 1961, was of lesser merit but still significant in this genre.

THEATRE OF THE ABSURD

The influence on young American playwrights of the absurdist plays of Eugene Ionesco, Samuel Beckett, and Jean Genet was profound.

These major European dramatists, first seen in 1955 in this country on Broadway in Beckett's controversial *Waiting for Godot* and Off-Broadway during the later fifties, stimulated a spate of plays in a similar vein. Already referred to, Jack Gelber's *The Connection* (1959), the notable forerunner of the genre, was followed in 1961 by *The Apple*. Jack Richardson also achieved acclaim principally for *The Prodigal* (1960) and *Gallows Humour* (1961).

Edward Albee, most successful of the early absurdists, went on to Broadway success with plays in an eclectic mixture of styles, having established his strength in 1959 with *The Zoo Story*. Albee's play and Gelber's *The Connection* are perhaps the most significant of the American absurd dramas. A powerful awareness of the meaninglessness of existence underlies the absurdist principle. The dramas involve terror and violence. Albee's *The Zoo Story* is typical. Two men meet in a park. One slowly and insidiously goads the other to kill him in an act of violence that is gratuitous and bizarre. Albee's *The Sandbox* (1960) and *The American Dream* (1961) are among the best one-act plays in the School of the Absurd.

YOUNGER PLAYWRIGHTS

A new crop of playwrights, stimulated by the ideas of the Theatre of the Absurd, found that some clubs, cellars, and basements of New York City were congenial places to experiment, thereby expanding the Off-Broadway theatre. Among the most promising young playwrights is Terence McNally whose plays—mostly one-act satirical comedies—include *Next Witness*, *Sweet Eros*, and *Noon* offered on Broadway in 1969.

Israel Horovitz, another talented young dramatist, won critical acclaim with his dark comedy *The Indian Wants the Bronx*. Subsequently, he has had a number of one-acters performed. These included *Rats*, *Morning* and *Line*, plays which reveal a notable gift for dramatic dialogue.

Other young playwrights include a number who first came to prominence in Cafe La Mama, the best known of the Off-Broadway

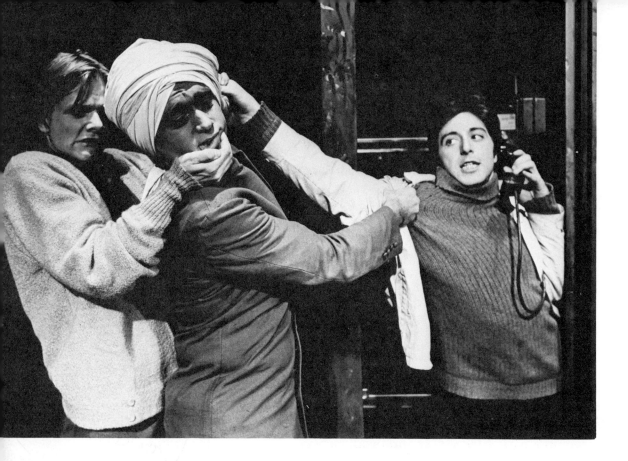

"THE INDIAN WANTS THE BRONX"   A chilling dramatization of wanton violence opened January 17, 1968, in this long one-
acter by Israel Horovitz. A foreigner, lost in the Bronx, is mauled and
terrorized by two neighborhood toughs, one of whom, Al Pacino, is
standing in a phone booth. The other hood is Matthew Cowles. John
Cazale plays the lost Pakistani. Thereafter Horovitz wrote "The Rats"
in 1968, "Morning" in 1969, and "Acrobats" and "Line" in 1971.

"ZOO STORY"   After a circuitous route—Edward Albee's one-act play had
been played and received with approval in major European cities—"The Zoo
Story" opened at the Provincetown Playhouse in 1960. Albee's bizarre one-
acter, a native example of the Theatre of the Absurd, smoulders innocuously at
first with the chance encounter of two men in a park. Then it erupts in violence. George Maharis (standing) contemplates the next move in a macabre
game that will drive William Daniels to kill him.

"OH! CALCUTTA!"   *The first unabashedly sexual revue, "Oh! Calcutta!" opened off-Broadway in June, 1968 in a 2nd Avenue theatre. Actors and actresses performed completely nude. The earlier back view of Ian Richardson in "Marat/Sade," which was*

theatre clubs. Begun in 1961 by an extraordinary and resourceful woman, Elaine Stewart, Cafe La Mama presented works by Leonard Melfi, Michael Locascio, Jean-Claude Van Italie, Rochelle Owens, Megan Terry, and Sam Shepard, among others.

Hair, the most engaging hippy musical of the decade, had its start in Joseph Papp's civic enterprise, the Public Theatre, before moving to Broadway. Charles Gordone, winner of the 1970 Pulitzer Prize for *No Place to Be Somebody,* which also premiered at the Public Thea-

followed by the daring nude scene in the hippie musical "Hair," gave some sanction to "Oh! Calcutta!" whose advent unleashed a spate of nude shows both on and off Broadway.

tre, saw his searching poetic drama move uptown. The vigor, brashness, and vitality of these youthful experimenters was filtering into the theatrical mainstream.

THE ARENA STAGE

Since the Second World War, the growing demand for permanent repertory companies has been responded to by Ford Foundation grants totaling over half a million dollars.

One notable theatre aided by such a grant is the Arena Stage of Washington, D.C. This theatre, directed by Zelda Fichandler, began in 1950 in a decrepit old movie house and now operates a brand-new theatre on the edge of the Potomac. It presents eight plays a season, from October to June, on a rectangular stage surrounded on four sides by rising rows of nearly 800 seats, with entrance tunnels at each of the four corners. This theatre has presented an extremely varied program, including works by Shaw, Chekhov, Brecht, Giraudoux, Anouilh, Andreyev, Edward Albee, Denis Johnston, John Arden, O'Neill, Thornton Wilder, Wallace Hamilton and Millard Lampell.

THE ACTOR'S WORKSHOP

The Actor's Workshop of San Francisco too, has benefited from a Ford Foundation grant. Established in 1952 by Herbert Blau and Jules Irving, then both faculty members of San Francisco State College, the theatre was first situated in a loft above a judo academy. The premier production was Philip Barry's *Hotel Universe.* Two years later, there followed a highly successful production of Miller's *The Crucible,* after which the company assumed professional status at the Marines' Memorial Theatre. Now a full-scale permanent company with solid subscription support from the Bay Area, The Actor's Workshop has produced some distinguished work, including the staging of Brecht's *Mother Courage,* Beckett's *Waiting for Godot,* O'Neill's *The Iceman Cometh,* and Genet's *The Balcony.*

In 1965, Blau and Irving departed to direct the Lincoln Center Repertory Company, taking some of the company with them; but the Actor's Workshop continues under directors Kenneth Kitch and John Hancock.

THE MINNESOTA THEATRE COMPANY

The founding of the Minnesota Theatre Company, now firmly established in the new Tyrone Guthrie Theatre in Minneapolis-St.

TYRONE GUTHRIE (1900-1971)   The noted actor, director, producer began his illustrious career associated with several regional theatres in Scotland and in England. After several years with the Old Vic and the Sadler's Wells theatre companies in a directorial and administrative capacity, in 1955 Guthrie was lured to Stratford, Ontario, where he founded the Shakespeare Festival. From 1962 until 1965, he led the newly formed theatre named for him at Minneapolis. Mr. Guthrie's fame as a director rests upon his inventiveness; he produced Shakespeare in modern dress and other Elizabethan classics in Edwardian costume.

Paul, provides an object lesson in what can be done when once a community's enthusiasm for intelligent drama has been awakened.

The Minnesota Theatre Company opened in 1963 under the direction of the noted stage director, Tyrone Guthrie, in a brand new

THE TYRONE GUTHRIE THEATRE   In 1963, through the efforts of Minnesota citizens and with the aid of foundation grants, the first publicly sponsored regional theatre was opened. Built to specifications set down by Tyrone Guthrie, this playhouse fosters intimacy with its patrons by means of a seven-sided stage that is practically surrounded by the audience. Mr. Guthrie became the Minnesota theatre's first director.

theatre designed in consultation with the company's own directors and stage designer. The project was financed by funds raised mainly by the citizens of the Twin Cities, and with the aid of grants from both the Walker and Ford Foundations.

The Tyrone Guthrie Theatre is of unusual design, with an asymmetrical pentagonal arena stage backed by a shallow apron, used

"THE MISER"   In its inaugural season, the Minnesota Theatre company presented Moliere's "The Miser" at the Tyrone Guthrie Theatre with Zoe Caldwell as Frosine and Hume Cronyn as Harpagon, seen here as husband and wife in Moliere's classic.

"THE HOMECOMING"   Harold Pinter, foremost English playwright in the
School of the Absurd, achieved his greatest Broadway success with "The Homecoming,"
produced in 1968. A deceptively simple drama, the play was brilliantly staged by Peter
Hall with members of the Royal Shakespeare Company, who took the roles of the grossly
sensual father, his three sons, and the daughter-in-law transformed into the family whore.
The drama, written in Pinter's peculiarly laconic style, develops a climate of indefinable
foreboding. Here, the family concubine is seen surrounded by her male consorts.

"THE GREAT WHITE HOPE"   Howard Sackler's poetic drama, poignantly captured the rise and fall of Jack Johnson, first American black heavyweight boxing champion. James Earl Jones in the lead role is shown in a moment of high spirits, as he cakewalks exuberantly with his handlers.

mainly for entrances and exits. The stage is fitted with large sliding doors which allow wagons, with preset furniture and props, to be pushed onto the stage when they are opened. When closed, the doors form a corrugated wall. The auditorium, which holds 1,437 seats, is on two levels; although a third of it slopes down uninterruptedly from the balcony. The story of how the theatre was created is well described in Tyrone Guthrie's lively book A NEW THEATRE, published in 1964.

The first season opened in 1963 with a program of four plays: *Hamlet, The Miser, The Three Sisters,* and *Death of a Salesman.* The company was led by Hume Cronyn, Jessica Tandy, George Grizzard, Rita Gam, and Zoe Caldwell. The success of these productions led to lengthened 1964 and 1965 seasons. Productions were on a high artistic level.

The McKnight Foundation has provided twelve annual fellowships to graduates of the University of Minnesota which enables these students to work for a season at the theatre as actors, designers, or in administration.

A non-profit organization, the theatre is well established in the community. A women's organization, "Stagehands," helps in liaison between the theatre management and the expanding subscription membership. Lectures, forums, and workshops are part of the off-season activities.

The success of Minnesota Theatre Company has led to increased interest in drama throughout the urban areas of the United States. Many new groups have started their own theatres, to which many visitors from all parts of the country are attracted. Groups with a common interest in drama are now organizing journeys by air and bus for a weekend of playgoing.

THE VIVIAN BEAUMONT THEATRE

The new Vivian Beaumont Theatre at Lincoln Center, made possible by a two million dollar donation by Mrs. Vivian Beaumont Allen,

*JULES IRVING (1925-00) AND HERBERT BLAU (1926-00)   In 1963,
the first New York Repertory Company of Lincoln Center for the Performing Arts opened in its temporary home—the ANTA Washington Square
Theatre—with the world premier of Arthur Miller's autobiographical play
"After the Fall." Following administrative and artistic differences, the first
directorial team of Elia Kazan and Robert Whitehead withdrew, and were
succeeded by Jules Irving and Herbert Blau, former directors of the San
Francisco Actors' Workshop. On October 21, 1965, in the Vivian Beaumont
Theatre, the group premiered with Blau's translation of Georg Büchner's
drama "Danton's Death." After some seasons of continued difficulties, Herbert Blau withdrew, leaving Jules Irving as the company's sole director.*

opened in 1965, the first new theatre to be built in New York for
over thirty years. A Ford Foundation grant assisted in the formation
of the Lincoln Center Repertory Company.

In the 1965-1966 season, Herbert Blau and Jules Irving, the new
directors, produced Büchner's *Danton's Death*, Wycherley's *The
Country Wife*, Jean-Paul Sartre's *The Condemned of Altona*, and
Brecht's *The Caucasian Chalk Circle*.

The theatre is part of a great cultural center, which also houses
the Metropolitan Opera, the New York Philharmonic Symphony
Orchestra, and the Juilliard School of Music. Designed by Eero

VIVIAN BEAUMONT THEATRE   This is a view of the interior of the Vivian
Beaumont Theatre, permanent home of The Repertory Theatre of Lincoln Center,
during a performance of Tennessee Williams' play "Camino Real." The theatre, de-

...signed by Eero Saarinen in collaboration with Jo Mielziner, was opened on December
21, 1965. The amphitheatre seats 1,083. No seat is farther than 64 feet from the stage.

New York Shakespeare Festival
Delacorte Theater   Central Park   Summer 1967

Produced by Joseph Papp
in cooperation with the City of New York
Hon. John V. Lindsay, Mayor   Hon. August Heckscher, Commissioner of Parks
presents William Shakespeare's

THE COMEDY OF
June 7 – July
(nightly except June 12, 19, 2

KING JOHN
July 5 – July 29
(nightly except July 17, 24)

TITUS ANDRONIC
August 2 – August
(nightly except August 14,

Performances at 8
ADMISSION

COMING TO YOUR NE

SHAKESPEARE FESTIVAL
MOBILE THEATER
VOLPO

Every Afternoon at 3:30
A Show for Kids
LALLAPA
For informat

Saarinen in association with Jo Mielziner, the theatre has many exciting new features. It has a thrust stage which can be moved forward at the push of a button. A flexible arrangement of panels can make, if desired, a proscenium for a traditional stage.

The thrust stage can be dropped, elevated, or rotated. There is a cyclorama at the back of the stage and two turntables. The expenses of scene-shifting have largely been overcome through automation.

The complicated lighting system is operated automatically by a punched-card system. Once the lighting plot for a complete play has been programmed, it is available for immediate use.

The theatre can easily store the settings and props for five productions. It provides seats for 1,083 playgoers; and when the thrust stage is retracted, for 1,140. No seat in the theatre is more than sixty-five feet from the stage. There is also a smaller auditorium seating 299, used for experimental plays and rehearsals.

SHAKESPEARE-IN-THE-PARK

New York City boasts an outdoor Shakespearean company, the New York Shakespeare Festival, which gives free performances in its own recently acquired Delacorte Theatre in Central Park. The group tours many neighborhoods, presenting performances in playgrounds, school auditoriums, and outdoor theatres, under the name of the Festival Mobile Theatre.

Several years ago, Joseph Papp, the producer, began the venture on a shoestring. The generally high caliber of the Shakespearean

JOSEPH PAPP (1921-   )   *The indomitable founder of the New York Shakespeare Festival Theatre began his career in 1954 as director of a Shakespearean workshop in the basement of an East Side church. Over the years, his determination to provide free theatre for the multitude attracted the attention of private philanthropies and of the city fathers. Open-air productions had been held on park grounds since 1957, but in 1962, the Delacorte Theatre was built in Central Park for a Shakespeare Festival. Most recently, New York City bought the Astor Library which, under the aegis of Papp, was internally restructured to form a complex of five experimental theatres.*

SHAKESPEARE-IN-THE-PARK   *A packed audience waits expectantly for the play to begin at the Delacorte Theatre at Central Park, in the heart of New York City. As part of his campaign to make New York City a cultural center for the masses, Joseph Papp arranged a free Shakespeare festival in 1957, and soon Shakespeare-in-*

the-Park became a regular summer feature. The new open-air theatre, built in 1962, has a thrust stage. The lighting and the acoustics are excellent (except for the occasional jets overhead). The scenery is minimal, but the costumes as lavish as in Shakespeare's time.

productions, given without charge to enormous audiences, has since attracted both municipal and private financial support.

Macbeth was presented in both English and Spanish in the summer of 1966, as was a children's show entitled *Pot Luck,* which New York's young playgrounders found enchanting. Mr. Papp and his companies have been responsible for bringing Shakespeare to one of the most diversified audiences in America.

THE PASADENA PLAYHOUSE

Founded in 1916 by Gilmor Brown, The Pasadena Playhouse has grown over the years and now has five auditoriums, extensive workshops, a new experimental theatre, a complete television studio. It also operates a school of the theatre which has produced many distinguished actors and directors.

OTHER REPERTORY COMPANIES

Founded in the same year by Raymond O'Neill, The Cleveland Playhouse is now run by Frederic McConnell.

Other repertory companies of note are The Alley Theatre in Houston, the Miller Theatre in Milwaukee, the Loeb Theatre at Harvard, the U.C.L.A. Extension Theatre in Los Angeles, and the Izenour-Schweikher Theatre at the Carnegie Institute of Technology in Pittsburgh.

AMERICAN SHAKESPEARE FESTIVAL THEATRE

The Shakespeare repertory group at Stratford, Connecticut, which operates under the official name of The American Shakespeare Festival Theatre and Academy, presents three or four of the Bard's works during a summer season. During the fall and winter months, this group tours various educational institutions.

The organization operates a beautiful theatre in Stratford, Connecticut, patterned after the Globe. The theatre lies in a rustic setting, where playgoers often picnic between a matinee and evening performance. The quality of the Stratford productions has been on a high level. Moreover, this fine theatre has provided actors, designers and directors with a place in which to try out their ideas. It has become a veritable training ground for American actors in Shakespeare interpretation, and the public has been afforded an opportunity to see intelligent—and new—presentations of Shakespeare's work.

COLLEGE DRAMA DEPARTMENTS

There is the vast proliferation of activity in the drama departments of colleges and universities. As well as providing degree courses in speech and drama, some university departments maintain professional theatres. For example, The University of Washington in Seattle operates three theatres and offers twenty-five productions throughout the year, six nights a week. The University also operates a touring company which prepares a repertory of three plays: a classic drama, a modern play, and a children's play.

Other universities that operate touring companies are Stanford, Indiana, North Dakota State, and North Carolina. Apart from producing the classics and well-known modern plays, one-act and sometimes full-length dramas written by students are produced. Productions are directed by the faculty, with students working in all the various phases of lighting, costume and scenic design, properties, acting, and stage management.

There have been some interesting new theatre buildings in the colleges in recent years. Among these should be mentioned Frank Lloyd Wright's Dallas Theatre Center for the graduate school of Baylor University. The University of Arkansas at Fayetteville has two theatres, one indoor and one outdoor.

The architect, Marcel Breuer, is responsible for the fine theatre at Sarah Lawrence College in Bronxville, N.Y. A 500-seat playhouse, it has been designed for great flexibility of use. The auditorium is arranged around three sides of a thrust stage, while there is also a proscenium and a traditional stage. At the rear of the stage, large sliding doors, when opened, enable the stage to be used as an open-air theatre.

The University of Washington in Seattle, which for many years operated an arena stage in its Penthouse Theatre, now has a new theatre with a ring stage, with various revolves and hydraulic lifts, backed by a plaster cyclorama, and with two shallow side stages.

Much of the progress in solving the technical problems of staging today in the new theatres with thrust or arena stages has been inspired by experimental college work.

AMERICA'S GREAT DESIGNERS

Today's America has probably produced some of the best designers of settings and costumes in the world. The designer, in close cooperation with the director, provides the background for the actors and thus illuminates and clarifies the main theme.

The pioneer work of Adolphe Appia and Gordon Craig has been absorbed into general practice. They employed simple and rather abstract setting, which by a flexible use of stage lighting, could quickly be changed to suggest a different mood. This technical possibility has been understood by contemporary playwrights; and many of their more recent works have made use of the dramatic possibilities of rapid changes of scene and mood through the dissolve and the flashback. While these techniques apply chiefly to the conventional proscenium stage, the new form of arena stage has also offered much scope in the development of new design.

ROBERT EDMOND JONES (1887-1954)

The first designer to reach eminence in America was Robert Edmond Jones. In 1915, for the production of *The Man Who Married a Dumb Wife,* a medieval comedy written by Anatole France, shown at Wallack's Theatre, Jones designed a simple set in somber tones of gray and black. This setting served as a foil to the brilliantly colored costumes, but yet contained an element of symbolism.

This element in Jones's designs has sometimes been overplayed,

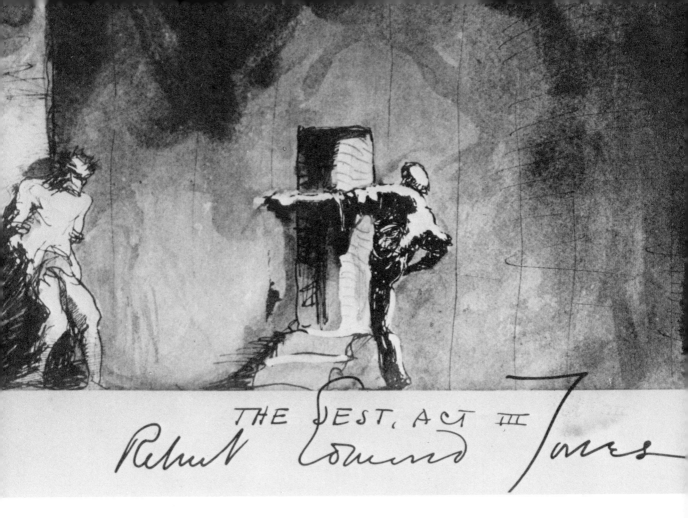

THE JEST, ACT III

Robert Edmund Jones

"THE JEST" *Depicted here is the setting by Robert Edmund Jones for Act III of the 1909 melodrama in blank verse by the Italian dramatist and disciple of D'Annunzio, Sem Benelli (1875-1949). Robert Edmund Jones, who revolutionized the art of stagecraft in America with his original ideas, produced a stark set for this Renaissance play of jealousy, vengeance, and fratricide, which was presented in New York in 1919 with John and Lionel Barrymore.*

as in his designs for *Macbeth* at the Apollo Theatre, in which Lionel Barrymore and Julia Arthur appeared in 1921. In this production, Jones introduced three enormous masks, which appeared high up in the sky and symbolized the forces of evil associated with the appearance of the witches. Most of the scenes in the castle were made up of arches set at rather odd angles, which imparted a disturbing element. At the time, this unusual treatment of a traditional tragedy was considered to have a quality of too powerful a symbolism for the conventional acting, which happened to be excellent. But Jones' set did excite much interest, and paved the way for the work of later innovators to find more acceptance.

Jones has made many dignified and simple settings in which detail is kept to an absolute minimum, and in which boldness achieves a dramatic value complementary to the play. Notable among these were the settings for Marc Connelly's *The Green Pastures,* and for *Othello,* originally staged by Jones in Colorado's Central City, but revived in New York in 1937.

NORMAN BEL GEDDES (1893-1958)   Settings characterized by the placing of abstract, simple geometrical forms around the stage, marked the work of Bel Geddes, heir to the ideas of Gordon Craig and Adolphe Appia for his heightened naturalistic design in "Arabesque" (1925), and "Lysistrata" (1930). "Dead End" (1934).

Jones also designed the more conventional settings for *Ah! Wilderness!* in the Theatre Guild's production of 1933.

Plays of a muscial character have inspired some of his best work, as in the Chinese temple set for *Lute Song* at the Plymouth Theatre produced in New York in 1946. The composite set was altered in different scenes chiefly through the lighting. The costumes, freely adapted from 14th century China, were designed to retain the essential impact without laborious detail.

Jones also took on the direction of plays and thus achieved a greater artistic unity, particularly in the performances of *Love for Love, Patience,* and *Camille.*

NORMAN BEL GEDDES (1893-1958)

Norman Bel Geddes, a contemporary of Jones, was a designer who also felt the influence of Gordon Craig. Like Jones, Bel Geddes directed as well as designed.

This designer has made much use of multiple settings, entirely composed of steps and rostrums. His design for *Hamlet,* which he directed at the Broadhurst Theatre in New York in 1931, was based on a series of small playing areas set at different levels, linked by steps. A few plain flats set at different angles masked the back and sides of the stage. The various levels could be used simultaneously. Lighting was the means of giving accent to the various parts of the setting.

Bel Geddes had earlier conceived of a vast production of Dante's *Divine Comedy* to be given in a special theatre to be built in Madison Square Garden. The designs for this production were planned, but remained unfulfilled. Bel Geddes also designed the settings for Reinhardt's production of *The Miracle* in which he converted the whole proscenium and stage into a soaring cathedral apse, achieving the effect of authentic medieval architecture with stained glass and carving.

Apart from *Hamlet,* his realized designs of note include O'Neill's

Lazarus Laughed, Lysistrata for the Theatre Guild, and Sidney Kingsley's *Dead End* presented at the Belasco Theatre in 1936. In the latter play, Bel Geddes turned to realism and set up riverside tenements and warehouses which caught the despairing tone of lost hopes.

LEE SIMONSON (1888-1967)

Beginning his designing career with the Washington Square Players, Simonson achieved his reputation chiefly through his work with the Theatre Guild. Like Bel Geddes, he used simple rostrums, ramps, and steps of different levels, as in Ernst Toller's *Man and the Masses* in which the grouping and movement of the players is considered an integral part of the setting.

For *Liliom,* Simonson devised simple stylized settings, nominally realistic, yet highly theatrical in effect. The robbery scene, designed to be enacted under the arch of a railway viaduct, added considerably to the tension of the drama. In the Heavenly Court scene, in which Liliom has to answer for his earthly misdeeds, the accent was on the very ordinary treatment of the walls, doors, and windows; yet there was no ceiling—the sky alone was seen above—and when the doors were opened, the sky appeared in the background.

In his designs for *Heartbreak House,* Simonson worked directly under the guidance of Bernard Shaw, who made several sketches indicating the kind of setting he visualized for his play.

O'Neill's *Marco Millions* gave Simonson splendid opportunities, not only in devising an ingenious solution to the problem of the many short scenes which had to be changed swiftly, but in capturing something of the flavor of Venetian, Chinese, Indian, and African art in the detail of settings and costumes. Simonson created one large setting with a large portal in the center. Two small additions completely altered the silhouette; they contained appropriate design motifs which symbolized the different localities.

LEE SIMONSON (1888-1967) One of the original members of the Theatre Guild, Simonson designed most of that company's productions in their early years.

Roar China was a Soviet play by Tretyakov which had been produced in Moscow by Meyerhold which dealt with a revolt of Chinese coolies against imperialism. The dominating element of Simonson's setting was a great representation of a warship, complete with turret and guns pointing out from the back of the stage. Between this and the forestage where a good deal of the action took place, there was a shallow tank on which several sampans floated. When the tank was moved into the center of the stage, the fully rigged sails of the sampans masked the warship, and they served as an effective curtain to punctuate the various scenes.

For O'Neill's *Dynamo*, Simonson devised a constructivist setting of four rooms, in one of which there stood a realistic generator of a modern power station. The result was powerful.

In his designs for *The Adding Machine* by Elmer Rice, Simonson used a few strangely distorted symbolic motifs to convey the mood of the play.

DONALD OENSLAGER (1902-   )   *Together with Robert Edmond Jones, Lee Simonson, and Jo Mielziner, this noted designer ushered in a new era of stagecraft in the contemporary theatre. Some of his major sets have been "Stage Door" (1936), "Of Mice and Men" (1937), "Peer Gynt" (1951), "Major Barbara" (1956) and "A Majority of One" (1959).*

Simonson has always attempted to catch the atmosphere of a play, and he has never done this more aptly than in S. N. Behrman's adaptation of Giraudoux's *Amphitryon 38*, which was so successfully produced in 1937 with the Lunts, in both London and New York. This witty and sophisticated retelling of the old Greek story of one of Zeus's many amatory excursions, caddishly undertaken in the guise of the lady's husband, gave the designer an opportunity for a remarkably stylish *jeu d'esprit.*

Other notable productions Simonson has designed have been

JO MIELZINER (1901-   )   A prolific stage designer, Mielziner's career includes the creation of some of the most notable settings of the contemporary theatre. He did the sets for: Molnar's "The Guardsman" (1924), "The Boys From Syracuse," "Gypsy" (1959).

Claudel's *The Tidings Brought to Mary,* Ibsen's *Peer Gynt,* Shaw's *The Apple Cart,* and Sherwood's *Idiot's Delight.* He has also made excursions into opera and ballet.

DONALD OENSLAGER (1902-   )

After graduating from Professor Baker's "47 Workshop," Donald Oenslager later became a teacher at Harvard. He has designed settings for many Broadway productions of importance, such as *You Can't Take It with You* and *Born Yesterday,* both sympathetic renderings. But Oenslager made more imaginative essays with his designs for the Shaw plays: *Major Barbara, The Doctor's Dilemma,* and *Pygmalion.*

His most broadly experimental work has often been done for college theatres—as in the settings for *Prometheus Bound* by Aeschylus, an imaginative symphony of lighting; and for O'Neill's *The Emperor Jones,* done for the Yale University Theatre.

MORDECAI GORELIK (1899-   )

The designer for many of the Group Theatre's earlier productions, including *Men in White, The Case of Clyde Griffiths,* and *Casey Jones,* Gorelik created convincing and unusual settings which added much to the interpretation of the main theme. Although these settings were broadly realistic, his later designs for more imaginative dramas afforded the designer greater scope for the creation of mood. Gorelik created a beautiful lighthouse setting for Ardrey's *Thunder Rock.* Likewise, for Odets' *The Flowering Peach;* and for Gazzo's *A Hatful of Rain,* Gorelik made contributions which have earned him a well-deserved reputation.

OTHER DESIGNERS

Aline Bernstein created some sensitively realized settings for period plays, notably in *Camille* for Eva Le Gallienne, and in *The Game of Love and Death* for the Theatre Guild.

Raymond Sovey, Cleon Throckmorton, Stewart Chaney, and Lemuel Ayres have produced colorful and exciting settings for many Broadway productions.

Boris Aronson (1900-   ) has designed impressive settings for many important plays, including Odets' *Awake and Sing* (1935), *The Country Girl* (1950), Tennessee Williams' *The Rose Tattoo,* Inge's *Bus Stop,* MacLeish's *J. B.* (1959), Irwin Shaw's *The Gentle People,* and particularly for Arthur Miller's *A View from the Bridge* (1955). In the latter, Aronson endowed the Brooklyn tenement scene with overtones of a monumental quality, something like a setting for a classical tragedy.

Off-Broadway, William and Jean Eckart have produced some imaginative work for the Phoenix Theatre, especially their set for *The Golden Apple by* John Latouche.

Oliver Smith has been responsible for the stylish settings of *My Fair Lady,* and has done fine work for many other productions, such as *Night of the Iguana* and *A Clearing in the Woods.*

Ralph Alswang has contributed settings to many unusual productions. His credits include the all-Negro *Lysistrata,* the *King Lear* of Louis Calhern at the National Theatre, *Peter Pan, Blood Wedding, Courtin' Time,* and *The Last Dance* by Strindberg.

JO MIELZINER (1901-   )

The most consistent and versatile of American set designers is without doubt Jo Mielziner, whose long list of productions spans forty years. During this period, Mielziner has shown a great range of style. He is responsible for the realistic tenement front of Elmer Rice's *Street Scene,* the fragile, semi-transparent settings for *The Glass Menagerie,* the heavy Victorian set of *The Barretts of Wimpole Street,* the brash vulgarity of the scenes in *Guys and Dolls.*

In his settings for Katherine Cornell's production of *Romeo and Juliet,* Mielziner chose the simple architectural treatment of the Italian primitives. He used pure colors in a light key rather than in heavy Renaissance style. For this production, Mielziner made use of pre-set scenes. As the action of one scene ended, the setting would disappear; and the setting for the next scene would be revealed, waiting directly behind it. In spite of the many scene changes, this device made possible a rapid flow of the drama.

Mielziner's settings for John Gielgud's *Hamlet* were ingenious in their simplicity. Governed by the need for a swift flow of action from scene to scene, the designer's craftsmanship accomplished precisely what was called for.

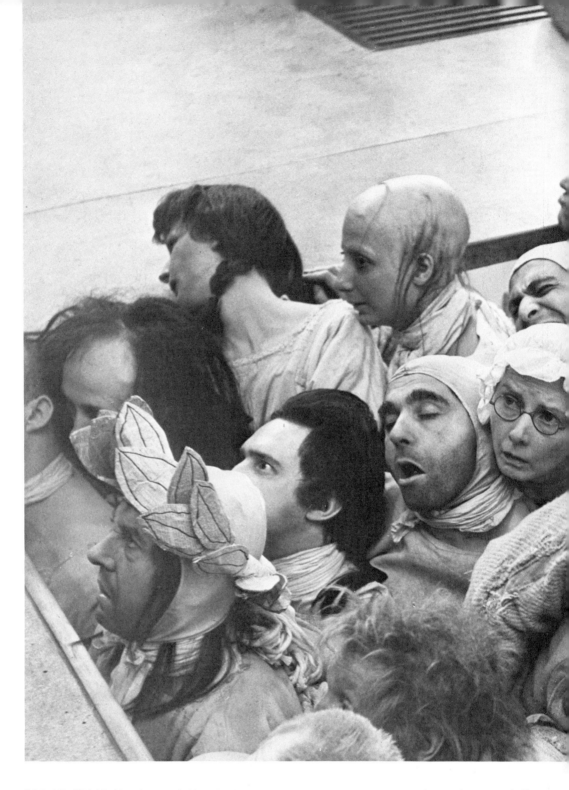

"MARAT/SADE"   The full title of Peter Weiss's startling drama, "The Persecution and Assassination of Marat as Performed by the Inmates of the Asylum at Charenton under the Direction of the Marquis de Sade," is as unconventional as was Peter Brook's stunning production of the play in 1966. The

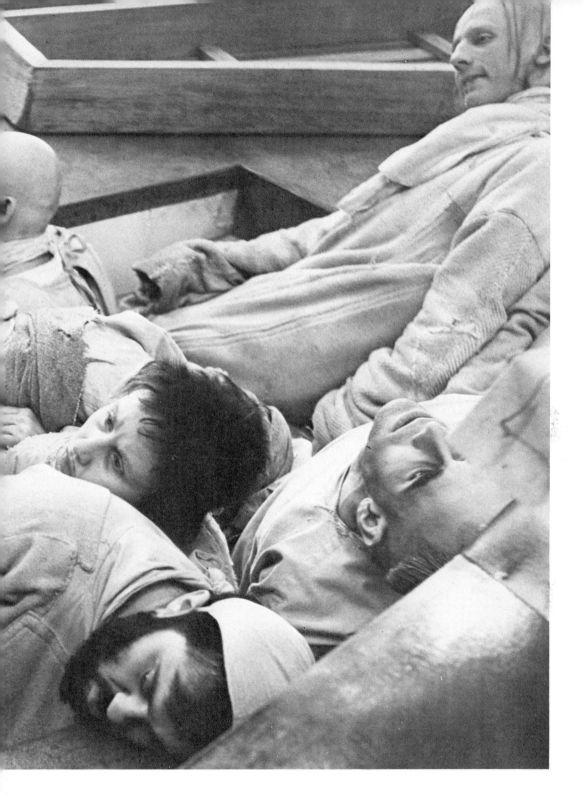

sensational English import sparked a decade of theatrical daring. Here, in the bath-house scene, inmates of the Asylum are acting out some of their violent urges in the aftermath of the French Revolution.

*"WINTERSET" (1935)   The Brooklyn Bridge broods over Jo
Mielziner's powerful stage design for Maxwell Anderson's 1935 play
"Winterset."*

For *Winterset* by Maxwell Anderson, Mielziner created the vast
brooding shadow of Brooklyn Bridge to characterize the inexorable
and tragic fate of the young lovers.

In Maxwell Anderson's *Journey to Jerusalem*, he devised an exciting method of projecting scenery that was a triumph.

Anouilh's *The Lark* was given a single permanent set. On the
circular wall across the back of the stage, scenes of village, countryside, court, and public square were suggested by means of light pro-
jections.

For Tennessee Williams' *Cat on a Hot Tin Roof,* Mielziner made use of symbolism, a simple set capturing the character of the old mansion of the South, by means of focusing attention on a few items of furniture.

For Arthur Miller's *Death of a Salesman,* the designer created a remarkable composite set composed of Willy Loman's house, surrounded by towering angular shapes of apartment buildings, crowding it on all sides. The kitchen, in the center of the house, contained a table, three chairs, and a refrigerator, but no other fixtures. To the right, stairs led to the upper bedroom of Loman's two sons. The roof was indicated by the outline of the gable. But although there was a fully built-up dormer window at the rear of the room, there were no walls and no actual roofing. Another bedroom was seen to the left of the kitchen, on a slightly higher level, again with a window. The curtained recesses suggested other parts of the house. In front of the house, the large apron stage fulfilled the dual purpose of representing Loman's backyard, and the locale of his imaginings and his scenes in the city. The set as a whole aptly expressed the strange mixture of dreams and reality which made Miller's play so memorable.

More than any other designer, Jo Mielziner has developed lighting. Mielziner has his own studio theatre where he works out lighting effects. To him, lighting may suggest the passage of time by its changing values, or a change of locale through differing intensity, or by projected shadows, or by the use of color transparencies. Mielziner can in a trice literally paint a scene with light more powerfully than an artist can pigment. Since he has always considered the projection of the underlying theme of the play his foremost task, his settings have been as varied in style as the plays themselves.

Mielziner was associated with the beginnings of the Lincoln Center Repertory Theatre in its earlier seasons at the A.N.T.A. Theatre, Washington Square, and was largely responsible for the design of the thrust stage and the modern equipment for the Vivian Beaumont Theatre, the company's ultimate home at Lincoln Center.

At this point in his career, Jo Mielziner is considered an institution.

The American Musical Theatre

EARLY HISTORY

Although American musical plays can be traced back to the 18th century, *The Black Crook* by Charles M. Barras, written in 1866, is considered the forerunner of the modern musical comedy. Combining song, dance, and ingenious scenic effects, Barras' melodrama was first presented at Niblo's Gardens in New York City on November 12, 1866. It became the season's rage, and inspired a host of imitators.

The corps de ballet created a sensation. "Girls!" a New York newspaper exclaimed, "Lithe, active beauties!" The girlie show had been born. Legs became the chief ingredient of the spectacles.

During the last quarter of the 19th century, musical plays were no more than a vehicle for sentiment, parody, and tunes of popular appeal.

As musical entertainment, the operetta, which came into vogue about 1870, grew even more popular than the musical comedy. The works of Gilbert and Sullivan, Johann Strauss, Jacques Offenbach, and other Continental purveyors of gaiety and charm were freely imported. By the end of the century, virtually every operetta set along

653

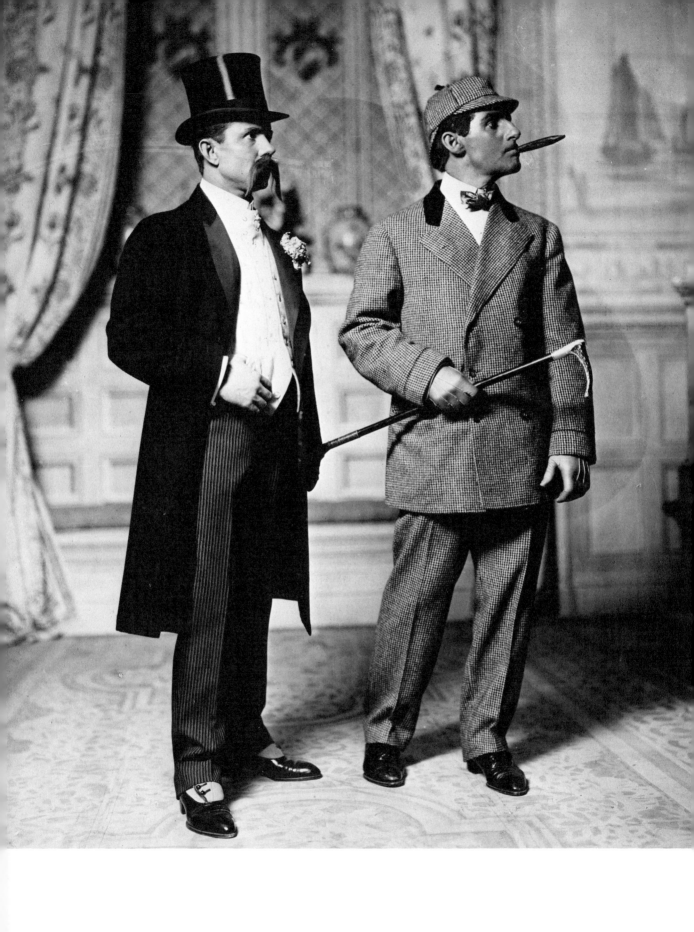

the Seine or the Rhine, or in Vienna, or in London or in Tokyo, had been transported to the United States. For example, between 1882 and 1889, 35 European operettas were performed at the Casino Theatre in New York City.

Influenced by the success of these imports, native American composers began working in the medium. The earliest major American operetta was *Robin Hood* (1890) with a score by Reginald de Koven. But it is with the German-trained Victor Herbert's *Prince Ananias* (1894) that the first significant composer for the American musical theatre made an appearance.

"THE RED MILL" (1906)   *This musical was written for the comic team of David Montgomery and Fred Stone who, in 1903, had scored an outstanding success in the Broadway extravaganza* THE WIZARD OF OZ. THE RED MILL *enjoyed the longest run (274 performances) of any Victor Herbert musical comedy shown during his lifetime. As Kid Conner and Con Kidder, two penniless Americans stranded in the little Dutch port of Katwyk-aan-Zee, David Montgomery and Fred Stone, disguised as Dr. Watson and Sherlock Holmes, consider their next move to abet the love affair of the burgomaster's daughter Gretchen and Captain van Damm.*

VICTOR HERBERT (1859-1924)

Although *Prince Ananias* had an attractive score, it was not until Herbert wrote *The Wizard of the Nile* (1895), a delightful vehicle for Frank Daniels, a popular comedian of the day, that the Dublin-born composer showed his musical prowess. In the following few years, Herbert's scores for the operettas *The Serenade* (1897) and *The Fortune Teller* (1898), remembered especially for the lullaby: "Gypsy Love Song," made him increasingly popular.

In 1903 with *Babes in Toyland* Victor Herbert established himself as the nonpareil composer of operettas. During the two following decades, Herbert poured out a stream of great melodies in such nostalgic confections as *Mlle. Modiste* (1905), *Naughty Marietta* (1910), *The Princess Pat* (1915) and *Orange Blossoms* (1922).

The commercial and popular success of "Ah Sweet Mystery of Life" from *Naughty Marietta* continues to the present day, rivalled only by such perennial favorites as "Thine Alone" from *Eileen* (1917) and "A Kiss in the Dark," from *Orange Blossoms*. Rooted in the Old World tradition of sentimental ballads and stirring marches, Victor Herbert's reign as king of the operetta drew to an end with the advent of World War I.

RUDOLF FRIML (1881-   )

The second important figure in the world of operetta reached the stature of Victor Herbert. Steeped in a Middle European musical heritage, the Czechoslavak-born composer toured the United States for several seasons as a concert pianist before making this country his permanent home in 1906. Years of relative obscurity followed, ending with the fortuitous withdrawal of Victor Herbert from a project that involved the temperamental opera star Emma Trentini. Recommended to Arthur Hammerstein, the producer, as a replacement, Rudolf Friml won immediate success with his score for *The Firefly* (1912), a work that revealed his great melodic gift. The score was studded with songs of an enduring quality: "Giannina Mia," "The Dawn of Love," "Sympathy." Oddly, it is "The Donkey Serenade," a Friml

VICTOR HERBERT (1859-1924)   Foremost among the three great writers of the
American operetta—a triumvirate which included Rudolf Friml and Sigmund Romberg
—Victor Herbert composed about 50 operettas in almost 40 years. Remembered for such
romantic ballads as "Kiss Me Again" from MLLE. MODISTE and "Ah, Sweet Mystery of
Life" from NAUGHTY MARIETTA, Herbert belongs to an era that ended with World War I.

SIGMUND ROMBERG (1887-1951) *A prolific and versatile composer, Romberg created 56 musical scores. His best effort was the Schubert extravaganza* THE WHIRL OF THE WORLD, *produced in 1914. After his death,* THE GIRL IN THE PINK TIGHTS *was produced in 1954. His was a record that has never been matched. With Romberg's death in 1951, a musical dynasty that had begun with Victor Herbert came to an end.*

tune later interpolated into the film version of the operetta, that became the show's standout.

For the next two decades, Rudolf Friml wrote about 20 operettas in the light-hearted vein of Victor Herbert, including *High Jinks* (1913), *Sometime* (1918), *Katinka* (1915), *You're in Love* (1917) and *Tumble Inn* (1919). Yet it is for three operettas most true to the Old World tradition of Franz Lehar's *The Merry Widow*, prototype of the European operetta at its romantic best, that Friml is remembered: *Rose-Marie* (1924), *The Vagabond King* (1925), and *The Three Musketeers* (1928).

SIGMUND ROMBERG (1887-   )

Last of the great trio of operetta composers, Hungarian-born Sigmund Romberg shared with Victor Herbert and Rudolf Friml a love of the

"THE DESERT SONG" (1926)   *William O'Neal, Margaret Irving, and Lyle Evans mix romance and rebellion in Sigmund Romberg's classic operetta, inspired by a newspaper account of a revolt among the Riffs of French Morocco. In spite of negative reviews, Romberg's songs, the exotic setting, and exotic characters gave the show a run of 465 performances.*

exotic world of Graustark, Ruritania, and Nordland. He, too, had a penchant for fairy tale settings. Before his initial success in 1915 with *The Blue Paradise,* Romberg was staff composer for J. J. Shubert, and he supplied musical numbers for Shubert productions at a furious clip. Between 1914 and 1917, he wrote 275 songs for some 17 musical shows including revues, extravaganzas, and musical comedies.

Following *The Blue Paradise,* Romberg wrote the first of his great box-office triumphs, *Maytime* (1917). So successful was the operetta that for the first time in Broadway annals a second company was formed during the show's run to play at a nearby theatre.

A string of operetta classics continued to flow from his pen: *Blossom Time* (1921), *The Student Prince in Heidelberg* (1924), *The Desert Song* (1926) and *New Moon* (1928), to name but a few. *New Moon,* the last of Romberg's works, sounded the finale for the light-hearted operetta. But with such immortal melodies as "Lover Come Back to Me," "One Kiss," "Wanting You," and "Softly as in a Morning Sunrise," *New Moon* sounded the closing note of a great era. From that time on, the musical theatre belonged to the musical comedy, revues, and the musical play.

GEORGE M. COHAN (1878-1942)

Before World War I, Victor Herbert and George M. Cohan pointed in the directions that the musical theatre would take in America. With *Babes in Toyland* (1903), Herbert established the romantic operetta; and with such plays as *45 Minutes from Broadway* (1906), George M. Cohan had begun the trend towards the fast-paced musical that was to become the hallmark of the American theatre and was to make him the darling of American audiences.

From his first musical *The Governor's Son* (1901), an extended vaudeville sketch, until the end of his great career, Cohan epitomized the native American performer. His easy confidence and relaxed manner set a standard that still prevails.

Following *The Governor's Son,* Cohan composed musical comedies that represent his best work. In 1904, Cohan scored his first

Broadway success with *Little Johnny Jones*. In 1906, there were *George Washington, Jr.* and *Forty-five Minutes from Broadway*. Then came *The Talk of the Town* (1907), *The Yankee Princess* (1908), *The Man Who Owns Broadway* (1910), *The Little Millionaire* (1911), and *Hello Broadway* (1914).

With America's entry into World War I, Cohan wrote "Over There" (1917), a song that became one of the country's favorite war hymns.

In the 1920's Cohan appeared in such shows as *Little Nellie Kelly, The Rise of Rosie O'Reilly, The Merry Malones,* and *Billie,* written in 1928, the last of his musical comedies.

With rare exceptions, most of Cohan's musical comedies of the 20s did not fare well. Although he bemoaned the fact that "people don't understand me anymore," the truth was that his brand of musical comedy had grown old-fashioned. New witty writers of great sophistication were emerging. By the end of the decade, the Cohan manner still had the brashness of the carnival pitchman, but the plays themselves seemed pallid.

Disheartened over his diminishing reputation, and in particular over the triumph of the actors in forming their union, the Actors Equity strike in 1919 found Cohan on the side of management. He threatened to withdraw completely from the stage.

However, despite his disenchantment, he continued writing and acting in plays, both musical and non-musical. Two significant acting successes marked his last years. In 1933, he appeared in Eugene O'Neill's *Ah Wilderness;* and in 1937, he played Franklin D. Roosevelt in the Kaufman, Rodgers and Hart collaboration, *I'd Rather Be Right.* But he was virtually in retirement. His last non-musical play *The Return of the Vagabond* closed in 1940 after seven performances. A little over two years later, George M. Cohan died.

The contribution of George M. Cohan to the musical theatre should not be underestimated. As the creator of breezy, fast-paced shows in which he performed with easy assurance, he infused a quality into the theatre that is indelibly American.

GEORGE M. COHAN (1878-1942) "Mr. Broadway" was the sobriquet given the man who is considered the father of musical comedy. From his first success LITTLE

JOHNNY JONES (1904) to his last work BILLIE (1928), Cohan displayed a unique ability to create plays in a distinctively racy American idiom.

FLORENZ ZIEGFELD (1867-1932)   In the 23 editions of the Ziegfeld Follies—1907 to 1931—America's master showman glorified "the American Girl" by placing gorgeously costumed damsels in a magnificent setting. Ziegfeld set a mark all revues aimed at but none surpassed.

FLORENZ ZIEGFELD (1867-1932) AND THE FOLLIES

During the first decade of the 20th century, Florenz Ziegfeld ushered in the world-famous Follies. His showmanship represented the most flamboyant and glamorous aspects of the theatre of the day.

On July 8, 1907, atop a theatre roof called the Jardin de Paris, Ziegfeld presented his Anna Held girls. His star was one Annabelle Whitford, a reigning beauty who appeared in bloomers as a Gibson bathing girl. An era was born.

FANNIE BRICE (1891-1951)   Celebrated for her Yiddish dialect songs in the 1910 Follies, the renowned star sang Irving Berlin's "Goodbye Becky Cohen." Fannie Brice (center) became one of the country's leading comediennes.

These divertissements continued yearly into the twenties. Production costs rose from $100,000 for the Follies of 1918 to $250,000 for the 1921 version. As the cost of production rose out of sight, Ziegfeld sensed that the heyday of the extravagant spectacular was on the wane.

Among the performers brought into the limelight by Ziegfeld were W. C. Fields, Will Rogers, Eddie Cantor, Leon Errol, and an inimitable comedienne by the name of Fannie Brice, who was to be por-

THE ZIEGFELD FOLLIES   *The supreme achievement of the most fabulous show-man America has ever known, the Ziegfeld Follies was the most expensive spectacle of its day. Pre-production costs ran from $13,000 in 1907 to a budget of $300,000 in 1927.*

So much in demand were tickets for these lavish shows that, in 1915, Diamond Jim Brady paid $750 for two opening night tickets. This photograph shows the chorus girls of the 1915 Follies who represented the months of the year.

trayed almost fifty years later by a star of like luminosity, one Barbra Streisand. In the 1910 Follies, Ziegfeld had introduced a fledgling song writer, a young man by the name of Irving Berlin.

EARL CARROLL (1893-1948) AND THE VANITIES

The Vanities was a lavish annual Broadway revue produced by Earl Carroll, who wrote the book, lyrics, and music of the first edition. Thereafter, the revues were produced annually from 1923 until 1936, except for 1929 when Carroll did *The Sketch Book Review* instead. Carroll specialized in spectacular tableaux of girls in transparent costumes. In 1936, Earl Carroll was accused by a segment of the public of staging obscene shows, and his productions faltered.

The most notable edition of the Earl Carroll productions was the 1930 version, which featured Jimmy Savo in a memorable Chaplinesque pantomime of "The Noted Chinese Actor, Satunmon." Patsy Kelly, then virtually unknown, lent able assistance. Jack Benny appeared as a radio announcer in a sketch "Station YRU;" and Harold Arlen contributed an amusing song.

The 1932 edition contributed several Harold Arlen tunes, among them the classic "I've Got a Right to Sing the Blues."

Earl Carroll's Vanities introduced a number of performers who would later become the luminaries of stage and radio, among whom were Milton Berle and Lillian Roth.

In 1938 Carroll left Broadway for Hollywood. He returned in 1940 for one last edition of his revues which, however, closed in three weeks. He was killed in a plane crash in 1947.

RUDOLF FRIML (1879-   )   In 1912, following a mediocre career as a serious composer, Friml wrote his first Broadway score, and immediately zoomed to fame on the wings of THE FIREFLY. *From then on, until his last operetta* ANINA *in 1934, the one-time concert-artist devoted himself almost exclusively to the musical theatre.*

"EARL CARROLL'S VANITIES"   *This well-clad chorus from the 1923 edition of*

the VANITIES—*normally an unclad show—is shown doing their famous Rainbow number.*

JEROME KERN (1885-1945)
After years of song plugging in Tin Pan Alley, Kern's first successful musical comedy THE GIRL FROM UTAH *(1914) thrust the gifted composer into the limelight. Although he wrote many hit shows, his genius is ultimately linked with* SHOW BOAT *(1926).*

JEROME KERN (1885-1945)

Kern had begun his long career in 1912 with *The Red Petticoat.* In 1915 he had begun collaborating with Guy Bolton. In 1917 they produced *Have a Heart.* Then, P. G. Wodehouse joined Bolton and Kern to form a trio that was later to evolve such outstanding hits as *Oh Boy* and *Leave It to Jane.*

The score of the 1920 Ziegfeld musical *Sally* was written by Kern and contained two outstanding hits: "The Church 'Round the Corner" and "Look for the Silver Lining."

In 1925 Kern wrote a snappy musical entitled *Sunny* in which Marilyn Miller, the darling of the day, starred.

During the 1930's Kern was responsible for some memorable shows: *The Cat and the Fiddle,* with the romantic ballad "The Night

"SALLY" (1920)   Marilyn Miller as the dishwashing waif, Sally, communes songfully with Leon Errol who plays Connie, a waiter and expatriate Balkan grand duke. Jerome Kern's score is remembered particularly for one song, "Look for the Silver Lining," which became so closely identified with Marilyn Miller that it became the title of her film biography. The Ziegfeld production had a record run of 570 performances.

Was Made for Love;" the operetta *Music in the Air,* in which the lyrical score opened with "I've Told Ev'ry Little Star;" the incomparable *Roberta,* highlighted by "The Touch of Your Hand" and "Smoke Gets in Your Eyes;" and his finale *Very Warm for May* (1939), a failure but remembered for the tune "All the Things You Are."

Then Kern went to Hollywood as a songwriter, winning two Academy Awards, the last one for *Centennial Summer*. In 1945 he returned to Broadway for a prospective musical to be produced by Rodgers and Hammerstein and for a revival of *Show Boat*. That year, before these projects came to pass, Kern died. Gifted tunesmith whose music is sung affectionately throughout the world, Kern's greatest contribution to the American Musical must be accounted to be his *Show Boat,* which was considered revolutionary in its day. Never before had a musical opened without an overture and with a gang of Negro stevedores complaining about their hard lot as they lifted bales of cotton. Today, both the score and the book seem romantic to excess; but the dark side of that play was a foretaste of the stage's realistic treatment of Negro life to come.

IRVING BERLIN (1888-   )

In the history of the American musical theatre and of Tin Pan Alley, Irving Berlin has enjoyed a unique career marked particularly by longevity, and also as the embodiment of a rags-to-riches story.

In 1906 when he was a teen-ager and had a job as a singing waiter in a Chinatown cafe, he wrote "Marie from Sunny Italy," his first lyric which brought him a royalty of 37 cents. Only a few years later, two tunes set to Berlin lyrics—'Sadie Salome Go Home" and "My Wife's in the Country"—were selling upwards of 200,000 copies each.

"SHOW BOAT" (1927)   Charles Winninger, as Cap'n Andy on his show boat "Cotton Blossom," calms the audience during a performance aboard ship of the play "The Parson's Bride" after the forest scout, in the box just above him, has threatened to shoot the villain in the play. Jerome Kern's famous musical version of the Edna Ferber novel ran for 572 performances in 1927.

W. C. FIELDS (1879-1946) IN "POPPY"   This 1923 musical comedy presented Fields as a con man (Eustace McGargle) who, as he traveled about in carnivals, milked the gullible of their money. Although considered an unpalatable role, it appealed to the former Follies star for its "grandiose humbug," and it served as the prototype of all future characterizations by W. C. Fields.

"KID BOOTS"   Caddie master Eddie Cantor at the Everglades Golf Club gives instructions to Dr. Josephine Fitch (Jobyna Howland), the physical training director of the club. A showcase for the popeyed comic, KID BOOTS is remembered solely for the Harry Akst song hit "Dinah," thereafter one of Cantor's favorites.

AL JOLSON (1888-1950) IN "BOMBO" (1921) The famous entertainer is shown here as Gus in this 1921 musical extravaganza. Loosely woven around the exploits of Christopher Columbus, the show made Jolson's blackface role a staple of his performance. The routine, developed in his early days with Dockstader's Minstrels, was a show stopper as Jolson sang "My Mammy." After Jolson, all performers of songs about mothers were dubbed "mammy singers."

By 1911 the 23-year-old tunesmith had thrown the country into a frenzy with "Alexander's Ragtime Band," which sold over a million copies. By then, Berlin was well on the way to becoming the titan of Tin Pan Alley.

Although many of his tunes were introduced in revues, notably in the Ziegfeld Follies of 1910 and 1911, it was not until 1914 that

IRVING BERLIN (b. 1888) The colossus of Tin Pan Alley, Irving Berlin catapulted to fame in 1911 with "Alexander's Ragtime Band," a tune that threw the country into a ragtime frenzy.

he composed his first complete musical score, *Watch Your Step,* a ragtime revue, starring the dance team Vernon and Irene Castle.

Other musicals followed: *Stop! Look! Listen!* (1915), *The Century Girl* (1916), and the inimitable army revue *Yip, Yip, Yaphank* (1918), remembered especially for that undying lament "Oh, How I Hate to Get Up in the Morning."

Between 1921 and 1924, in his own theatre The Music Box, the now famous composer produced revues, composing both the music and the lyrics. Some of the ageless numbers created by Berlin were "Say It with Music," the revue's theme song; "Lady of the Evening" from the 1922 edition; "What'll I Do?" from the 1923 version sung by the then unknown Grace Moore, soon to be recognized as a great Metropolitan Opera star; and "All Alone."

Irving Berlin's two topical musical shows with books by Moss Hart, *Face the Music* (1932) and *As Thousands Cheer* (1933), touched on contemporary social and political issues. *Face the Music* is chiefly remembered for the great tune "Soft Lights and Sweet Music." *As Thousands Cheer* had the torrid Ethel Waters blasting out "Heat Wave" and "Easter Parade." *Louisiana Purchase*, written in 1940, marked Berlin's last venture in a satirical show.

Following his rousing army revue *This Is the Army* (1942), Irving Berlin reached the apex of his achievement with *Annie Get Your Gun* in 1946. Ethel Merman was heard at her extroverted best as Annie Oakley, brassily outsinging Ray Middleton in such tuneful treats as: "Anything You Can Do," lilting "They Say It's Wonderful," and belting out the anthem "There's No Business Like Show Business."

Although Berlin's later plays—*Miss Liberty* (1949), *Call Me Madam* (1950), and *Mr. President* (1962)—were undistinguished, his place in the history of the musical theatre is assured.

In 1968, Irving Berlin's eightieth birthday was celebrated on Ed Sullivan's TV show; and an entire hour and a half was dedicated to this beloved American songwriter.

He will undoubtedly be remembered in coming generations for two great songs: "God Bless America," first introduced by Kate Smith at an Armistice Day celebration in 1938, and the undying holiday classic "White Christmas."

"ANNIE GET YOUR GUN"   As the best shot in Buffalo Bill's Wild West Show, Ethel Merman, seen here as the sharp-shooting backwoods girl, complains lustily that "You Can't Get a Man with a Gun." Based on the legendary exploits of Annie Oakley, this 1946 musical was Berlin's first show to run over 1,000 performances on Broadway.

THE GRAND STREET FOLLIES AND THE GARRICK GAIETIES

After its inception in 1922 at the Neighborhood Playhouse, the Grand Street Follies was produced year in and year out. These witty productions yielded a crop of top performers which included Aline McMahon, Dorothy Sands, Jessica Dragonette, Joanna Roos, and a young song-and-dance man by the name of James Cagney.

In 1925 the Garrick Gaieties brought a number of young Theatre Guild luminaries to the fore. The first edition of this review witnessed the emergence onto the stage of a duo named Rodgers and Hart. Their memorable tunes were carolled by Sterling Holloway, Romney Brent, House Jameson, Libby Holman, Lee Strasberg, and Alvah Bessie, to name but a few.

COLE PORTER (1893-   )

In 1916 that most urbane personality Cole Porter wrote *See America First*. The show was a failure. In 1919, he followed with *Hitchy-Koo;* and in 1924, with the *Greenwich Village Follies;* in 1928, with *Paris;* and in 1929, with *Fifty Million Frenchmen,* which was a solid hit. This musical offered the great tune "You Do Something to Me." In 1929 Cole Porter produced *Wake Up and Dream,* which contained the outstanding song "What Is This Thing Called Love?"

In the thirties, Porter reached the apex of his career with such plays as *The Gay Divorcée,* in which Fred Astaire rendered the hit "Night and Day." There followed *Anything Goes,* in which Ethel Merman trumpeted "You're the Top" up to the very balcony. Porter's

GERSHWIN AND ROMBERG   A young George Gershwin, seated at the piano, entertains some friends. The older man leaning against the piano is Sigmund Romberg, the famous composer af operettas.

"GARRICK GAIETIES"   The 1925 edition of this intimate
revue with Sterling Holloway (center) spoofed plays, performers,

and especially the parent company, The Theatre Guild, with which the young performers were associated.

next great effort *Leave It to Me* (1938) presented playgoers with a new, young hoofer by the name of Gene Kelly, and introduced a then unknown songbird named Mary Martin, who skyrocketed to fame with the naughty "My Heart Belongs to Daddy."

In the 1948-49 season, Porter presented *Kiss Me Kate,* a biting musical remake of *The Taming of the Shrew,* followed by *Can Can* in 1953, and *Silk Stockings* in 1955, the last two works of no great significance.

Porter's last show was *Silk Stockings.* Tragically, his right leg was amputated in 1958. The embittered man refused to attend his 70th birthday celebration at the Metropolitan Opera House, and died in 1964.

Cole Porter wrote his own lyrics, and is accounted as one of the greatest figures in the musical world. His hit tunes were legion, and the melodies he created are heard around the world.

RICHARD RODGERS (1902-   ) AND LORENZ HART (1895-1943)

In 1920 Richard Rodgers and Lorenz Hart first came to public attention as contributors of songs to *Poor Little Ritz Girl,* nominally composed by Sigmund Romberg. During that year this duo produced a crop of great tunes which established their reputation. "Here in My Arms" was the hit song of *Dearest Enemy* (1925); "The Blue Room" was the hit song of *The Girl Friend* (1926); and "My Heart Stood Still" was the hit song of *A Connecticut Yankee* (1929). During the thirties the great Rodgers and Hart team went on to produce its best work. They, along with the Gershwins and Cole Porter, who was his own lyricist, ruled the stage of that day. As tunesmiths, they were unexcelled. From their time on, the musical grew in respectability, as

"LADY BE GOOD!" (1925)   *Walter Catlett, as J. Watterson Watkins, thinks up a "get rich quick" scheme for the down-and-out dancing team of Dick and Susie Trevor, played by Fred Astaire and Adele Astaire. This 1925 musical, which ran for 330 performances, marked the first successful musical comedy by the Gershwin brothers. This production featured one of Gershwin's greatest melodies— "Fascinating Rhythm."*

"THE GAY DIVORCÉE"   The Cole Porter smash hit chronicled the story of an
unhappy wife who hires a co-respondent to help her get a divorce. This scene from the

1932 production shows Luella Gear shocked to discover Claire Luce, the wife, with both the alleged co-respondent, Fred Astaire, and the real seducer, Erik Rhodes.

lyricists Lorenz Hart, Ira Gershwin, and Cole Porter are accounted the wittiest, the most poetic, and the most sophisticated word-masters ever to pen a ditty. They have yet to be surpassed.

In the 1930's Rodgers and Hart hit their full stride. They wrote *Jumbo* and *Babes in Arms,* which contained the celebrated number "The Lady Is a Tramp." Then followed *The Boys from Syracuse,* which contained the tender tunes "Falling in Love with Love," "Sing for Your Supper," and "This Can't Be Love."

RICHARD RODGERS (1902-   ) AND OSCAR HAMMERSTEIN II (1895-   )

In 1942 when Theresa Helburn of the Theatre Guild approached Rodgers with the idea of making a musical out of Lynn Rigg's GREEN GROW THE LILACS, Rodgers grew enthusiastic. However, his lifetime partner, Lorenz Hart, demurred. The partnership, Rodgers knew, was over. Hart's illness—he was to die of alcoholism on November 22, 1943—made him incapable of working.

In one of the more fortunate happenings of the musical theatre, Rodgers approached Oscar Hammerstein II with the project; and a working relationship, destined to change the scope of the musical theatre, began.

Hammerstein was not an unknown. He had been active as a lyricist and librettist since the early 20's, but it was not until his collaboration with Jerome Kern on *Show Boat* in 1927 that he came into prominence. Several successes followed: *Sweet Adeline* (1929), a Kern and Hammerstein venture, notable solely for Helen Morgan's tearful rendering of "Why Was I Born?" and "Here Am I;" and *Music in the Air* (1932), with the team's delightful airs "I've Told Ev'ry Little Star" and "The Song Is You." But in 1935, Hammerstein entered a lean period lasting until 1943, during which time failure followed failure. The names of the shows of that period appeared one day in Hammerstein's famous ad in VARIETY, after *Oklahoma*'s successful opening: "I've Done It Before and I Can Do It Again" blazed a banner headline, with the flop shows listed: *Very Warm for May,*

"NO, NO, NANETTE" (1925)   Wellington Cross as Billy Early, a wealthy Bible publisher, and his lawyer Jimmy Smith (Charles Winninger) get a dressing down for flirting while on holiday at Atlantic City, while Billy's daughter Nanette cowers from her mother's anger. This Vincent Youmans' success introduced two classics: "Tea for Two" and "I Want to be Happy."

Sunny River, The Gang's All Here, East Wind, and others long since forgotten. The only bright note in that time was Hammerstein's winning an Academy Award in 1941 for the hit tune "The Last Time I Saw Paris."

All that changed on March 31, 1943, when the curtain went up on Oklahoma. Blending dance, music, and book into a beguiling

"NO, NO, NANETTE"   *Jack Gilford and Ruby Keeler kick up their heels in the 1970 revival of Vincent Youmans's 20's musical. Miss Keeler's performance marks her Broadway comeback after an absence of more then 40 years. She last appeared on*

Broadway in 1929 in "Show Girl". Another Hollywood stalwart in this nostalgic show was Patsy Kelly.

"OF THEE I SING"   *Having decided on "love" as their campaign issue, the politicians behind presidential candidate John P .Wintergreen (William Gaxton) are pleased as he delivers the campaign song "Of Thee I Sing" to the Madison Square Garden audience. Sitting at his side, his newly-acquired wife (Lois Moran) adds the appropriate family note.*

whole, it was the first time in the history of the musical stage that songs, story, and dance were inseparable parts of a theatrical entity. The show was as revolutionary at the box-office as it was in form. Its Broadway run of 2,248 performances grossed $7 million; the original investment was $83,000. The national company toured in about 250 cities during 10 years and grossed another $20 million. It was calculated that 18 years after it had opened, gross proceeds from all media in which *Oklahoma* had appeared—radio, T.V., film, and the like—approached the $100 million mark.

In 1945 Rodgers and Hammerstein followed their initial triumph with *Carousel.* Although not as prodigious a success as *Oklahoma,* the musical adaptation of Ferenc Molnar's play *Liliom* was highly esteemed.

Of their following six musicals, *Allegro* (1947), *Me and Juliet* (1953), *Pipe Dream* (1955) and *Flower Drum Song* (1958) were lesser Rodgers and Hammerstein musicals; but *South Pacific, The King and I,* and *The Sound of Music* were triumphs.

The year 1949 saw the opening of perhaps the best-loved Rodgers and Hammerstein musical *South Pacific.* Based on James Michener's TALES OF THE SOUTH PACIFIC, the show had tills ringing merrily as Mary Martin lathered and warbled "I'm Gonna Wash That Man Right Outa My Hair" and Ezio Pinza, the noted opera basso, crooned "Some Enchanted Evening."

The King and I, presented in 1951, was a delightful change of pace for the team with its Oriental locale and its East-meets-West clash of the two central characters. Adapted from Margaret Landon's story ANNA AND THE KING OF SIAM, the musical had Yul Brynner as the King, and Gertrude Lawrence, in her last appearance before her death in 1952, as the Governess, singing the tender ballad "Hello, Young Lovers," the delightful melodies "Getting to Know You," "Shall We Dance?,"the King's plaintive "Is a Puzzlement," and a host of other musical treats.

Ironically, the team's last show, *The Sound of Music* (1959), though one of their greatest box-office bonanzas was not a critical success. Accused of being too operetta-like and sentimental, the

"THE KING AND I"   *Yul Brynner (center) as the King of Siam and Mary Martin*
as an English governess, surrounded by a chorus of the King's children in "The King

and I," the 1951 Rodgers and Hammerstein musical comedy based on Margaret Landon's best-seller, ANNA AND THE KING OF SIAM.

RICHARD RODGERS (1902-) AND LORENZ HART (1895-
1943)   *Although their long and productive association had begun
early in 1918, it was not until 1925 that the team became known
through their bright revue the* GARRICK GAIETIES. *For the next 25 years
—a period of longevity unequaled by any other duo—Rodgers and Hart
produced a string of 27 musicals that included such memorable hit
shows as* ON YOUR TOES *(1936),* THE BOYS FROM SYRACUSE *(1938), and*
PAL JOEY *(1940).*

criticism inspired Oscar Hammerstein's retort: "What's wrong with
being sentimental?" Apparently very little, for the musical play—
which was based on the chronicle of the Trapp Family Singers—
delighted audiences for 1,443 performances with its melodic pleasures
as sung by Mary Martin and Theodore Bikel.

"THE BOYS FROM SYRACUSE" *Jimmy Savo as Dromio asks his master Antipholus of Syracuse (Eddie Albert) for several drachmas to see the sights of Ephesus. In the Rodgers and Hart 1938 version of Shakespeare's* COMEDY OF ERRORS, *George Balanchine's choreography and George Abbott's staging added a fast-paced theatrical dimension to one of the best Rodgers and Hart scores.*

It was the last show for the most celebrated duo of the contemporary musical theatre. On August 23, 1960, Oscar Hammerstein II died of cancer.

The sentiment expressed by one of his peers, "All of us who worked in the theatre always walked more proudly because Oscar Hammerstein was of the theatre," typifies the esteem in which this giant of the American theatre is held.

After Hammerstein's death, Richard Rodgers composed *No Strings* in 1962 with his own lyrics, and "Do I Hear a Waltz?" with lyricist Stephen Sondheim.

VINCENT YOUMANS (1899-1946)

Although his productive life was short—in 13 years he composed less than 100 songs—Vincent Youmans wrote some of the most representative musical shows of the 1920's.

He made his debut as co-composer of *Two Little Girls* (1921), a beginning for which he owed much to his friend George Gershwin. Both young tunesmiths were working at the time for Harms, a music publisher. Impressed by his friend's tunes, the irrepressible Gershwin played them for Alex Aarons, the show's producer; and Youmans was hired. Shortly thereafter, Youmans established himself as one of Broadway's foremost composers with *Wildflower* (1924). Then in 1925 came *No, No, Nanette,* in which Youmans seemed to capture the effervescent spirit of the decade. In 1970, 35 years later, *No, No, Nanette* was revived to resounding hurrahs, with a cast starring Ruby Keeler, Patsy Kelly, Jack Gilford, and Helen Gallagher.

The composer contracted tuberculosis in 1927, and his creative output was seriously curtailed. Despite the strain of increasing invalidism, he continued producing spirited musical comedy scores. *Hit the Deck* followed in 1927, and included the lovely tunes: "Sometimes I'm Happy" and "Hallelujah." The ambitious *Rainbow* (1928), an undertaking in the tradition of *Show Boat,* was a failure, but is remembered for the great songs: "More Than You Know," "Without a Song," and "Great Day."

COLE PORTER (1892-1964)   *Foremost writer of the lavish, bawdy, fast-paced musicals of the 30's, the noted composer-lyricist was hailed by Walter Winchell on the opening of his show* ANYTHING GOES *(1934) as "King Cole Porter." Porter's hallmark — a sly lyric wed to a suave tune—has set the standard of sophistication for the musical theatre.*

Smiles, an Adele and Fred Astaire vehicle, with the radiant Marilyn Miller sharing the limelight, flopped despite the great Fred Astaire dances to the tunes of "Top Hat and Tails" and "Say, Young Man of Manhattan"—two numbers which became the brilliant routines in the film *Top Hat.* This play also contained the memorable tune "Time on My Hands." Though he was growing increasingly ill, Youmans was called in to help perk up the floundering *Humpty Dumpty* on its pre-Broadway tryout. Renamed *Take a Chance* (1932), it became one of Ethel Merman's earlier triumphs.

Forced to retire permanently from the theatre at 35, Youmans continued to write music even while he was bedridden. After his death in 1946 at age 47, 175 manuscripts were found in his trunk. One hopes that these songs might one day be wedded to a proper book and lyrics to bring alive once again the magic of Vincent Youmans' great melodies.

EARL CARROLL (1893-1948)
In 1923, the former songwriter determined to outstrip Ziegfeld in promoting feminine pulchritude and opened the first of his "Vanities." Across the stage door he placed a sign with which the Carroll Vanities have always been associated: "Through these portals pass the most beautiful girls in the world."

GEORGE GERSHWIN (1898-1937)

The youngest song plugger ever to thump a piano in Tin Pan Alley was a 15-year-old high school dropout—George Gershwin. This was in 1913. Within a few years, Gershwin's tunes began popping up in revues and musical comedies; and by 1919, his first complete musical comedy score *La, La Lucille* was noted for melodies that had ginger. But it was Al Jolson's zesty rendering of "Swanee"—which sold over a million copies of sheet music—which really put the young composer on the map.

Engaged by George White as sole composer for the prospective George White's Scandals, Gershwin was soon recognized as the freshest, most original writer of theatre music on Broadway. Between 1920 and 1924, a score of notable tunes issued from the annual Scandals. "On My Mind the Whole Night Long," "I Found a Four Leaf Clover," and "Somebody Loves Me" were among them.

More significant was Gershwin's attempt to insert a 20-minute jazz opera *Blue Monday* into the 1922 Scandals. Though this number was pulled out of the show after opening night, it foreshadowed Gershwin's masterpiece *Porgy and Bess*.

A string of hit shows followed. *Lady Be Good* in 1924 marked the first time that George and his brother Ira (1896-   ) worked together as composer and lyricist. The pair became immortalized with such memorable tunes as "Oh, Lady Be Good" and "Fascinating Rhythm."

Ten months later, there followed an event of the first magnitude: the premier of George Gershwin's "Rhapsody in Blue" with the composer at the piano. At the end of 1924, George Gershwin, as one journalist put it, was "a giant with one foot on Broadway and the other in Carnegie Hall."

The hit shows that swiftly followed include: *Oh Kay* (1926) which starred Gertrude Lawrence, seen in the United States for the first time, and Victor Moore. The show featured the Gershwin melodies "Do, Do, Do" and "Someone to Watch Over Me." In 1927 *Funny Face,* a vehicle for Adele and Fred Astaire, sparkled with such confections as "'S Wonderful," "Funny Face," "High Hat," and "The Babbitt and the Bromide."

Gershwin was determined to break the conventional limits of the musical comedy play. As early as 1926 he had been attracted to DuBose Heyward's novel PORGY; but not until 1933 did his folk opera begin to take shape. On October 10, 1935, the play opened to lukewarm critical appraisal. When the play closed after 124 performances, it was obviously a financial flop as well as a popular failure. It was not until the revivals of 1942 and 1953—the last starring a superb cast highlighted by Leontyne Price and William Warfield—that the warmth and originality of *Porgy and Bess* was recognized, and the work acclaimed a masterwork of the American musical theatre.

The news of George Gershwin's death of a brain tumor at 38 stunned the music world. In a brief career spanning only 20 years, he had created works of incomparable range and virtuosity. Without question, Gershwin, who also wrote music which was to achieve classic stature, was one of the most gifted composers that America ever produced. His brother Ira wrote the lyrics to his shows and went on to become associated in later years with the greatest tunesmiths of that era.

"PORGY AND BESS" (1935)   *The folks who live in the tenements called Catfish Row are getting ready for a picnic on Kittiwah Island. In this scene from the original production of Gershwin's folk opera which ran for only 124 performances, Sportin' Life*

(*John W. Bubbles*) *stands on the table; Porgy (Todd Duncan) and Bess (Anne Brown) are seated. Gershwin's folk opera grew in stature through two major revivals in 1942 and in 1953. It has been acclaimed as "a masterwork of the lyric theatre."*

KURT WEILL (1900–1950)   *Kurt Weill's musical scores are linked to libretti characterized by moral indignation over injustices. "The Threepenny Opera," written in 1933, shows Weill's genius in full flower. Weill wrote the music to Paul Green's anti-war fable "Johnny Johnson" in 1936.*

MUSICAL COMEDY DURING THE THIRTIES

The stock market crash of 1929 brought an end to innocence. It also brought to the theatre of the thirties a new social consciousness. Teeming with vitality, the new musical satires were a major factor on the stage. Although the plays have aged badly because their topical references are now stale, there is in the best of them an insouciance and gusto that is the hallmark of the period. *Of Thee I Sing* won the Pulitzer Prize in 1931. The book was written by George S. Kaufman

RICHARD RODGERS (1902-) AND OSCAR HAMMERSTEIN (1895-1960) "The most profound change in 40 years of musical comedy has been—Rodgers and Hammerstein," said Cole Porter. Through their pioneering work in OKLAHOMA, *the team brought the musical theatre to full maturity.*

and Morrie Ryskind, and the music and the lyrics by the Gershwins. In 1933 the same team produced *Let 'em Eat Cake.*

In 1937 the somewhat venerable George M. Cohan was featured as Franklin D. Roosevelt in *I'd Rather Be Right,* an odd turnabout for this politically conservative performer.

Although the Broadway musicals of the thirties were dominated by the superior achievements of George Gershwin, notable workers in the conventional vein produced estimable results. Irving Berlin con-

"BRIGADOON" (1947)   Highlanders begin a traditional dance in the Lerner and
Loewe musical fantasy about a little Scottish town that, having disappeared in 1747,

reappears for a single day in every century.

tributed *Face the Music* and *As Thousands Cheer,* both written in collaboration with Moss Hart. Arthur Schwartz, Howard Dietz, and George S. Kaufman brought in *The Bandwagon,* which starred Fred Astaire, Adele Astaire, and Frank Morgan. This musical was notable for its hit song "Dancing in the Dark."

KURT WEILL (1900-1950)

In 1933 Kurt Weill and Bertold Brecht produced *The Threepenny Opera,* a masterful evocation of Berlin during the twenties; but it failed after twelve performances. Not until its 1953 revival was the inimitable play recognized as a distinctive work of the theatre. In 1936 Weill's sweet-sour compositions embellished the Group Theatre's production of Paul Green's *Johnny Johnson.* In 1938 the satirical *Knickerbocker Holiday,* written by Weill in collaboration with Maxwell Anderson, confirmed Kurt Weill as a top composer.

In 1949 Weill wrote the soul-stirring music of *Lost in the Stars,* the musical version of Alan Paton's best-selling CRY THE BELOVED COUNTRY, a dramatic novel concerned with the low estate of the Blacks in apartheid South Africa.

THE MUSICAL COMEDY IN THE 1940's AND THE 1950's

The rolling juggernaut of Hitler's war machine made the public aware of a reality merely hinted at in the musical satires of the thirties. Now came the end of the plush, confectionary musicals. More thoughtful books, and music more integrated with the script and with the dramatic action of the book now became the trend. *Pal Joey,* written in 1940 through the collaboration of Richard Rodgers, Lorenz Hart, and John O'Hara, was a milestone. For the very first time, a musical comedy presented a heel as the hero in a tough, unromanticized world.

"MY FAIR LADY"   *Julie Andrews as the Cockney flower girl Eliza and Rex Harrison as the phonetics specialist Professor Henry Higgins meet outside Covent Garden in the Lerner and Loewe version of "Pygmalion." One of the most successful productions in the history of the musical theatre, "My Fair Lady" after its 1956 opening had the longest run of any musical up to that time. Translated into 15 languages, this musical play won ovations in 21 countries and grossed more than 80 million dollars.*

"SOUTH PACIFIC" (1949)   Ezio Pinza and Mary Martin enjoy
"Some Enchanted Evening" in the 1949 Rodgers and Hammerstein
musical based on James A. Michener's "Tales of the South Pacific."
The romantic tale of the sophisticated French planter, Emile De
Becque, and Nellie Forbush, the army nurse from Little Rock, set on a
balmy Pacific isle during wartime, had a run of 1,925 performances.
"South Pacific" became the second musical to win a Pulitzer Prize for
drama.

"SOUTH PACIFIC" (1949)   The ladies take time out from their off-duty chores to celebrate Nellie Forbush's finding romance in the South Pacific wartime arena. Mary Martin and her colleagues sing "I'm in Love with a Wonderful Guy."

Carousel, written by Oscar Hammerstein and Richard Rodgers in 1945, was another outstanding success. However, one of the biggest hits ever to appear on the musical stage followed in 1949. *South Pacific* had the tills ringing merrily as Mary Martin lathered and warbled "I'm Gonna Wash That Man Right Outa My Hair." Enzio Pinza, a noted operatic star, excelled. His rendition of "Some Enchanted Evening" reverberated on radio sets from one end of the country to the other.

Air-Conditioned

NATIONAL

"America's First Theatre"

GUYS & DOLLS

A MUSICAL FABLE of BROADWAY

The tide of change was sweeping in new talent. In 1944, Leonard Bernstein wrote the pungent, melodic score to *On the Town,* and followed with *Wonderful Town* in 1953, *Candide* in 1956, and with the brilliantly-conceived *West Side Story,* a solid hit, in 1957.

Other musicals, some of less stature perhaps, that owe much of their success to the literary sources on which they were based, were Loesser's *The Most Happy Fella* which was taken from Sidney Howard's play *They Knew What They Wanted.* Jerry Herman's *Hello Dolly* was based on Thornton Wilder's *The Matchmaker.* Both of these productions enjoyed a not inconsiderable vogue.

FRANK LOESSER (1910-1969)

In 1948 Frank Loesser had written the lyrics and score to his first show *Where's Charley.* He hit the top of the pile rather quickly, for in 1950 *Guys and Dolls* was rated as one of the great productions of all time. A brilliant assemblage of raffish characters, headed by Sam Levine, brought Damon Runyon's world to life and absolutely captivated audiences. The tunes were catchy and singable, and the action and pace were completely engaging. Loesser also contributed the songs to *How to Succeed in Business Without Really Trying,* which won the Pulitzer Prize.

Other musicals, some of less stature perhaps, that owe much of their success to the literary sources on which they were based Loesser's *The Most Happy Fella* was taken from Sidney Howard's play *They Knew What They Wanted,* Jerry Herman's *Hello Dolly* was based on Thornton Wilder's *The Matchmaker.* Both of these enjoyed a not inconsiderable vogue.

"GUYS AND DOLLS" PLAYBILL Frank Loesser's "musical fable of Broadway," based on Damon Runyon stories, presented a gallery of shiftless Broadway types dedicated to dice throwing and horse-playing. In this chronicle of the redemption of a gambler, Sky Masterson, at the hands of a Salvation Army lass, Sarah Brown, Loesser struck solid gold. The musical had a triumphant run of 1,200 performances and has become a classic of the musical theatre.

"GUYS AND DOLLS" (1950) In a sewer which serves as the temporary home for the "oldest established permanent floating crap game in New York," Sky Masterson (Robert Alda) is throwing the dice. Nathan Detroit (Sam Levine) (kneeling to his right) has found this location in order to provide the action demanded by Big Julie (B. S. Pully) (standing behind Alda). Nicely Nicely Johnson (Stubby Kaye) kneels alongside Big Julie.

ALAN JAY LERNER (1918-   ) AND FREDERICK LOEWE (1904-   )

During the fifties, a new pair hit pay dirt. Alan Jay Lerner, librettist, and Frederick Loewe, composer, teamed up to put together two moderate successes: *Brigadoon* and *Paint Your Wagon.* They then followed with one of the most literate shows ever to grace the boards: *My Fair Lady* (1956), featuring Rex Harrison and Julie Andrews. The show seemed to run interminably and went on through six years to hang up a record of 2,717 performances. The hit was translated into 15 foreign languages and was produced in practically all capitals throughout the civilized world. Small wonder, for the play featured a host of infectious tunes: "I Could Have Danced All Night," "I've Grown Accustomed to Her Face," "On the Street Where You Live."

My Fair Lady was Shaw's *Pygmalion* dressed up in musical comedy clothes. The score projected the play effortlessly and unpretentiously, and brought together in one harmonious blend all the major talents it employed. Moss Hart, at the top of his powers, was the director. Rex Harrison portrayed with superlative skill the professorial Henry Higgins; and Julie Andrews rendered Eliza, the flower girl, with captivating freshness and an impeccable cockney accent.

The team followed in 1960 with *Camelot,* and unexceptional show, except for several notable songs: "Camelot" and "If Ever I Should Leave You." After Loewe's retirement, Lerner continued, with Burton Lane, to supply literate and witty lyrics to such musical plays as *On a Clear Day You Can See Forever* (1965). In 1969, with his composer André Previn, he did the fabulous *Coco,* the story of the famous modiste, starring Katherine Hepburn.

"SOUND OF MUSIC"   As Maria, the governess of the Von Trapp children, Mary Martin teaches her delighted charges to sing. Despite critical reservations about the musical's resemblance to an old-fashioned operetta, the sentimental chronicle of the Trapp family's flight from Austria, was a smash hit at the box office in 1959 and its run nearly reached the 1500 mark.

"A FUNNY THING HAPPENED ON THE WAY TO THE FORUM" (1962)
Zero Mostel as the wheeling-dealing slave, Pseudolus, in ancient Rome is being measured for a fit against the back of a lovely courtesan. When told the measurement is perfect, Mostel murmurs "Yes, but how often will we find ourselves in this position?" The bawdy romp, based on various plays of Plautus, was given a notable assist through the music and lyrics of Stephen Sondheim.

"WEST SIDE STORY" (1957) *In a "fair-fight," representatives of the Jets and the Sharks square off in the Leonard Bernstein-Jerome Robbins contemporary version of the "Romeo and Juliet" story. Unique in the history of the musical drama for its choice of theme, the amalgam of Bernstein's music and the brilliant choreography of Jerome Robbins created a new high in the art of the musical theatre.*

"FIDDLER ON THE ROOF"   The Sheldon Harnick-Jerry Bock musical play, based on stories by Sholem Aleichem, brought the world of the Jewish ghetto to life. Tevye, played by Zero Mostel, a pious dairyman who talks familiarly to God, was immortalized by the incomparable comic actor. The record run of the musical, continuing from its opening in 1964 to the present, bids fair to make it the longest running hit show in Broadway history. Here, Zero Mostel as Tevye imagines how nice it would be to be wealthy, in the song "If I Were a Rich Man."

MUSICAL COMEDY DURING THE SIXTIES

In 1964 the team of Sheldon Harnick and Jerry Bock presented a version of the Sholem Aleichem stories. The featured character was one Tevye, a devout dairyman who, with his family, was uprooted from his native village by Czarist forces because he was a Jew. Zero Mostel seemed to have been made for the part. He cavorted on the stage and sang with a charm and abandon that moved audiences to paroxysms of both tears and glee. As these pages are being written, *Fiddler on the Roof* is still being played to packed houses. During the past seven years the show has had 2,718 performances on the New York stage. But this is only part of the story. Translations have been made into almost every major language. What is surprising is that the show is such a hit in such far-off places as Japan. However, it seems that *Fiddler* evokes a certain empathy which transcends race. It is a story of the downtrodden; and the audience unfailingly responds, no matter what the idiom, to the underdog. But what makes *Fiddler* the worldwide hit that it is is its profusion of singable tunes: "Matchmaker, Matchmaker," "Tradition," "If I Were a Rich Man," and "Sunrise, Sunset."

THE MUSICAL COMEDY: AN APPRAISAL

Undoubtedly the musical comedy is America's unique contribution to world theatre. Reenacted throughout the world and frequently revived, these great shows have been universally admired but never successfully imitated. The melodies of noted musicals have entered the culture of countries of every political stripe. The song hits of Broadway are heard in the marketplaces of Istanbul and in the alleys of Calcutta. The tunes are played and enthusiastically relished in the middle of Africa. New musicals like *Hair* are reproduced in Tel Aviv and in Tokyo.

This writer regards *My Fair Lady, Guys and Dolls, South Pacific,* and *Fiddler on the Roof* as the four greatest musical comedies of all

JAMES RADO AND GEROME RAGNI   These actor-authors rocked the theatre world with their "tribal love-rock musical."

"HAIR" (1968)   After an immensely successful eight-week run at Joe Papp's New York Shakespeare Festival Theatre, the show was transferred to Broadway. It is running in every major world capital from Sydney to Paris, grossing $18 million a year. The three black girls—Mary Davis, Melba Moore, Emmaretta Marks—sing about how they like white boys. During a rendition of the show's title song, Debbie Offner is being swung through the air by fellow tribesmen.

"HAIR" (1968)   Gerome Ragni spoofs the middle-class audience in the most startling musical play of the 60's. A haphazard plot that combined views on hippies, love children, the Vietnam war, and racism, embellished by the rock score of Galt MacDermott, made "Hair" the representative musical of the youth generation.

time. Perhaps the reader may have another list; but no matter in what order the nominations are made, practically all critics—both American and foreign—pay homage to the musical comedy as the great American achievement of the stage.

The Index

A. E. (see Russell, G. W.)
A.N.T.A. Washington Square Theatre (New York), 597, 629, 651
A.P.A., The, 614, 616 (see also Phoenix Theatre, N.Y.)
Aarons, Alex, 700
Abbey Theatre (Dublin), 440, 443-445, 446, 529, 575
Abbott, George, 519, 699
Abe Lincoln in Illinois, 544, 545
Abraham Lincoln, 454, 496
Abthorpe, Thomas, 314
Academy Award, 675, 691
  Centennial Summer, 675
  Last Time I Saw Paris, The, 691
acoustics
  in Greece, 40
  in Rome, 58
Acrobats, 618
Acropolis, 33
acting style
  in ancient Greece, 31, 42
  in Middle Ages, 81, 82, 85
  Commedia dell'Arte, 138-141
  18th century, 212, 213, 215-216, 224, 229, 238, 240, 241

  19th century, 244, 266-267, 276, 278, 283, 287, 293, 327, 331, 354, 357-358, 364, 405-406, 407, 411, 417, 420, 506, 512, 515
  20th century, 566-567
  (see also Ensemble acting)
"Actor Prepares, A'n," 392, 407
actors
  in ancient Greece, 22, 25, 40-47, 51
  in ancient Rome, 58, 59, 61, 64
  and The Christian Church, 65
  in Middle Ages, 74, 76, 85, 86
  Commedia dell'Arte, 138-139
  18th century, 227, 240
  (see also Boy actors; Women on the stage)
Actors Equity, 661
actors' income, 94, 102, 127, 185, 483, 576, 578
Actors' Studio, 504
Actor's Workshop, The, 622, 629
actresses (see Women in the theatre)
Adamov, Arthur, 474
Adams, Maude, 361, 371, 380
Adding Machine, The, 537, 577, 643
Addison, Joseph, 296, 298

Adelphi (London), 264

Adler, Luther, 557, 566, 570-571

Adler, Stella, 392, 566

Admirable Bashville, The, 439

Admirable Crichton, The, 432

"Admiral's Men, The," 97, 111, 112, 113

admission fees
    in ancient Greece, 54-55
    in Elizabethan England, 94, 102
    18th century, 206, 241
    19th century, 250, 251-255
    20th century, 483, 578, 636, 667

Adventure Story, 452

Adventures of Harlequin and Scara-mouche, The, 297

Aeschylus, 17, 20, 23, 24-27, 28, 29, 30, 33, 39, 51, 53, 646

After All, 453

After the Fall, 596-597, 629

Agamemnon, The, 24, 25

Ages of Man, The, 487

Agitatoria, 49

"Ah, Sweet Mystery of Life," 656, 657

Ah, Wilderness!, 529, 641, 661

Aiken, George L., 344

Ainley, Henry, 292

Ajax, 27

Akst, Harry, 677

Alabama, 385

Alabaster, William, 99

Albee, Edward, 601-603, 617, 618-619, 622

Albert, Eddie, 699

Alcestis, 28

Alchemist, The, 106, 109

Alda, Robert, 716-717

Aldridge, Ira, 326, 327, 328

Aldwych Theatre (London), 504

Aleichem, Sholem, 722, 723

Alexander, Sir George, 292, 431

Alexander, Katherine, 593

"Alexander's Ragtime Band," 678, 679

Alexandrinsky Theatre, 396, 410, 414

Alhambra Theatre (London), 280

"All Alone," 680

All for Love, 184

All My Sons, 591

All Over, 602

All the Comforts of Home, 385

"All the Things You Are," 675

Allegro, 695

Allen, Vera, 562

Allen, Vivian Beaumont (Mrs.), 628

Alley Theatre (Houston), 636

Alleyn, Edward, 103, 111, 112, 117, 120

Allgood, Sara, 446

Alma-Tadema, Sir Lawrence, 283

Alswang, Ralph, 647

Ambassadors Theatre, The (London), 511

Amédée, 474

American Blues, The, 583

American Company, The, 302-306, 308, 309, 310, 312, 313, 314, 315, 317

American Dramatists' Club, 378 (see also Dramatists' Guild)

American Dream, The, 601, 617

American National Theatre and Academy (see A.N.T.A.)

American Roscius, 59

American Shakespeare Festival (Stratford, Conn.), 636-637

American Theatre (New York), 338

Ames, Winthrop, 519

amphitheatre (see theatre buildings)

Amphitruo, 548

Amphitryon 38, 548, 562, 644

Anatomist, The, 455

Anders, Glenn, 525

Anderson, Maxwell, 509, 532, 534, 536, 541, 557, 650, 711

André, 311, 314

André, Major John, 308

Andrea, 381

Andreini, Francesco, 142, 149, 157, 162

Andreini, Isabella, 142, 157, 162

Andrews, Julie, 710-711, 719

Andreyev, Leonid, 576, 577, 622

Androcles and the Lion, 440, 577

Andromeda, 38

Andronicus, Livius, 57

Anglih, Margaret, 389

Animal Kingdom, The, 560

animal mimicry, 18, 19, 42, 44, 70

animals on stage
    in ancient Greece, 37

in ancient Rome, 58
19th century, 255, 261, 344
Anina, 669
ANNA AND THE KING OF SIAM, 695, 697
Anna Christie, 522
Anna Held girls, 664
Anne of a Thousand Days, 536
Annie Get Your Gun, 680, 681
Another Part of the Forest, 549
Anouilh, Jean, 466, 577, 622, 650
Anthony Street Theatre (New York), 325
Antigone, 27, 28, 398
Antoinette Perry Award, 616
Anything Goes, 683, 701
"Anything You Can Do", 680
APA-Phoenix, 614, 616
Apollo Theatre, 639
Appia, Adolphe, 413, 638, 640
Apple, The, 616, 617
Apple Cart, The, 440-441, 442, 645
apron stage, 176, 183, 222, 240, 246-247, 257, 319, 329, 345, 363, 484, 509, 624, 651 (see also Thrust stage)
aquatic melodrama, 275, 276
Arabesque, 640
Archer, William, 436
Anchon, 47
Arden, John, 501, 622
Ardrey, Robert, 572, 646
Are They the Same at Home?, 456, 457
Arena Stage, The (Washington, D.C.), 621-622
arena stage, 515, 621-622, 624, 638
Aretino, Pietro, 87
Ariosto, Ludovico, 87
Aristophanes, 17, 18, 23, 26, 29, 33, 35, 38, 47, 172
Aristotle, 21, 27, 42, 56
Arizona, 384
Arkansas, University of, 637
Arlecchino (see Harlequin)
Arlen, Harold, 669
Arliss, George, 381, 428-429
Armoured Train 14-69, The, 408, 420-421
Arms and the Man, 436, 485, 487, 496, 497, 577
Armstrong's Last Goodnight, 501
Arnaud Theatre (London), 512

Arnaud, Yvonne, 512
Aronson, Boris, 646
Arrabal, F., 474
Arragh-na-Pogue, 349
Arrau (playwright), 474
Arthur, Julia, 639
Artists of Dionysus, 43
Arts Theatre (London), 478
As a Man Thinks, 386
As Thousands Cheer, 680, 711
As You Like It, 167, 260, 494, 563
Ascent of F.6, The, 463
Ashcroft, Peggy, 426, 452, 487
Assassin, The, 572
Association of Producing Artists, The, 614
Astaire, Adele, 686-687, 701, 703, 711
Astaire, Fred, 683, 686-687, 688-689, 701, 703, 711
Astley's Amphitheatre (London), 255, 481
Aston, Anthony, 296
Astor Library (New York), 633
Astor Place Opera House, 334, 345
Astor Place Riot, 327, 328, 333
At Homes, 272
Atellana, 49
Athens, 17, 22, 24, 29, 30, 31, 32, 33, 56
Atkins, Robert, 483, 484, 485
Atkinson, Rosalind, 499
Auctioneer, The, 381
Auden, W. H., 463
audiences
    in ancient Greece, 54-56
    in ancient Rome, 63, 64
    during Restoration, 179, 180, 192, 200
    18th century, 199, 200, 206, 208, 238, 239, 240, 241
    19th century, 251-255, 257-258, 270, 273, 276, 280, 282, 334-336, 363, 389, 452, 506, 517, 578, 611
Augustus, 61, 62, 64 (see also Riots in the theatre)
Australia, 270, 357
Authors Act, 259
automation, 633
Autumn Crocus, 452

Autumn Garden, The, 549, 605
Awake and Sing, 567-568, 646
awards (see Antoinette Perry Award;
    Nobel Prize; Pulitzer Prize; Theatre
    Guild Award)
Ayres, Lemuel, 646

B

"Babbitt and the Bromide, The," 703
Babes in Arms, 690
Babes in Toyland, 656, 660
Bacchae, The, 26, 29
Back to Methuselah, 440, 442, 577
backboard, 172
backcloth (see Backdrop)
backdrop, 27, 33, 34, 86-87, 159, 162,
    196, 277, 315, 363
Bacon, Francis, 114-115
Bacon, Jane, 485
Bad Seed, The, 536
Baddeley, Angela, 483, 495
Badger's Green, 455
Bagnold, Enid, 473
Baker, George Pierce, 518-519, 521,
    560, 645
Balanchine, George, 699
Balcony, The, 622
balcony (see Gallery; Staging)
Bald Prima Donna, The, 474
Ballad of the Sad Cafe, The, 603
ballerina, 156, 158
ballet, 203, 222, 315, 490, 653
Banbury Nose, The, 459
Band Box Theatre, 579
Bancroft, Marie Wilton, 278, 280, 282,
    291, 293
Bancroft, Squire, 280, 282, 291, 293
Bandwagon, The, 711
Bankhead, Tallulah, 550-551, 553
Barbara Frietchie, 371, 386
Barefoot in the Park, 609
Barnum's American Museum (New
    York), 345
Barras, Charles M., 653
Barretts of Wimpole Street, The, 454
Barrie, James M., 361, 430, 432-433,

435, 441, 484
Barry, Elizabeth (Mrs.), 177, 187, 188,
    192, 194
Barry, Philip, 519, 560-563, 622
Barrymore, Ethel, 367, 380, 386
Barrymore, Georgiana Drew, 367
Barrymore, John, 367, 369, 639
Barrymore, Lionel, 367, 639
Barrymore, Maurice, 367, 376
Barrymore, William, 481
Bartholomew Fair, 109
Bartolozzi, Lucia Elizabeth (see Ma-
    dame Vestris)
Bates, Alan, 477
Bates, Blanche, 380, 381
Bateson, Timothy, 478
Bath House, The, 411
Battle of Angels, 583
Bayliss, Lillian, 482, 483, 484, 490,
    494-495
Baylor University, 637
Be Yourself, 563
Bear, The, 401
Beau Brummell, 369, 386
Beaumont, Francis, 107, 109, 114-115,
    181, 186, 210, 509
Beautiful People, The, 573
Beaux' Stratagem, The, 178, 184, 186,
    296, 304
Beck, Julian, 616
Beckett, Samuel, 474-475, 478, 616,
    617, 622
Bedbug, The, 411, 419
Bedford, Brian, 616
Beeston, William, 170
Beggar on Horseback, 541, 563
Beggar's Opera, The, 205
Behan, Brendan, 506, 511
Behn, Aphra (Mrs.), 195
Behrman, Samuel Nathan, 518, 548,
    562, 644
Bel Geddes, Barbara, 588
Bel Geddes, Norman, 640-642
Belasco, David, 380, 381-382, 383
Belasco Theatre (New York), 382, 568,
    642
Belgrade Theatre (Coventry), 512
Bells, The, 285, 287
Benavente, 578

Benchley, Robert, 519
benefit performances, 190-191, 264-265, 301, 303, 308, 312, 358
Benelli, Sem, 639
Benny, Jack, 669
Benson, Frank, 292-293
Benthall, Michael, 499
Bergman, Ingrid, 512, 536
Berle, Milton, 669
Berlin, Irving, 543, 665, 669, 675-680, 707, 711
  and Moss Hart, 711
Berliner Ensemble, The, 504-506
Bernhardt, Sarah, 278, 366
Bernstein, Aline, 646
Bernstein, Leonard, 715, 720
Bertinazzi, Carlin, 164
Besier, Rudolf, 454
Bessie, Alvah, 683
Betterton, Mary Sanderson, 189, 194
Betterton, Thomas, 175, 177, 184-190, 191, 194, 200, 310
Betty, William Henry West (Master), 244-248
Between Two Worlds, 537
Beyond the Horizon, 522
Biancolelli, Guiseppe Domenico, 139, 142, 143
Bidwell, Barnaby, 311
Big Night, 558
Bikel, Theodore, 698
Billie, 661, 663
Binyon, Lawrence, 484
Bio-mechanics, 411
Bird Cage, The, 603
Bird in Hand, 454
Bird, Montgomery, 330
Birds, The, 18, 30, 38
Birmingham Repertory Theatre (England), 442, 453, 454, 487
Birthday Party, The, 476
Bittersweet, 448
Black Comedy, 500, 512
Black Crook, The, 653
Black Eye, The, 455
blackface role, 678
Blackfriars, The, 98, 99, 102, 106, 121, 122, 129
blackout, 283, 348

Blair, Mary, 525
Blakely, Colin, 461, 504, 505
Blau, Herbert, 622, 629
Blithe Spirit, 449
Blitzstein, Marc, 582
Blackade of Boston, The, 306
Blood Wedding, 647
Bloomgarden, Kermit, 557
Blossom Time, 660
Blow Your Own Trumpet, 459, 484, 496
Blue Bird, The, 401, 407
Blue Monday, 702
Blue Paradise, The, 660
"Blue Room, The," 687
Bluebeard, 255
boat car, 19
Bock, Jerry, 722, 723
Bogart, Humphrey, 544
Bohnen, Roman, 557
Boleslavski, Richard, 575
Bolton, Guy, 672
Bombo, 678
Bondman, The, 189
Bone Squash, 341
Booth, Barton, 212, 229
Booth, Edwin Thomas, 322, 336, 351, 355, 356-359, 362-363, 364, 368, 369, 376
Booth, John Wilkes, 322, 352, 358, 362
Booth, Junius Brutus (1796-1852), 322, 323, 354-355, 356, 357, 358, 481
Booth, Junius Brutus, Jr. (1821-1883), 322, 355, 358
Booth, Richard, 355
Booth, Shirley, 562
Booth's Theatre (New York), 358-359, 363
Born Yesterday, 645
Both Your Houses, 536
Bottomley, Gordon, 472, 484
Boucicault, Dion, 274, 348, 349-350, 381, 434, 442
Bound East for Cardiff, 521
Bourgeois Gentleman, The, 165
Boweny Theatre, 333, 336, 341, 345
box set, 278, 358
boxes, 240, 251, 255, 277, 316, 329, 363
Box-Ma-Box, 603

boy actors, 120-122, 124, 126, 192
Boy David, The, 433
Boys from Syracuse, The, 645, 690, 698, 699
Boy Growing Up, A, 457
Bracegirdle, Ann (Mrs.), 177, 186, 192, 194, 195
Bradford, Roark, 547
Braithwaite, Lillian, 448, 483
Brand, 408, 424
Brand, Phoebe, 557, 570-571
Brando, Marlon, 584-585
Brecht, Bertold, 504, 506, 509, 515, 548, 622, 629, 711
"Breeches" part, 184, 209, 210, 211, 264-265
Brent, Romney, 683
Breuer, Marcel, 637
Brice, Fanny, 665
Bridie, James, 442, 454
Brig, The, 509
Brief Moment, 548
Brigadoon, 708-709, 719
Brighella, 144, 146, 155, 167
Bright Star, 560
Brighton, 378
BRIGHTON ROCK, 462
Bristol Old Vic (England), 499
Britain's Daughter, 484
Brittania Triumphans, 130
Broadhurst Theater (New York), 641
Broadway Theater, 334, 345
Bromberg, J. Edward, 566
Brook, Peter, 502-503, 510, 605. 648
Brougham, John, 376
Brougham's Lyceum Theatre, (New York), 345
Broun, Heywood, 519
Brown, Anne, 705
Brown, Ford Madox, 283
Brown, Gilmor, 636
Brown, John Mason, 519, 541
Brown, Kenneth H., 509
Brown, Pamela, 495, 499
Browning, Robert, 258
Bruce, Robert, 114-115
Brutus, 325
Brynner, Yul, 695, 696-697
Bubbles, John W., 705

Büchner, 575, 629
Buckton, Florence, 473, 485
"Building a Character," 407
Bulgakov, Leo, 575
Bull, Peter, 478
Bullock, Christopher, 299
Bulwer-Lytton, Lord, 264, 338
Bunch of Keys, A, 386
Burbage, Cuthbert, 100
Burbage, James, 98, 100, 113, 117
Burbage, Richard, 100, 113, 117, 120, 135
Burglar, The, 385
Burgoyne, General John, 306
burlesque, 21, 30, 44, 61, 167, 208, 255, 260, 274
Burletta, 260-261, 276
Burne-Hones, Sir Edward, 283, 287
Burnett, Frances Hodgson, 384
Burning Glass, The, 458
Burrell, John, 496, 497
Burton's Theatre (New York), 345, 350
Bury the Dead, 572
Bus Stop, 604, 646
buskins, 36
Busybody, The, 296
Butova (actress), 407
Butter and Egg Man, The, 541
Byron, Arthur, 380
Byron, H. J., 278

C

Cadell, Jean, 495
Caesar and Cleopatra, 439, 442, 577
Caesar, Julius, 61, 62
Café La Mama, 617, 620
Cagney, James, 683
Call It a Day, 452
Call Me Madam, 680
Caldwell, Erskine, 563
Caldwell, Zoe, 624-625, 628
Calhern, Louis, 647
Camden, William, 114-115
Camelot, 719
Camille, 366, 641, 646

Camino Real, 587, 630
Campbell, Herbert, 282
Campbell, Patrick (Mrs.), 286, 287, 292, 424, 426, 440
Can Can, 687
Canaries Sometimes Sing, 448
Candida, 436, 439
Candide, 715
candle snuffers, 197
Canons of Hippolytus, 65
Canterbury Cathedral, 463
Canterina, 158
Cantor, Eddie, 665, 677
Capek, 577
Capon, William, 225
Captain, The, 137, 148-149, 152, 167
Captain Brassbound's Conversion, 439, 443
Captain Jinks of the Horse Marines, 386
Carbonaria, 49
Careless Husband, The, 186
Caretaker, The, 476, 477
Carnegie Hall (New York), 703
Carnegie Institute of Technology, 636
Carnovsky, Morris, 525, 557, 566, 570-571
Carousel, 695, 713
Carroll, Earl, 669, 702
  "Vanities," 669, 670, 671, 702
Carroll, Paul Vincent, 444-445
Carter, Leslie (Mrs.), 381
Carver, Mary, 475
Carving a Statue, 462
Case of Clyde Griffiths, The, 646
Casino Theatre, 655
Cass, Henry, 473, 491
Casson, Lewis, 434, 485, 496
Caste, 279
Castle Garden (New York), 345
Castle of Perseverance, 83, 85
Castle, Vernon and Irene, 679
Casey Jones, 646
Cat and the Fiddle, The, 672
Cat on a Hot Tin Roof, 587, 588, 589, 651
Catfish Row (see Porgy and Bess)
Cato, 296, 298, 309
Caucasian Chalk Circle, The, 629

Cavalcade, 448
Cave Dwellers, The, 573
Cazale, John, 618
Cecilia and Clorinda, 174
censorship
  in Rome, 61
  in England, 169, 170-171, 208, 259, 424, 436
Centennial Summer, 675
Central City (Colorado), 640
Central Park Shakespeare Festival (see Shakespeare-in-the-Park)
Century Girl, The, 679
Cerf, Bennett, 532
Chairs, The, 474, 475
Chalk Garden, The, 473
Chaney, Stewart, 646
Channel Road, The, 541
Chapman, George, 109, 113
Charity Ball, The, 381
Charles I, 169, 170, 171, 184, 191, 192, 193
Charles II, 164, 167, 169, 173, 174, 192, 195, 199, 201, 298
Charley's Aunt, 223
Charlot's Revue, 448
Charon, Jacques, 498
Chase, Mary, 616
Chauve-Souris Company, 573
Chayefsky, Paddy, 604, 605
Ché, 609
Cheats of Scopin or The Tavern Bilkers, The, 203
Chekhov, Anton, 396, 397, 398, 399, 400-406, 407, 424, 440, 446, 484, 504, 575, 578, 580, 622
Cherry Orchard, The, 406, 409, 490, 575, 580
Chestnut Street Theatre (Philadelphia), 312, 316, 318-319, 322, 325
Chevalier, Albert, 282
Chichester Festival Theatre (England), 512, 513
Chicken Soup with Barley, 471, 472
Children of Darkness, 614
Children's Hour, The, 549, 552
Chiltern Hundreds, The, 453
Chinese Prime Minister, The, 473
Chips with Everything, 472, 473

Chiton, 39
Chlamys, 36
Choephorae, The, 24
"Choir Boys of St. Paul's," 122
"Choir Boys of the Chapel Royal," 122
choral odes, 21
Choregi, 50
Choregus (see Choregi)
chorus, 18, 19, 21, 23, 25, 32, 33, 38, 44-47, 50
chorus leader, 22, 23, 25, 47
Chris Christopherson, 522
Christian opposition to the theatre, 65, 67, 68, 76, 94-96, 143, 169, 295, 301, 310, 344
Christie, Agatha, 511
Christmas pantomime, 64, 167, 282
Christy's Minstrels, 340, 341
Chums, 383
Church plays, 72-74 (see also Liturgical drama)
"Church 'Round the Corner, The," 672
Cibber, Colley, 186, 200, 201, 203, 204, 205, 299, 376
Cibber, Susannah (Mrs.), 209, 212, 215, 217, 237
Ciceri, Charles, 315
Cicero, 58
Circle-in-the-Square, 530, 533, 613-614
Citizen Kane, 583
City, The, 387
City Corporation (London), 96, 97, 98, 99
City Dionysia, 29, 33, 47
Civic Repertory Theatre, The, 578, 580-581
Civil War, American, 358
Claracilla, 173
Clash by Night, 572
classical theatre
    of Greece, 17-56
    of Rome, 57-65
Claudel, 577, 645
Clearing in the Woods, A, 603, 647
Clements, John, 499
Cleveland Playhouse, The, 636
Climbers, The, 386
Clive, Colin, 455
Clive, Kitty, 220

closet drama, 63
Clouds, The, 26, 30
clowns, 167, 249-250
Clurman, Harold, 392, 556, 557, 558-559, 567
Clytemnestra, 25
Cobb, Lee J., 557, 566, 570-571, 593, 598
Cockpit, 170, 185 (see also Phoenix)
Cocktail Party, The, 464
Coco, 719
Coco, James, 608, 610
Coghlan, Charles, 376
Coghlan, Rose, 376
Cohan, George M., 629, 660-661, 662-663, 707
Colbert, Claudette, 525
Coleman, (Mrs.), 192
Colleen Bawn, The, 349
Collier, Constance, 447, 548
Collins, Russell, 566
Collins, Wilkie, 372
Colman, George, 229, 230
Colvin, Padraic, 444
Columbine, 137, 157, 167
Come Back Little Sheba, 604
Come Blow Your Horn, 609
Comédie-Française, 163, 165, 367, 377, 497, 610
Comédie-Italienne, 163
comedy, 17, 24, 29, 30, 41, 42, 43, 44, 46, 47, 49, 52, 138 (see also Costumes; Masks)
    of manners, 167, 181, 184, 200, 430-432, 447
    origins of, 24, 29-30
    styles of, (see Burlesque; Farce; Comedy of manners; Music hall)
    use of stock characters in, 31, 32, 63, 137, 138, 139, 167
Comedy of Errors, 699
Comedy Theatre (New York), 576
Comical Revenge, The, 184
Commedia dell'Arte, 64, 137, 167, 181, 195, 202, 203, 495
Complaisant Lover, The, 462
Commonwealth Protectorate, 169, 171, 177, 185
competitions in ancient Greece, 21, 22,

23, 24, 26, 27, 47, 50, 51, 52, 53, 54
Compton, Fay, 496
Condemned of Altona, The, 629
Confidential Clerk, The, 464
Congreve, William, 167, 177, 179, 181, 184, 186, 206, 207, 449, 504-505
Connecticut Yankee, A, 687
Connection, The, 615, 616
Connell, Leigh, 533
Connelly, Marc, 541, 547, 563-566, 640
  and Frank B. Elser, 566
  and George S. Kaufman, 541, 563
Conrad, Robert T., 330
Conroy, Frank, 576
Cons, Emma, 481-482
Conscious Lovers, The, 300
Constant Couple, The, 178, 184, 209, 210, 211
Constant Wife, The, 447
Constantin, 146
Contrast, The, 310
Constructivism, 412, 413, 414, 415, 417, 643
convention, theatrical
  in Greece, 31, 33-34, 35, 36
  in Rome, 33-34
  (see also Costumes; Masks)
Cooke, George Frederick, 243-244, 317, 320, 321, 325, 330
Cooper, Thomas Abthorpe, 315, 316-317, 321, 330
Copeau, Jacques, 573
copyright, 259, 378, 439
Coquelin (actor), 366
Corcoran, Katherine, 383
Coriolanus, 217, 244, 495
Corn Is Green, The, 457, 458
Corneille, Pierre, 165
Cornell, Katharine, 576, 647
Corri, Charles, 482
Cossart, Ernest, 525
costume
  Greek, 19, 20, 27, 31, 36-40, 41, 44, 45
    color conventions in, 31, 36
  Roman, 45, 46, 49, 51, 52, 54
  Middle Ages, 69-70, 71, 72, 82, 85-86
  Elizabethan, 104-105, 110, 111, 124-

127, 130, 131
Commedia dell'Arte, 139, 149, 142, 144-157, 202
  Restoration, 194, 196
  English 18th century, 202, 217, 218-219, 220, 223, 224, 225-227, 230, 232, 238
  English 19th century, 244, 249, 250, 256, 257, 266, 268, 270, 271, 273, 275, 276, 277, 279, 281, 284, 286, 288-289, 290, 291
  American 18th century, 307, 309
  American 19th century, 320, 326, 327, 329, 331, 337, 340, 342-343, 346, 352, 360, 361, 365, 370, 381, 374-375, 388
  Russian, 396-397, 401, 402, 416, 421
  English 20th century, 428, 431, 438, 450, 451, 460, 465, 470, 473, 477, 478-479, 485, 488, 489, 492, 493, 494, 495, 496, 498, 500, 501, 502-503, 505
  American 20th century, 518, 526, 530, 533, 535, 538, 542, 546, 550, 552, 554, 561, 562, 564, 570, 574, 580, 582, 584, 588, 594, 598, 606, 610, 611, 612, 613, 618, 620, 623, 625, 626, 627, 630, 631, 635, 642, 648, 654, 662, 665, 666-667, 669, 670, 674, 676, 677, 678, 681, 684, 686, 688, 691, 692, 694, 696, 699, 704, 708, 710, 712, 713, 717, 718, 720, 721, 722, 724, 725
  (see also Buskin; Chlamys; Himation; Make-up; Masks; Phallus; Soccus)
Cotten, Joseph, 562
Cotton, Sir Robert Bruce, 114-115
Counsellor-at-Law, 537
Country Girl, The, 646
Country Wife, The, 178, 184, 224, 376, 494, 629
court influence on theatre, 97, 129, 132, 170, 179, 180, 192, 199 (see also Masque)
Court Theatre (London), 433, 442, 500, 595 (see also Royal Court Theatre)
Courteline, 577
Courtin' Time, 647
Covent Garden Theatre (London),

174, 202, 205-208, 209, 211, 212, 213, 215, 225, 226, 227, 229, 230, 231, 243, 245, 246-247, 249, 250, 251, 255, 259, 261, 264-265, 267, 268, 274, 283, 313, 314, 316, 317, 333, 349, 354, 355, 490
Coventry cycle, 79
Coviello, 150
Coward, Noel, 448-449, 451
Cowboy and the Lady, The, 386
Cowie, Laura, 426
Cowl, Jane, 544
Cowles, Matthew, 618
Cradle Song, 614
Cradle Will Rock, The, 582
Craig, Gordon, 407-413, 416, 638, 640, 641
crane (stage machinery), 35
Crane, William H., 378
Crawford, Cheryl, 556, 558-559
Cream in the Well, The, 553
Creon, 28
Critic, The, 231
Cromwell, Oliver, 169, 172
Cronyn, Hume, 624-625, 628
Crosman, Henrietta, 381
Cross, Wellington, 691
Crow, Jim, 338, 339
Crowden, Graham, 500
Crucible, The, 593, 594-595, 622
Cruelty of the Spaniards at Peru, The, 171, 172
Cruger's Wharf Theatre, 302
Cruickshank, Andrew, 484, 496
CRY THE BELOVED COUNTRY, 509, 711
Cumberland, Richard, 309
curtain, 58, 94, 98, 124, 159, 182, 196, 506
Curtmantle, 466, 467
Cushman, Charlotte, 336-339
Cyclorama, 283, 633, 638
Cyrano de Bergerac, 369

D

Da Silva, Howard, 571
Dallas Theatre Center, 637

Daly, Arnold, 436
Daly, Augustin, 368, 372-373, 374-375, 376
Daly's Theatre (London), 376
Daly's Theatre (New York), 373
Damon and Phillida, 300
Danchenko, Vladimir Nemirovich-, (see Nemirovich-Danchenko)
"Dancing in the Dark," 711
dancing, in theatrical performances
    in ancient Greece, 18, 32, 47, 51
    in Elizabethan Theatre, 118, 123, 127, 128-129
    Commedia dell'arte, 143, 156, 158
    18th century, 202, 203, 259, 281
    19th century, 338-344, 345
    20th century, 506, 653-726
    (see also Masques)
Daneman, Paul, 478
Dangerous Corner, 456
Daniel, Samuel, 131
Daniell, Henry, 548
Daniels, Frank, 656
Daniels, William, 618-619
D'Annunzio, Gabriele, 366, 639
Dante, 641
Danton's Death, 575, 629
Darby's Return, 312
Dark Ages, 63
Dark at the Top of the Stairs, The, 604, 606-607
Dark Is Light Enough, The, 466
Dark of the Moon, 613
Dark Tower, The, 541
Davenant, Charles, 174, 175, 179, 189
Davenant, (Lady), 189
Davenant, Sir William, 94, 169, 170-173, 174, 175, 177, 179, 181, 185, 187, 189, 192, 221, 259
Davenport, Fanny, 368, 371, 376
David Garrick, 278
Davis, Mary, 724
"Dawn of Love," 656
Day by the Sea, A, 458
Days to Come, 549
Days Without End, 529
deBeaumarchais, Pierre-Augustin Caron, 324
deKoven, Reginald, 655

DeLoutherbourg, Philip James, 225
deMille, Henry C., 381
Dead End, 640, 642
Dean, Alexander, 519
Dear Brutus, 433
Dear Liar, 286
Dear Octopus, 452
Dearest Enemy, 687
Death of a Salesman, 592-593, 598-599, 628, 651
Death of Bessie Smith, The, 601
Death of Rolla, The, 314
Deep Blue Sea, The, 452
Dekker, Thomas, 113, 114-115, 122, 509, 582
Delacorte Theatre, 633, 634-635 (see also Shakespeare-in-the-Park)
Delane (18th c. actor), 220
Delaney, Shelagh, 480, 511
Delicate Balance, A, 603
Dell, Floyd, 521
Delsarte, François, 377
Desert Highway, 456
Desert Song, The, 658-659, 660
Design for Living, 448
Desire Under the Elms, 523, 524
deus ex machina, 35 (see also Crane)
Deval, Jacques, 544
de Valois, Ninette, 490
Devil and Mr. Bolfry, The, 455
Devil to Pay, The, 298
Devil's Disciple, The, 370, 371, 436, 439, 577
Devine, George, 468, 496, 500
de Witt, Johann, 95, 99, 100, 116, 127
Diamond Jim Brady, 667
Diary of Ann Frank, The, 605
Dibdin, Thomas, 261
Dickens, Charles, 258, 350, 457
Digges, Dudley, 446, 525, 537, 576
Dietz, Howard, 711
"Dinah," 677
Dinner at Eight, 541
Diogenes, 172
(see also Religious festivals)
Dionysus, 17, 18, 19, 32, 45, 56
Diorama, 276
Disappointment, or The Force of Credulity, The, 306

Dithyrambic
festival, 21
hymn, 21
Dithyrambs, 18, 19, 22, 30
Divine Comedy, 641
"Do I Hear a Waltz?," 700
"Do, Do, Do," 703
Dobie, Alan, 473
Dockstader, Lew, 342-343
Dockstader's Minstrels, 678
Doctor, The, 139, 151, 167
Dr. Angelus, 455
Doctor Faustus, 108, 111, 484, 510, 582, 614
Doctor in Spite of Himself, The, 165
Doctor's Dilemma, The, 440, 577, 646
Dog Beneath the Skin, The, 463
Doggett, Thomas, 177, 19;
Dolce, 87
Doll's House, A, 426, 429
Don Quixote, 158
Donat, Robert, 465
"Donkey Serenade, The," 656
Donne, John, 114-115
Doré, Gustave, 283
Dorset Garden (London), 175, 179, 189, 197 (see also Duke's Theatre)
Dot, 350
Double-Dealer, The, 177
Douglas, 187, 256, 309
Douglass, David, 302, 303, 304, 306, 308
Douglass, David (Mrs.) (formerly Mrs. Lewis Hallam), 299, 302, 307
Dowling, Eddie, 560, 574-575
Doyle, Sir Arthur Conan, 385
"Drag" part, 223
Dragonette, Jessica, 683
Dragon's Mouth, 457
Drama Critics' Award, 572, 575
Time of Your Life, The, 572, 575
dramatic festivals (see Religious festivals)
Dramatists' Guild, 378 (see also American Dramatists' Club)
Drayton, Michael, 106
Dream Girl, 537
Drew, Georgiana, 367
Drew, John, 361, 366-367, 368, 376, 380

Drew, John (Mrs.), 366, 367
Drifting Apart, 383
Drinkwater, John, 453-454, 463, 496
Drivas, Robert, 611
Drury Lane (London), 170, 174, 177,
    186, 193, 201, 203, 208, 212, 213,
    215, 217, 220, 221, 224, 230, 231,
    232, 233, 234, 235, 236, 237, 240,
    245, 257, 259, 261, 262, 266, 267,
    282, 283, 299, 317, 332, 333, 354,
    355, 448, 511
    (see also Theatre Royal)
Druten, John Van, 452
Dryden, John, 181, 184, 193, 231, 298
Dublin Roscius, 59
Duchess of Malfi, The, 117
Duchess Theatre (London), 477
Duel of Angels, 466
Duenna, The, 231, 310
Duke of Buckingham, 231
"Duke of York's Players," 177
Duke of York's Theatre (London), 434
Duke's Theatre (London), 171, 175,
    176, 182, 183, 195 (see also Dorset
    Garden)
Dulcy, 563
Dumas, Alexandre, 372, 578
Duncan, Todd, 705
Dunlap, William, 309, 311, 312, 313,
    314, 315, 317
Dunne, J. W., 456
Dunnock, Mildred, 599
Dunsany, Lord, 442
Durranmatt, Friedrich, 546
Duse, Eleonora, 366, 575
Dybbuk, The, 575
Dynamo, 525, 577, 643
Dyskolos papyrus, 41

E

Earl of Dorset, 114-115
"Earl of Leicester's Men, The," 97, 98
Earl of Rochester, 187
Earl of Southampton, 114-115
"Earl of Worcester's Men, The," 118
East Lynne, 358, 380

East Wind, 690
"Easter Parade," 680
Eastward Ho, 109
Eaton, Walter Prichard, 519
Eckart, Jean, 647
Eckart, William, 646
Edward II, 109
Edwardes, George, 376
Edwards, Hilton, 446
Egan, Jenny, 595
Egypt, 41
Eileen, 656
Elder Statesman, The, 464
Electra, 27
Elen, Gus, 282
Elezaisousae, The, 26
Eliot, T. S., 463-466
Elizabeth I, 124, 125, 126, 129, 132
Elizabeth the Queen, 534
Elizabethan theatre, 31, 57, 81, 93-135
Elliston, Robert William, 260-261
Elser, Frank B., 566
Emery, Katherine, 552
Emmett, Daniel, 341
Emperor and Galilean, 424
Emperor Jones, The, 522, 646
Empire Theatre (London), 280
Empire Theatre (New York), 380
Empress of Morocco, The, 182, 183
"End of the Affair, The," 462
Endgame, 474, 512
Enemy of the People, An, 426, 427,
    495, 600
England, 68, 70, 85, 90, 91, 164
    Elizabethan, 93-135, 167
English Stage Company, 468, 500, 595
Ensemble acting, 395, 407 (see also
    Berliner Ensemble; David Garrick)
Entertainer, The, 469
Epicene or The Silent Woman, 106, 109
Epicharmus, 42
Epidaurus, 35
Epitrepontes, 41
Epstein, Alvin, 613
Erchmann-Chatrian, 285
Ericson, Leif, 557
Errol, Leon, 665, 672
Ervine, St. John, 444
Esmeralda, 384

Etherege, Sir George, 181, 184
Eumenides, The, 24, 27
Euripides, 17, 26, 28-29, 30, 33, 34, 44, 50, 53, 54, 57, 442
Evadne, 28
Evans, Lyle, 658-659
Evans, Dame Edith, 431, 450, 458, 485, 494, 499
Evans, Maurice, 455, 491, 494
Ever Since Paradise, 456
Evershed-Martin, Leslie, 513
Every Man in His Humour, 109
Everybody in the Garden, 603
Everyman, 85, 484, 575
Everywhere I Roam, 566
Evreinoff, 577
Exter, Alexander, 416

F

Face, the Music, 543, 680, 711
Fair Penitent, The, 301
Faith Healer, The, 389
Fall of the City, The, 600
Fallen Angels, 448
"Falling in Love with Love," 690
False Shame, 314
Family Reunion, The, 463
Fanny's First Play, 440, 443
Fantesca, 156
farce, 44, 61, 138, 179
Farmer, Frances, 557, 566, 570-571
Farmer Takes a Wife, The, 566
Farquhar, George, 178, 184, 186, 202, 210, 211, 298, 299, 304
"Fascinating Rhythm," 687, 703
Fatal Marriage, The, 187, 235, 237, 243
Father of an Only Child, The, 302
Faversham, William, 380
Fawcett, John, 264-265
Fechter, Charles, 278, 279, 280
Federal Street Theatre (Boston), 315, 316, 324
Federal Theatre Project, 537, 578, 579, 582
Fenton, Frank, 561
Ferber, Edna, 541, 675

Fertility festivals, 21
Fervent Years, The, 567
Festival Mobile Theatre, 633
Feydeau, Georges, 498
Ffrangcon-Davies, Gwen, 431, 454
Fichandler, Zelda, 622
Fiddler on the Roof, 722, 723
Field, Betty, 537
Field, Nat, 121
Fielding, Henry, 208, 442, 508
Fields, W. C., 665, 677
Fifth Avenue Theatre, 373
Fifty Million Frenchmen, 683
Figulus, 49
Fings Ain't Wot They Used T'Be, 511
Finlay, Frank, 461
Finney, Albert, 469, 471, 501
Fiorillo, Tiborio, 152, 163
fire in the theatre, 232, 246, 250, 299, 308, 316, 324-325, 329, 373
Firefly, The, 656, 669
First Man, The, 522
Fisk, James, 373
Fiske, Minnie Maddern, 360, 371, 428-429
Fitch, Clyde, 369, 371, 380, 382, 386, 387
Fitzgerald, Barry, 446
Flanagan, Hallie, 578
Flashing Stream, The, 458
flats, 86-87, 172, 182, 196, 483, 641
Flea in Her Ear, A, 498
Fleetwood, Charles, 212, 215
Fletcher, John, 107, 109, 114-115, 181, 186, 210, 509
Flies, 358
Flight to the West, 537
Flora, or Hob in the Well, 297
Florence, W. J., 358, 376
Florence, W. J. (Mrs.), 358
Flower Drum Song, 695
Flowering Peach, The, 646
Flowers of Virtue, The, 566
folk drama, 72
Fonda, Henry, 566
Fontanne, Lynn, 448, 450, 451, 526-527, 528, 563, 577, 644
fool (see Jester)
Foolish Notion, 560

footlights, 116, 197, 225, 251, 257, 305, 348
Forbes-Robertson, Jean, 426
Forbes-Robertson, Johnston, 291, 293, 439
Forbes-Robertson, Lady Gertrude, 484
Force of Calumny, The, 314
Ford Foundation, 621, 622, 629
Ford, John, 113, 117
Ford's Theatre (Washington, D.C.), 322, 352, 362
Forrest, Edwin, 322, 327, 328, 330-336, 356
Forrest, Colonel Thomas, 306
Forrester, Ross, 525
FORSYTE SAGA, THE, 433, 434
Fortune, The, 102, 117
Fortune Teller, The, 656
45 Minutes from Broadway, 660, 661
49-ers, The, 563
"47 Workshop," 518, 560, 645
Foster, Stephen, 341
"Four Quartets," 463
Four Seasons, The, 471
France, 69, 75, 80, 143, 149, 162, 163, 164, 171, 173, 195, 221
France, Anatole, 638
Francesca da Rimini, 366
Fraser, Ronald, 500
Freedley, Vinton, 579
French theatre, 57
French Without Tears, 450
Fried, Walter, 557
Friml, Rudolf, 656-658, 668, 669
Frogs, The, 18, 23, 26, 30
Frohman, Charles, 361, 379-380, 382, 386
Frohman, Daniel, 361, 377, 379, 381, 382
Front Street Theatre (New York), 313
Frou-Frou, 376
Fry, Christopher, 466-467
Funny Face, 703
Funny Thing Happened on the Way to the Forum, A, 720-721
Furies, The, 24, 25, 27
Futz, 609

G

Galileo, 509
Gallagher, Helen, 700
gallery, 84, 94, 95, 99, 100, 101, 116, 123, 221, 222, 240, 246-247, 251, 255, 257, 305, 316, 483, 513
Gallows Humour, 617
Galsworthy, John, 279, 427, 430, 433-434, 435, 442
Gam, Rita, 628
Game of Love and Death, The, 646
Ganassa troupe, 162
Gang's All Here, The, 691
Garden District, 589-590
Garfield, John, 566, 570-571
Garrick, David, 164, 167, 179, 202, 212-217, 220-223, 225, 227, 228, 229, 230, 233, 234, 237, 238, 240, 249, 268, 287, 299, 302, 310, 313, 376 (See also David Garrick)
"Garrick Gaieties," 683, 684-685, 698
Garrick Theatre (New York), 573, 576
Gate Theatre (Dublin), 446
Gaul, George, 525
Gaxton, William, 694
Gay Divorcée, The, 683, 688-689
Gay, John, 205, 264
Gazzo, 646
Gear, Luella, 688, 689
Geddes, Norman Bel, 640-642
Gelber, Jack, 615, 616
Gelosi troupe, 142, 149, 162
Genet, Jean, 474, 616, 622
Geneva, 441
Gentle People, The, 572, 646
George III, 227
George Barnwell, 298
George Washington, Jr., 661
Germanova, Maria, 407
Germany, 282, 283
Gershwin, George, 556, 682-683, 700, 702-703, 704, 705, 707
Gershwin, Ira, 690, 703
Gershwins, 687, 707
"Getting to Know You," 695

Ghosts, 423, 424, 426, 435, 576, 578
"Giannina Mia," 656
Gibson girl, 664
Gibson, William, 605
Gideon, 605
Gielgud, Sir John, 431, 456, 458, 485-487, 496, 514, 603, 647
Gifford, Henry, 212, 214, 299
Gilbert and Sullivan, 653
Gilbert, George H. (Mrs.), 376
Gilbert, John, 376
Gilder, Rosamund, 579
Gilford, Jack, 692-693, 700
Gillette, William, 380, 382, 384, 385
Gingold, Hermione, 483
La Gioconda, 366
Giraudoux, Jean, 466, 548, 577, 622, 644
Girl Friend, The, 687
Girl from Utah, The, 672
Girl in the Pink Tights, The, 658
girlie show, 653
    birth of, 653
Girl of the Golden West, The, 381
Gish, Lillian, 381, 439
"Giving Out," 258
Gladiator, The, 337, 330, 332
Glasgow Citizens Theatre, 455
Glaspell, Susan, 521
Glass Menagerie, The, 582, 583, 585, 647
Gleam, The, 453
Globe Theatre (London), 96, 100, 102, 103, 117, 121, 122, 127, 450, 636
"God Bless America," 680
Godfrey, Thomas, 306
Gogol, Nikolai, 509
Golden Apple, The, 647
Golden Boy, 568-571
Goldoni, 578
Goldsmith, Oliver, 226, 229, 230, 310, 484
"Good Companions, The," 456
Good Soldier Schweik, The, 556
"Goodbye Becky Cohen," 665
Goodman, Edward, 576
Goodman's Fields Theatre, (London), 212, 214, 299

Good-Natured Man, The, 226, 229
Gordon, Ruth, 494, 548
Gordone, Charles, 620
Gorelik, Mordecai, 646
Goring, Marius, 496
Gorki, Maxim, 399, 404, 407, 408, 575
Governor's Son, The, 660
Graham, Morland, 483
Grand Army Man, A, 381
Grand Street Follies, 683
Grandville-Barber, Harley, 433, 442, 443, 468, 496
Grass Is Greener, The, 453
"Great Collaborator, The," 541
"Great Day," 700
Great Divide, The, 388, 389
Great Fire, 177
Great God Brown, The, 523
Great Plague, 177
Great White Hope, The, 605, 627
Greece, 17-56, 57, 63, 137, 138
GREEN GROW THE LILACS, 690
Green Grow the Lilacs, 553
Green, Jane, 230
Green Pastures, The, 547, 563, 564-565, 640
Green, Paul, 541, 556, 557, 706, 711
    and Kurt Weill, 556
Green Room, The, 228
green, symbolism of, 228
Greene, Graham, 462
Greene, Robert, 105, 108
Greenwich Village Follies, 683
Greet, Ben, 483
Gregory, Lady, 443, 444
Greih, J. T., 423, 435
Griboyedov, Alexander, 408
Gribunin, V. F., 407
Grimaldi, Joseph, 249-250, 254, 481
Grimaldi or The Life of an Actress, 349
Grizzard, George, 602, 628
Group Theatre, 392, 556-559, 566, 568, 569, 572, 575, 646, 711
Gorelik, Mordecai, 559
Guardsman, The, 546, 645
Guardsmen, 228
Guild Theatre (New York), 579

guilds,
    in ancient Greece, 43
    in Middle Ages, 76
Guinea Pig, The, 453
Guinness, Alec, 495, 499, 600
Guitry, Sacha, 575
Guthrie, Tyrone, 485, 490, 494, 496,
    497, 499, 622, 623, 624, 628
Guy Mannering, 337, 338
Guys and Dolls, 647, 714, 715, 716-717,
    723
Gwenn, Edmond, 434
Gwynne, Nell, 180, 192, 193
Gypsy, 534, 645
"Gypsy Love Song," 656

H

Habimah players, 575
Hackett, James Henry, 324
Hackett, James K., 379
Hagen, Uta, 602
Haigh, Kenneth, 470
Haines, Joseph, 191
Hair, 620, 621, 723, 724, 725, 726
Hairy Ape, The, 522-523
Halévy, Ludovic, 372
Hall, Peter, 478, 504, 626
Hall, Willis, 472
Hallam, Adam, 299
Hallam, Lewis, (1714-1756), 298-302
Hallam, Lewis, Jr., (1740?-1808), 299,
    300, 302, 303, 304, 309, 310, 312,
    313, 314
Hallam, (Miss), 299
Hallam, Lewis (Mrs.) (later Mrs.
    David Douglas), 299, 302, 307
Hallam, William, 298, 302
"Hallelujah," 700
Hambleton, T. Edward, 614, 616
Hamilton, Wallace, 622
Hamlet, 113, 117, 118, 119, 120, 122,
    123, 124, 129, 135, 185, 188, 215,
    243, 245, 248, 265, 266, 267, 278,
    279, 283, 291, 309, 310, 317, 325,
    332, 333, 338, 356, 358, 362, 369,
    376, 377, 407, 408, 413, 483, 485,

487, 491, 495, 628, 641, 642
Hammerstein, Arthur, 656
Hammerstein, Oscar, II, 553, 675, 690-
    700, 707, 712, 713
    and Jerome Kern, 690
Hancock, John, 622
Hannen, Nicholas, 496, 497
Hansberry, Lorraine, 605
Happy Man, The, 453
Harding, John, 475
Hardwicke, Sir Cedric, 439, 440, 454
Hare, John, 280
harlequin, 137, 139, 140, 142, 143, 144,
    145, 149, 151, 154, 157, 158, 159,
    166, 167, 202, 203, 249
Harlequin Doctor Faustus, 202
Harlequin Sorcerer, 202
Harlequinade
    (See Harlequin; Pantomime;
        Christmas Pantomime)
Harms, 700
Harnick, Sheldon, 722, 723
Harper (actor), 315, 316
Harrigan, Edward, 382
Harris, Henry, 189, 191
Harrison, Richard B., 547
Harrison, Rex, 710-711, 719
Hart, Charles, 191, 193
Hart, Lorenz, 661, 683, 687-690, 698,
    699, 711
Hart, Moss, 541, 543, 680, 711, 719
Harvard University, 518, 560, 636, 645
Harvey, 616
Hatful of Rain, A, 646
Haunted, The, 528
Hauptmann, Gerhart, 398, 406, 442
Have a Heart, 672
Having a Wonderful Time, 566
Hawkes, Jaquetta, 457
Hawkins, Jack, 496
Hay Fever, 448
Haydon, Julie, 574-575
Hayes, George, 485
Hayes, Helen, 536, 616
Haymarket Theatre (London), 208,
    209, 238, 259, 271, 278, 280, 313,
    316, 432, 487
Hazel Kirke, 377
Hearst Greek Theatre, 62

Heart of Maryland, The, 381
Heart of Midlothian, The, 350
Heartbreak House, 440, 442, 577, 642
Hearts of Oak, 383
"Heat Wave," 680
Heckert, Eileen, 439
Hedda Gabler, 398, 426, 428-429
Heflin, Van, 562
Heir-at-Law, 350
Heiress, The, 487
Helburn, Theresa, 519, 690
Held by the Enemy, 385
Hell Mouth, 77, 81-82
Hellenistic Period, 20, 26, 32, 37, 45
Hellman, Lillian, 548-553
   and DuBose Heyward, 553, 556, 605
Hello Broadway, 661
Hello Dolly, 548, 715
"Hello, Young Lovers," 695
Helpmann, Robert, 465, 495
Heming, John, 100, 120
Henrietta, 378
Henry IV, 102, 489, 493, 507
Henry V, 268
Henry VI, 106
Henry VIII, 189, 252-253, 336, 490
Henry, John, 306, 309, 310, 312, 313,
   314
Henry, Maria (Mrs.), 312
Henslowe, Philip, 103, 117, 124
Hepburn, Katharine, 441, 560, 561,
   562, 563, 719
Her Majesty's Theatre (London), 292
Herbert, Victor, 655, 656, 657, 658, 660
Herculaneum, 45, 46
"Here Am I," 690
Here Come the Clowns, 560
"Here in My Arms," 687
Herman, Jerry, 715
Herne, James A., 382, 383-384
Herne, Katherine Corcoran (Mrs.), 383
Heros, 41.
Heyward, DuBose, 553, 556, 577, 703
   and Dorothy Heyward, 577
Hibernian Roscius, 59
"High Hat," 703
High Jinx, 658
High Tor, 536, 541
Highland Call, The, 556

Hill, Arthur, 602
Hill, Jenny, 282
Himation, 36, 51
Hingle, Pat, 601, 606-607
Hippolytus, 29
His Grace of Graumont, 386
History of Sir Francis Drake, The, 171
"History of the American Theatre, A,"
   311
Hit the Deck, 700
Hitchy-Koo, 683
Hoadley, Bishop, 299
Hodgkinson, John, 313, 314
Hodgkinson, John (Mrs), 313
Hogarth, William, 180, 218-219
Hold Everything, 613
Holiday, 560
Holland, 79
Holloway, Baliol, 485, 499, 525
Holloway, Sterling, 683, 684
Holman, Libby, 683
Home, 487, 514
Home at Seven, 456
Home of the Brave, 603
Home, William Douglas, 453
Homecoming, The, 477, 528, 626
Homer, 24
Honest Whore, The, 113
Hopkins, Anthony, 498
Hopkins, Arthur, 369
Horne (playwright), 309
Horovitz, Israel, 617, 618
horses on stage
   in ancient Greece, 37
Hostage, The, 506
Hôtel de Bourgogne, 162, 163
Hotel Universe, 560, 622
House of Connelly, The, 556, 557
House of Regrets, 459
house-keepers, 102
Houseman, John, 582
Howard, Bronson, 373, 376, 378, 379
Howard, Leslie, 544
Howard, Sir Robert, 299
Howard, Sidney, 519, 577, 715
Howard, Trevor, 499
Howells, William Dean, 382, 383
Howland, Jobyna, 677
Hoyt, Charles, 382, 386

Hughes, Margaret, 191
Hull, Henry, 381
Hull, Josephine, 542-543
Hume, Sam, 519
Humourous Lieutenant, The, 174, 193
Humpbacked Lover, The, 271
Humpty Dumpty, 701
Hunt, Hugh, 499
Hunted, The, 528
Hunter, Glen, 576
Hunter, W. C., 458
Huston, Walter, 52, 523, 536
Hymn to the Rising Sun, 556

I

I Am a Camera, 605
"I Could Have Danced All Night," 719
"I Found a Four Leaf Clover," 702
I Have Been Here Before, 456
"I Want to be Happy," 691
Ibsen, Henrich, 292, 360, 369, 398,
    408, 423-429, 435, 446, 484, 495,
    496, 576, 577, 578, 600, 645
Iceman Cometh, The, 529-531, 614, 622
I'd Rather Be Right, 541, 543, 661, 707
Ideal Husband, An, 432
Idiot's Delight, 544, 545, 645
"If Ever I Should Leave You," 719
"If I Were a Rich Man," 722, 723
Il Cinthio, 87
I'm Talking About Jerusalem, 471, 472
"I'm Gonna Wash That Man Right
    Outta My Hair," 695, 713
"I'm in Love with a Wonderful Guy,"
    713
Imaginary Invalid, The, 160-161, 165
Importance of Being Earnest, The, 430,
    431, 432, 450, 487
improvisation, 64, 118
improvised theatre
    (See Commedia dell'Arte;
      Improvisation)
In Abraham's Bosom, 556
In a Garden, 560
In Good King Charles' Golden Days,
    442

In the Zone, 521, 576
Inadmissible Evidence, 469, 471
Incident at Vichy, 597, 600
Inconstant, The, 178
Independent Theatre Group, 423, 435
Indian Queen, The, 186, 193
Indian Wants the Bronx, The, 617, 618
Inge, William, 604, 646
Innamorata, 155, 166
Innamorato, 157
Invitation to a March, 603
Innyard theatres, 93-94, 100
Inspector Calls, An, 457
Interludes, 91
Ionesco, Eugene, 474, 475, 601, 612,
    616
Iphigenia in Taurus, 29
Ireland, 243, 245, 283, 440, 443
Irving, Henry, 281, 283-287, 289, 291,
    293, 363, 366, 410
Irving, Jules, 622, 629
Irving, Margaret, 658-659
Irving, Washington, 351, 353
"Is a Puzzlement," 695
Isabella, 237
Isherwood, Christopher, 463
It Depends What You Mean, 455
Italian Theatre, 129, 132, 159, 162,
    163, 167, 196
    (see also Commedia dell'Arte)
Italy, 65, 87, 132, 137, 162, 173, 221
Ivanov, 401, 487
Ivanov, Vsevolod, 420
"I've Grown Accustomed to Her Face,"
    719
"I've Told Ev'ry Little Star," 675, 690
"I've Got a Right to Sing the Blues,"
    669
Ives, Burl, 588
Izenour-Schweikher Theatre, 636

J

J. B., 601
Jackson, Sir Barry, 442
Jackson, Freda, 495
Jacobi, Derek, 500

James I, 125, 194
Jameson, House, 683
Jane Shire, 302
Jardin de Paris, 664
Jarrett and Palmer London Company, 346-347
Jeans, Ursula, 495
Jeb, 572
Jefferson, Joseph (1774-1832), 322
Jefferson, Joseph (1829-1905), 341, 348, 350, 351, 352, 353, 376
Jest, The, 639
jester, 70
Jew of Malta, The, 108
Joan of Lorraine, 536
"Joey," 249
John Bull's Other Island, 440
John Gabriel Borkman, 426, 578
John Golden Theatre, 525
John Street Theatre, 304-305, 308 (see also Theatre Royal, New York)
Johnny Johnson, 541, 556, 706, 711
Johnson, Celia, 499
Johnson over Jordan, 487
Johnson, Dr. Samuel, 212, 229
Johnston, Denis, 444, 446, 622
Jolson, Al, 678, 702
Jonah and The Whale, 455
Jones, Barry, 544
Jones, Henry Arthur, 279, 292
Jones, Inigo, 90, 106, 130, 131, 132, 135, 170, 194, 221
Jones, James Earl, 627
Jones, Robert Edmond, 369, 519, 521, 522, 523, 524, 528, 563, 566, 576, 638-641, 644
Jongleurs, 71
Jonson, Ben, 106, 107, 109, 114-115, 122, 132, 135, 170, 181
Journey to Jerusalem, 536, 650
Journey's End, 455, 496
Joy, Nicholas, 562
Joyous Season, The, 560
Judgment Day, 537
Julius Caesar, 333, 358, 362, 582
Jumbo, 690
"Jump Jim Crow," 338, 339
Juno and The Paycock, 445, 460, 461
Justice, 434

K

Kachloff, Vassily (see Katchalov)
Kaiser, Georg, 577
Kamerny Theatre, 413, 416, 417, 418
Katchalov, Vassily, 407, 575
Katherine and Petruchio, 261
Katinka, 658
Kaufman, George S., 541, 661, 706, 711
    and Edna Ferber, 541
    and Moss Hart, 541, 543
    and Alexander Woollcott, 541
    and Marc Connelly, 541, 563
Kaye, Stubby, 716-717
Kazan, Elia, 557, 566, 571, 591, 597, 601, 629
Kazner, Kurt, 613
Kean, Charles, 268, 269-270, 271, 274, 276, 277, 287, 327, 348, 381
Kean, Edmund, 262-263, 264-267, 270, 321, 323, 325, 327, 330, 354, 355, 481
Kean, Thomas, 298
Keeler, Ruby, 692-693, 700
Keen, Malcolm, 483
Keene, Laura, 350, 351, 352, 354, 357, 362
Kelly, Gene, 687
Kelly, Patsy, 669, 693, 700
Kelly, Robert, 538-539
Kemble, Charles, 252-253, 264-265, 268, 317
Kemble, John Philip, 237-238, 243, 244, 245, 246, 250, 251, 252, 253, 254, 256, 267, 312, 317
Kemble, Roger, 233, 237
Kemble, Stephen, 252-253, 316
Kemp, William, 100, 118, 120, 121
Kendall, Madge, 366
Kendall, William, 366
Kenna, Mr. and Mrs., 313
Kennedy, Arthur, 595, 598, 599
Kent, Edgar, 525
Kent, Kenneth, 456
Kentucky Minstrels, The, 341
Kern, Jerome, 672-675, 690
    and Oscar Hammerstein II, 690

Key Largo, 536
Kid Boots, 677
Killigrew, Charles, 174
Killigrew, Thomas, 173, 174, 177, 178,
    185, 189, 191, 259
Kilty, Jerome, 286
King and I, The, 695, 696, 697
King and No King, A, 113
King Arthur, 484
King Edward VII, 292
King John, 268
King Lear, 113, 117, 135, 215, 267,
    328, 330, 496, 502, 503, 510, 647
King of Nowhere, The, 455
King Richard III, 212, 214, 215, 216,
    267
"King's Men, The" 102
"King's Players," 177, 192
Kingsley, Sidney, 558, 642
Kirkland, Jack, 563
Kirkland, Sally, 611
Kismet, 370
"Kiss in the Dark, A," 656
"Kiss Me Again," 657
Kiss Me Kate, 687
Kitch, Kenneth, 622
Kitchen, The, 471
Knickerbocker Holiday, 536, 711
Knights of the Burning Pestle, The, 109
Knights, The, 26
Knipper-Chekhova, Olga, 400, 402,
    407, 575
Knoblock, Edward, 456, 519
Komisarjevsky, Theodore, 414
Komisarjevskaya, Vera, 410, 414
Komos, 18, 26
Kott, Jan, 503
Krapp's Last Tape, 474
Kruger, Otto, 521
Kyd, Thomas, 108, 110, 117
Kynaston, Edward, 185, 191

L

La Città Morta, 366
La, La Lucille, 702
Lacy, John, 191

Lady Be Good!, 686-687, 703
Lady from the Provinces, The, 575
Lady from the Sea, The, 426
Lady Gregory, 443, 444
Lady in the Dark, 543
"Lady Is a Tramp, The," 690
Lady of Lyons, The, 338, 357
"Lady of the Evening," 680
Lady Windermere's Fan, 287, 431
Lady's Not for Burning, The, 466, 487
La Fausse Prude, 163
Lahr, Bert, 605, 613
L'Aminta, 87
Lampell, Millard, 622
Lanchester, Elsa, 490, 491
Land, Robert, 498
Landon, Margaret, 695, 697
Lane, Burton, 719
Lang, Matheson, 483
Langtry, Lily, 287
Langner, Lawrence, 521, 576
La Princesse Brambille, 413
Lark, The, 466, 650
Larrimore, Earle, 528
Last Dance, The, 647
Last of Mrs. Cheyney, The, 448
Last of the Red Hot Lovers, The, 608
    609
"Last Time I Saw Paris, The," 691
Latent Heterosexual, The, 605
Latin manuscripts, 63
Latoudie, John, 647
Laughlan, Agnes, 495
Laughton, Charles, 454, 490-491
Laurents, Arthur, 603, 604
Laurie, John, 503
L'Avare, 624-625
    (see *The Miser*)
Lawrence, Gertrude, 695, 703
Lawrence, T. E., 441
Lawson, John Howard, 558
Lazarus Laughed, 523, 642
League of Youth, The, 424
Leave It to Jane, 672
Leave It to Me, 687
Lee, Nathaniel, 299
LeGallienne, Eva, 426 578, 580, 646.
Leger, Fernand, 415
legitimate theatres,

(see Patent Theatres)
Lehar, Franz, 658
Leigh, Andrew, 483, 485
Leigh, Vivien, 452, 495
Leighton, Margaret, 452, 488, 497
Lenea, 47
Leno, Dan, 282
Lensky, Alexander, 402
Lerner, Alan Jay, 708, 711, 719
   and Frederick Loewe, 708, 711, 719
   and Burton Lane, 719
Lesson, The, 474
"Let 'em Eat Cake," 707
Levine, Sam, 716-717
Levitt, John, 473
Lew Dockstader's Minstrels, 342-343
Lewis, James, 376
Lewis, Leopold, 285
Lewis, Robert, 557
Leybourne, George, 282
Libation Bearers, The, 24
Liberty Jones, 560
licensing, 98, 259-260, 264, 299-300
   301, 302, 306, 315, 316
licensing acts, 208, 259-260, 264, 280
Life and Death of Buonaparte, The,
   261
Life of Man, The, 576
lighting, 116, 127, 129, 132, 196-197,
   222, 223, 241, 251, 277, 282-283,
   293, 308, 315, 325, 345, 348, 349,
   364, 382, 398, 412, 421, 483, 485,
   506, 518, 547, 585, 633, 635, 638,
   641, 646, 651
   (see also Automation; Footlights)
Liliom, 578, 642, 695
Lillo, George, 298, 299
Lincoln, Abraham, 322, 352, 362
Lincoln Center for the Performing Arts,
   629, 651
Lincoln Center Repertory Company,
   579, 597, 622, 629, 630-631, 651
Lincoln Center Repertory Theater
   (see Lincoln Center Repertory Company)
Lincoln's Inn Fields (London), 177,
   179, 201, 202, 203, 204, 205, 208
Linden Tree, The, 457
Line, 617, 618

Linley, Elizabeth, 230-231
Linley, Dr., 230, 231
Little Eyolf, 426
Little Foxes, The, 549, 550-551, 552-
   553
Little Johnny Jones, 661, 662-663
Little Millionaire, The, 661
Little Minister, The, 361, 432
Little Nellie Kelly, 661
Littlewood, Joan, 468, 480, 506, 511
liturgical drama, 72-74
Livesey, Roger, 495
"Living Newspaper," 537
Living Room, The, 462
Living Theatre, The, 509, 615, 616
Livius Andronicus, 57
Lloyd, Marie, 282
Locascio, Michael, 620
Lock Up Your Daughters, 508
Lodge, Thomas, 108
Loeb Theatre (Harvard), 636
Loesser, Frank, 715
Loewe, Frederick, 708, 711, 719
Lohr, Marie, 447
Lomas, Herbert, 496
London Assurance, 274, 349
London Merchant, The, 298
Lonergan, Lenore, 562
Long and the Short and the Tall, The,
   472
Long Day's Journey Into Night, 521,
   530, 532, 533, 614
Long, John Luther, 381
Long Sunset, The, 456
Long Voyage Home, The, 521
Lonsdale, Frederick, 448
Look Back in Anger, 468, 469, 470, 488
"Look for the Silver Lining," 672
Lord Chamberlain, 208, 259, 264, 424,
   436
"Lord Chamberlain's Men, The", 100,
   106, 113
Lord Chumley, 381
Lord Conyngham, 264
Lost Colony, The, 556
Lost in the Stars, 711
Louis XIV, 160-161, 165
Louisiana Purchase, 680
Love à la Mode, 215

Love and a Bottle, 178
Love and Honour, 185
Love for Love, 177, 184, 186, 298, 301, 487, 491, 504, 505, 641
Love in a Tub, 184
Love in a Wood, 178
Love in Idleness, 450
Love of Four Colonels, The, 459
Lover, The, 155
"Lover Come Back to Me," 660
Lovers' Vows, 314
Love's Lost Shift; or, The Fool in Fashion, 201
Love's Old Sweet Song, 573
Lower Depths, The, 399, 404-405, 407, 409, 575
Luce, Claire, 688-689
Ludlow, Noah M., 324
Lun, 203
  (see also John Rich)
Lunt, Alfred, 448, 450, 451, 525, 562, 577, 644
Lunts, 544, 546, 548
Lute Song, 641
Luther, 469-471
Luzhsky, V. V., 407
Lyceum Theatre (London), 274, 278, 285, 289, 291, 293, 363
Lyceum Theatre (New York), 345, 378, 379, 477, 614
Lyly, John, 108
Lynch, Alfred, 500
Lynn, Eleanor, 557
Lyric Theatre (London), 456
Lyric Theatre, Hammersmith (London), 454
Lysistrata, 640, 642, 647

M

M.P., 279
Macbeth, 117, 215, 220, 226, 235, 251, 256, 261, 281, 317, 323, 328, 330, 334, 336, 337, 358, 485, 639
Maccus, 152
Macgowan, Kenneth, 519, 521, 522
MacDermott, Galt, 726

Machiavelli, Niccolo, 87
Macintosh, Kenneth, 498
MacKaye, Percy, 519
MacKaye, Steele, 349, 376, 377-378
MacLeish, Archibald, 600-601, 646
MacLiammoir, Micheal, 446
Macklin, Charles, 213, 215, 220, 224, 226
Macready, William Charles, 266, 267-270, 271, 274, 276, 327, 328, 333-336, 337, 481
Madame Bovary, 417
Madame Butterfly, 381
Madame Vestris (see Vestris)
Madame Violante, 209
Mlle. Modiste, 656, 657
Madison Square Garden (New York), 641
Madison Square Theatre, (New York), 349, 377, 379, 381, 384, 385, 386
Madras House, The, 443
Malden, Karl, 571
Maeterlinck, Maurice, 292, 401, 402, 442
Magnani, Anna, 587
Maharis, George, 618-619
Maid's Tragedy, The, 113, 509
Major Barbara, 440, 577, 644, 646
Majority of One, A, 644
make-up, 249-250, 281
Malade Imaginaire, Le, 160-161, 165
Malcolm, 603
Malina, Judith, 616
Malleson, Miles, 499
Malone, Mr. (18th century actor), 301
Malvern Festival, 442-443
Mamba's Daughters, 556
"mammy singers," 678
Man and Superman, 439, 443
Man and the Masses, 642
Man of Destiny, The, 436, 439
Man of Mode: or, Sir Fopling Flutter, The, 184
Man of the World, The, 215
Man Who Came to Dinner, The, 541
Man Who Had All the Luck, The, 591
Man Who Married a Dumb Wife, The, 638
Man Who Owns Broadway, The, 661
Mandragola, 87

Mann, Ted, 533

Manning, Mary, 446

Mansfield, Richard, 369, 370, 386, 436

mansion, 74, 75, 78-79, 83, 84, 85

Many Loves, 616

Marat/Sade (The Persecution and Assassination of Marat as Performed by the Inmates of the Asylum at Charenton under the Direction of the Marquis de Sade), 510, 605, 609, 620, 648-649

Marcellus, Theatre of, 62

March, Frederic, 427

Marco Millions, 523, 525, 577, 642

Margaret Fleming, 383

"Marie from Sunny Italy," 675

Marines' Memorial Theatre, 622

Marinsky Theatre, 414

Marivaux, Pierre de, 163, 167

Marks, Emmaretta, 724

Marlowe, Christopher, 105, 108-109, 112, 117, 454, 582

Marlowe, Julia, 368, 371, 380

Marriage à la Mode, 184

Marriage Brokers, The, 509

Marriage by Moonlight, 383

Marryat, Florence, 372

Marshall, E. G., 613

Marston, John, 109, 113, 122

Martin, Mary, 687, 695, 696-697, 698, 712, 713, 718-719

Martin, Nan, 601

Martin Beck Theatre (New York), 525, 528, 593

Mary of Scotland, 534, 535, 536

Mary Rose, 433

Mary Stuart, 454

Masefield, John, 442, 463

"Masks, The", 412

masks

    in Greek theatre, 20, 21, 31, 37, 38, 39, 40, 42, 43, 44, 45, 46

    in Roman theatre, 50, 54, 59

    in Middle Ages, 71, 82

    in Commedia dell'Arte, 137, 138, 144, 145, 146, 148, 149, 150, 151, 152

    in the 20th century, 523

Masque of Kings, The, 536

masques, 90, 128-129, 130, 131, 132, 135, 170, 172, 177, 194, 196

Massey, Raymond, 545, 601

Massinger, Philip, 113, 262, 323

Master Betty, 244-248

Master Builder, The, 426, 578

Matchmaker, The, 548, 715

"Matchmaker, Matchmaker," 723

Mathews, Charles (1776-1835), 272, 274, 349

Mathews, Charles James (1803-1878), 270-274, 451

matinees, 280

Matthews, A. E., 447

Maude, Charles, 434

Maugham, William Somerset, 446, 447, 487

Mavor, O. H. (see James Bridie)

Maxine Elliott Theatre (New York), 552

May, Elaine, 610

Mayakovsky, Vladimir, 419

Mayday or New York in an Uproar, 310

Mayden Queene, The, 193

Mayer, Edwin Justis, 614

Mayo, Frank, 379

Maytime, 660

McConnell, Frederic, 636

McCowan, Alex, 503

McCullers, Carson, 603

McEwan, Geraldine, 498

McGee, Florence, 552

McKenna, Siobhan, 446

McKnight Foundation, 628

McMahon, Aline, 683

McNally, Terence, 610, 611, 617

McVicker, Mary, 358, 359

Me and Juliet, 695

Medea, 28

Medieval theatre, 63, 67-86

Meilhac, Henri, 372, 376

Meisner, Sanford, 557

Melfi, Leonard, 620

Melmoth, Charlotte (Mrs.), 314

melodrama, 261, 276, 314, 346-347

Mermaid Theatre (London) 506, 508, 509

Memorial Theatre, Stratford-on-Avon, 485, 501, 504, 507

Memory of Two Mondays, A, 596, 600
Men and Women, 381
Men in White, 558-559, 646
Menander, 31, 41, 43, 46, 49, 57
Mendelsohn, Felix, 495
Menken, Helen, 534-535
Mercenary Match, The, 311
Merchant of Venice, The, 102, 121, 224, 233, 261, 300, 325, 381, 398, 483
Merchant, Vivien, 477
Merchant of Yonkers, The, 548
Mercury Theatre, 579, 582
Meredith, Burgess, 536
Merivale, Philip, 544
Merman, Ethel, 680, 681, 683, 701
Merrill, Beth, 381
Merrily We Roll Along, 541
Merry Malones, The, 661
Merry, Anne (Mrs.), 314
Merry Widow, The, 658
Merry Wives of Windsor, The, 129
Merton of the Movies, 563
Messallina, 134
Messel, Oliver, 494, 496
Metamora, 331
method, the, 392, 395, 407
   (see also Stanislavsky System)
metre, poetic, 21
Metropolitan Opera, 629
Metropolitan Opera House (New York), 687
Metropolitan Theatre (San Francisco), 357
Meyerhold, Vsevolod, 411, 412, 413, 414, 415, 416, 643
Mezzetino, 146, 147
Michener, James, 695, 712
Middle Comedy, 29, 30
Middle of the Night, 605
Middleton, Ray, 439, 680
Midsummer Night's Dream, A, 102, 108, 120, 495, 510, 575, 613
Mielziner, Jo, 528, 536, 593, 630-631, 633, 644, 647, 650-651
Milbourne, Mr. (scene painter), 316
Miles, Bernard, 508
Miles, G. H., 330
Milk Train Doesn't Stop Here Any-

more, The, 590
Miller, Arthur, 427, 583, 590, 591-600, 604, 622, 629, 646, 651
Miller, Gilbert, 579
Miller, Henry, 371, 379, 380, 388, 389
Miller, Marilyn, 672, 701
Miller Theatre (Milwaukee), 636
Millionairess, The, 441, 563, 577
Mills, John, 495
Milton, Ernest, 483
Milton, John, 171
mimes, 63, 70, 71, 137
   (See also Commedia dell'Arte; Pantomime)
Minnesota Theatre Company, The, 622, 623, 624, 628
minstrel show, 338, 339, 340, 341-344, 350, 678
minstrels, 67-72, 137
   schools for minstrels, 69-70
   town minstrels, 70-72)
Miracle, The, 575, 641
miracle plays (see Mystery plays)
Miracle Worker, The, 605
Misalliance, 440
Misanthrope, The, 165, 178
Miser, The, 624-625, 628
Miss in Her Teens, 302
Miss Julie, 512
Miss Liberty, 680
Miss Mabel, 456
Mitchell, Cameron, 598-599
Mlle. Modiste, 656, 657
Modest Soldier, The, or Love in New York, 312
Modjeska, Helen, 371, 376
Moeller, Philip, 525, 528, 576
Mohun, Michael, 191
Molière, 31, 160-161, 162, 163, 165, 167, 178, 324, 578, 616, 624-625
Molnar, Ferenc, 546, 577, 578, 645, 695
Moment of Truth, The, 459
Money, 280
Monoply theatres (see Patent Theatres)
Monsieur Beaucaire, 369
Montague, H. J., 376
Montgomery, David, 654-655
Month in the Country, A, 512
Moody, William Vaughan, 387-389

Moon of the Caribees, The, 521
Moon for the Misbegotten, A, 521, 530, 531
Moore, Grace, 680
Moore, Melba, 724
Moore, Victor, 703
morality plays, 83, 85-86
Moran, Lois, 694
More Stately Mansions, 521, 614
"More Than You Know," 700
Morgan, Charles, 458
Morgan, Helen, 690
Morgan, Frank, 711
Morley College, 482
Morley, Robert, 495
Morning, 617, 618
Morozov, Sara, 393, 406
Morris, Clara, 376
Morris, Mary, 519, 521, 523, 566
Moscow Art Theatre, The, 391-407, 408, 409, 410, 413, 414, 418, 504, 566, 573, 575
Moscow Small Theatre, 402
Moskvin, Ivan, 402, 407, 575
Most Happy Fella, The, 715
Mostel, Zero, 613, 720-721, 722, 723
Moth and the Flame, The, 386
Mother Courage, 622
Mother Goose, 249, 250
Mountfort, Susanna (Mrs.), 177, 194
Mountfort, William, 191
Mourning Becomes Electra, 528, 529, 577
Mousetrap, The, 511
Mower, Margaret, 576
Mr. Antonio, 368
"Mr. Broadway," 662
Mr. Wilkinson's Widows, 385
Mr. President, 680
Mrs. Warren's Profession, 436, 576
Much Ado About Nothing, 118, 357, 494
Muni, Paul, 537, 593
Munro, C. K. 442
Murder in the Cathedral, 463, 464, 465
Murdoch, Iris, 457
Murray, Professor Gilbert, 41
Murray, Walter, 298
Music Box, The, 680

music hall, 61, 167, 280-282, 345
Music in the Air, 675, 690
music, in theatrical performances
    in ancient Greece, 18, 19, 20, 21, 32, 44, 47, 51
    in Elizabethan Theatre, 127, 128-129
    in Commedia dell'Arte, 142, 156, 158, 163
    in Restoration, 172, 196
    in 18th century, 202, 203, 208, 214
    in 19th century, 259, 260, 261, 280-282
    in American Theatre, 297, 309, 315, 338-344, 345, 495, 506, 453-726
Music Master, The, 381
musical comedy, 511, 543, 553, 653-726 (see also Burlesque)
musical instruments, 18, 19, 20, 69, 84
Mustapha, 187
My Fair Lady, 440, 642, 710-711, 719, 723
"My Heart Belongs to Daddy," 687
"My Heart Stood Still," 687
My Heart's in the Highlands, 572, 573
MY LIFE IN ART, 407
MY LIFE IN THE RUSSIAN THEATRE, 398
"My Mammy," 678
"My Wife's in the Country," 675
mystery plays, 73, 78-79, 80-85, 86, 87

N

Naevius, 49, 57
Nassau Street Theatre (New York), 298, 300
Nashe, Thomas, 108
Nathan Hale, 386
National Theatre (London), (see Old Vic)
National Theatre (New York), 345, 647
National Theatre Company, The (see Old Vic)
NATIVE SON, 556
Naughty Marietta, 656, 657
Nazimova, Alla, 426
Negro, 675

Neighborhood Playhouse, 683
Nelson, Ruth, 557
Nemirovich-Danchenko, Vladimir, 392-394, 396-397, 398, 414
Nero, 61, 63
Nesbitt, Cathleen, 496
New American Company, The, 312-313, 314, 315, 316
New Comedy, 29, 30-32, 57, 42, 43, 46, 49, 51, 52
New Exhibition Room, 315
New Life, A, 537
New Moon, 660
NEW THEATRE, A, 628
New Theatre (Charleston, Virginia), 298
New Theatre (London), (see Old Vic)
New Tivoli (London), 280
New Way to Pay Old Debts, A, 262, 323
New York Philharmonic Symphony Orchestra, 629
New York Repertory Company (see Lincoln Center Repertory Company)
New York Shakespeare Festival, 633 (see also Shakespeare-in-the-Park)
New York Shakespeare Festival Theatre (Delacorte Theatre), 724
New York Theatre, 354, 372
Newcombe, Mary, 494
Next, 610, 617
Ney, Marie, 485
Niblo's Garden (New York), 345, 653
"Night and Day," 683
Night Music, 572
Night Must Fall, 457
Night of the Iguana, 589, 647
Night over Taos, 534, 536, 557
"Night Was Made for Love, The," 672
1931, 557
No, No, Nanette, 691, 692-693, 700
No Song, No Supper, 248
No Strings, 700
No Time for Comedy, 548
Noah, 487
Noakes, John, 473
Nobel Prize, 529
    Eugene O'Neill, 529
Nohes, James, 191

Noon, 610, 617
Norman, Frank, 511
North Carolina University, 637
North Dakota State University, 637
Nottingham Playhouse (England), 512

O

O Mistress Mine, 450, 453
O. P. Riots, 251-255, 256
O'Casey, Sean, 445, 460, 461
Octoroon, The, 348, 350, 351
Odd Couple, The, 609
Odets, Clifford, 566, 567-572, 646
Oedipus Coloneus, 27, 509
Oedipus complex, 28
Oedipus the King, 27-28, 509
Oenslager, Donald, 519, 521, 644-646
Of Mice and Men, 644
Of Thee I Sing, 541, 694, 706
Off-Broadway, 610-611, 613-616, 617-621
Offenbach, Jacques, 653
Offner, Debbie, 724-725
Oh Boy, 672
Oh! Calcutta!, 609, 620-621
"Oh, How I Hate to Get Up in the Morning," 679
"Oh Kay," 703
"Oh, Lady Be Good," 703
Oh What a Lovely War, 511
O'Hara, John, 711
Ohio Roscius, 59
Oklahoma! 553, 690, 691, 695, 707
OL' MAN ADAM AN' HIS CHILLUN, 547
Old Bachelor, The, 177
Old Comedy, 29, 30, 40
Old Vic, 275, 443, 456, 461, 465, 480-485, 487, 490, 491, 494, 495 496-497, 498, 499, 500, 512, 593, 623
Oldfield, Anne, 186
Oldmixon, Georgina (Mrs.), 316
Oliver Cromwell, 454
Oliver Twist, 337
Oliver, Sir Laurence, 452, 461, 466, 469, 489, 492, 493, 494, 495, 496, 497, 499, 512

Olympic Theatre (London), 264, 271, 273

On a Clear Day You Can See Forever, 719

On Approval, 448

"On My Mind the Whole Night Long," 702

On the Spot, 490

"On the Street Where You Live," 719

On the Town, 715

On Trial, 537

On With the Dance, 448

On Your Toes, 698

Once in a Lifetime, 541

"One Kiss," 660

O'Neal, William, 658, 659

O'Neill, Eugene, 371, 418, 446, 518, 519, 532, 576, 577, 614, 622, 641, 642, 643, 646, 661

O'Neill, Eugene (Mrs.), 532, 614

O'Neill, Henry, 521

O'Neill, James, 371, 519

O'Neill, Maire, 446

O'Neill, Raymond, 636

Onkos, 45

Open Air Theatre, Regent's Park London, 485

Opera House, The, 310 (see also Southwark Theatre)

operetta, 653, 655, 656, 657, 658, 660, 668, 669, 695

Optimistic Tragedy, The, 417

Orange Blossoms, 656

orchestra (in Greek theatres) 32, 33

Oresteia, The, 23, 24, 25

Orestes, 27

Orlando Furioso, 87

Orphan, The, 186, 187, 297, 298

Orpheus Decending, 583

Osborne, Hubert, 519

Osborne, John, 468, 500

Ostler, William, 121

Othello, 113, 117, 124, 135, 192, 215, 262-263, 267, 309, 317, 325, 326, 327, 328, 330, 363, 364, 460, 487, 492, 640

O'Toole, Peter, 500

Otway, Thomas, 184, 186, 187, 297

Our American Cousin, 322, 351, 352, 362

Our Betters, 447

Our Boys, 376

Our Town, 547, 549, 554-555, 614

Ours, 279

Ouspenskaya, Maria, 575

"Over There," 661

Owen, Reginald, 447

Owens, Rochelle, 620

P

Padlock, The, 328

Page, Geraldine, 614

Paint Your Wagon, 719

Pal Joey, 698, 719

Palace Theatre (London), 504

Palais-Royal, 161

Palladio, Andrea, 88, 162

pallium, 51

Palmer, A. H., 385

Pantagleuze, 614

Pantalone, 137, 147, 148, 150, 151, 159, 167

Pantaloon, 484 (see Pantalone)

pantomime, 61, 64, 141, 167, 202, 203, 208, 227, 249, 250, 255, 259, 260, 261, 270, 282, 297, 299, 313, 315

Papp, Joseph, 620, 632-633, 724

Papposilinus, 20

Paradise Lost, 568

parasite, 42

Paris, 683

Parson's Wedding, The, 174

Paris Bound, 560

Park Theatre (New York), 315, 317, 321, 322, 323, 324-325, 328, 329, 333, 345

Party, The, 558

Pasadena Playhouse, The, 636

Passion Play, 575

Passion of Joseph D., The, 605

Past Imperfect, 453

pastoral, 90, 109

Patent Theatres, 170, 174, 201, 209, 212, 259, 260, 261, 264, 268, 273, 274, 280, 298

patents, 170, 171, 243, 259, 260, 274, 280, 293

Patience, 641
Paton, Alan, 509, 711
Paul Pry, 271
Payment Deferred, 490
Payne, John Howard, 324, 325
Peace, The, 35
Pedrolino (see Pierrot)
Peele, George, 108
Peer Gynt, 369, 424, 484, 496, 644,
    645
Pemberton, Reese, 497
Penthouse Theatre, 638
Pepys, Samuel, 164, 185, 189, 228
Percy, Esme, 495
performances
    in ancient Greece, 51, 52,
    in ancient Rome, 57-58
    and the Christian Church, 65
    in the Middle Ages, 72-74, 76, 79-80,
        85
    Renaissance, 87
    Elizabethan, 94
    Restoration, 180-181
    18th Century, 206-208, 240-241
    19th Century, 251-255, 258, 281-282,
        333-336
Peri Keiromene, 41
Period of Adjustment, 590
Perkins, Osgood, 519
*Persecution and Assassination of Marat
    as Performed by the Inmates of the
    Asylum at Charenton under the Di-
    rection of the Marquis de Sade, The,*
    510, 605, 609, 620, 648-649
Persians, The, 24
Peter Pan, 361, 432, 441, 647
Peters, Paul, 581
Peters, Rollo, 576
Petrified Forest, The, 544, 545
Phaedra, 28
phallus, 21, 31, 38, 40, 43, 137, 150
Phelps, Samuel, 274-276, 293, 481
Philadelphia Story, The, 560, 561,
    562, 563
Philanderer, The, 436
Philaster, 113
Philharmonic Dramatic Academy
    (Moscow), 392, 414
Phillips, Augustine, 100

Philoctetes, 27
Phoenix-APA, 614, 616
Phoenix-Theatre (London), 170, 171,
    172, 173
    (see also Cockpit)
Phoenix Theatre (New York),
    614, 616, 642
Phoenix Too Frequent, A, 466
Photo Finish, 461
Phylakes, 44, 49
Pichel, Irving, 519
Pickford, Mary, 381
Pickwick, 285
Picnic, 604
Pierrot, 137, 154-155
Pillars of Society, The, 426, 429
Pinero, Sir Arthur Wing, 279, 286, 287,
    292, 367
Pinter, Harold, 475-477, 480, 626
Pinza, Ezio, 695, 712, 713
Pipe Dream, 695
Pirandello, Luigi, 474, 509, 616
pirating, 258-259, 350, 378
Pisistratus, 22
Pit, The, 206, 238, 239, 240, 251, 255,
    273, 277, 304
Pizarro, 231, 244, 314
Placide, Alexandre (Mr. and Mrs.),
    313, 315, 324
plagiarizing, 258-259, 350
plagues, 97, 98, 177
Plain Dealer, The, 178
Plaintiff in a Pretty Hat, The, 453
Planché, J. R., 268, 273
platforms (see Theatre buildings)
Plautus, 41, 42, 57, 137, 138, 548, 720
Play, 279
playbills, 211, 214, 248, 264-265, 277,
    332, 340, 353, 358-359, 714
Playboy of the Western World, The,
    444
Players' Club, 351, 363
Playfair, Nigel, 454
Playhouse Theatre, (London), 496
playhouses (see Theatre buildings)
"Plays, Pleasant and Unpleasant," 436
Plaza Suite, 609
Pleasance, Donald, 477
Plough and the Stars, The, 445

Plowright, Joan, 471
Plummer, Christopher, 601
Plymouth Theatre (New York), 641
Poel, William, 482, 484
poetry in drama, 463, 467
   (see also Greece, 17-56)
"Polichinelly," 164
Pollock, Ellen, 441
Polyneices, 28
Poor Little Ritz Girl, 687
Poor Soldier, The, 310, 312
Pope, Alexander, 215, 229
Pope, Thomas, 100, 120
Poppy, 677
Porgy, 553, 577, 703
PORGY, 703
Porgy and Bess, 556, 702, 703, 704-705
portable stages
   in Greece, 22
   in Middle Ages, 78-79, 81
   Commedia dell'Arte, 158, 166
   (see also Theatre buildings)
Porter, Cole, 683-687, 688, 690, 701, 707
Portman, Eric, 452
posters, 346-347
Pot Luck, 636
Potting Shed, The, 462, 487
Powell, Dawn, 558
Powell, (American actor), 316
"Power and the Glory, The," 462
Power of Darkness, The, 399
Powers, Tom, 528
Pownall, Mrs. (actress), 314
Present Laughter, 449
Pretenders, The, 424
Previn, Andre, 719
Price, The, 600
Price, Leontyne, 703
Price, Nancy, 471, 483
Price, Stephen, 317, 321
Priestley, J. B., 442, 456-457, 487
prima donna, 157
Prince Ananias, 655, 656
Prince of Parthia, The, 306
Prince of Wale's Theatre (London), 278, 291
Princess, The, 174

Princess Pat, The, 656
Princess Turandot, 418
Princess's Theatre (London), 268, 270, 274, 278, 279
Prisoner of Zenda, The, 368
Prisoners, The, 173, 174
Pritchard, Mrs. Hannah, 220
Private Life of Henry VIII, The, 490
Private Lives, 448
prizes (see Competitions)
Prodigal, The, 617
production costs
   in ancient Greece, 50
   in Middle Ages, 76
   during Restoration, 185
   19th Century, 251, 255, 285, 364
   20th Century, 483, 633, 636, 665, 666
Professor, The, 384
Promises, Promises, 609
Promotheus, 25
Promotheus Bound, 24, 25, 646
prompter, 75, 80
properties
   in Greece, 27, 34, 35
   in Middle Ages, 70
   Commedia dell'Arte, 158
   Elizabethan, 123
   18th century, 218-219, 309
   19th century, 250
   20th century, 484, 628, 633
Proposal, The, 401
proscenium, 84, 176, 183, 195, 222, 232, 251, 257, 319, 345, 484, 508, 509, 633, 638
proscenium doors, 176, 183, 195, 207, 221, 222, 232, 246, 247, 305, 319, 329
Provincetown Players, 521-522, 524, 611, 618
Provok'd Husband, The, 186
Provok'd Wife, The, 179, 184, 223
Public Theatre, The, 620
Puccini, Giacomo, 381
Pulcinella, 150, 152, 153
Pulitzer Prize, 522, 536
   Anna Christie, 522
   Beyond the Horizon, 522
   Both Your Houses, 536

Death of a Salesman, 593
Green Pastures, 566
Idiot's Delight, 544
In Abraham's Bosom, 556
J. B., 601
Men in White, 559
No Place To Be Somebody, 620
Of Thee I Sing, 706
South Pacific, 712
Street Scene, 537
Time of Your Life, The, 572, 575
You Can't Take It With You, 541
Pully, B. S., 716-717
Punch and Judy, 64, 167
  (See also Pulcinella)
Punchinello (see Pulcinela)
puppet theatres, 167
Purdy, James, 603
Puritans, 94, 97, 169, 171, 172, 180,
  295, 296, 297
Pygmalion, 287, 440, 577, 646, 711, 719

Q

Quaker, The, 252
Quality Street, 361, 432
Quare Fellow, The, 511
Quayle, Anthony, 495, 501, 600
Queen Anne, 194, 199
Queen Henrietta Maria, 170, 171
Queen Victoria, 269-270, 277
Queen's Husband, The, 544
"Queen's Men, The," 97
Queen's Theatre (London), 251, 278
Quick, John, 230
Quin, James, 207, 212, 215, 216, 217,
  229
Quintero, Jose, 533, 578, 613, 614
"Quintessence of Ibsenism, The," 437

R

Rabb, Ellis, 614, 616
Rachel, Mlle., 278
Racine, Jean, 165, 324
Rado, James, 724

Ragni, Gerome, 724, 726
Rahere, 68
Rainbow, 700
Rainbow number, 670-671
Raisin in the Sun, A, 605
raked stage, 319
Raleigh, Sir Walter, 114-115
Ranbrugh, Irene, 447
Rats, 617, 618
Rattigan, Terence, 450, 452, 453
realism, 278, 280, 293, 364
Rebellion, 453
Recruiting Officer, The, 178, 184, 202,
  209, 296, 298
"Recueil Fossard," 158
Red Bull Playhouse, 116
Red Mill, The, 654-655
Red Petticoat, The, 672
Redgrave, Michael, 494, 512, 572
Redman, Joyce, 497, 504, 505
Reed, John, 521
Régnier, François, 377
Rehan, Ada, 368, 371, 326
Rehearsal, The, 231
rehearsals, 189, 268, 293, 328, 395-
  397, 566
Reinagle, Alexander, 312, 316
Reinhardt, Max, 575, 641
Réjane, Gabrielle-Charlotte, 366
Relapse, The, 179
religious drama (see Church; Liturgi-
  cal drama; Miracle play; Mystery
  play; Hell mouth)
religious festivals, 17, 18
  in ancient Greece, 21, 22, 29, 33, 47,
    53, 55, 56
  (see also Competitions)
Relph, George, 497
Reluctant Debutante, The, 453
Reluctant Peer, The, 453
Renaissance, 63, 84, 86, 87-91
Repertory Theatre of Lincoln Center
  (See Lincoln Center Repertory
    Company)
Republic Theatre (New York), 382
Restoration, 85, 120, 169-197, 199, 200,
  206, 222, 228, 241, 258, 259, 430
Return of Peter Grimm, The, 381
Return of the Vagabond, The, 661
Reunion in Vienna, 544, 545, 546

Revere, Anne, 552
Reverend Griffith Davenport, The, 383
"Rhapsody in Blue," 703
Rhinoceros, 474, 612
Rhodes, Erik, 688-689
Rhodes, John, 185
Riccoboni, 142
Rice, Elmer, 446, 537-541, 544, 577, 643, 647
Rice, Thomas D., 338, 339, 341, 344
Rich, Christopher, 201
Rich, John, 201, 202, 203, 204, 205, 206, 207, 208, 209, 212, 213, 215
Richard II, 264, 265, 485, 491
Richard III, 113, 247, 261, 298, 321, 322, 323, 326, 354, 355, 357, 381, 484, 485
Richards, N., 134
Richardson, Ian, 503, 620
Richardson, Jack, 617
Richardson, Sir Ralph, 447, 456, 458, 487, 488, 491, 495, 496, 497, 499, 514
Richelieu, 358, 362
Ricketts, Charles, 490
Riders to the Sea, 444
Rigg, Diana, 503
Riggs, Lynn, 553, 690
Right You Are If You Think You Are, 509
Ring Around the Moon, 466
riots in the theatre, 60, 238, 240, 251, 255, 256, 327, 333-336
Rip Van Winkle, 348, 351, 352, 353
Rise of Rosie O'Reilly, The, 661
Ristori, Adelaide, 366
Rivals, The, 229, 230, 231, 309, 351
River Like, 458
Rix, Brian, 511
Road to Rome, The, 544
Roadside, 553
Roar China, 643
Robards, Jason, 530-531, 547, 614
Robbins, Jerome, 720
Robert and Elizabeth, 454
Robert E. Lee, 454
Roberta, 675
"Roberts-Campbells plays," 383
Robertson, Agnes, 349, 350
Robertson, Tom, 278-279, 280, 282

Robeson, Paul, 487, 522
Robin Hood, 655
Robinson, Judith, 606-607
Robinson, Lennox, 444
Robson, Flora, 424, 490
Robson, May, 379, 380
Robson, Stuart, 378
Rock, The, 463
Rocket to the Moon, 572
Rodd, Marcia, 608
Rodgers, Richard, 553, 661, 675, 683, 687-690, 698, 699, 711, 712, 713
    and Lorenz Hart, 661, 683, 687, 690, 698, 699, 711
    and Oscar Hammerstein II, 675, 690-700, 707, 712
    and Stephen Sondheim, 700
Rogers, Paul, 477
Rogers, Will, 529, 665
Romanoff and Juliet, 461
Romberg, Sigmund, 657, 658-660, 682-683, 687
Rome, 33, 57-65, 67, 137, 138, 152
Romeo and Juliet, 102, 118, 127, 220, 261, 264-265, 338, 358, 359, 416, 485, 647
Roos, Joanna, 683
Roots, 471, 472
Roscius, 59
Rose, The, 99, 102, 117
Rose Tattoo, The, 587, 646
Rose-Marie, 658
Rosen, Julius, 372
Rosmersholm, 426, 429
Roth, Lillian, 669
Rowe, Nicolas, 299, 301-302
Roxana, 99
Royal Circus (London), 260
Royal Coburg Theatre (London), 481
Royal Court Theatre (London), 468, 470, 500
Royal Dramatic Theatre, 533
Royal Family, The, 541
"Royal Family of Broadway," 366-367
Royal Hunt of the Sun, The, 512
Royal Shakespeare Company (England), 471, 495, 501, 502, 507, 510, 626
Royal Victoria Theatre (London), 481
Ruben, Jose, 576

Rugged Path, The, 545
Russet Mantle, 553
Rucellai, 87
Runyon, Damon, 715
Russell, Annie, 371
Russell, George William, 444
Russell, Lillian, 371
Russians, The, 496
Ruy Blas, 278, 362
Ryskind, Morris, 707

S

S. S. Glencairn, 521
" 'S Wonderful," 703
Saarinen, Eero, 629, 630, 631, 633
sack of Rome, 65
Sackler, Howard, 605, 627
"Sadie Salome Go Home," 675
Sadler's Wells (London), 249, 274, 275, 276, 490, 495, 623
Sag Harbor, 383
Saint Apollonia, 75
St. Denis, Michel, 459
St. Helena, 455
Saint Joan, 440, 577
St. James's Theatre (London), 278, 292, 431, 510-511
St. James Theatre (New York), 377
Salisbury Court, 177
Salle, Mlle., 227
Sally, 672
Salome, 432
Salvation Nell, 360
Salvini, Tommaso, 364, 366
Samia, 41
Sandbox, The, 617
Sands, Dorothy, 683
Sanford, Erskine, 577
Sarah Lawrence College, 637
Saratoga, 378
Sardou, Victorien, 372
Saroyan, William, 572-575
Sartre, Jean-Paul, 629
satire, 21
Saturday's Children, 534
satyr chorus, 19, 20, 22
satyr-plays, 20, 21, 24, 30

satyrs, 19, 20
Sound of Music, The, 695, 698, 718, 719
Saunders, Florence, 483
Savo, Jimmy, 669, 699
Savoy Theatre (London), 282, 443, 487
"Say It with Music," 680
"Say, Young Man of Manhattan," 701
Scala, Flaminio, 141-142
Scala Theatre (London), 278
Scamozzi, Vincenzo, 88
Scapino, 145, 146
Scaramouche, 149, 152
scenerii, 138, 141
scenery and settings,
  in ancient Greece, 27, 34, 51
  in ancient Rome, 58
  in Middle Ages, 72-75, 78-79, 80, 81
  Renaissance, 86-87
  Elizabethan, 122-124, 131, 132, 135
  Commedia dell'Arte, 158, 162
  Restoration, 170, 171, 172, 173, 182, 183, 196
  English 18th century, 207, 217, 223, 225, 232, 240-241
  American 18th century, 304-305, 309, 315, 316, 319
  English 19th century, 246-247, 250, 256, 257, 260, 268, 269, 276, 277, 278, 280, 282-283, 285, 293
  American 19th century 345, 358, 363, 382
  Russian, 398, 403, 410-412, 414-421
  English 20th century, 483, 484-485, 494, 496, 506, 515
  American 20th century, 518, 524, 525, 526, 528, 538, 540, 542, 547, 550, 552, 554, 559, 561, 562, 563-566, 570, 580, 582, 585, 586, 593, 594, 597, 598, 601, 606, 612, 628, 630-631, 633, 634-635, 638-651, 653, 662, 665, 674, 684, 691, 692, 694, 696, 704, 708, 710, 713, 717, 718, 720
  (see also Backboard; Backdrop; Box set; Curtains; Cyclorama; Diorama; Flats; Flies; Gallery; Lighting; Properties; Shutters Stage; Stage devices; Staging;

Theatre buildings Trap door; Trolley; Wings)

Schnitzler, 578

scholar-playwrights, 91, 106, 108, 135

School, 279

School for Scandal, The, 229, 231, 232, 310, 614

School for Wives, 165, 616

Schwartz, Arthur, 711

Scofield, Paul, 503, 510

Scornful Lady, The, 113, 210

Scotland, 454-455

Scott, Sir Walter, 338

Scottish National Players, 455

screens, 34, 232

Seagull, The, 396, 398, 400, 402, 404-405, 406, 414

Sears, David 446

seating
    in ancient Greece 33, 34, 53, 54, 55, 56
    in England, 206, 228, 251, 255, 257, 273, 277, 319, 329, 363, 483, 513, 622, 624, 628, 631, 633
    (see also Audience Boxes; Gallery; Performances; the Pit)

Second Mrs. Tanqueray, The, 286, 287

Second Man, The, 548

Secret Service, 385

See America First, 683

Sejanus, 109

Seneca, 57, 63, 108

Separate Tables, 452

Serenade, The, 656

Serena Blandish, 548

Serlio, Sebastiano, 86-87, 90

settings (see Scenery and Settings)

Settle, Elkanah, 182, 183

Seven Against Thebes, 24

Seven Descents of Myrtle, The, 590

Severed Head, The, 457

Seyler, Athene, 491

Sganarelle, 105

Shadow of a Gunman, 445

Shaffer, Peter, 500, 512

Shakespeare Festival,
    Stratford, Connecticut, 636-637
    Stratford, Ontario, 623

Shakespeare-in-the-Park, 632, 633, 634-635, 636

(see also Festival Mobile Theatre; Joseph Papp; Delacorte Theatre; Astor Library; New York Shakespeare Festival)

Shakespeare Memorial
    Theatre, Stratford-on-Avon, 485, 501, 504, 507
    (see also Royal Shakespeare Company)

Shakespeare Theatre (Liverpool), 512

SHAKESPEARE OUR CONTEMPORARY, 503

Shakespeare Theatre (Ontario, Canada) 513

Shakespeare, William, 24, 97, 98, 100, 102, 103-108, 109, 113, 114-115, 117, 118, 119, 120, 121, 122, 123, 126, 127, 129, 130, 131, 132, 135, 148, 167, 170, 177, 181, 189, 196, 208, 213, 220, 226, 227, 234, 238, 244, 256, 261, 262, 268, 274, 281, 285, 290, 291, 292, 299, 328, 339, 358, 370, 376, 380, 398, 406, 443, 446, 482, 483, 484, 487, 496, 499, 500, 501, 504, 563, 575, 578, 632, 633, 634, 636, 637, 699

"Shall We Dance?" 695

Shannon, Effie, 379

Shaughraun, The, 348, 349

Shaw, George Bernard, 286, 287, 289, 291, 369, 371, 424, 425, 435-443, 446, 487, 488, 496, 563, 576, 577, 622, 642, 645, 646, 719

Shaw, Irwin, 557, 572, 646

Shaw, Mary, 436

Shaw, Robert, 500

Shaw, Ronald, 477

She Stoops to Conquer, 226, 229, 310

She Would and She Would Not, 376

She Would If She Could, 184

Sheldon, Edward, 360, 518

Shenandoah, 378, 379

Shepard, Sam, 620

Sheppy, 446, 447, 487

Sheridan, Richard Brinsley, 167, 229-232, 237, 243, 257, 310, 314, 442, 484

Sheridan, Thomas, 229, 231, 234

Sherlock Holmes, 385

Sherriff, R. C., 455-456

Shirley, James, 131

Shoemaker's Holiday, 113, 504, 582
Shor, Elaine, 610
Shore Acres, 383
Show Boat, 672, 675, 690, 700
Show Girl, 693
Show Off, The, 614
Shubert brothers, 382
   (see also Jacob Shubert; Lee Shubert; Sam Shubert)
Shuter, Edward, 230
shutters, 182
Siddons, Sarah (Mrs.), 227, 233-238, 243, 244, 250, 251, 252, 253, 255, 256, 257, 312, 317
Siddons, William, 233
Sidewalks of New York, The, 349
Siege of Rhodes, The, 171, 172, 173, 192
Sifton, Claire and Paul, 557
Silk Stockings, 687
Silver Box, The, 433
Silver Tassle, The, 445
Simon, Neil, 608, 609
Simonov, Konstantin, 496
Simonson, Lee, 519, 525, 576, 642-645
Simov, Victor, 398
"Sing for Your Supper," 690
Singer, John, 120
sinking stage, 278
"Sir Henry Unton's Wedding," 129
Sirocco, 448
Sketch Book Review, The, 669
Skin of Our Teeth, The, 547-548, 549
Skinner, Otis, 368, 370, 386
Sklar, George, 581
Slapstick Tragedy, 590
Slavins Original American Troupe, 346-347
Sleeping Clergyman, A, 455
Sleeping Prince, The, 452, 453
sliding stage, 283
Smiles, 701
Smith, Art, 557
Smith, C. Aubrey, 447

Smock Alley Theatre (Dublin), 237
"Smoke Gets in Your Eyes", 675
Smug Citizens, 399
Soccus, 39, 51
Society, 279
Socrates, 26
Sofonisba, 87
"Soft Lights and Sweet Music," 680
"Softly as in a Morning Sunrise," 660
"Some Enchanted Evening," 695, 712, 713
"Somebody Loves Me," 702
"Someone to Watch Over Me," 703
Sometime, 658
"Sometimes I'm Happy," 700
"Song Is You, The," 690
Sons and Soldiers, 572
Sophocles, 17, 23, 26, 27-28, 29, 33, 34, 53, 57, 398, 509
Sothern, E. A., 278, 351, 352
Sothern, Edwin Hugh, 368, 371, 379
Soubrette, The, 157
Sondheim, Stephen, 700, 720
sound effects, 203, 506
South Pacific, 695, 712, 713, 723
Southern Theatre (Louisville), 339
Southerne, Thomas, 187, 237
Southwark Theatre, The, 304, 308, 309, 310
   (see also Opera House)
Sovey, Raymond, 646
Spanish Art Theatre, 575
Spanish Fryar, The, 298
Spanish Tragedy, The, 108, 110, 117
Speaight, Robert, 455
spectacle, 63, 64, 135, 208, 215, 255, 261, 270, 276, 313, 344, 345, 653
Squire, William, 465
Staff, May, 296
stage,
   in Greece, 22, 33
   in Rome, 58
   in Middle Ages, 75, 78-79
   Renaissance, 84

English 19th century, 246-247, 251, 257, 278, 283

English 20th century, 484, 508, 509, 513

American before 1900, 304-305, 319, 345, 363

American—20th century, 624, 630-631-634-635, 638

(see also Apron stage; Arena stage; Curtain; Gallery; Portable stages; Proscenium; Proscenium doors; Raked stage; Scenery and settings; Sinking stage; Sliding stage; Stage boxes; Stage devices; Staging; Theatre buildings; Thrust stage)

stage boxes, 176, 183, 195, 221, 232, 246-247, 257, 319, 363

stage devices,
    in Green Theatre, 35, 51
    in Rome Theatre, 58
    in Middle Ages, 81-82
    Elizabethan, 111, 122, 123, 132
    in Commedia dell'Arte, 159, 162
    Restoration, 171, 172, 177
    18th century, 203, 218-219, 225
    19th century, 282-283, 329, 363, 364, 377, 378
    20th century, 633, 638
    (See also Crane; Curtain; *Deux ex machina,* Trap door; Trolley; Screens; Lighting; Stage effects)

Stage Door, 541, 644

stage effects, 225
    (See also Blackout; Curtain; Lighting; Scenery and settings; Sound effects; Stage devices; Staging)

stage settings (see scenery and settings)

Stage Society, 423, 436

"Stagehands," 628

Stagg, Charles, 296

staging
    in ancient Greece, 27, 32-36, 40
    in Rome, 58-59
    in Middle Ages, 72-75, 78-79, 85

240-241

English 19th century, 246-247, 257, 260, 268, 276, 277, 282, 283, 293

American (before 1900), 345, 372, 382, 406, 414-421

English 20th century, 484-485, 506, 508, 515

American 20th Century, 518, 523, 547, 554, 562, 585, 598, 601, 616, 630-631, 635

    (see also Costumes; Curtains; Gallery; Lighting; Portable stages; Properties; Scenery and settings; Sound effects; Stage; Stage devices; Theatre buildings)

Stallings, Laurence, 532

Stanford University, 637

Stanislavska, Marie Lilina, 407

Stanislavsky, Constantin, 392-408, 413, 414, 418, 506, 575

Stanislavsky Rehearses Othello, 407

Stanislavsky System, The, 392, 395, 407, 575
  (see also The Method)

Star Theatre (New York), 379

Star Wagon, The, 536

Starr, Frances, 381

Stead, Estelle, 483

Steele, Sir Richard, 299

Stevedore, 580-581

Stewart, Elaine, 620

Stewart, James, 616

stock characters, 31, 32, 42, 51, 63, 167
  (see also Commedia dell'Arte)

stock plots (see Commedia dell'Arte)

Stoll Theatre (London), 511

Stone, Fred, 654-655

Stone, John Augustus, 330

Stop! Look! Listen! 679

Storey, David, 514

Story for Strangers, A, 566

Stow, John, 114-115

Stowe, Harriet Beecher, 344, 345, 346-

Stratford-on-Avon Memorial Theatre, 485, 501, 504, 507
Strauss, Johann, 653
Straw, The, 522
Street Scene, 537, 538-539, 540-541, 647
Streetcar Named Desire, A, 584, 585
Streisand, Barbra, 669
Strife, 434
Strike Up the Band, 541
Strindberg, Arthur, 424, 446, 512, 577, 647
Strode, W. Chetham, 453
Stallings, Laurence, 532
Student Prince in Heidelberg, The, 660
Success Story, 558
Suddenly Last Summer, 589
Sullivan, Ed, 610
Sullivan, Francis L., 485
Summer and Smoke, 585, 614
Sunken Bell, The, 398
Sunny, 672
Sunny River, 690
"Sunrise, Sunset," 723
supers, 40
Suppliant Women, The, 24
Surrey Theatre (London) 260, 261, 481
Susannah and the Elders, 455
Swan Theatre (London), 95, 99, 100, 106, 127
"Swanee," 702
Sweeney Agonistes, 463
Sweet Adeline, 690
Sweet Bird of Youth, 590
Sweet Eros, 609, 611, 617
Swift, Johnathan, 205
Swinley, Ian, 456
Sydney, Basil, 483
Sylvester, 114-115
"Sympathy," 656
Synge, John, 444

T

Tairov, Alexander, 417, 418
Take a Chance, 701

TALES OF THE SOUTH PACIFIC, 695, 712
Talk of the Town, The, 661
Tamberlaine the Great, 105, 108, 117
Taming of the Shrew, The, 291, 483, 495, 687
Tancied and Sigismunda, 248
Tandy, Jessica, 494, 496, 584-585, 628
Taplin, Terence, 473
Tarkington, Booth, 368
Tarleton, Richard, 118
Tartuffe, 165
Tasso, Torquato, 87
Taste of Honey, A, 480, 511
Tate, Nahum, 328
Taylor, Laurette, 560, 583
Taylor, Tom, 351, 358
"Tea for Two," 691
Teatro Olimpico, Vicenza, 88-89
Tempest, The, 127, 130, 131, 132, 491, 496
Tempest, Marie, 292
Temple of Love, The, 170
Ten Nights in a Barroom, 349
Tenth Man, The, 605
Terence, 41, 42, 57, 71, 84, 138
Terry, Ellen, 287, 288-289, 291, 366, 410, 439, 484
Terry, Megan, 620
Texas Steer, The, 386
Theatre, The (London), 98, 100
theatre buildings
   in Greece, 22, 32, 33, 34, 35
   in Rome, 48, 58-59, 60, 62, 64
   in Middle Ages, 72-75, 78-79, 80, 81, 83
   in Renaissance, 84, 87, 88-89, 90
   Elizabethan, 93, 94, 95, 96, 98, 99, 100, 101, 102, 103, 116, 132, 134
   Commedia dell'Arte, 158, 159, 166
   Restoration, 175, 195, 200
   18th century, 204, 207, 221, 222, 232, 241
   England 19th century, 246-247, 251, 257, 276, 282-283
   English 19th century, 293
   American (before 1900) 300, 304-305, 308, 316, 318-319, 329, 345, 363, 373, 389
   Russia, 394

England, 20th century, 480, 506, 507, 508, 509

American 20th century, 517, 577, 610, 611, 614, 621, 622, 623, 624, 628, 630-631, 633, 634-635, 636-637, 638

Theatre Group, 475

Theatre Guild, 436, 440, 525, 528, 536, 537, 546, 556, 559, 562, 563, 572, 575-577, 578, 641, 642, 643, 646, 685, 690

Theatre Guild Award, 583, 591

Theatre of Aspendus, Rome, 58

Theatre of the Absurd, 474-503, 605, 612, 613, 615, 616, 617, 618, 626

Théâtre-Italien, 139

Theatre Regulations Act, 264

Theatre Royal (Bath), 316

Theatre Royal (Bristol), 499

Theatre Royal (London), 174, 177, 180, 187, 201, 211, 248, 265, 299 (see also Drury Lane)

Theatre Royal (New York), 308

Theatre Royal, Stratford (East London), 468

Theatre Workshop, 468, 480, 506, 511

theatres (see Theatre buildings)

Thebes, 28

Theodora, 65

Theodoric, 65

Theodorus, 42

There Shall Be No Night, 544

There's Always Juliet, 453

"There's No Business Like Show Business," 680

thespian, origin of word, 22

Thespis, 19, 22, 23, 33, 39, 51

Thespis car, 19

They Came to a City, 457

They Knew What They Wanted, 577, 715

"They Say It's Wonderful," 680

"Thine Alone," 656

Thirst, 521

"This Can't Be Love," 690

This Happy Breed, 449

This Is the Army, 680

This Year of Grace, 448

Thomas, Augustus, 382, 384, 385-386

Thomas, Dylan, 457

Thompson, James, 217, 248

Thorndike, Eileen, 483

Thorndike, Russell, 483, 485

Thorndike, Dame Sybil, 424, 440, 458, 483, 485, 495, 496, 497

Three Musketeers, The, 658

Three Sisters, The, 403, 406, 408, 409, 414, 575, 628

Threepenny Opera, The, 706, 711

Throckmorton, Cleon, 646

thrust stage, 515, 630-631, 633, 634, 635, 637, 638

Thunder Rock, 572, 646

Ticket of Leave Man, The, 358

Tidings Brought to Mary, The, 645

Tiger at the Gates, 466

Till the Day I Die, 567

Tilley, Vesta, 282

Time and the Conways, 456

Time of the Cuckoo, The, 603

Time of Your Life, The, 572, 573, 574-575

"Time on My Hands," 701

Timor the Tartar, 261

Tin Pan Alley, 672, 675, 678, 679, 702

Tiny Alice, 487, 603

'Tis Pity She's a Whore, 117

Titus Andronicus, 104-105

To the Ladies, 563

Tobacco Road, 563

Tobias and the Angel, 455

Tobin, Dan, 562

Toller, Ernst, 577, 642

Tolstoy, Leo, 398, 399, 402, 406, 614

Tom Thumb, 309

Tom Thumb the Great, 208

Tomorrow and Tomorrow, 560

Tone, Franchot, 553, 566

Tonight at 8:30, 448

Tonight We Improvise, 616

Too Much Johnson, 385

Too True To Be Good, 438-439, 441, 443

Top Hat, 701

"Top Hat, White Tie, and Tails," 701

Torch Theater (London), 510

Touch of a Poet, A, 521, 531, 614

"Touch of Your Hand, The," 675

touring actors (see Traveling players)
Tovarich, 544
Toys in the Attic, 552
Trachinian Women, The, 27
Tracy, Spencer, 545
"Tradition," 723
tragedy, 17, 21, 22, 24, 27, 29, 30, 47
  (see also Costumes; Masks)
tragi-comedy, 107, 109, 113
Tragical History of Dr. Faustus, The,
  108, 111
translations, 57, 616
trap door, 35, 111, 122, 123, 203
Trapp Family Singers (see *Sound of
  Music*)
traveling players, 22, 63, 67, 86, 93,
  97, 98, 132-133, 169, 218 219, 291,
  292, 293, 295, 296, 297, 300, 317
  (see also Commedia dell'Arte)
Travers, Henry, 576
Tree, Sir Herbert Beerbohm, 290, 292,
  432
Trelawney of the Wells, 279, 367, 495
Trentini, Emma, 656
Tretyakov, Sergei, 643
trilogy, 23, 24, 25
Trip to Chinatown, A, 386
Tripler's (New York), 345
Trissino, Gian Giorgio, 87
Triumph of Peace, The, 131
Trojan Women, The, 29
trolley, 35
Trollope, Anthony, 372
Truckline Cafe, 536
Truth, The, 387
Trygaeus, 35
Tsar Feodor, 398, 402, 409
Tulip Tree, The, 458
Tumble Inn, 658
Tunicularia, 49
Turgenev, 575
Turleigh, Veronica, 495
Twaits, William, 322
Twelfth Night, 108, 121, 167
Twenty-third Street Theatre,
  (New York), 380
Twin Rivals, 178
Two Bouquets, The, 566
Two for the Seesaw, 605

Two Little Girls, 700
Two on an Island, 537
Tyler, Royall, 310

U

U.C.L.A. Extension Theatre, 636
Uncle Tom's Cabin, 344-345, 346-347
Uncle Vanya, 400, 406, 487, 496, 497
Under the Gaslight, 372, 374-375
Underwood, John, 121
Union Square Company, 378
United States, 267, 268, 269, 274, 287,
  293, 295, 389, 436, 515
University of Arkansas, 637
University of Washington (Seattle),
  637, 638
Ure, Mary, 470
Usher, Luke, 324
Ustinov, Peter, 459, 461, 496

V

Vagabond King, The, 658
Vajda, 577
Vakhtangov, Eugene, 418
Valley Forge, 536
Van Druten, John, 452
Van Italie, Jean-Claude, 620
Vanbrugh, Irene, 292
Vanbrugh, Sir John, 179, 181, 184, 223
Vance, Alfred Glanville, 282
VARIETY, 690
Variety Theatre, 282, 345
vaudeville, 61, 63, 282
Vedrenue, J. E., 442
Venice Preserved, 184, 187, 317
Venus Observed, 466
Very Warm for May, 675, 690
Vestris, Mme., 264, 270, 274, 278, 349
  481
Vieux-Columbier Company, 573
View From The Bridge, A, 596
Visit, The, 546
Vivian Beaumont Theatre, 579, 628,

629, 630-631, 633, 651
   (see also Lincoln Center)
Voice of the Turtle, The, 453
Vicar of Wakefield, The, 261
Vicenza, Teatro Olimpico, 88-89, 162
Victoria Theatre (Burnley, England),
   495
Victorian theatre, 228, 264, 267-293
Vikings of Helgeland, The, 424
violence, 64
Violante (Madame), 209
Virgin Goddess, The, 454
Virginia Mummy, The, 341
Vitruvius, 90
Volpone, 106, 109
Von Hofmannsthal, 575
von Kotzbue, August Friedrich Fer-
   dinand, 314
von Mosev, Gustav, 372
Vonnegut, Marjory, 576
Vortex, The, 448
Voysey Inheritance, The, 443

W

wagon (see Portable stages; Mansions)
Waiting for Godot, 474, 478, 605, 613,
   617,62
Waiting for Lefty, 567, 569
waits, 70
Wake Up and Dream, 683
Walker Foundation, 624
Walker, June, 566
Walkley, A. B., 440
Wallach, Eli, 612
Wallach, Henry John, 323
Wallach, James William
   (1791-1864), 323, 376
Wallach, Lester, 323, 376, 377
Wallach Theatre, (New York), 377,
   345, 638
Walnut Street Theatre (Philadelphia),
   330
Walpole, Robert, 208
"Wanting You," 660
War and Peace, 614
War of the Worlds, 583

Warfield, David, 381
Warfield, William, 703
Warre, Michael, 497
Warren, William, (1767-1832), 322,
   325, 349
Washington Square Players, 575-577,
   611, 642
Washington Square Theatre,
   (A.N.T.A.), 597, 629, 651
Wasps, The, 18
"Waste Land, The," 463
Watch on the Rhine, 549
Watch Your Step, 679
Waterloo Bridge, 544
Waters, Ethel, 556, 580
Waters of the Moon, 568
Way of the World, The, 177, 184, 186,
   206, 207
Wayne, David, 439
We, the People, 537
Weaver, John, 203, 204
Webb, John, 170, 172
Webster, John, 113, 117
Weill, Kurt, 536, 556, 706, 711
   and Maxwell Anderson, 711
Weiss, Peter, 648
Welles, Orson, 579, 582-583
   and John Houseman, 582
Wells, H. G. 583
Werfel, Franz, 577
Wesker, Arnold, 471, 472
West Indian, 309
West Side Story, 715, 720
Westen, Lucille, 358
Westley, Helen, 525, 528, 537, 576
What Every Woman Knows, 361, 433
"What Is This Thing Called Love?"
   683
What Price Glory?, 532
What Say They, 455
"What'll I Do?" 680
When We Are Married, 456
When We Dead Awaken, 426
Where's Charley, 715
Whiffen, (Mrs.) (actress), 379
Whirl of the World, The, 658
Whitbread, Samuel, 233
Whitford, Annabelle, 664
"White Christmas," 680

White Countess, The, 457
White Devil, The, 117
White, George, Scandals, 702
White Wings, 560
Whitehall Theatre (London), 511
Whitehead, Robert, 629
Whorf, Richard, 562
Who's Afraid of Virginia Woolf, 601, 602, 603
"Why Was I Born?" 690
Widowers' Houses, 436, 437
Widsith, 68
Wife, The, 381
Wignell, Thomas
Wilbur, Richard, 616
Wild Duck, The, 426
Wild Oats, 310
Wilde, Oscar, 287, 292, 430, 431-432, 435, 49, 450
Wilder, Thornton, 547-549, 554, 622, 715
Wildflower, 700
Wilks, Robert, 17, 212, 229
Williams, Emlyn, 457-458
Williams, Harcourt, 483, 487, 497
Williams, Hugh, 453
Williams, Margaret, 453
Williams, Tennessee, 582, 583-590, 591, 604, 614, 630, 646, 651
Williams, William Carlos, 616
Williamson, Nicol, 469, 471
Wilson, Harry Leon, 563
Wilson, Robert, 120
Wilton, Marie
    (See Marie Wilton Bancroft)
Winchell, Walter, 701
Wind of Heaven, The, 458
Wingless Victory, 534, 536
wings, 172, 182, 196, 223, 277, 315, 345
Winninger, Charles, 675, 691
Winslow Boy, The, 450, 453
Winter Garden (New York), 350, 356, 358, 362, 363
Winter's Tale, The, 287-291
Witching Hour, The, 385-386
Winterset, 534, 536, 650
Wisdom Tooth, The, 563
"Without a Song," 700

Without Love, 560, 563
Witness, 610
Wizard of the Nile, The, 656
Wizard of Oz, The, 655
Wodehouse, P. G., 672
Woe from Wit, 408
Woffiington, Peg, 184, 208-209, 210, 211, 213, 220
Wolfe, Thomas, 519
Woman of No Importance, A, 432
women on the stage, 40,
    in Rome, 61, 63, 65
    in England, 85, 167, 192
    in Europe, 85, 157, 167, 192
    (see also Boy actors)
Wonderful Town, 715
Wood Demon, The, 400
Wood, William B., 322, 325
Wood's Museum, 373
Woodthorpe, Peter, 477, 478
Woollcott, Alexander, 541, 543
Wools (actor), 315, 316
Worth, Irene, 503, 603
Wren, Christopher, 175, 179, 189
Wright, Frank Lloyd, 637
Wright, Richard, 556
Wright, Teresa, 606-607
Wycherley, Margaret, 537
Wycherley, William, 178, 181, 184, 376, 494, 629

X

X=O: A Night of the Trojan War, 454

Y

Yale University, 518
Yale University Theatre, 646
Yankee Princess, The, 661
Yard of Sun, A, 467
Yates, (18th-century actor), 220
Yeats, William Butler, 442, 443, 463
Yip, Yip, Yaphank, 679
You and I, 560

"You Can't Get a Man with a Gun," 680
You Can't Take It With You, 541, 542-543, 614, 645
"You Do Something to Me," 683
You Never Can Tell, 439
Youmans, Vincent, 691, 692, 700-701
Young, Roland, 544, 576
Young Roscius, 59, 244-249
Young Mrs. Winthrop, 378
Young Woodley, 453
Youngest, The, 560
Your Humble Servant, 368
You're in Love, 658
"You're the Top," 683

Z

Zanni, 150, 159
Zaza, 381
Zhdanova, (actress), 407
Ziegfield
    Florenz, 664-668, 702
    "Follies," 664, 665, 666, 667, 669, 678
    musical, 672
    production, 672
Zoo Story, The, 601, 602, 617, 618-619
Zweig, Stefan, 577